THE GoLDEN MAZE

Also by Richard Fidler

Ghost Empire

'A brilliant reconstruction of the saga of power, glory, invasion
and decay that is the one-thousand year story of Constantinople.
A truly marvellous book.' – Simon Winchester

Saga Land (co-authored with Kári Gíslason)

'I adored this book – a wondrous compendium of
Iceland's best sagas.' – Hannah Kent

RICHARD FIDLER

THE GoLDEN MAZE

A BIOGRAPHY OF PRAGUE

ABC
BOOKS

United Nations
Educational, Scientific and
Cultural Organization

Prague - City of Literature
Designated UNESCO
Creative City in 2014

The ABC 'Wave' device is a trademark of the
Australian Broadcasting Corporation and is used
under licence by HarperCollins*Publishers* Australia.

HarperCollins*Publishers*
Australia • Brazil • Canada • France • Germany • Holland • Hungary
India • Italy • Japan • Mexico • New Zealand • Poland • Spain • Sweden
Switzerland • United Kingdom • United States of America

First published in Australia in 2020
by HarperCollins*Publishers* Australia Pty Limited
ABN 36 009 913 517
harpercollins.com.au

A catalogue record for this book is available from the National Library of Australia.

ISBN 978 0 7333 3526 6 (hardback)
ISBN 978 1 4607 0692 3 (ebook)

Cover design by Nathan Burton
Maps: pages viii–ix by Maxime Plasse; page x by the author
Index by Kerryn Burgess
The lines from Jaroslav Seifert's poem 'Lovers, those evening pilgrims...' translated by
Edward Osers, used by permission of Catbird Press
Typeset in Minion Pro Regular by Kelli Lonergan
Printed and bound in Australia by McPherson's Printing Group
The papers used by HarperCollins in the manufacture of this book are a natural, recyclable
product made from wood grown in sustainable plantation forests. The fibre source and
manufacturing processes meet recognised international environmental standards, and carry
certification.

To the students of 1989

'The truth will prevail.'

– Jan Hus, fifteenth-century Bohemian religious reformer,
  burnt at the stake

'It was my belief that the truth would prevail,
but I did not expect it to prevail unaided.'

– Edvard Benes, second president of Czechoslovakia,
  exiled after the Nazi occupation

'The truth prevails, but it's hard work.'

– Jan Masaryk, Czechoslovak foreign minister, found dead
  in 1948 in the courtyard below his bathroom window

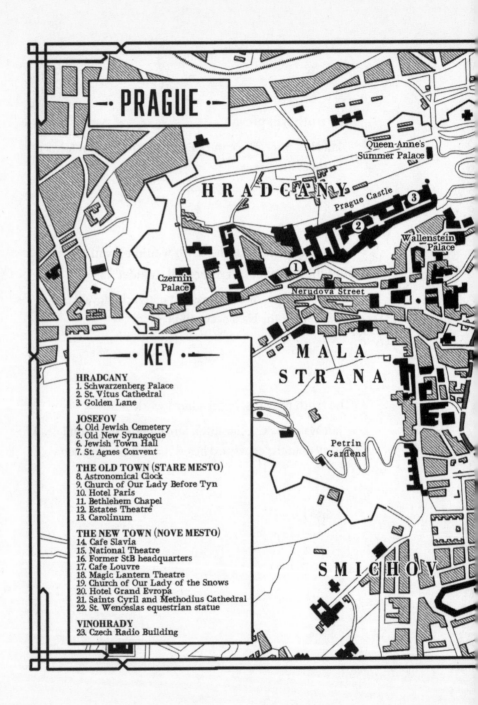

— PRAGUE —

Queen-Anne's
Summer Palace

H R A D C A N Y

Prague Castle ③
②
①

Wallenstein
Palace

Czernin
Palace

Nerudova Street

**M A L A
S T R A N A**

Petrin
Gardens

S M I C H O V

— KEY —

HRADCANY
1. Schwarzenberg Palace
2. St. Vitus Cathedral
3. Golden Lane

JOSEFOV
4. Old Jewish Cemetery
5. Old New Synagogue
6. Jewish Town Hall
7. St. Agnes Convent

THE OLD TOWN (STARE MESTO)
8. Astronomical Clock
9. Church of Our Lady Before Tyn
10. Hotel Paris
11. Bethlehem Chapel
12. Estates Theatre
13. Carolinum

THE NEW TOWN (NOVE MESTO)
14. Cafe Slavia
15. National Theatre
16. Former StB headquarters
17. Cafe Louvre
18. Magic Lantern Theatre
19. Church of Our Lady of the Snows
20. Hotel Grand Evropa
21. Saints Cyril and Methodius Cathedral
22. St. Wenceslas equestrian statue

VINOHRADY
23. Czech Radio Building

CENTRAL EUROPE

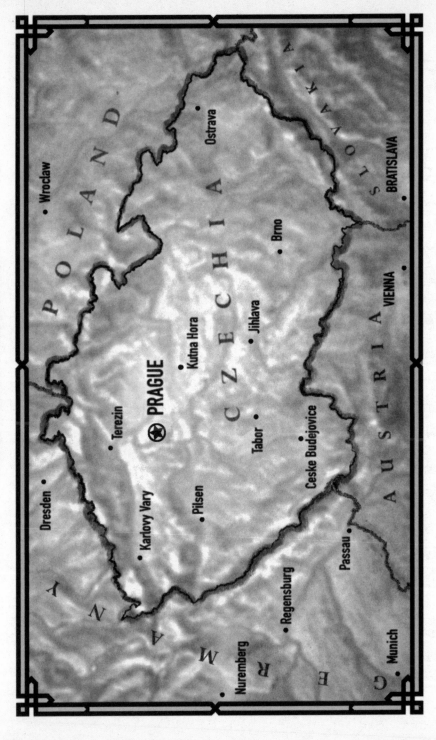

CONTENTS

INTRODUCTION

S OMEWHERE BEYOND THE orbit of Mars, among the countless boulders, and planetoids of the asteroid belt, lies a rock, around 70 kilometres wide, known by astronomers as 264 Libussa. The asteroid was named after the legendary witch queen of Bohemia, who was said to have founded the city of Prague.

Libussa, according to the legend, was uncommonly wise and blessed with the gift of prophecy. Her exploits were first recorded in a chronicle written a thousand years ago. Queen Libussa, it was said, stood on the edge of a steep cliff one day, looking down at the Vltava River and the forest beyond, when her attendants saw that her breath was short and that her eyes had become strange and dreamy. Stretching her arms towards the wilderness, Libussa gave voice to the prophecy welling up from within: 'I see a great city. Its glory will touch the stars.'

Turning to her attendants, she said, 'In the forest below there is a clearing. There you will find a man making the best use of his teeth at midday. *That* is the place where this city will be founded.'

The courtiers went down into the valley, and in a clearing they found some men in the process of building a house. It was midday and so they were eating their lunch. One of the men, however, was still at work, sawing a block of wood.

The courtiers had found their man.

'What are you making?' they asked.

'A threshold,' he replied. 'A threshold for a house,' a *prah* in the Czech language.

Which is how the city that grew up there came to be known as Praha, Prag or Prague.

A THRESHOLD, in a children's tale, is a device that serves as a point of transition from the everyday world into the dream realm. Ideally, it's a commonplace object: a looking-glass, a wardrobe in an attic, a broken gate at the bottom of a meadow. So many visitors to Prague over the centuries have noticed this uneasy liminal quality; the uncanny stillness of the streets on a winter's night can make the waking world appear thin and diaphanous. Even the drab Soviet-era apartment blocks of Prague can seem airless and haunted.

Patrick Leigh Fermor, who came in the early 1930s, was unsettled by Prague's strangeness: 'There were moments,' he wrote, 'when every detail seemed the tip of a phalanx of inexplicable phantoms.'[1] Troubling creatures that haunt the world's imagination have found their way across Prague's threshold: a golem made from river mud, a human transformed into a cockroach, a factory-made humanoid. An easy ten-minute walk through the city can take you from a clock that runs backwards to another where the skeleton of Death chimes the hour every hour; along the way you pass through squares once splashed with the blood of heretics, houses where alchemists attempted to transmute base matter into gold, and churches strafed with Nazi bullets.

Those who come to Prague from New-World metropolises like Sydney, Toronto or Los Angeles are sometimes touched by an odd sense of déjà vu, a vague impression of homecoming that can eventually be located in our memories of the old European folk tales given to us as children. But Prague's imaginative landscape is no Disneyland; it's the natural home of the older, more troubling versions of those tales, where Cinderella's step-sisters lop off parts of their feet to fit the glass slipper, and Little Red Riding Hood is compelled to dance naked for the wolf before it eats her alive.

Andre Breton, high priest of the Surrealist movement, was given a hero's welcome when he came to Prague in 1935. Walking the streets, he instantly grasped that Prague's surrealist masterpiece was the city itself, a colossal work of automatic writing, scribbled over time from some collective subconscious impulse. Prague was, he said, 'one of those cities that effectively pin down poetic thought, which is always more or less adrift in space ... When viewed from a distance, with her towers that bristle like no others, it seems to me to be the magic capital of old Europe.'[2]

'Keyholes are glittering in the sky,' wrote Prague's most lyrical poet Jaroslav Seifert,

> *and when a cloud covers them*
> *somebody's hand is on the door-knob*
> *and the eye, which had hoped to see a mystery,*
> *gazes in vain.*

- I wouldn't mind opening that door,
except I don't know which,
and then I fear what I might find.[3]

THE ORIGINS OF THIS BOOK can be traced to the Velvet Revolution, when I found myself among the happiest people in Europe, revelling in the peaceful overthrow of a decrepit police state. It was one of the most exciting moments of my life. At the time, I knew something of Prague's twentieth-century history: enough to feel a shiver of dread as I passed by the secret police headquarters on Bartolomejska Street, but the origins of the city itself were a mystery to me. Prague in those days was grimy and tendril-like, it seemed that no human hand had been needed to construct it; that it had somehow risen up from the soil like a stone garden, summoned by Libussa's chthonic spell: *I see a great city. Its glory will touch the stars.*

Prague's history is dotted with extraordinarily ambitious people who have striven to touch those stars. In the years when Emperor Rudolf II ruled from Prague Castle, he gave his patronage to astronomers, alchemists and magicians, hoping they might penetrate the inner workings of the universe and discover the occult correspondences binding it together.

Prague has also served as a playground for fanatics acting in the service of heaven – or someone's idea of heaven on earth. Nazis, Stalinists, and Catholic crusaders have all tried to bend human nature to their will and to erase whole categories of human existence. Those who blocked the road to paradise, or failed to cheer loudly enough in the parade, were executed in a prison courtyard or on the stones of the Old Town Square, in the very place where tourists now gather to watch the famous Astronomical Clock chime the hour.

The story of Prague offers a stark warning against the totalitarian urge, if we care to hear it. I once imagined that totalitarianism was a peculiar phenomenon of the twentieth century. But Prague bears the scars of earlier murderous crusades that set out to win souls for heaven, led by men who dreamt they could straighten the crooked timber of humanity by striking it hard with a hammer.

And yet, such monsters form only part of the story; Prague Castle has also been home to rulers who are sometimes lionised as 'philosopher-kings' (or 'philosopher-queens', in the case of the legendary Libussa); flawed individuals who accepted the challenge of power, and whose words and deeds summoned people to listen to the better angels of their nature.

A Brief Word About Names and Places

ONE BRIGHT MORNING in early 2018, I was standing in front of the Gothic Powder Tower, on the border of Prague's Old Town, chatting with a guide named Marketa, and I made the mistake of lumping her country in with the Eastern Bloc of Soviet satellite nations during the Cold War. I should have known better. She raised her eyebrows and asked me if I knew the easiest way to annoy a Czech person.

'Describing your country as eastern European?' I replied, already chastened.

'Exactly,' she said. 'Look at your map. This is *central* Europe.'

Visitors are often surprised to discover that Prague – a Slavic-language city – lies further west on the map than Vienna or Stockholm. It's a good deal quicker to fly to London from Prague than it is to go to Moscow. Looking at the map you see it's one of the

Europe as a queen, with Bohemia as her heart.
Sebastian Munster, 1570.

most centrally located landlocked cities in Europe. The Czech author Bohumil Hrabal thought this was why Praguers were so well read: lacking access to the sea, they compensated with an ocean of words.

PRAGUE CASTLE, the great keep of Bohemia's rulers, was founded in the early Middle Ages. Since then, Prague has served as the capital, or as a provincial capital, of a bewildering assortment of kingdoms, republics and imperial entities.

Prague became the seat of Bohemia's first ruling dynasty, the Premyslids, in the ninth century. Shortly afterwards, Bohemia was incorporated into a conglomeration of central European principalities and city-states known as the Holy Roman Empire, where it would remain for a thousand years. In the fifteenth century, a European super-dynasty, the Habsburgs, came to dominate the empire, and Bohemia became a subsidiary of the family's vast international holdings. The empire was dismantled by Napoleon, but after Waterloo, the Habsburgs were able to patch most of it back together as the newly badged Austrian Empire, and then again as the Austro-Hungarian Empire.

During these years, a Czech nationalist movement arose to demand greater independence from their indifferent Habsburg rulers in Vienna. At the end of the First World War, when the defeated Austro-Hungarian Empire collapsed, the Czechs made a run for the exit, hand in hand with their Slovak cousins. And so a new nation with an excessively long double-barrelled name was born: Czechoslovakia. In Prague, the proclamation of independence was greeted with rolling celebrations in Wenceslas Square; so much so, that after the third day, the new government issued an edict asking citizens to quit singing and drinking and get back to work.[4]

THE FIRST CZECHOSLOVAK REPUBLIC was a tadpole-shaped nation that brought together the Czech lands of Bohemia and Moravia in the west, with Slovakia and a sliver of Ruthenia in the east, and combined them into a single democratic nation, with Prague as its capital and largest city. Today, Czechs look upon this era between the wars as a golden age of democracy, prosperity and culture.

Sadly, this republic lasted just twenty years before it was shattered by Adolf Hitler. Under Nazi occupation, the Czech lands were reconstituted as the Protectorate of Bohemia and Moravia, and incorporated into the Third Reich.

After the defeat of Hitler, a revived Czechoslovak democratic republic lasted just three years before being extinguished by the communist coup of 1948. Czechoslovakia was made a vassal state of the Soviet Union, and Prague became the capital of the Czechoslovak Socialist Republic. This gloomy state of affairs lasted for four decades, until democracy was restored with the Velvet Revolution of 1989.

THE NEW PRESIDENT, Vaclav Havel happily proclaimed in his first New Year's address: 'People, your government has returned to you!'[5] But what name, they wondered, should they give their newly liberated nation? To begin with, Havel argued that the word 'Socialist' should be struck from the nation's title, and there was little disagreement about this. The term 'Czechoslovak', however, was trickier. The Slovaks, a separate people with a different, although mutually intelligible language, felt the 'slovak' component of that compound word, with a lower-case 's', was tacked-on and slightly demeaning. The nation, they insisted, should be named the Czecho-Slovak Republic. Havel came back with a counter-offer of Republic of Czecho-Slovakia, but that was rejected. At last they arrived at an acceptable compromise, which seemed to confer equal dignity on both peoples: The Czech and Slovak Federative Republic. That was a name that was never going to trip off anyone's tongue and so out of habit most people just went on using the old name of Czechoslovakia.

In the end, Slovakia decided to leave anyway and take its half of the name with it. On New Year's Day 1993, the Czechs and Slovaks went their separate ways in an amicable split nicknamed, inevitably, the Velvet Divorce. The departure of Slovakia left a remnant Czech state in need of yet another new name. Unfortunately, Bohemia with all its romantic connotations couldn't work because it excluded the other Czech province of Moravia. One professor joked the new entity should be called Left-Over-Stan. Eventually the government settled on the Czech Republic. Simple, easy to say.

And yet, and yet … there was a niggling feeling among the country's leaders that its dignity required the nation to be expressed as a *noun* rather than a mere adjective, and so in 2016 the government decreed that their state would be styled as Czechia. This awkward new name fell instantly into disuse, and citizens and politicians have slipped back to calling their nation the Czech Republic.[6]

The Five 'Quarters'

THE HISTORIC CENTRE of Prague is made up of five separate towns, which grew up walled off from each other and were eventually stitched together into a single city. Hradcany, the castle district, home of the mighty St Vitus Cathedral and the site of Prague's original settlement, sits high on a headland overlooking the rest of the city. In the shadow of the castle lies Mala Strana – the Lesser Town – established as a home for craftsmen and merchants in the service of the castle. Crossing the legendary Charles Bridge, with its avenue of stone and bronze saints, leads you into Prague's Stare Mesto – the Old Town – and the medieval Old Town Square, bordered by the Tyn Church, the Old Town Hall and the Astronomical Clock. Between the Old Town Square and the river lies Josefov, the Jewish quarter, the smallest of the five precincts, founded in the thirteenth century. Today almost nothing remains of its medieval past, aside from the old synagogues, the town hall and the Jewish cemetery, where the headstones jut out like broken teeth.

Prague's Nove Mesto – the New Town – curves around the Old Town like a cupped hand. The New Town is not so new; it was founded in 1348 by Emperor Charles IV, who endowed the city with the bridge, the university and the square that bear his name. Its biggest landmark is Wenceslas Square, created originally as the city's horse market. Beyond the square is the elegant precinct of Vinohrady, which once held the king's vineyards. Further afield are the rapidly gentrifying precincts of Zizkov, Karlin and Holesovice.

A Strange and Scarcely Accessible Language

THE CZECH LANGUAGE can seem very opaque to the native English speaker. First-time visitors will be confronted with unfamiliar yet critically important words such as 'VÝCHOD', 'PIVNICE' and 'ŽENY' ('Exit', 'Beer Cellar', and 'Women's Toilets', respectively).

This awkward distance between the languages might explain why the English-speaking world knows less of the Czechs than it does of the French, Germans and Italians. The Slavs of central Europe, wrote Milan Kundera, 'have remained the least known and the most fragile part of the West – hidden, even further, by the curtain of their strange and scarcely accessible languages'.[7]

Czech is a Slavic language rendered in Latin script, which makes use of diacritical marks to ensure correct pronunciation. On the page, the name 'Jiří' seems to be similar to 'Jerry', but it's actually the Czech version of George; the 'J' is sounded like a 'Y', and the accented 'ř' is followed by a 'zh'. So 'Jiří' should come out like 'Yerrr-zhi'. The composer Antonin Dvořak's surname is likewise pronounced 'Dvorr-zhak'.

The letter 'c' is like 'ts'. So Vaclav Havel's name is pronounced 'Vahts-lav Hav-ell'.

The 'č' in Hradčany is a 'ch' sound, so the castle's name is correctly pronounced as 'Hrrad-chany'. The letter 'z' is the same as in English, but the 'ž' is more of a 'zh', as in 'pleasure'.

Some Czech words like Vltava seem to be in dire need of a vowel. In such cases it can be helpful to simply imagine a short 'uh' sound where the missing vowel should be: 'Vuhl-ta-va'.

There's plenty more detail to explain, but I won't detain you any further as I've elected to remove the diacritical markings in this book, as the hooks, lines and dots tend to snag the reader's eye, and native English speakers will struggle to arrive at a correct pronunciation anyway. For clarity's sake, in some places I've chosen to anglicise a name; for example, Libuše, the legendary philosopher-queen of Prague, is written as 'Libussa'. I hope Czech speakers will forgive me for any mistreatment of their language.

PRAGUE IS THE ANCIENT capital of the Czechs, a people that struggled for centuries to assert their distinctive culture and language. But the city's position at the heart of Europe made it a natural point of intersection where various tribes could meet, co-mingle, intermarry and hybridise their ideas. For all its 'Czech-ness', Prague has always been a multi-lingual, multicultural city, where the borders of national identity blur at the edges. When SS-Obergruppenfuhrer Reinhard Heydrich ordered his men to carefully sift Prague's population into discrete racial categories, they discovered to their dismay that Czechs, Germans and Jews of Prague were hopelessly mixed. Intermarriage was common and it was difficult to know for sure who was a true Aryan and who was not. Most baffling for the Nazis were the so-called 'amphibians' – Czechified Germans and Germanised Czechs – equally at home in both cultures.

The city's most famous author, Franz Kafka, was born into a Jewish Czech family ('Kafka' means jackdaw in Czech), but he spoke and wrote almost entirely in German, and used German place names in his letters, referring, for example, to the river that courses through the city as the Moldau rather than the Vltava. Towards the end of his life, he took up the study of Hebrew.

PRAGUE IS NEVER MENTIONED by name in any of Kafka's novels and short stories, but it's impossible to extricate his literary imagination from the peculiar atmosphere of the city it grew in. Prague makes the world seem slippery, transmutable. When you leave, you might imagine you're holding a dream of it within you, but perhaps it's the other way around. 'Prague doesn't let go,' Kafka wrote to a friend when he was nineteen. 'This little mother has claws.'[8]

CHAPTER ONE

1990

Façade of the Grand Hotel Evropa.

The Grand Hotel Evropa

ON A COLD JANUARY evening in 1990, I entered the café of Prague's Grand Hotel Evropa and took a seat by the window. The hotel was a honey-golden Art Nouveau palace on Wenceslas Square. Shortages of paint, plaster and carpet had left the place rundown. Even so, the hotel retained something of its pre-war glamour.

The café's clientele that night was a mix of office workers, shoppers, black-market currency hustlers and foreigners like me, drinking coffee and beer, discussing the latest astonishing news from that morning's papers. On a tiny stage, a string quartet of old men in dinner jackets played gypsy music. I ordered a beer and waited for my travelling companions to show up. Then above the din in the room, I heard the beat of a drum from outside growing louder.

I WAS TWENTY-FIVE YEARS old and this was Europe's season of miracles. Over the preceding six months, a wave of mass protests had rolled across the police states of central and eastern Europe and expelled their failing governments one by one. First Poland, then Hungary, East Germany and now Czechoslovakia. The regimes, foisted on those nations by Stalin at the end of the Second World War, had been sustained by the organs of state security and, in the last resort, by Soviet military power. Now, after four decades, the Soviet leader Mikhail Gorbachev had let it be known he was no longer prepared to prop up his client governments with tanks and troops. Deprived of the tools of coercion and violence, the regimes had simply disintegrated under popular pressure.

The *annus mirabilis* of 1989 had reached a climax in November, when the hated Berlin Wall was demolished by ecstatic crowds on both sides of the divide, while armed *Volkspolizei* looked on impassively. As the revolutionary wave rolled on to Prague, the capital of Czechoslovakia, journalists struggled to keep up with the quickening tempo. One of them famously quipped: 'In Poland it took ten years, in Hungary ten months, in East Germany ten weeks; perhaps in Czechoslovakia it will take ten days.'[1]

IN PRAGUE, THE MASSES of protestors were led by students, musicians, workers, actors and, above all, by writers. 'The city came alive with words,' wrote one local author. 'Words covered the shop windows, the walls, the halls, and the corridors of the subway, which until that point had been a silent mausoleum to the ruling ideology'.[2] For Ivan Klima, whose novels were published everywhere except in his own country, it seemed 'the heavens of freedom, imperceptible only a short time ago, had finally opened before us'.[3] The heady rush of liberation was most keenly felt among Czechs who were of the same generation as me: not yet thirty, not old enough to have suffered the disappointments and humiliations that had soured the lives of their parents and grandparents.

On 24 November, the playwright and opposition leader Vaclav Havel had appeared on a balcony in Wenceslas Square, standing next to the hero of the failed Prague Spring of 1968, Alexander Dubcek, while 300,000 people cheered and jingled their keys, creating an eerie noise that sounded to observers like a swelling mass of Chinese bells – a message to the Communist Party that its time was up. Only six months earlier, Havel had been a prisoner. A general strike was called for 27 November at noon, and four days later, the Communist Party folded: it announced it would relinquish power and dismantle the one-party state. Few had imagined it could happen so rapidly, so bloodlessly. Someone had described this swift and peaceful change of power as a Velvet Revolution, and the phrase, with its vaguely erotic connotations, had stuck. By the time I arrived in mid-January, the work of overthrowing the communist monopoly on power was done. Havel had been elected president by the parliament, and the country was readying itself for a return to democracy.

FROM INSIDE THE HOTEL CAFÉ, I heard the pounding bass drum getting louder. I looked up and saw a dozen or so students holding up a banner, chanting a slogan as they walked past. Twenty more protestors followed, then a hundred more. Stepping outside, I saw a trail of demonstrators, extending all the way back to the statue of St Wenceslas. I was excited and perplexed. The old regime had been done away with. What were these people marching for?

Attaching myself to the fringes of the crowd, I asked questions in an awkward mish-mash of English, German and Czech. A couple of students passed me on to a young man who spoke good English. He was cleanshaven, with a padded blue jacket and a white ski-cap. I had to yell above the din to ask what was going on.

'We're protesting!' he shouted. 'Against the StB!'

The StB, the secret police. The most hated institution in the country. For four decades, the StB had practised surveillance, blackmail and torture to enforce compliance with Communist Party rule. I said I thought the StB had already been dissolved.

'No!' he said. 'They're still spying on people. We see them everywhere! Even now!'

'But … but who are they reporting to?'

'No one! Someone! Who knows?'

The front section of the march had now reached the northern end of Wenceslas Square and was turning left into Narodni Street. I asked where we were heading.

'StB headquarters,' he said. 'We want them to understand they can no longer make us afraid.'

'You *know* where the secret police headquarters are?'

'Of course!' he said. 'Everyone knows. It's the place no one ever wanted to go.'

I followed the demonstration down to the StB's citadel: a hulking Art Deco building the colour of dried blood. Behind it, on Bartolomejska Street, stood their interrogation centre, a five-storey building covered in grimy rectangular tiles nicknamed the Kachlikarna – the tile stove. The chants of the protestors became louder, more resonant, in the narrow street. My companion looked tense.

'What's going to happen now?' I asked.

'I don't know. Something terrible, maybe,' he said, scanning the windows and rooftops. 'We hear rumours the StB have guns stashed in roofs across the city.'

This was not an unfounded fear. Earlier that week in Romania, black-shirted secret police had fired semi-automatic weapons into crowds of protestors on the streets of Bucharest and Timisoara. Outside the Romanian embassy in Mala Strana, an artist had assembled a commemoration for the dead: the word 'TIMISOARA' carved in block letters, plastered with sheets of blood-soaked paper. The Czech secret police were almost as hated as their Romanian counterparts and could conceivably lash out if they thought they were cornered.

I cast a worried look up and down the street and saw how easy it would be to block off either end, then fire into the crowd from the rooftops. The darkened windows of the Kachlikarna offered no clue. There was no response from inside, and so after twenty minutes of chanting, the protestors began to disperse.

THE YOUNG MAN IN the blue jacket introduced me to Marta, a middle-aged woman dressed in loose-fitting clothes, who was leaning against a car, smoking. Marta told me her husband had once been the Czech ambassador to Canada. She said they had considered staying in North America after the 1968 Soviet invasion, but they eventually resolved to return to their country and face the grey lethargy of the 'normalisation' period. As former foreign service workers, they fell under the constant watch of the StB.

'This is the thing I want you to understand about the StB,' she said to me. 'They didn't want *anybody* to trust *anybody*. They made it so you couldn't trust your friends. Or even your family.'

I asked her how this worked. She thought for a moment then said, 'You're talking with some friends and you make a simple joke about the government. One of those friends is secretly an informant. This person reports your joke to the StB and a note is put in your file. Just for safekeeping.'

She drew on her cigarette nervously as she said this.

'Then one morning,' she continued, 'maybe a month later, there is a phone call. They invite you in for a friendly conversation, but there's no need to worry, it's just a few details. A car arrives at your apartment and they bring you here.' She waved her hand at the Kachlikarna without looking at it.

'In the interrogation room, there are forms to fill in. You must write down the names of all your friends and associates. Then they show you some information about yourself.'

'Like what?'

'Like an affair you might be having. Or once had. Or a friendship with an undesirable person. Then they invite you to name the person you got the joke from. Eventually you might be asked to write a whole-hearted statement of support for the party and its leadership. That too is put in your file.'

'What about the "friend" who reported you?'

'That person might get to the front of the queue for a better apartment or a car. Or their daughter might get a place at university. They find the weak spot in shame or fear or ambition always.'

I told Marta I didn't understand why the StB would expend so much energy persecuting someone who had made a joke, who could be no threat to the state. What was the point?

'The point,' she said, sadly, 'was to destroy trust between people. You need trust to make an opposition.'

DESPITE OUR FEARS that night, the StB made no desperate last stand against the revolution. As cynical realists, they were more interested in covering over the traces of their past and preparing themselves for business opportunities in the post-communist world.

There were even suspicions the StB had played a role in destabilising the regime and its leader Milos Jakes, by leaking a video of a ridiculous speech Jakes had given to a regional party conference, where he had complained he felt 'as lonely as a fence post'. He confused a boiler with a broiling chicken. Czechs and Slovaks found Jakes's wounded self-righteousness hilarious. Vaclav Havel's brother Ivan said the opposition 'literally laughed the communist government out of power'.[4]

IN THOSE YEARS, I was part of a music-comedy trio, dividing our time between Australia and the UK. Our style was often described as confrontational and 'dangerous', but we'd never endured state surveillance, harassment or imprisonment. We had begun as street performers who would wade into the crowd to get people to sing, or to steal children as a donation for the guitar case. We brought this intense, aggressive style of performance to the stage, letting no audience member feel safe. Early on, we noticed that on a good night, there was an odd political dynamic at work: when the crowd gave itself over to laughter, it surrendered itself to the comic authority of the performers. Seen from one angle, there was something weirdly fascistic about it. Our stage costumes changed, became more militaristic. We adopted the aesthetics of Soviet propaganda, producing posters in the flat primary colours and block letters of socialist realism. I was fascinated by the way the clean lines of totalitarian art could smooth over the jagged edges of reality.

On stage, we would goad the audience, demand audience participation, then harangue them for acting like sheep. We were even more ruthless with each other on stage. Whatever we vehemently asserted as 'truth', would be contradicted just as vehemently. In media interviews, we made up preposterous lies and were amazed to see them printed uncritically in *The Times* and *City Limits*. Sometimes we were mistaken for fascist sympathisers, when, of course, the very opposite was true.

In late 1989, our group was engaged to play a three-week season at the Bloomsbury Theatre in London, just as the revolutionary wave was cresting in Europe. I had to watch the collapse of the Iron Curtain from the sidelines in my London flat. I saw news footage of people dancing on the Berlin Wall, of construction machines yanking out its concrete segments like rotting teeth, and I longed to be there with them. As soon as the season in London finished, my then girlfriend, Josephyne, and I rushed to Berlin and then to Prague, where the action was still unfolding.

IT WAS MY FIRST time in Prague, and we were struck at once by the city's fabled loveliness, the absence of advertising and the carnival atmosphere in the streets, bars and cafés. People walked at a fast clip, some with flyers or posters wedged under their arms. Every other Praguer wore the smiley-face badge of the protest coalition Obcanske Forum – 'Civic Forum' – but not everyone was smiling. There were a few sullen, disappointed faces in the streets also brandishing bright OF badges on their lapels; they were, I suspected, apparatchiks who had done well under the old regime but knew well enough to nod obediently at whoever was in charge. There were also those in the high-rise estates and in the countryside who were frightened by the change, worried with good reason that the new freedoms would leave them stranded and unsupported. At the time, their misgivings would have seemed paltry to me, caught up as I was in the moment.

A guide book recommendation had led me to the Grand Hotel Evropa, but I wasn't sure if the 'v' in 'Evropa' was a misprint. I'd tried to book ahead, but no one answering the phone had any English and I had no Czech, so we just showed up at the front desk on arrival.

The room rate was cheap, so we were delighted to discover we'd arrived at something like a palace, with liquid, curvaceous lines, grand mirrors and gilded finishings. Its timeworn quality only made it more appealing to us. The room was sparsely furnished, with threadbare carpets and patchy wallpaper. There was no TV, only a radio tuned to a single station. The waiters and cleaners were friendly, but the uniformed staff at reception were so spectacularly rude and unhelpful that interacting with them became a perverse form of entertainment. The woman at the front desk had heavy-lidded eyes that froze with disdain whenever I asked for her help.

'Can you tell me please where I can make an international phone call?'

'It's impossible from this hotel.'

'Is there anywhere outside the hotel I can do this?'

'You think I spend my days finding out such things for your benefit?'

She, and the rest of the desk staff also wore the cheerful OF badges, even though half of them would have certainly worked as secret police informants.*

THE GRAND HOTEL EVROPA was constructed in 1872 and refurbished at the turn of the century in the fashionable Art Nouveau style. Franz Kafka delivered the first public reading of his short story 'The Judgement' in the café there in 1912. Composer Leos Janacek stayed in 1918 and he too complained about the rude service.[5] A similarly palatial Prague hotel forms a backdrop for Bohumil Hrabal's wonderful novel *I Served the King of England*, in which his main character Ditie takes a job as a waiter. On his first day, his boss pulls him up by one ear and tells him, 'Remember, you don't see anything, and you don't hear anything. Repeat what I just said.' Ditie does as he's told, then the boss pulls him up by the other ear. 'Remember too,' he says, 'you've got to see everything and hear everything.' Ditie is taken aback but he dutifully promises also to see everything and hear everything.[6]

JOSEPHYNE AND I HAD befriended two other twenty-something travellers who, like us, had rushed to Prague to witness this moment in history. That night, the four of us decided to treat ourselves to dinner in the hotel's basement restaurant, which had been a major gastronomic destination for Europeans in the pre-communist era. Dressed in our scungy jeans and jumpers, we felt a little out of place as we descended the grand staircase into a fine dining room with

---

* An investigation that month by the new interior minister revealed that every such hotel contained a secret room equipped with video monitors connected to cameras in the hotel restaurants and lobbies. If the Grand Hotel Evropa had such a room, I never encountered it.

mahogany wainscoting, intricately carved pillars and architraves, and a vaulted ceiling of jade-coloured glass.

We were met at the foot of the stairs by a very tall waiter, with a starched white apron tied to his waist and a large, strawberry-coloured birthmark across one side of his face. He was young but his manners were very old-fashioned and correct. As we sat down at our table, he flicked out four napkins dramatically and laid them gently on our laps. 'Welcome,' he said in clipped English, 'to the famous restaurant of the Grand Hotel Evropa. As you look around, you will see it is designed as a replica of the dining room on the ship *Titanic*.'

The menu offered dumplings in gravy as an entrée, followed by a choice of pork schnitzel, chicken schnitzel or veal schnitzel. More dumplings and cabbage accompanied this. Dessert was dumplings filled with apricot jam. We decided to give the Bulgarian wine a miss, in favour of the famous Czech pilsner, which was perfect.

THAT DAY, 16 JANUARY, was the anniversary of a shocking incident that had taken place in Wenceslas Square twenty-one years earlier: a student, Jan Palach, had poured gasoline on his head and set fire to himself to protest the Soviet invasion of 1968. After dinner, we decided to visit the site where Palach had performed this self-immolation at the top of the square. Praguers, for the first time in two decades, were free to honour Palach's memory, and the site on the pavement had become a shrine to his martyrdom: a thick bed of melted wax and dead leaves, covered in a mass of candles, cards and flowers.

It was close to midnight when we arrived and there were only a few people standing with us. We stared at the flickering candles until two young Czech soldiers approached us.

'*Pivo? Pivo?*'

They wanted us to help them find beer.

They were still in their late teens; their winter uniforms looked too big and heavy for their skinny frames. They had only a few scraps of English, we had even less Czech. The taller one politely introduced himself as Jan.

'American?' he asked. I told him we were Australian.

'Oh!' He closed his eyes and recited a litany of Australian cities in a heavy Slavic accent, 'Sydney ... Melbourne ... Brisbane ... Adelaide.'

'Wow!' I said. 'You really know your geography.'

Jan nodded energetically.

'I like your music. *Assidissy*! *Assidissy*!' then, '*Ahn-goose, Ahn-goose*.' He began to play a wailing air guitar, then duck-walked across the stones of Wenceslas Square in the style of Angus Young, AC/DC's lead guitarist. Josephyne was bent over laughing, which pleased Jan, who was clearly the clown of his battalion. Jan's soldier friend rolled his eyes. 'He listens to the German radio,' he said by way of explanation.

Then a middle-aged man with a briefcase who had heard our conversation came forward with the name of his favourite Australian popstar: '*Kylieminog*,' he said emphatically. '*Kylieminog*. Nizzze girl. Nizzze girl.'

We invited Jan and his friend to join us back at the hotel, which was fortunately still serving *pivo* at that late hour. Mr Briefcase invited himself along too, but sat at an adjacent table, periodically raising his glass to us. A round of fine pilsner was served in heavy glass steins the size of vases, and quickly finished off. We had another round and Jan and I became emotional.

'We are friends now,' Jan said.

'Yes, we are,' I replied, looking across the table at his friend, who was grinning and trying to flirt with Josephyne.

'Please,' Jan implored me. 'Listen to me please, Richard: Australia, Czechoslovakia, America ... *one* world please *one* world.'

He was utterly sincere.

He held me by the shoulders and repeated his mantra of peace:

'Please. Listen to me Richard: Australia, Czechoslovakia, America, Germany, Russia … one world, please, one world.'

I nodded along and then Mr Briefcase was suddenly between us, pounding his fist on the table, making the beer glasses jump.

'*No!*' he roared. 'No Russians! No Russians!'

He glowered at us, then pulled some yellow flyers from his briefcase, a political tract in closely typed Czech. He slapped them on the table and marched out of the bar.

No one was quite sure what had just happened.

Jan paused for a moment, held me by the shoulders again, and repeated, in a softer voice this time, 'Please. Listen to me Richard: Australia, Czechoslovakia, America, Russia, one world, please, one world.'

WHEN I FINISHED HIGH SCHOOL, I had not expected to reach the age of thirty. This conviction was partly a symptom of natural teenage melancholy, but it arose more profoundly from the darkening world situation of the early 1980s.

The era of détente between the nuclear superpowers had passed, and there was renewed resolve in the Western democracies to confront Soviet aggression. The Soviet deployment of intermediate-range nuclear weapons in Europe was countered by a similar deployment by NATO, and with that, the reaction time to a report of a nuclear attack was shortened to mere minutes.

Just as worryingly, the leaders of both the United States and the USSR appeared to be suffering from cognitive decline. In

October 1981, US president Ronald Reagan carelessly mentioned he could envision a limited nuclear war in Europe, which was taken to mean he believed such a conflict was winnable, but then he stepped back from the claim. When he denounced the Soviet Union as an 'evil empire', the KGB director Yuri Andropov tried to convince his fellow Politburo members that America was planning a nuclear strike on their homeland.

The Soviet leader, Leonid Brezhnev was, like Reagan, in his seventies. In his few public appearances, he looked stiff and grey. Waving mechanically at his people from Lenin's tomb, he appeared prematurely embalmed himself. To me, it seemed the world was run by unyielding old men who could afford to be careless about a future they would not live to see.

The national security strategy of both superpowers at the time rested on a doctrine known as MAD: Mutually Assured Destruction. The best assurance of peace came from the understanding that neither power would be so suicidal as to launch a nuclear attack, knowing a massive retaliatory strike would soon follow. But the theory of MAD rested on two critical assumptions: that the decision-makers with the launch codes were rational, and their early warning systems were sound. I was sure of neither of those things.

In November 1979, the United States was alerted to a missile attack from a Soviet submarine. Jets were scrambled and bases were placed on alert before the military realised that a technician had mistakenly inserted a war-game program into the North American Aerospace Defense Command's computer.

The following June, president Jimmy Carter's national security advisor, Zbigniew Brzezinski, was woken in the night by his military aide and informed that 220 Soviet missiles were in the air and on their way. Brzezinski asked the aide to confirm the report. He called back and corrected the earlier figure: there were 2200 missiles in the air. Washington would be hit within minutes. Brzezinski readied himself to call the president and advise him to launch a counterstrike. He decided not to wake his sleeping wife. Better she should die in her sleep. Then the phone rang again. A relieved aide advised Brzezinski it was a false alarm, caused by a minor computer glitch.

Having the fate of the human existence hinge on such flimsy safeguards was not an acceptable way to live. Thinking of the future filled me with dread.

THE END OF THE COLD WAR arrived in 1989 not with a bang, nor a whimper, but with a party. It felt like the world had been given a reprieve from a death sentence and our future was returning to us. The joy was felt most profoundly in East Berlin and Prague, whose regimes had been among the cruellest in the Soviet bloc. Liberation had been so long awaited, and then so quick and bloodless in its realisation. Throughout those weeks, William Wordsworth's famous lines on the French Revolution kept springing to my mind:

Bliss was it on that dawn to be alive,
But to be young was very heaven!

Those words from his poem 'The French Revolution as it Appeared to Enthusiasts at its Commencement', foreshadowed the awful disillusionment that sank in after the Jacobin terror. But in Prague, two centuries later, the painful lessons of history had been learnt. There would be no guillotine in Wenceslas Square. And the new president, Vaclav Havel, was the furthest thing from a Robespierre imaginable.

SHORT IN STATURE, shaggy and unkempt, President Havel was a Bohemian in every sense of the word: a writer of sharp absurdist dramas and a lover of psychedelic rock and roll. As president, he was delighted to welcome Lou Reed and Frank Zappa to the palace. In January, while wandering around the castle, I saw him striding through the courtyard, followed by a retinue of staff members and journalists, one of whom he was chatting with flirtatiously while dragging on his cigarette.

At formal functions at the castle, Havel was shy and polite; he was much more at home backstage at a theatre or at his favourite pub, the Golden Tiger, enjoying witty conversation over cigarettes and beer. Irresistibly drawn to the company of attractive women, Havel's promiscuity annoyed his friends and his much-admired wife, Olga, his lifeline to the outside world during his years as a political prisoner.

He was as astonished as anyone by the events that had elevated him from a prison cell to the palace. 'I am the kind of person,' he said after taking office, 'who would not be in the least surprised if, in the very middle of my Presidency, I were to be summoned and led off to stand trial before some shadowy tribunal, or taken straight to a quarry to break rocks.'[7]

Havel to the Castle, 1989.

HAVEL HAD BECOME an internationally renowned playwright in the 1960s. His absurdist dramas parodied the nonsensical language of bureaucracy and exposed the petty humiliations routinely dished out by totalitarian governments.

Havel's work was banned in Czechoslovakia after the Soviet invasion of 1968. In 1979, he was jailed for four years for his dissident activities and was released only when he became seriously ill with pneumonia. His health was always shaky after that, but he continued to smoke, nonetheless. By the mid-1980s, Havel had become the regime's sharpest critic and a figure of unimpeachable moral courage. Like Nelson Mandela, his years as a prisoner had given him insight into the psyche of his jailers and made him aware of their weaknesses.

The Velvet Revolution, sparked by a vicious police attack on a student march, led Havel and his colleagues to form Civic Forum, a broad coalition of citizens demanding liberal democracy. As the regime blustered, teetered and collapsed, posters of Havel's gentle, smiling face began to appear across the city, accompanied by a block-lettered demand: HAVEL NA HRAD – 'Havel to the Castle'. The Communist Party bowed to public demand, and in December 1989, the dissident playwright was inaugurated as president at Prague Castle, the ancient stronghold of emperors, kings and commissars.

AS HIS NATION'S HEAD OF STATE, Havel consented to a haircut, a suit and a tie, but a part of him remained true to his impish, counter-cultural instincts. He explored his new palace like an excited kid, zooming through its endless corridors on a wooden scooter.

One day he found a locked door for which there was no key, so he had a staff member break it open. They found a closet with a desk and a telephone: a hotline link to the Kremlin. Havel, greatly amused, picked up the phone and was answered by a Russian-speaking woman. When he asked to be put through to President Gorbachev, he was put on hold. Then the line went dead, permanently.[8]

VACLAV HAVEL'S PLAYFULNESS sat above a great well of moral seriousness. On New Year's Day 1990, just four days after his inauguration, he delivered the traditional New Year's Day Presidential Address to the Nation. People watching state television that day saw a new, more dignified Havel: the president's unruly blond hair had been brushed, his moustache had been trimmed and he had donned an uncomfortable suit and tie. He spoke nervously, drawing in deep breaths, but his opening words were bracing:

> *My dear fellow citizens.*
> *For forty years you heard from my predecessors on this day*
> *different variations on the same theme: how our country was*
> *flourishing, how many million tons of steel we produced, how*
> *happy we all were, how we trusted our government, and what*
> *bright perspectives were unfolding in front of us.*
>
> *I assume you did not propose me for this office so that I, too,*
> *would lie to you. Our country is not flourishing.*

Havel spoke of the nation's ruined environment, its moribund industries and the poor state of people's health. Then he identified a deeper problem, the root cause of the national malaise:

> *The worst thing is that we live in a contaminated moral*
> *environment. We fell morally ill because we became used to*
> *saying something different from what we thought.*[9]

HAVEL INSTINCTIVELY RECOILED from slogans and clichés, but he grasped the need for some words that might unite his people and raise their moral expectations. At a student rally earlier in December, he had improvised a line at the end of his speech: 'Truth and love must overcome lies and hatred.'[10] While there were those who rolled their eyes at the apparent naïveté of such a statement, his words lifted the spirits of the protest movement and made them proud of what they had achieved.

One month after that speech, Josephyne and I were walking through the Old Town Square on our way back to the hotel. It was past midnight, and the square was cold and still. The Tyn Church, illuminated by golden spotlights, looked like a hologram. As we turned the corner near the Astronomical Clock, we saw a group of students, mulling wine over an open brazier, and they called us over. They appeared to be wearing every item of clothing they owned to stay warm. A woman in a woollen cap passed us a cup of the sweet, spicy wine. Her boyfriend raised his plastic chalice and said, '*Pravda a laska*!' I looked at the woman in the woollen cap.

'Truth and love,' she translated.

'Truth and love,' we replied, raising our cups in return.

FOR WORDSWORTH, the first heady years of the French Revolution unlocked such passionate, intense feelings within him that he felt like he was falling in love. 'Oh! pleasant exercise of hope and joy!' he wrote, 'For mighty were the auxiliars which then stood upon our side, we who were strong in love!'[11] The goals of the Velvet Revolution – the restoration of a normal democratic society – were far more modest than the dizzy, utopian dreams of its French counterpart from two centuries earlier, but I understood the sentiment. To be swept into a joyful revolution in this beguiling, heavenly city really did feel like falling in love: there was the thrilling sense of the impossible becoming real, the paradoxical feelings of being relaxed and excited at the same time, the pleasure of waking each morning wondering: what on earth will happen today?

Not every observer felt the same sense of unadulterated joy. Joseph Skvorecky, the exiled novelist, sang the revolution's praises in a minor key: 'The generation of twenty-year-olds who were bloodied by the police and went on to topple the power monopoly of the Communist Party are experiencing pure bliss untainted by any – even tiny – drops of sadness. That's how it should be … But,' he noted:

as one turns to the generation of their parents, now in their early forties, the picture changes. Two generations ago, when they were twenty themselves, this generation was as euphoric as their sons and daughters are today. But the Big Lie descended on Czechoslovakia and those who were starting life in 1968 lost their most creative, and potentially happiest years … It all appears to be a huge joke played by history. The joke, however, is ebony black.[12]

The author at Hradcany, January 1990.

*

I LEFT PRAGUE IN February 1990 to return to work in London, while Czechoslovakia struggled to stabilise, confront its ugly past and to jump-start a market economy.

I returned briefly in the summer of 1991 with Khym, whom I had just met and was soon to marry. I wanted to show her the city that had affected me so deeply.

The Grand Hotel Evropa was thankfully unchanged, still an unrenovated bargain. Sex workers now loitered in the lobby instead of secret policemen. In the room, I heaved my suitcase onto the springy bed and picked up the English-language tourist news sheet lying next to it. In between the travel tips and restaurant ads, I saw a headline: 'What Are We to do about the Gypsy Problem?' In language that seemed to consciously or unconsciously evoke memories of the Holocaust, the unnamed columnist asked whether the time had come to remove the thieving Gypsies from Prague 'once and for all'. I passed it to Khym, who read it with widening eyes.

Minutes later, we heard shouting and scuffling outside the window. Pulling aside the net curtains, we looked down onto Wenceslas Square and saw two skinheads punching and kicking a Gypsy teenager who was yelping on the ground. He could have been no more than fourteen years old. His attackers had shaved heads, tight-fitting denim jackets and bloodied knuckles. One wore reflective sunglasses that fell off him momentarily in the violence. Two police officers came running from around the corner. The skinheads grinned, stepped back and held up their hands in mock surrender. The police helped the whimpering Gypsy kid to his feet, while the skinheads walked away, smirking.

Prague was just a year and a half into the post-communist era. The carnival atmosphere of 1989 had dissipated, replaced by the buzz of commercial activity as the Czechs raced to catch up with Western European standards of living.

It would have been foolish and naive to be disappointed by the encroachment of international consumerism; the Velvet Revolution had been at least as much about freedom from the shabbiness of the communist economy as it was about political liberation. Still, I hoped Prague might somehow evade having its face stamped with the same generic corporate logos as every other city in Europe.

Khym and I took a late-afternoon walk. The day had been hot but the evening was unusually cool for July. We crossed the Charles Bridge, where a basso-voiced busker with a balalaika sang a sad old Russian folk tune at the stone feet of Jan Nepomuk, the saint of Bohemia. A thin mist floated over the Vltava. I followed Khym down to the riverbank where she crouched down and tossed some bread crumbs to a pair of swans.

After four days we left. A year later we were married. In another five years, we had kids and our years of easy travel were curtailed, our lives taken up with work and raising young children. Memories of those feverish weeks in Prague became increasingly remote and unreal to me, like the thread of a story I couldn't pick up again.

I CAME BACK TO PRAGUE after a long absence in 2018, and again in 2019, and remained for several months. This time, I did not stay in a *Jugendstil* palace on Wenceslas Square, but in the outer suburbs, in a pebblecrete apartment block near the Barrandov film studios. The location was somewhat less romantic, but the flat was airy and warm, and the local tram brought me to the centre of Prague in no time.

The griminess had gone; the old buildings had been repaired and repainted. The weird communist shops that sold nothing in particular had been replaced by shops selling battalions of matryoshka dolls, Bohemian glassware, Becherovka and Kafka t-shirts (but not his books). Well, alright, what did I expect to find after a cyclone of tourism had swept through the place? Yet late at night, as I walked through the quiet, empty streets, there it was again, that unsettling feeling, the prickling sense of expectation.

PRAGUE IS A CITY of powerful symbols whose meanings constantly shift. A heretic in one century is a martyr in another. Statues of national heroes are erected and then secretly buried for safekeeping. A red star can be a shining beacon of emancipation until it becomes a symbol of hypocrisy and foreign tyranny. History here is written in pencil, erased, rewritten and erased again.

Prague is a fabulous palimpsest of stories. But to trace its origins, you have to strip back all the accretions of the centuries. Walk down from Wenceslas Square, through the Old Town, across the stone bridge, and imagine all these things vanishing behind you as you pass. Walk up the hill towards the castle. Then it too vanishes and there's nothing there, only a grassy bluff overlooking the bend of a river and a dark forest. On the headland, a priestess whispers, *I see a city ...*

======= CHAPTER TWO =======

THE STONE CROWN OF THE WORLD

PREHISTORY TO 1378 CE

THERE WAS A TIME when there was no castle, no city, trams or cars. No bridges spanned the waters of the Vltava; there was only the river and the wilderness.

At the end of the fifth century BCE, a tribe of Celtic people migrated into the lush basin around the river bend. The ancient Romans knew these people as the Boii, and named their territory Boiohaemum, or Bohemia.[1] The Boii turned the soil with iron ploughs, made pottery on a wheel and built fortified villages alongside the river, where they manufactured ornate jewellery and weapons.

Sometime around the reign of Augustus Caesar, Germanic tribes known as the Marcomanni entered the Bohemian lands. The Boii mostly fled or were simply absorbed into German clans. Over the following centuries, the presence of the Germans waned and the western Roman empire imploded, setting the tribes of Europe moving across the peninsula. In the sixth century, a new people, the Slavs, entered the Bohemian lands.

THE SLAVS CAME FROM the east, from the lands around the Carpathian Mountains. The word 'Slav' was once thought to be derived from the Latin word for 'slave' – sclavus – because so many Slavs had been captured and forced into slavery by the Moors of Spain. It's now thought the word is more likely to have evolved from the Slavonic word slovo, meaning 'word' or 'speech', suggesting a community of people who speak meaningfully to each other.*

The Slavic tribes were known to the Byzantine historian Procopius, who encountered them while serving under the Roman general Belisarius. The Slavs, he wrote, 'are all exceptionally tall and stalwart men ... they are not ruled by one man, but they have lived from of old under a democracy, and consequently everything which involves their welfare, whether for good or for ill, is referred to the people'.[2]

THE SLAVIC TRIBES WHO wandered into Bohemia were pleased to find themselves surrounded by fertile land, with navigable rivers for fishing, and forests with plenty of game. They settled alongside the remaining Germanic tribes and, over time, they became the predominant group in the area, not by sudden military conquest, but by the slow spread of established farmlands and forts.[3]

BY 800 CE, A thriving Slavic community had taken hold on Hradcany Hill, the bluff above the Vltava River. Its castle was at that stage no more than a large stone-and-timber fort with a great

---

* The Old Church Slavonic word for foreigners is nemici, which relates to nemu, or 'mute'. The Czech word for Germans, nemci, has the same origin.

log house at its centre, sitting above a river crossing on an overland trade route between western Europe and Asia. A trading post grew up outside the castle fortifications, attracting ironmongers and leatherworkers. Merchants built stone-and-timber houses on the slope of the bluff running down to the river, the area of today's Mala Strana district.

Just as the Bohemian settlements dotted around Prague began to cohere under a common Czech language and customs, they came under intense pressure from the new superpower on their borders: the empire of the Franks, led by their king and emperor Charlemagne.

CHARLEMAGNE, or 'Charles the great', had built his empire through the conquest and domination of western European lands once ruled by the Romans. At the beginning of the ninth century, his realm encompassed most of modern-day France, Bavaria, Saxony and northern Italy. Charlemagne's conquering armies were followed by waves of missionaries sent to Christianise his newly subjugated lands.

On Christmas Day 800 CE, Charlemagne was crowned Emperor of the Romans by the pope, making him the first ruler of a patchwork realm that would come to be known as the Holy Roman Empire. It had little in common with its ancient pagan namesake, but for its rulers, the prestige of the Roman name was irresistible.

In 805, Charlemagne's armies defeated the Bohemian Slavs, who were compelled to pay tribute of 500 pieces of silver and 120 oxen to their new imperial overlord. The Bohemians regarded their conqueror with a mix of resentment and awe; their generic word for king – *kral* – is taken from 'Karel', the Czech version of his name.[4]

In giving his pious thanks to God for his victory, Charlemagne ordered the conquered Slavs to become Christian, and in 845 fourteen Bohemian chieftains showed up, reluctantly, at the city of Regensburg to be baptised. This was how it would go for the Bohemian Slavs from now on: the price for living in the heart of Europe would be either to fight an ongoing struggle against the greater powers around them, or to carve out some autonomy from within a larger Germanic entity.

The Bohemian Slavs eventually took on the name of their predominant tribe, the Czechs, derived from a word meaning 'people' or 'kinsmen'.* And it's here the historical record begins to intersect with the folk legends of how they came to be.

The Promised Land

THE OLDEST RECORDED version of these legends was written in the twelfth century by the priest and historian Cosmas of Prague. Cosmas gathered the old tales that had been passed from generation to generation, then dressed them up in the fine cloth of antiquity to give them grandeur and dignity. His work *The Chronicle of the Bohemians* is the foundation of the Czech national story, and his 'history' is held, even today, by many Praguers as the true origin of their people and their city.

The Bohemians, Cosmas wrote, were a tribe of Slavs from beyond the Tatra Mountains, who took their name from their leader, a chieftain named Bohemus. After years of wandering through the wilderness, the Bohemians came to a halt in the fields and forests around Rip Mountain, where the land was full of game, the freshwater streams held plenty of fish, and the meadows hummed

---

*   Much the same way that Germans called themselves *Deutsche*, and the Welsh use the term *Cymry*, meaning 'people' or 'fellow countrymen', as opposed to foreigners or *Auslanders*.

with thousands of bees. Bohemus brought out little wooden effigies of the Slavic gods and fixed them to the ground. Then he lay his face upon the soft grass and asked the land to keep them safe and give them many descendants.

Cosmas records that the Bohemians built houses, cowsheds and stables around a village green. They ate acorns and wild game and drank sparkling fresh water from the spring. He describes their society as a kind of primordial communist paradise, where there was no conflict, everything was shared, everyone walked about naked in the sunshine and changed sexual partners every night, breaking 'the iron shackles of love' with each new dawn.[5]

After many happy years, Bohemus expired and the chieftainship of his people fell to a man named Krok. When Krok died, he left no male heir, so the people looked to his youngest daughter, Libussa, who was uncommonly wise and believed to have the gift of prophecy. It was she, according to the legend, who founded the first Bohemian dynasty and the heavenly city of Prague.

LIBUSSA LIVED IN A CASTLE on the bluff overlooking the river, where people came to seek her counsel and to settle their quarrels. Rather than adjudicate from a high seat, Libussa would hear the pleas of her people while reclining on a bed of finely embroidered cushions.

One day, two neighbours came to her court to resolve a dispute over the boundaries of their properties. Libussa heard their arguments, but when she decided in favour of the younger man, the older farmer lost his temper.

'What kind of justice can we expect from a woman?' he asked. 'Her hair is long, but she is short on brains. Shame on us men! Where else does a woman rule, except here?'

The old man's effrontery shocked the court, but no one said anything in Libussa's defence. She flushed, then leant forward.

'It's true what you say,' she said. 'I am a woman and I rule not with a rod of iron, but with compassion, which you mistake for weakness.'

Then she turned to her court. 'As for you,' she said, 'your silence tells me you also want a man to rule over you. Very well. Come back tomorrow and I will marry the man you choose to be your lord.'

THE NEXT MORNING, the clan leaders arrived with their kinsmen. Everyone wondered which man would be chosen to marry Libussa and become their prince.

'The moment has come,' she said in a stony voice, 'when you must tell me who you want for your prince. But I warn you: a man will not rule as I have. He will take your children to become his soldiers or his slaves. He will tax your linen and furs, and seize your horses and cattle to pay for his armies. In return, you will not have to bear the shame of having a woman as your ruler.'

No one in the courtyard spoke.

'So go ahead and choose a man, but be sure you do so carefully. It is easy to put a man on the throne, but much harder to drag him off it. Choose!'

'Tell us who we should choose!' they cried out. 'Advise us, Libussa, as you always have!'

A dreamy expression fell over Libussa's eyes. Pointing to the mountains, she said in a flat, high voice, 'Beyond those hills there is a stream and a crossroads. Take my white horse to that junction, untether it and follow it wherever it leads. It will take you to a man who eats from an iron table. Give that man my crimson robe and slippers and bring him here, for this man will be your lord, and our children will rule this land.'

TWO MESSENGERS SET OUT with Libussa's white horse. It led them from the junction into a field where they found a farm worker eating bread and cheese on an iron plough. His name was Premysl and he really was a very fine looking young man.

The two messengers dressed Premysl in the crimson robe and slippers, and brought him to the castle, where Libussa was ready to receive him.

Libussa and Premysl smiled knowingly at each other. Libussa took his hand and drew him to her and they kissed passionately. Then she led him into the castle, and he spent the night in her bed chamber, as he had many times before.

The wedding festivities lasted three days. Premysl was made prince of Bohemia. He and Libussa had three sons. The first kings of Bohemia, the Premyslids, are descended from them.

TODAY, LIBUSSA WATCHES protectively over her city from multiple vantage points. Go to the House at the Golden Nail on Karlova Street in the Old Town and look up: there she is, high up on a ledge accompanied by three falcons, looking down tenderly at the unsuspecting passers-by. Her statue is the colour of butter. Go inside the vestibule of the Old Town Hall and see her rendered in a mosaic, her arms extended, summoning the city skyline from the earth. In the necropolis of Vysehrad Fortress she is rendered in stone, holding her husband Premysl protectively with one arm, the other arm gesturing to a future only she can see.

The Women's War

LIBUSSA AND PREMYSL are said to have introduced a golden age for the Bohemians. Premysl was the prince, but Libussa, surrounded by her female courtiers, remained the most powerful figure in the land. According to Cosmas, Bohemian women served as warriors, hunted wild animals and chose men who pleased them whenever they wanted them. Women had their own fortress, a castle named Devin, which sat opposite the men's fortress of Vysehrad on the bank of the river.

After Libussa's death, matriarchal power broke down. More than a few men mocked the women's powerlessness. Vlasta, who had been Libussa's closest friend, called the women of Bohemia to arms. At Devin, she trained the strongest as horse archers, the oldest as strategists, and the most beautiful to act as spies and decoys. As they readied themselves for battle, they vowed that their brothers and fathers were nothing to them now.

The men at Vysehrad saw the women practising with their weapons and rode out to attack. Vlasta told the women not to take fright and that it was better to fight and die than to be a slave. The men expected an easy victory, but they were drunk and Vlasta's warrior-women mercilessly cut them to pieces.

The women now extracted their murderous revenge by waging a campaign of terror through the countryside. In farmhouses, men were found lying dead with daggers in their chests. One of Vlasta's decoys, a beautiful woman named Sarka, lured an arrogant young warrior into a glade and captured him. His corpse was found broken on a wheel outside Vlasta's castle.

The men, now full of rage and fear, marshalled a full-strength attack on Vlasta's castle, and this time the women were defeated. Vlasta was killed in the fighting.

Sarka escaped from the slaughter, but refused to live under the rule of men. She wandered west from Prague into a wilderness, where she climbed up to a high cliff and leapt from it to her death in the valley below.

Today, Sarka gives her name to a nature reserve on the western outskirts of Prague known as Wild Sarka. A path through the hills leads to a bluff known as Girl's Jump, where men and women come to stand together on the precipice, and perhaps they look uneasily at each other when they do.

✳

The Stone Throne

LIBUSSA AND PREMYSL are held in Czech tradition to be the founders of the Premyslids, the first ruling dynasty of Bohemia. But the earliest of the Premyslids to emerge from the fog of legend into documented history was a ruler named Borivoj, who declared himself Duke of Bohemia in 867 and built a castle on Hradcany Hill soon afterwards. There he ruled from a princely throne carved from stone in his ducal palace.[6] Within the castle, Borivoj kept a retinue of a few hundred warriors and favourites, a knightly caste that evolved into an independently powerful landed nobility. The power of the duke or king would always exist in a state of tension with the Czech nobles, who reserved their right to elect their ruler.

DUKE BORIVOJ, like most Bohemians, was a pagan, which put him increasingly out of step with the other princes of central Europe. One chronicle records that when Borivoj visited the Christian prince of nearby Moravia, he could not be given a seat of honour at the table; as a pagan, he was obliged to eat on the floor with the goatherds and the other heathens. The experience was so unseemly that the following day, Borivoj, his wife, Ludmila, and his retinue of thirty warriors asked to be instructed in the Christian faith and baptised. At Hradcany, Borivoj ordered a church to be built on top of Zizi, an old pagan sacred site.

Baptism of Duke Borivoj, from the fourteenth-century Bible of Velislav.

BORIVOJ AND LUDMILA'S conversion to the god of the Christians was greeted sullenly by the leading families of Bohemia. Most of the nobility remained loyal to their old gods, whom they believed inhabited the springs, rivers and mountains. Their gods had much in common with the Norse deities of Scandinavia: Perun, the thunder god, took his name from a lightning-splintered tree; Svantovit, the god of war and fertility, had four faces which saw everything in the world; there was Veles, a bearded god who smelt of damp wool and shepherded the souls of the dead into the afterlife.

The shift to Christianity had begun in earnest in 862, when the prince of Greater Moravia wrote to the emperor in Constantinople, asking him to send teachers to the Czech lands 'to explain to us the Christian truths in our own language'.[7]

The emperor was pleased to send two brothers from Thessalonica, Cyril and Methodius, who were acquainted with Slavic languages. While in the Czech lands, Cyril set to work creating a new script that could hold Slavic words to the page more effectively than the Greek or Latin alphabets. The result was an elegant new alphabet known as Glagolitic. With this script, the brothers were able to introduce scripture, liturgy and written law to the Slavs, which brought them into the cross-currents of medieval thought and culture. Over time, Cyril's Glagolitic script evolved into a new alphabet that looked much more like Greek and was thus easier to adopt. It was named Cyrillic in honour of the saint who brought Christianity to the Slavs in their own language, and it prevails today in Russia, Ukraine, Bulgaria and Serbia.

The Slavic rite flourished in Bohemia and Moravia for more than a century, but the collapse of Greater Moravia severed contact with the Byzantine world, and Bohemia adjusted to the Roman Catholic rite and Latin alphabet brought in by German missionaries. Cyril and Methodius were nonetheless canonised, and today the brothers are venerated in both the Catholic and Orthodox churches.

Glagolitic script from the first page of the Gospel of John, from the Codex Zographensis.

*

The Rude Wind's Wild Lament

THE MOST FAMOUS OF the early Premyslid rulers, 'Good King Wenceslas', was not a king at all, but a duke. Bohemia's rulers had not yet earned the right to call themselves kings.

Wenceslas ('Vaclav' in Czech) was raised as a pious Christian by his paternal grandmother, Ludmila. But the boy's piety grated with his pagan mother Drahomira, who complained that her son's mind had been 'twisted by clerics'. He ought to be a prince, she said bitterly, 'but they have made him a monk'.[8]

On his father's death in 921, twelve-year-old Wenceslas was crowned duke of Bohemia, but it was his grandmother Ludmila, not his mother, who was made regent. Rather than be pushed aside, Drahomira hired two assassins to kill her mother-in-law. They found Ludmila at prayer and strangled her with her veil.

Drahomira tried to rally support from the Czech nobles, but her coup flopped, and she was sent into exile. The martyred Ludmila was made a saint.

THE VICES OF POWER, it was said, held no sway with Wenceslas. The duke vowed to rule with justice for all and with charity for the poor. Tenth-century accounts of his life attest to his deep piety: Wenceslas was said to have worn a hairshirt to constantly remind him of the suffering of Christ; and to have personally harvested grapes and grain to make his own wine and bread for the Eucharist.[9] He was seen walking to church at night, barefoot in the winter snow, his mind so enraptured in prayer that the chill of the snow did not trouble him.

Meanwhile, the balance of power was shifting around Bohemia. In 929 Bohemia was invaded from the west by the German king Henry the Fowler. The Germans withdrew when Wenceslas agreed to pay Henry an annual tribute and accept his suzerainty. The bowing of a Bohemian duke to the greater power of a German king would be cited one thousand and ten years later by Adolf Hitler as justification for his invasion of the Czech lands.

Making the best of things, Wenceslas invited German priests into his realm and bestowed generous gifts of furs and silver upon them. Henry, in turn, gave Wenceslas a precious holy relic, the withered arm of St Vitus, a Christian martyr from Sicily.* Wenceslas built a small Romanesque church at Hradcany and dedicated it to St Vitus. The church would later be enlarged and rebuilt into the massive, spiky Gothic cathedral that stands on the grounds of Prague Castle today.

WENCESLAS'S EMBRACE of his German allies was not a popular move at court. Czech nobles fumed at the influx of Germanic language and culture into Bohemia. A group of disgruntled nobles gathered around Boleslav, Wenceslas's ambitious younger brother, to urge him to take the throne for himself.

In late September 935, Boleslav invited Wenceslas to visit him at his castle for a feast. Wenceslas enjoyed a merry evening drinking ale with his brother and his guests. As he mounted his horse to leave, Wenceslas was warned there was a plot against him but refused to believe it.

---

* In northern Europe, the feast day of St Vitus was often celebrated by people dancing around his statue, which gave rise to the expression 'St Vitus's Dance' to describe a neurological disorder that induces sudden jerking movements in the face, hands and feet.

The next morning, on 28 September, Wenceslas set out on foot for morning mass, but in the church courtyard, he was bailed up by his brother and three men with drawn swords.

Wenceslas said uncertainly, 'You were a good host to us last night.'

'Yesterday I served you well,' replied Boleslav, 'but this must be my service for you today.' Then he hit his brother on the head. Wenceslas tried to stagger into the church, but the other men pierced him with their swords and Wenceslas fell dead in the vestibule.[10]

BOLESLAV ASSUMED POWER with the support of the nobles, but his role in the murder of his brother cast a deep shadow on his reign. Boleslav made a show of repenting his terrible sin and arranged for his brother's corpse to be brought to Prague for interment at St Vitus's Church. The men sent to transport the remains claimed that several supernatural events occurred along the way. The stories troubled Boleslav and ensured that Wenceslas would be canonised as a saint.

Duke Boleslav's reign was a hard slog. He renounced the alliance with the Germans and refused to pay tribute to Henry's successor, King Otto I, which led to long years of border incursions, sieges and open warfare.

Boleslav soon realised Bohemia could not be properly defended by a patchwork of local militias, and he set about bringing the Czech nobles to heel. He embarked on a systematic campaign of conquest, ruthlessly tearing down their hillforts and constructing new castles under his command.[11] The network of fortresses brought security and stability to Bohemia, allowing trade to flourish, and for the settlement of Prague to grow accordingly. Although his older brother is venerated as the patron saint of Czech nationhood, it was Boleslav the fratricidal villain who unified Bohemia and gave it a sense of nationhood.

IN 950, BOLESLAV FINALLY bowed to the logic of German power and agreed to pay tribute to Otto, just as his brother had done. Bohemia was thereafter incorporated into the Holy Roman Empire, under the supreme authority of a German king. But Boleslav was able to carve out an independent position within the empire, and his truce with the Germans allowed him to expand into Silesia and Lesser Poland.

IN BOHEMIA, A CULT grew up around Wenceslas's relics. In the nineteenth century, an English songwriter wrote the carol 'Good King Wenceslas', which remembered his barefoot trek in the snow, and made his kindly reputation synonymous with the spirit of Christmas. The great square in Prague that bears his name (which is more like a broad boulevard) is crowned by a heroic statue of the bookish Wenceslas which portrays him absurdly as a manly warrior on horseback. Another statue of Wenceslas on the Charles Bridge shows him with his hands clasped in prayer, looking longingly to the heavens.

The feast day of St Wenceslas falls on 28 September. Every year on the anniversary of his death, his skull is brought up from its crypt, girdled by a crown, and draped with a gauzy veil across its face.

Skull of St Wenceslas.

The Grave of the Warrior

IN 1925, WITH THE millennial anniversary of Wenceslas's death approaching, an archaeological dig was commissioned on the grounds of Prague Castle. It was hoped that the discovery of artefacts from Wenceslas's time would reveal the sturdy roots of the Czechs in Bohemia and connect them to the dignity of their legendary past.

Three years into the dig, a young archaeologist named Ivan Borkovsky was working in the third courtyard, scraping away at the surface, when he uncovered a shallow grave. As he brushed away the dirt and rocks, Borkovsky saw a male skeleton laid out inside a crumbling oak coffin. The skeleton was surrounded with fine grave goods: an axe, several knives, a leather bag containing a flint, a wooden bucket with metal hoops, and a handsome but heavily corroded metre-long sword in a scabbard.

The finding was deemed significant enough to have the entire burial plot winched up from the ground intact, and brought into the Gothic Old Royal Palace, where it could be preserved and studied more closely.

There was great excitement when scientists dated the grave to the late tenth century, the era of Wenceslas and Boleslav. Who was this warrior? The location of his burial site and the grave goods indicated he was a figure of some importance. Was he a prince, a nobleman or a mere swordsman? And most importantly for the authorities, was he Czech or was he German?

Borkovsky recognised strong similarities to Viking graves he'd seen elsewhere, which presented him with an awkward personal dilemma: Borkovsky was a Ukrainian, who had come to Prague to escape the Stalinist terror. At the time he discovered the skeleton, he was applying for permanent residency in Czechoslovakia and he worried that if he spoke up and identified the warrior as a Viking – that is, as *Germanic* – the Czech authorities would be offended and throw him out of the country. So, when his boss at the National Museum, Karel Guth, published an article suggesting the skeleton might be that of the first Premyslid ruler, Duke Borivoj, Borkovsky kept his doubts to himself.

THE NAZI OCCUPATION of Prague in 1939 turned all these considerations on their head. Czech nationalism was out and German nationalism was very much in. The new Nazi masters didn't hesitate to claim the dead warrior as one of their own, and his purported Germanic origins were played up to support the legitimacy of their occupation of Bohemia. His prestigious burial site, they argued, proved that Hradcany was Germanic in origin, not Slavic, and that made Hitler the castle's rightful owner. A Nazi spokesman rhapsodised over the 'eternal stream of blood' which bound modern Germans to the Nordic warriors who had once fought for German soil in Bohemia.[12]

German archaeologists angrily accused the Ukrainian of suppressing the truth of the warrior's origins. Taking the hint, Borkovsky published a paper in 1941 supporting the warrior's identity as a Viking.

It was only a temporary reprieve. Four years later, the Nazis were expelled from Prague by the Soviet army. The new official view was that the warrior was *unquestionably* a Slav. Borkovsky was threatened with being sent to a Soviet gulag for his pro-German paper as well as for his pre-war anti-Stalin views. In his defence, the archaeologist pleaded he'd been forced to publish under Nazi pressure, and indicated his willingness to write a second paper to correct the record.

The new article safely concluded that the early date of the burial precluded the presence of Vikings in Bohemia. The warrior was therefore, he wrote, almost certainly a Slav, and probably related to the Premyslids. Not leaving anything to chance, Borkovsky remarked that the quality of the grave goods was indicative of the advanced cultural level attained by the early Slavic settlers. With that, he was off the hook again.

Throughout the communist years, the grave of the warrior was kept in storage, safely out of sight, presumably in case someone noticed his Viking sword. It wasn't until 2004, fifteen years after the collapse of communism, that it could be placed on display in the Old Royal Palace.

The Grave of the Warrior, Old Royal Palace, Prague.

New technology has recently forced the troublesome skeleton to yield some of his secrets. Strontium isotope analysis of his teeth revealed that he came from the Baltic coast, an area populated in the tenth century by Vikings, Slavs and Baltic tribes. The presence of a Viking-style sword and axe, alongside Czech domestic objects – the bucket and knives – suggests he existed within a complex, hybrid culture, among people inclined to use the best tools available, no matter what their provenance, just as Praguers have done for centuries.[13]

*

City of Stone and Lime

AS PRAGUE EXPANDED, trade activity moved from Hradcany Hill and Mala Strana to the other side of the river, forming the nucleus of Prague's Old Town. Market places sprang up around the Old Town Square, and a manor house for foreign merchants was built around a fortified courtyard named the Tyn Yard. Stone merchant-houses, tanneries and breweries grew up along what is now Celetna and Karlova streets.

By the end of the first Christian millennium, Prague had become a thriving centre of commerce, trading in basic staples, exotic luxury goods and slaves. In 965 CE, a Jewish traveller from Spain named Ibrahim ibn Yaqub passed through the city and recorded his impressions:

> *Prague is built with stone and lime; it is the largest trade centre*
> *in this land. To this city come Russians and Slavs from the city of*
> *Cracow, with their goods. And from the land of the Turks come*
> *Muslims, Jews, and Magyars with goods and merchants' weights.*
> *From these merchants they buy slaves, tin, and various furs.*
> *Their land is the best in the north and the richest in food.*

Ibrahim was a merchant, a scholar and slave-trader, and possibly a spy for the Muslim caliph of Cordoba. He observed the medieval Praguers as they went about their daily lives like an anthropologist:

> *Their women when married, do not commit adultery. But when*
> *a girl falls in love with some man or other, she will go to him and*

quench her lust. If a husband marries a girl and finds her to be
a virgin he says to her, 'If there were something good in you, then
you would certainly have found someone to take your virginity.'
Then he sends her back.

The people of the city, Ibrahim noted, had no baths. Instead, they
would build a wooden shed, seal up the walls with tar, and build
a stone stove in one corner. Once inside this medieval sauna, 'they
pour the water on the glowing coals in the stove until steam rises up.
Each of them holds a bundle of dried herbs; with them he fans the
air toward himself. And then their pores open and a torrent of sweat
comes out, flowing over their bodies until not even a trace of ulcer or
skin eruption remains.'[14]

IN 973, THE POPE recognised Prague's growing importance by
establishing it as a diocese with its own bishopric, but Adalbert, the
first Czech bishop, came to despair of his heathen flock. Although
Bohemia was officially Christian, the faith was still mostly confined to
the nobility, while the merchants and the common people remained
stubbornly pagan. 'The flock entrusted to me does not wish to listen
to me,' Adalbert complained in a letter to Rome. Bohemia was, he
said, 'a country where strong fists rule instead of justice.'[15]

Adalbert came from the powerful Slavnik clan. When Duke
Boleslav entered into a feud with the Slavniks, the bishop fled Prague
in fear of his life. Boleslav, somewhat embarrassed, persuaded
Adalbert to return to his post, but this second stint as bishop was
cut short by a hideous incident. One night, a noblewoman accused
of adultery came to his door begging for protection against an angry
mob. Adalbert granted her the sanctuary of his church, but when the
mob arrived, they demanded he hand her over. When he refused,

they pushed him aside and found the woman clinging to the altar. She was dragged out onto the steps of the convent and killed.

Adalbert ex-communicated the murderers and then left Prague for good to wander through Europe as a missionary. He travelled north, to the dank marshlands and forests of the Baltic coast to preach God's truth to the Old Prussians, the last pagan people of Europe. But his presence was unwelcome: the local chieftains condemned him as a spy and a coloniser. Adalbert was decapitated, and his corpse thrown into the Baltic Sea. His remains later washed ashore in the Vistula delta.[16]

The King of Poland, who had known and admired Adalbert, was appalled. He offered to purchase Adalbert's remains, but the pagans demanded the corpse's weight in gold as their price, an astronomical sum. The Polish king agreed, and the martyr's remains were brought to the city of Gniezno and buried there in the year 1000. Adalbert was duly canonised as a saint.

IN 1039, A BOHEMIAN army raided Gniezno and seized Adalbert's bones as plunder. The relics were brought to Prague and re-interred at the castle, where they remain to this day.* On feast days, his skull is sometimes brought out under a glass dome for public viewing.

Today, a dramatic baroque statue of St Adalbert stands on the Charles Bridge, clutching the gospels with one hand, while gently blessing bridge walkers with the other; a monument to a martyr honoured more by his fellow Bohemians in death than in life.

---

* The Poles of Gniezno dispute this story; they insist the Bohemians were fooled into taking the wrong bones, and that the true relics of Adalbert remain enshrined in Gniezno.

The People's Crusade in Prague

IMAGINING MEDIEVAL PRAGUE today while standing in its streets is, to begin with, an extractive process; the background traffic ceases and is replaced by footfalls, trundling cartwheels and the slow plodding of a horse; in the air there is birdsong and the chime of a church bell; from the houses there is the clatter of wooden plates, feet thumping down some stairs, the creaking of a door.

There are no sewers, only gutters, and so the stench in the street stings the nose, as does the sweet, rancid tang from the hides of a tannery. But there is also the passing scent of a wood fire from a brazier, brewer's yeast from a kitchen window, and a trace of incense wafting from an open church door.

The Vltava is there of course, but there is no stone bridge and no brick embankments; the river courses alongside banks of mud and long grass. There is no New Town, no spires of St Vitus soaring up from Hradcany, only rotundas and stone bastions poking above the clay-slate walls; the handsome baroque facades in Mala Strana are replaced by cruder timber-and-stone frontages; the streets are unpaved; pigs and hens are penned up next to the houses.

People are smaller and dirtier than they are now, and pockmarked by disease. For most of them, the distinction between the natural and the supernatural is non-existent – angels and demons are as real as birds, beasts and insects. At night, the darkness and silence are broken by the feeble light of a candle in a window and the echo of a persistent hacking cough. When people look up at the night sky, they see a screen upon which God does his handwriting.

IN THE YEAR 1095, Europeans looked to the heavens and observed a meteor shower, a comet and a lunar eclipse. The celestial activity clearly portended that some momentous crisis was at hand.

Reports filtering in from the east confirmed that Islam was on the march again, and that the armies of the Muslim Seljuk Turks now occupied Jerusalem. In response to a request for help from the Emperor of Constantinople, Pope Urban II made an incendiary speech, calling for a crusade, a war of the cross, to expel the 'base and bastard' Muslim infidels from the Holy Land.

Urban's speech unlocked vast latent energies within Europe's half-starved, overworked masses. In the months that followed, French and German nobles assembled and provisioned their armies for the long march to the east. But there were charismatic preachers among the poor who scorned the idea of careful preparation; to them, such precautions seemed timorous, even faithless. They told their flocks that Christ's warriors would only need to march to the Holy Land and surely the Muslims would be scattered by the trumpet blasts of angels. Such preachers inspired thousands of peasants and petty criminals to pick up whatever weapons or farm implements they could get their hands on and to follow them to Jerusalem. They massacred every Jewish settlement they encountered along the way. These shambling armies became known as the People's Crusade.

One horde of the pauper crusaders wandered through the Rhine Valley following a goose they believed was filled with the Holy Spirit. Another group, led by a charismatic priest named Volkmar, entered Bohemia and on 30 May 1096, they arrived at the gates of Prague.

THE TIMING, FOR THE inhabitants, was exquisitely awful: the duke and his army were away campaigning in Poland. With no force to restrain them, Volkmar's crusaders fell upon the Jewish settlement at the foot of Prague Castle, cutting throats, stealing goods and performing baptisms at knife-point. Clergymen begged the crusaders to stop the atrocities but were ignored. After days of blood and horror, Volkmar's crusaders left the city for Hungary. When order was restored in Prague, the Jews who had been forcibly converted were permitted to return to Judaism.[17] Meanwhile, the King of Hungary sent in his army to cut the crusaders to pieces. Not one of the armies of the People's Crusade would ever make it to the Holy Land.

THE FLEDGLING JEWISH community rebuilt itself, but in 1142 their settlement at the foot of Hradcany was burnt to the ground once again, and Prague's first synagogue went down with it. The community elected to move across the river into a tightly packed wedge of streets between the Old Town Square and the Vltava.

Medieval law decreed Jews to be collectively guilty for the murder of Christ and that they should be held in servitude to the king, which constrained where they could go and how they could behave. Jews were free to move around Prague during the day, but in the evening and on Christian festivals the gates of the ghetto were locked to protect the inhabitants from sudden outbreaks of violence. Conspicuously wealthy Jews were a tempting target for greedy dukes and resentful commoners. A pogrom – a massacre of the Jewish community – would typically be sparked by a spurious allegation of Jewish sacrilege or treachery.

PRAGUE'S JEWISH QUARTER, known today as Josefov, is still its smallest district. Most of the medieval ghetto was demolished in the slum clearances of the nineteenth century, and the maze of gimcrack tenements was replaced with respectable Beaux Arts apartment buildings. The main avenue, Parizska – Paris Street –

has become the high-end shopping precinct of post-communist Prague, lined with boutiques selling branded luxury goods found in airport transit lounges all over the world. But a left turn down the steps of a narrow lane called Red Street leads you into the heart of old Jewish Prague.

The solemn Old-New Synagogue on Maiselova Street has been the focus of Jewish religious and social life in Prague since its completion in 1270.* It sits diagonally across from Prague's Jewish Cemetery, an angular compressed space, filled with ancient tombstones that bob up from the soil like floating debris. The stones are inscribed in Hebrew and capped with symbols that represent the deceased: a book for a cantor, scissors for a tailor. A bunch of grapes indicates a happy and prosperous life.

The two thousand visible tombstones represent only a small fraction of the dead buried below the surface. After the cemetery was founded, the small patch of land soon filled up, so the surface had to be filled in and levelled off, creating room for a new layer of graves. In some places, the layers run twelve deep.

ON MY FIRST VISIT to Prague in 1990, I wondered how the synagogues and cemetery had survived the six years of Nazi occupation. And now I know. Hitler's SS left the buildings untouched so that after the war, when all the Jews were dead or gone, the ghetto could become an open-air Nazi tourist attraction – a museum of an extinct race. Here, visitors would buy ice-creams and wander past the synagogues, candelabras and Torah scrolls of the annihilated race, and 'silently rejoice over the progress of civilisation'.[18]

---

* It was originally called the New Synagogue but the name was changed when newer temples were built nearby.

Headstones at Prague's Jewish Cemetery.

King Wenceslas and Saint Agnes

PRAGUE GREW UPWARDS and outwards throughout the twelfth and thirteenth centuries. The Old Town Square became fully enclosed with stone houses, while a small German community sprang up around St Peter's Church. The first stone bridge to span the Vltava, the Judith Bridge, was completed in 1172, linking Mala Strana with the Old Town. As the population swelled, the spaces between the districts began to close up, and by the end of the thirteenth century, the name Prague was commonly used to refer to the collection of towns as a whole.

In 1235, the Old Town was enclosed by a seven-metre-high stone wall, with ramparts and a drawbridge, which stood back from a broad, deep moat. Today, the line of the city walls can be traced along the busy shopping street Na Prikope – 'On the Moat' – which separates the Old Town from Wenceslas Square.

The discovery of rich silver deposits in nearby Jihlava and Kutna Hora turned Prague into a boom town. The kingdom of Bohemia, flush with wealth, became the most powerful dominion within the

Holy Roman Empire, and in 1212, the emperor issued a charter, the Golden Bull of Sicily, that conferred the hereditary title of king upon Bohemia's rulers. The document recognised Bohemia as the pre-eminent territory of the Holy Roman Empire, and its king as the first of the empire's prince-electors.

KING WENCESLAS I was the first of four Bohemian kings to be named after the murdered saint. His court at Prague Castle adopted the chivalric culture fashionable in Europe at the time, amusing themselves with bouts of hunting and jousting and songs of courtly love performed by wandering German poets.

Wenceslas's reign was crowned with military triumph. In 1241, the king rode out with his knights to aid Henry II of Silesia in his struggle against the invading Mongol army, the Golden Horde of Batu Khan, which had devastated eastern Europe. Unable to wait for Wenceslas's arrival, Henry impetuously launched into battle. The attack was a fiasco: his army was completely destroyed and the city of Cracow was burnt to the ground. Wenceslas retreated with his still-intact army to the narrow Klodzko Valley. In the cramped mountainous passage, the Mongol riders were unable to manoeuvre, and the Bohemians fought them off. The Golden Horde lost interest in Bohemia and headed south to raid Hungary.

King Wenceslas returned to Prague a hero.

DESPITE THIS TRIUMPH, King Wenceslas's name was destined to be eclipsed by his youngest sister Agnes.

From early childhood, Agnes was betrothed to a series of royal suitors but every one of the engagements was called off. She was first engaged at the age of three to a Silesian prince and sent to a Polish convent to be suitably educated, but her fiancé died before she came of age. At eight, Agnes was again betrothed, this time to the ten-year-old son of the Holy Roman Emperor Frederick II, but after six years the proposed marriage was cancelled. Her next suitor was King Henry III of England, but negotiations between Prague and London came to nothing. Then Emperor Frederick himself proposed marriage, but Agnes had had enough and, after consulting the pope, she turned him down. Agnes was now 23 years old and ready to live on her own terms. In 1231, she left the confines of Prague Castle and came down to the Old Town, where she entered a convent. Inspired by the example of Saint Francis of Assisi, Agnes gave away her wealth and had her hair shorn. In between bouts of fasting, she existed on a diet of raw onions, bread and fruit. She regularly prepared food for the poor and washed the clothes of lepers.[19]

In 1234, she used a donation of land from her brother to found a hospital and a beautiful convent next to the river. The cloister was the grandest Gothic structure in the city other than Prague Castle itself, but the women within its walls practised radical Christian poverty and charity. In 1238, Agnes organised the nurses and physicians at the hospital into a new military order dedicated to nursing, known as the Knights of the Cross with the Red Star. She lived out her life as abbess of the cloister until her death on 2 March 1282.

AGNES'S CLOSEST FRIEND and mentor was another nun, Sister Clare of Assisi, who gave her name to the order known as the Poor Clares. The two women never met face-to-face, but shared an intimate correspondence for decades. Like Agnes, Sister Clare longed for the spiritual freedom of absolute poverty. Clare spoke of Agnes as 'the other half of my soul and the special shrine of my heart's deepest love'. Spiritual yearning melded with sublimated erotic longing in their letters, as these brides of Christ called out to their heavenly saviour:

O heavenly spouse!
I will run and not tire,
until you bring me into the wine-cellar,
until your left hand is under my head
and your right hand blissfully embraces me;
and you will kiss me with the most blissful kiss of your mouth.[20]

SEVERAL MIRACLES WERE later attributed to Agnes, but she would have to wait a good seven centuries before she was canonised. She finally achieved sainthood in November 1989, just as the Velvet Revolution was erupting on the streets of Prague. Many Catholics believed the timing was no coincidence, and in 2011, the princess-nun of Prague was acclaimed as the Patron Saint of the Overthrow of Communism. Her convent was restored in the 1980s and now serves as Prague's glorious Museum of Medieval Art.

The Iron and Golden King

AGNES, FOR ALL HER ASCETICISM, never entirely withdrew from family politics, and in 1250, she stepped in to reconcile her brother, the king, with his treacherous son, Prince Otakar.

The young, ambitious Otakar was described as 'a handsome youth, of swarthy complexion, middling stature, broad chest, full lips, vivacious and wise'.[21] The fifteen-year old prince had been passing his days drinking and hunting when a cabal of disgruntled nobles inveigled him into a plot to overthrow his father. Given Otakar's aggressive, impatient nature, it's unlikely he needed much persuading.

In 1248, while King Wenceslas was out of town, the rebels installed

Otakar at the castle, hailing him as *Rex Iuvenis Boemorum* – Younger King of Bohemia. Otakar ruled for just eighteen months before his father gathered some soldiers, seized back his crown and flung his impertinent son into prison. The rebellious nobles were beheaded or broken on a wheel.

Otakar spent some weeks in prison until Agnes interceded on his behalf. As Wenceslas's only living son and heir, Otakar was too useful a political asset to be left out in the cold for long, so he was released on probation. The king appointed him Margrave of Moravia and married him off to Margaret of Babenburg to seal the family's claim to Austria and Styria. Margaret was nearly thirty years his senior, but Otakar had no choice but to consent to the union.

A year later, Wenceslas I died and his son was crowned King Otakar II Premysl of Bohemia at Prague Castle on 23 December 1253.

KING OTAKAR II, was just twenty years old when he took the throne, but by virtue of his acumen, aggression and good fortune, he became the greatest of the Premyslid kings and, briefly, the most powerful man in central Europe.[22]

Otakar began his reign with a show of military strength, leading a 60,000-strong coalition of armies in a crusade against the pagan Prussians of the Baltic coast. The Prussians were easily crushed and forced to accept baptism at sword-point. Afterwards, the royal fort of Koenigsberg – King's Mountain – was named in his honour.*

BOHEMIA'S GROWING STRENGTH aroused the jealousy of King Bela IV of Hungary, who made his own claim to the provinces of Austria and Styria. In the summer of 1260, Bela brought a

---

* Now the gloomy Russian city of Kaliningrad.

35,000-strong army to the Austrian border, near the town of Kressenbrunn. Otakar summoned his own coalition of 30,000 soldiers, and the two forces confronted each other on either side of the Morava River. Neither king dared to risk crossing the water to attack, so both armies glared at each other in the summer heat for several days without making a move.

Otakar offered to break the stalemate by backing up a little, to give Bela's troops a chance to cross the river unharmed and allow them to fight on equal terms on open ground. The Bohemians stepped back and Bela's horsemen began to cross the river, but when the Hungarian light cavalry got to the other side, they became excited and charged at the retreating Bohemians. Otakar took this as a breach of the agreement and wheeled his heavy cavalry around to attack while Bela's men were still crossing the river. The outraged Bohemians mauled the Hungarian light horsemen and pushed them into the flowing water. Those who were not cut down drowned trying to escape, while the remnants of Bela's army looked on helplessly from the other bank. Within an hour, ten thousand of Bela's men lay dead or drowned.

OTAKAR'S VICTORY at Kressenbrunn compelled Bela to cede his claim to Styria. The peace was sealed by a royal wedding. Otakar's childless marriage to the aged Margaret was annulled, and in 1261, he wed Bela's granddaughter, the sixteen-year-old princess Kunhuta. The wedding at Prague Castle was followed by a coronation of the bride, and a feast on Letna Hill, overlooking the city.

Like his father, Otakar made Prague Castle a home for artists, poets and German troubadours, who sang in praise of their king's wisdom and virtue. In 1262, he issued his *Statuta Judaeorum*, which gave Otakar the right to tax his Jewish subjects as he pleased and to restrict where they could live and how they could work. In return, the Jews were granted the right to manage their own civil affairs. The decree also obliged the king to protect Jews from Christian violence and against the blood libel – the medieval slander that accused Jews of harvesting the blood of Christian children to make their Passover bread.

In 1269 Otakar acquired more lands through strategic diplomacy in Carinthia, modern-day Slovenia, and Friuli near Venice, and for the one and only time in its history, Bohemia was no longer land-locked. Otakar's dominion extended all the way to the shores of the Adriatic Sea.

OTAKAR WAS NOW HAILED throughout Europe as the Iron and Golden King: iron for his military success and gold for his wealth. But the awe of the German princes and bishops surrounding Bohemia was tinged with resentment and fear.

Otakar's great good fortune had been to come to power during an imperial interregnum, when the various states and principalities of the Holy Roman Empire could not agree on who should wear the crown as emperor, and so no rival could emerge. The ramshackle empire had become an ill-fitting jigsaw puzzle of German, French, Italian and Czech kingdoms, duchies, church lands and territories, each with its own ruler, some of whom had the right to elect the Holy Roman Emperor, who reigned over the whole thing.

As the most powerful ruler within the empire, Otakar naturally wanted that imperial dignity for himself, and in 1273 he put himself forward to the imperial electoral college. The successful candidate would be named king of the Romans until the pope could formally crown him in Rome as Holy Roman Emperor. Otakar seemed the obvious choice, but the college wanted a counterweight to his overweening power, and to Otakar's astonishment they elected a minor German noble, Rudolf of Habsburg, instead.

Let Others Wage War

RUDOLF OF HABSBURG was an unprepossessing figure, yet by the age of fifty-five, he had become deft at tripping up powerful opponents such as Otakar, using their greater weight against them. In the coming centuries, such tactics, mixed with good luck, cunning and a knack for judicious marriages, would win the Habsburgs a multi-national empire that spanned the globe. While other dynasties bled themselves dry with war, the Austrian Habsburgs prided themselves on their family motto: *Let others wage war: you, happy Austria, marry.*[23]

The House of Habsburg traces its origins to the eleventh century, when a minor noble named Radbot of Klettgau built a castle named Habsburg in modern-day Switzerland. Over time, his descendants took on the name of the fortress. The dynasty would produce only a few outstanding leaders and a great many mediocre ones. Such was the stress on keeping power within the family, the Habsburgs often married within their clan, a habit that, over time, distorted their physiognomies, producing heirs with heavily swollen jaws and protuberant lips. Inbreeding would eventually incapacitate the Habsburgs to such a degree that by the nineteenth century, they found it almost impossible to reproduce.[24]

Nonetheless, despite their apparent mediocrity, the Habsburgs would come to dominate the continent for centuries. As defenders of the Catholic faith, they fended off repeated incursions by the Ottoman empire, and ruthlessly suppressed the spread of Protestantism in their lands. While other famous families flared briefly then fizzled out like roman candles, the Habsburgs plodded along generation after generation until their dominion extended over most of Europe and to their far-off colonies in Asia and the Americas.

IN 1273, ALL THAT LAY in the distant future. Count Rudolf of Habsburg was still a very minor player compared to Otakar, the Iron and Golden King; but in the contest for the imperial crown, Rudolf outfoxed Otakar in classic Habsburg fashion: securing the support of the prince-electors of Saxony and the Palatinate by betrothing two of his daughters to them. Otakar, who was absent in Hungary, was misled by his ambassadors into thinking he had the numbers in the electoral college and was shocked when Rudolf won the vote unanimously.

Otakar denounced the election process as improper and refused to accept a lowly count as emperor-elect. Rudolf, undeterred, demanded that Otakar hand over the Premyslids' recently acquired lands in Austria, Styria and Carinthia to the imperial crown. When Otakar refused, he was placed under the imperial ban, which legally deprived him of his rights and possessions until he submitted to Rudolf's authority.

In 1276, Rudolf invaded Austria at the head of five armies. Otakar marched out to meet him, but a rebellion among the Czech nobles at home pulled him back to Bohemia and he was forced to sue for peace. Otakar agreed to give up all his territories other than Bohemia and Moravia, which he now had to graciously 'accept' from Rudolf on bended knee as fiefdoms of the emperor.

Humiliated, Otakar plotted his revenge against the Habsburg schemer who had somehow undone his life's work. On 26 August 1278, Otakar's armies confronted Rudolf's on a grassy plain at Marchfeld in Austria. The Bohemians charged into battle, crying, '*Praha*!' while Rudolf's men shouted, 'Rome and Christ!'[25]

Rudolf's knights led the attack, accompanied by lightly armoured Cuman horse archers from the Eurasian steppe, who rode in fast, fired their lethal arrows and then raced off before Otakar's men could retaliate. Otakar led his Bohemian heavy cavalry forward and drove the Austrians back towards a stream. Rudolf, now aged sixty, was caught in the fighting when his horse was cut down under him, and only narrowly escaped with his life.

Otakar seemed close to victory, until a reserve group of German knights hidden on the sidelines attacked the Bohemian flank. Otakar's men, confused in their heavy armour, turned and fled into the nearby vineyards, leaving their king stranded on the field of battle. Otakar, exhausted and almost entirely alone, fought on, until a young Austrian nobleman struck him down with a blow to the head. The Cuman raiders looted his armour and clothes, and then mutilated his body.

Otakar's remains were gathered up and eventually entombed in St Vitus Cathedral. In 1976, the tomb was opened and his skull was carefully examined. The axe-blow that killed him was clearly visible.

The Last of the Premyslids

THE DEATH OF THE KING was followed by years of chaos in Prague, as Rudolf carved up Otakar's lands and parcelled them out to his friends and family. Rudolf's sons were given the Austrian territories, shifting the centre of Habsburg power to Vienna, where it would remain. The emperor kept Moravia for himself.

Bohemia had to be handled more carefully. Rudolf had to acknowledge Otakar's son as the rightful heir to the throne, but Wenceslas II was not quite seven years old and so Rudolf installed his ally Otto of Brandenburg in Prague Castle as regent. The boy-king was sent to Brandenburg as a hostage, while Otto's armies pillaged Bohemia.

Lawlessness and violence in the countryside brought famine and pestilence to Prague. Within weeks, the plague cut down a quarter of the city's population, leaving empty houses and workshops. Two thousand bodies were flung into a pit next to the Church of St Peter. A story was later told of a plague victim who revived in the pit, and kept himself alive by consuming the flesh of the bodies laid on top of him until discovered. For a while, it seemed as though the whole kingdom might disintegrate.

WENCESLAS II, THE BOY-KING of Bohemia, was permitted to return to a slowly recovering Prague in 1280. At fourteen he married Judith of Habsburg, another of Rudolf's daughters, and at eighteen, he was ready to rule independently.

Recognising the need to lift the spirits of his subjects, he organised a dazzling coronation ceremony in 1297. The king and queen were crowned on a glorious summer's day in a ceremony at Hradcany, which was followed by festivities across the city. Dukes, princes and other nobility dined in a richly decorated wooden feasting hall, which extended from Petrin Hill to the river. In the Old Town, musicians and acrobats performed for the revellers. Wine flowed from public fountains and people danced in the squares. A group of men removed their clothes and held a running race through the narrow streets. A chronicler recorded that everyone went home with a happy heart, despite the pickpockets in the crowd.[26]

WENCESLAS II PROVED TO be as able as his famous father. He took care to maintain good relations with Rudolf, his father-in-law, who in turn agreed to restore Bohemia's vote in the imperial electoral college. The wealth from the silver mines allowed Wenceslas to expand the boundaries of the Bohemian realm once again. In 1300, after annexing Upper Silesia, Wenceslas was invited to accept the crown of Poland. A year later, when the Arpad dynasty died out, a group of Hungarian nobles offered him their crown as well.

The Premyslids now held all three crowns of central Europe, a stunning turnaround in fortunes. But once again, the power imbalance provoked a backlash in Vienna and Rome, and the king was forced to withdraw the family's claim to the Hungarian crown.

When Wenceslas II died of tuberculosis in 1305 he was replaced by his fifteen-year-old son, Wenceslas III, who preferred drinking with his friends than attending to matters of state. Wenceslas III's grasp on the Polish crown began to slip when a rival claimant, the entertainingly named Wladyslaw the Elbow-high, took the city of Cracow from him. Wenceslas raised an army and was on his way to take it back when he was stabbed to death in his tent by an unknown assassin on 4 August 1306.

And with that, the long line of Premyslid rulers, who had reigned in Prague for more than four centuries, was finally extinguished.

ONCE AGAIN BOHEMIA fell into a messy, protracted succession crisis, which became, in essence, a struggle between Wenceslas's two sisters, Anna and Eliska, and their rival husbands. The crown changed hands four times in as many years. The crisis was only resolved when Eliska arrived at the gates of Prague accompanied by her fourteen-year-old husband, John of Luxembourg, and several imperial regiments. The burghers of the Old Town, tired of the instability, opened the gates of the city, and Anna's gormless husband, Henry of Carinthia, was forced to flee. John and Eliska were crowned King and Queen of Bohemia on 4 December 1310.

PRAGUE CASTLE HAD BEEN damaged in a fire, and so the royal couple were obliged to move into the House at the Stone Bell on the Old Town Square.* In 1316, Eliska gave birth to a son named, inevitably, Wenceslas, but the young King John, who had been raised in Paris, was unhappy in Prague. He spoke no Czech, and never bothered to learn. John, in turn, was disliked by the nobility for his lavish expenditure, his unwillingness to learn the language and his reliance on the German advisors sent to him by his father.

THE RELATIONSHIP BETWEEN king and queen soured as well. John disliked his forceful wife, who was four years older and treated her young husband accordingly. Eliska saw herself as the defender of the Premyslid family heritage, which made him feel like an interloper. In 1319, John received intelligence, real or imagined, that Eliska was planning to overthrow him and rule Bohemia as regent through their three-year-old son. John pre-emptively arrested his wife and exiled her to a castle in northern Bohemia. His blameless son, Wenceslas, was imprisoned in a dungeon at Loket Castle. The boy would never see his mother again.

King John now longed to leave Bohemia, but he was unwilling to lose the income and prestige that came with his crown. A compromise was reached with the nobles: the king was to hand over management of the kingdom to them; in return, he could keep his crown and would be granted a regular income.

FREED OF HIS KINGLY RESPONSIBILITIES, John abandoned Prague to pursue his dreams of conquest in Denmark, eastern Europe and northern Italy. To raise more gold, he pawned his royal castles.

---

* Today it houses the City Gallery of Prague, where the bell still hangs.

When those funds ran out, he raided the tombs of St Wenceslas and St Adalbert, stripping them of their gems and treasures. John, the first of the Luxembourg kings of Bohemia, made something of a reputation for himself in Europe as a brave warrior-king, but his legacy in Prague was that of a parasite and a vandal. It would be up to his eldest son to redeem the family name.

Young Charles

KING JOHN HAD COME to fear and resent his son Wenceslas, whose Premyslid blood had endowed him with a stronger claim to the Bohemian crown than his foreign father. John intended to keep him well away from Prague, and in 1323, he sent the seven-year-old boy to Paris to be raised in the court of the French king, Charles le Bel.

Wenceslas received an excellent education in Paris, and eventually became fluent in five languages: Latin, Czech, German, French and Italian. His most significant influence in these years was his tutor, the court priest Pierre de Rosières, a diplomat and scholar, who would one day become Pope Clement VI. The priest introduced the young prince to the life of mind and took him to lectures at the Sorbonne. At thirteen, Wenceslas was betrothed to Blanche de Valois, who was the same age, and the union would prove to be a happy one. At his confirmation, he asked to change his name to Charles, in honour of his host the king.

IN 1331, KING JOHN sent his son to northern Italy to represent the Luxembourg family interests there. Charles had grown into a tall, lean teenager, and by his own account, he spent lavishly on his pleasures and slept with many women. He participated in jousting tournaments under an assumed name, and suffered an injury to his jaw, which left an ugly scar on his left cheek.

In the course of his two-year sojourn in Italy, Charles learnt how to fight with a sword, build up a town's defences and to negotiate a treaty. At Modena, he led an army to an unlikely victory in a battle which dragged on from early afternoon until sundown. Charles was wounded in the shoulder and his horse was killed from under him. Afterwards, he was knighted in the field with 200 of his comrades.[27]

Charles curtailed his dissolute lifestyle (or so he claimed) after an electrifying vision one night in the village of Terenzo. He dreamt an angel appeared at his bedside and pulled him up by his hair into the sky. The angel pointed down to a scene of battle and commanded, 'Look and see!' Below, Charles saw a great army of horsemen amassing at a castle gate led by the Dauphin of Vienna, an ally of his father's. Then he saw another angel swoop down with a flaming sword to slash at the dauphin's groin, leaving him to bleed to death.

'For his sins of impurity he has been struck down by God!' said the angel, still dangling Charles by the hair. 'Beware then, and tell your father that he too should beware of the same sin. Or worse will befall him and you.'

Charles claimed he tried to tell his father of the angel's warning, but was dismissed. Several days later, news arrived at Parma that the Dauphin of Vienna had indeed been killed while besieging a castle. He had been hit by an arrow in the thigh.[28]

CHARLES RETURNED TO BOHEMIA in 1333, after an absence of eleven years to administer the lands of the Bohemian crown in his father's name. In Prague, he was told his mother Eliska had died three years earlier of tuberculosis. The news left him feeling untethered from the land of his birth. 'When I came to Bohemia,' he wrote, 'I found neither father nor mother nor brother nor sister nor anyone I knew. Also, I had completely forgotten Czech, which I later relearnt.'[29]

Both he and Blanche were eighteen now, and he brought her to Prague as soon as possible so they could live together as husband and wife. They found Prague in a shameful state of neglect, plundered of its wealth to pay for his father's largely pointless campaigns in Italy and elsewhere. Charles ordered urgent reconstruction of the castle, and tried to win back the crown lands mortgaged by John, but was undercut by his father, who was jealous of Charles's evident ability and growing popularity.

A year later, father and son were reconciled. John had contracted ophthalmia and his eyesight was rapidly dimming. He was ready now to transfer his ambitions to Charles, whom he named Margrave of Moravia and governor of Bohemia. Even then he did so meanly, forging a contract that required Charles to pay his father five thousand pieces of silver a year in return for the privilege of the office.[30]

CHARLES, DESPITE HIS YOUNG AGE, moved as though he had no time to waste. He persuaded the pope to upgrade the status of Prague to an archbishopric, and to appoint his friend Ernest of Pardubice to the office. Then Charles set about giving the archbishop a suitable church for his prayers. On 21 November 1344, he laid the foundation stone for a great new St Vitus Cathedral to be built on the site of the old church established by St Wenceslas four centuries earlier.

Charles appointed the French architect Matthias of Arras to design a soaring Gothic masterpiece, which would rise dramatically from the heights of Hradcany to dominate the skyline of Prague. The cathedral was to be a mausoleum for Bohemia's kings, a shrine for its holy relics, a vault for its royal treasures and a showcase of the joys of the afterlife.

Charles also began a renovation of the Royal Palace at Prague Castle, rebuilding and expanding it in imposing Gothic style, with interlaced vaulted ceilings. The Black Tower, which served as the original eastern gate into the castle, was given a gilded roof and renamed the Golden Tower. When it caught the sun, it glittered like a beacon to the people in the city below.

CHARLES DREAMED of transforming Prague into a great imperial capital, but to do that he would have to become an emperor. In July 1346, he was elected king of the Romans with the support of his old tutor, Pope Clement VI, setting him up to challenge the sitting Holy Roman Emperor, Louis the Bavarian. But he had another battle to fight before he could think about wresting the imperial crown from Louis's grasp: in August that year, Charles set out for France with his father, to fight alongside their French allies against the English at the Battle of Crécy.

CRÉCY LIES SOUTH OF CALAIS, not far from the Channel coast. The impressive French forces, led by their king, Philip VI, arrived on the field of battle, spearheaded by Europe's finest cavalry and Italian infantry with crossbows. The English, although greatly outnumbered, were supported by their powerful longbowmen.

The battle began late in the afternoon, when the Italian crossbowmen let out a war cry and marched towards the English lines. Once within range, they stopped and fired, but their crossbow strings were wet with rain and the bolts fell short. With a whoosh, the quick-firing English longbowmen launched thousands of armour-piercing arrows in a shower 'so thick that it seemed as snow'.[31]

The wounded crossbowmen fell to their knees while their comrades panicked and ran, crashing into the French cavalry, who cursed them as cowards and trampled over them to get to the fighting.

King John of Bohemia, now known as John the Blind, went into the fray dressed in full battle armour. His mount was strapped to the horses of two retainers, who led him towards the fighting. John flailed away sightlessly with his sword for a short while; then he was knocked off his horse and killed. The battle ended in total defeat for the French. John's body was found on the field the next day alongside those of his retainers and their horses, still bound together.

The Third Rome

CHARLES ESCAPED THE battlefield at Crécy with several stab and arrow wounds. Once recovered, he returned to Prague, ready to accept the crown of Bohemia and rule entirely in his own right. Charles arrived in high spirits, dressed in a fashionable French jacket cut short to reveal his shapely legs. For this he received a written reprimand from his friend the pope for his un-kingly attire.

Physically, Charles was an impressive specimen: tall and powerfully built, but his battlefield wounds had left him with a slight stoop and a forwardly protruding neck.[32] Charles, supremely confident and astute, had the politician's gift of being able to stand outside his own skin and perceive himself as others did. Crécy convinced him that war was a foolish, wasteful business, and thereafter he avoided battle, preferring to achieve his goals through shrewd diplomacy and the mystique of kingly splendour. Unlike his father, the new king took delight in his kingdom, which he described as, 'a green garden to our eyes and the personal delight of our majesty'.[33]

In preparation for his coronation on 2 September 1347, Charles commissioned a dazzling new crown of St Wenceslas, studded with nineteen chunky sapphires, forty-four spinels, thirty emeralds, twenty pearls and a single fat ruby.*

The coronation of King Charles and Queen Blanche was followed by a lavish banquet, held in a special feasting hall adorned with magnificent tapestries. The feast was attended by nobles who arrived on horses with banners and heraldry, and who served, as was customary, at the king's table.[34]

CHARLES WAS ALREADY king of the Romans, but the exalted title of Holy Roman Emperor was still held by his bitter enemy Louis of Bavaria. Charles was readying himself for a fight when Louis did him the service of dropping dead from a stroke while on a bear hunt. Civil war within the empire was averted, and the path was cleared for Charles to assume the imperial crown, with Prague as his imperial capital.

Almost overnight, the city became a massive building site, as stonemasons, architects and labourers set to work, transfiguring Prague into the city that would one day be hailed as 'the loveliest gem in the stone crown of the world'.†[35]

Taking the Sorbonne as his model, in 1348 Charles founded a university in the Old Town to provide a caste of educated officials

---

* Today, the crown is held inside a secret chamber in St Vitus Cathedral. The door is sealed with seven locks; each key held by seven different official keyholders who must all convene to open the chamber door.

† The praise came from Goethe, who, despite having every intention to do so, never actually got around to visiting the city.

for his administration. Prague University, later renamed Charles University, was the first of its kind in central Europe. It gathered a community of scholars from as far away as England, Scandinavia and the Balkans into the heart of Prague and infused the city with science and philosophy.

Like the Sorbonne, the university was to have four faculties: theology, medicine, philosophy and law. Socially, the students and academics were divided into four 'nations' – Bohemian, Bavarian, Saxon and Polish. A college named for Charles – the Carolinum – was established near the fruit market in the Old Town.

TO SOLVE THE PROBLEM of overcrowding, Charles ordered the construction of a new town for Prague. A broad crescent of land hugging the perimeter of the Old Town was cleared, sweeping up from the fortress of Vysehrad to the northeastern bank of the river. Existing timber shacks and slums in the construction zone were demolished and replaced with stone buildings, paved streets and squares. An elongated horse market (now Wenceslas Square), was established in the New Town, along with a cattle market (the present-day Charles Square) and a hay market near today's main railway station.

Nothing was put to waste. All the dirt and debris pulled up to build the New Town was carted into the Old Town to raise the street level to protect it from being swamped every time the Vltava flooded. As a result, the ground floors of the Old Town houses and buildings became basements and catacombs, and the first floors became street fronts. The mismatched street level can be seen today in the Jewish quarter, where the Old-New Synagogue appears to be sinking, when in fact the pavement has risen around it.

Charles enclosed his New Town inside a system of walls and fortifications, with twenty-four defensive towers and four gates. When the fortifications were complete, he ordered the construction of another defensive wall running down the slope of Petrin Hill, dubbed the Hunger Wall, because its builders were able to feed their families with their wages during a famine in 1361. To the east of the New Town's walls, Charles established expansive vineyards on the land which would one day become the elegant inner-city suburb of Vinohrady.

CONSTRUCTION OF THE New Town proceeded at a rapid pace, but progress on the new St Vitus Cathedral stalled after the death of Matthias of Arras in 1352. Charles found a replacement in Peter Parler, a 24-year-old German architect, who rewarded his patron's faith by creating a spectacular vault over the choir in St Vitus with criss-crossing skeletal stone ribs, and swooping arcs and shadows. Parler's Gothic aesthetic came to be known as the Beautiful Style. 'What Augustus did for Rome,' wrote an Italian chronicler, 'Charles IV did for the capital city of Bohemia.'[36]

CHARLES WANTED PRAGUE to become a great centre of Christian pilgrimage like Rome, Constantinople and Jerusalem. Holy relics with claims to extraordinary antiquity were brought into the city: bones from Abraham the Patriarch; a fragment of the tablecloth from the Last Supper; and several drops of a milky substance purporting to be from the breast of the Virgin Mary herself.[37] These precious objects were encased in exquisite reliquaries of gold, silver and crystal, adorned with precious stones.

Charles hoarded these relics with a collector's mania. One chronicler recorded a visit he made to a convent, where the nuns, at his request, brought out the precious finger of Saint Nicholas for him to hold in his trembling hand. Charles pulled out his pocketknife and greedily sliced off a tiny sliver of the ancient finger for himself. But the chronicle records that when Charles looked at his knife, he saw smears of fresh blood on the blade. Chastened by this miracle, the emperor returned the sliver of flesh, which instantly rejoined the finger as though it had never been cut away.[38]

IN 1354, CHARLES and his retinue set out from Prague for Rome for his long-delayed imperial coronation. They crossed the Alps in the new year, stopping in the northern Italian cities where Charles had once soldiered as a young man. He entered Rome on 5 April 1355 without fanfare, dressed more as a pilgrim than as an emperor-elect. There was, however, no pope in the city to crown him. The current pontiff, Innocent VI, ruled from the papal enclave in Avignon, France. It was an odd state of affairs that neither the head of the Church of Rome nor the Holy Roman Emperor actually lived in the Eternal City. The absence of the pope had emptied Rome of its legions of cardinals, bishops and clerics. Grass was poking up between the stones of the city's famous squares.

Charles was met on the steps of St Peter's Basilica by the Cardinal of Ostia, who had been authorised to perform the coronation on the pope's behalf. After vowing to uphold the rights of the Roman church, Charles was anointed with sacred oil. The octagonal crown was placed upon his head and he received the imperial orb, sceptre and sword. As soon as the coronation banquet was over, Charles left the city with his entourage. His quick departure dismayed prominent Romans like the poet Petrarch, who wanted Charles to devote himself to the revival of Italy, just as he had with his beloved Bohemia.

CHARLES HAD BEEN IRKED by the pointlessly arcane process that elected him king of the Romans, and within a year of his coronation, he overhauled the Holy Roman Empire's creaking framework. In 1356, he codified and simplified the election process. In future, emperors would be elected by a college of seven: the archbishops of Cologne, Mainz and Trier, the Prince of Saxony, the Count-palatine of the Rhineland, the Margrave of Brandenburg and the King of Bohemia, who would remain the pre-eminent elector and 'arch-cupbearer of the holy empire'.[39]

Charles Bridge, towards the eastern tower.

Palindrome in Stone

ON THE MORNING of 9 July 1357, Charles appeared on the embankment of the Vltava in the pre-dawn dark. At precisely 5.31 am, he presided over the consecration of a foundation stone for a new bridge across the river. The specific moment in time was thought to be auspicious – the numerals of the year, the day, the month, the hour and the minute when run forward and back, formed an elegant palindrome:

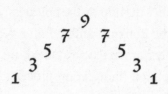

The palindrome rose up in increments to the middle like a bridge, then descended safely to the other bank. This happy set of numbers, it was hoped, would lend the stone structure extra strength.

Prague's new bridge, designed by Peter Parler, was to be higher, broader, stronger and in every way more magnificent than the old Judith Bridge which preceded it and which had been destroyed by floods and river ice fifteen years earlier. Spanning half a kilometre across the river, Parler's bridge rested on sixteen broad arches, and was bracketed at both ends with two beautiful Gothic towers. Aside from a simple cross, the ramparts were bare; the famous avenue of baroque statues would come centuries later. It was officially named the Charles Bridge in the nineteenth century.

The bridge was, and is, the glory of Prague. For six centuries it has served as a promenade, a meeting place, and a commercial thoroughfare, binding the left and right banks of the city together. The bridge is endlessly delightful and changes its nature according to your perspective: from the riverbank it seems heavy, stolid, almost geological; seen from the distant heights of Letna Park it appears as weightless as a chain of paper dolls.

Today, the Charles Bridge is congested year-round with tourists, hawkers and buskers, which is not so very different from how it was in medieval times. But the bridge is at its best in the lonely, still hours between midnight and dawn, when the river can be heard rushing through the arches and the silhouetted statues seem to move when you're not looking.

ALONG THE BRIDGE WALL on the Old Town embankment, the head of Bradac, the Bearded Man, can be seen poking out from the stone. Bradac watches the water level day and night. Medieval Praguers knew that when the waters rose above his nose it was time to seek higher ground.

The Vltava has burst its banks periodically over the centuries, carrying away carts, horses, pigs, goats and humans in its watery grasp. The English poet Jane Elizabeth Weston, a resident of seventeenth-century Prague, described the weird spectacle of river water rushing through the streets:

> *Here is a man, here is a bed, and here his wife swims.*
> *You see beams and pine trees, you see houses swimming along;*
> *monstrous things are tossed in the rushing channels.*[40]

Let My Soul Pierce the Stars

CHARLES IV MARRIED four times. His first wife, Blanche, was his favourite, but she died in 1348 after a short illness, leaving him without a male heir. A year later, he married Anna of Bavaria, who gave birth to a son but the baby died after a year, and then Anne died too, falling from a horse and breaking her neck.

The twice-widowed Charles then married his second cousin, the fourteen-year-old Anna of Schweidnitz, which allowed him to incorporate the neighbouring Silesian lands into his kingdom. Seven years later, Anna, gave birth to a son and heir named, predictably, Wenceslas, but Anna did not live to see her son's second birthday; she died in childbirth a year later, at the age of twenty-three.

Charles then engineered a fourth and final diplomatic marriage to Elizabeth of Pomerania. Empress Elizabeth was forthright and possessed enormous physical strength: she was said to enjoy entertaining dinner guests by bending swords and horseshoes with her bare hands.[41] She and Charles would have six children together, including Sigismund, a future emperor, and Anne, who would one day become the queen consort of Richard II of England.

AS HE ENTERED MIDDLE AGE, Charles began to suffer from chronic gout, which caused him terrible, debilitating pain in his feet. At court, he was irritable and distracted, failing to look his guests in the eye as he whittled away at a piece of wood with a small knife.

On his 1378 journey to France, he had to be carried on a litter borne by servants. Ever conscious of his image, at the gates of Paris he mounted a horse to make a dignified entrance to the city alongside the French king. While staying at the Royal Palace, Charles had to be carried up and down stairs in the arms of a retainer.[42] In November, on his return to Prague, Charles fell from his horse and broke his leg. Pneumonia set in and he died. He was sixty-two years old, and had ruled as King of Bohemia for thirty-two years.

THE FUNERAL PROCESSION WAS, unsurprisingly, a spectacle of great majesty and solemnity. The emperor's corpse, swathed in a crimson robe, lay in its catafalque on a golden cloth, protected by a funerary canopy held aloft by a dozen armoured knights.

A procession of forty black-clad carriages of noblewomen, led by Empress Elizabeth, was followed by the empire's standard-bearers, clergymen, academics and students. At the rear was a single knight, bearing Charles's helmet and sword.

The procession made its way through a city utterly transformed by the man acclaimed as *pater patriae,* the father of his country. His bones rest in the royal crypt of the great church he commissioned but never saw completed.

In 1849, the university put up a bronze statue of Charles next to the bridge that bears his name. The man who endowed the city with so many treasures is not presented as a warrior, but as a kindly benefactor: he beams down at his subjects from his four-metre-high pedestal with a tender, fatherly expression; his pose is relaxed, the sword is sheathed; he holds out the foundation bull of the university to his city like a coming-of-age gift to a most beloved child.

His final testament is inscribed on his tombstone:

I, the fourth Charles, an emperor unbeaten by the great horrors of the world, now overwhelmed by death, under this grave I am hidden. Noble Lord, please, let my soul pierce the stars.[43]

Statue of Charles IV, on the Square of the Knights of the Cross with the Red Star, Prague.

=== CHAPTER THREE ===

THE NIGHT OF ANTICHRIST

1378–1550

The Ploughman of Bohemia denounces Death.
Fifteenth-century woodcut.

The Ploughman and the Weaver

THE INSECURITY OF EVERYDAY life in medieval Prague tended to produce extremes of temperament: human tenderness vied with revulsion for the corruption of the flesh. Admiration for the beauty and grace of the human body, rendered so affectionately in Bohemian religious painting and sculpture, had to be reconciled with the everyday presence of deformity and disease. At the turn of the fifteenth century, two Bohemian authors, one German, the other Czech, struggled to come to grips with a world so darkly shadowed by death and misfortune.

'The Ploughman of Bohemia' was a short tract written like a courtroom drama. The humble ploughman (who ploughs the page with his pen) grieves for his dead wife, Margaretha, and denounces the figure of Death before God as the destroyer of love and human dignity. Death, in reply, snorts with contempt for the prattling ploughman. 'Gack, gack, gack, gabbles the goose,' he says. 'Howl, howl, says the wolf.' Death scoffs at human dignity:

A human is conceived in sin, nourished with impure, unspeakable feculence in the maternal body, born naked and smeared like a beehive; a mass of refuse, a churn of filth, a dish for worms, a stinkhouse ... Let recognise who will: every human created to completion has nine holes in his body; out of all these there flows such repellent filth that nothing could be more impure.

'Pah to you, you evil sack of shame!' snaps the ploughman. Humans, he retorts, are noble creatures, endowed with eyes that reach 'the clarity of the heavens'; ears that differentiate 'a host of sweet sounds'; and a mind filled with thoughts that can climb towards heaven.

It is left to God to adjudicate the winner of the debate. Although the ploughman has the argument, God decides that Death must have the victory, as it does over everyone in the end.[1]

THE POPULARITY OF 'The Ploughman of Bohemia' provoked a response titled 'The Little Weaver'. The author, a 'weaver of words', has a different complaint. His lover is not dead; she has merely left him for someone else. His quarrel is with Misfortune, who reminds the weaver that while heaven and hell are realms of absolute certainty, human existence is raddled with instability. Misfortune is therefore a hard moral necessity that teaches all mortals to be humble and to love justice. Without Misfortune, a man would be nothing more than a selfish lump:

> *He would not be afraid of any events, which is impudence.*
> *He would not know where he is going, and consequently would*
> *not know what is good and bad, which is stupidity. He would not*
> *know poverty, because he would live forever in pleasure, which is*
> *gluttony ... He would not act to benefit anyone, which is negligence.*
> *He would not even recognize God, which is bestiality.*[2]

THE SENSE OF DOUBT, of the need for a sad reckoning with the harsh uncertainties of the world, was all of a piece with the growing hardships of the age. Charles's successor, his seventeen-year-old son, Wenceslas IV, had none of his father's luck or ability. Multiple disastrous vectors – a declining economy, instability within the empire, divisions within the church – all converged on Bohemia early in his reign. Rather than grapple with these problems, the hapless Wenceslas spent his days hunting and drinking, expecting things would somehow work themselves out. His subjects nicknamed him Wenceslas the Idle. When discontent boiled over into murderous violence in Prague, he was unable or unwilling to stop it.

IN 1389, ON HOLY SATURDAY, a rumour spread through the city that a priest had been attacked in the Jewish quarter. It was said the priest had been on his way to bring holy communion to a dying woman when some Jewish hooligans had beaten him up, and the Eucharist wafer was soiled on the street.

The Jews deemed guilty for the violence were arrested, but as reports of the sacrilege spread, an angry mob gathered in the Old Town Square armed with stones, clubs and torches. An order from the king to keep the peace was ignored and the mob invaded the Jewish quarter. Houses were burnt, adults and children were beaten to death and others pushed into the fires. Houses, synagogues and even Jewish gravestones in the cemetery were smashed and looted.

The death toll was placed at anywhere between 400 and 3000 souls. It was to be the worst attack on Prague's Jews until the Holocaust. Rabbi Avigdor Kara, whose father was killed that day, wrote an elegy that is still sung in Prague on Yom Kippur:

> *Many were destroyed, who knows their number?*
> *Young men and girls. Old people and babes-in-arms.*
> *You, oh Lord, need not be reminded.*
> *You will judge them.*[3]

Wenceslas spoke out against the massacre, but no one was punished for it and the castle ensured it would profit from the violence. The king decreed that all the looted goods from the Jewish quarter should be turned over to his treasury. The total value of the loot amounted to five barrels of silver.

THE ONE UNIVERSAL POINT of moral authority in a world disrupted by plague, hunger and other calamities was the church, but that too was showing signs of decay.

Under Charles, the church had become the richest institution in Prague, attracting the talented, the earnest and the opportunistic alike, but the clergy's blatantly corrupt behaviour was soiling its public reputation. Positions in the curia were often sold to the highest bidder. To recoup their money, priests demanded crippling fees from the poor for funerals and other ceremonies. Too many of them neglected pastoral care in favour of drinking, womanising and gambling in taverns. Troubled by reports of clerical misbehaviour, Archbishop Ernest of Prague set up an office of corrections and punished the worst offenders, but corruption in the lower ranks was mirrored at the church's very apex, the papacy, which gorged itself on income from the sale of indulgences.

THE MARKET IN INDULGENCES was made possible by the invention of the concept of purgatory, the realm in the afterlife where a soul would endure purifying fire as penance for the sins accreted in the course of a lifetime. The concept was emotionally powerful, but commercially dormant until someone suggested that the church might issue an indulgence for sin, a kind of token that would shorten the painful interval of purgatory and speed the soul on to the reward of heaven.

The scheme rested on the notion that the Vatican held a vast treasury of virtue, amassed like surplus capital over the centuries. It seemed a shame to keep it all locked up in Rome, when it might be profitably invested in Christian enterprises elsewhere to generate even more virtue. The pope would therefore sell a tiny portion of his surplus spiritual gold in return for good works of some kind.

Initially, the sale of indulgences was used to fund charitable causes: feeding of the poor, or building a hospital or sanatorium for lepers. But truly pious Christians were expected to offer the church some kind of *ex gratia* payment for an indulgence, a formality that rapidly evolved into a market for the remittance of sin.

It wasn't long before inventive theologians, acting like hedge-fund managers, came up with new angles, such as the sale of indulgences to help the souls of the already dead. With greater complexity came greater abuse. Kings and princes demanded a piece of the action from indulgences sold in their realms. In some places, the indulgence was issued to the grateful sinner on a piece of paper, like currency.[4] Indulgence hawkers sharpened their sales pitches. In Saxony, a Dominican friar sang from town to town, 'When a penny in the coffer rings, a soul from purgatory springs.'[5]

*Satan distributing indulgences, illumination from a
Czech manuscript, the Jensky Kodex.*

THE TRAFFIC IN INDULGENCES relied upon the willingness of people to accept whatever their priests told them as God's revealed truth. But Charles IV's education reforms had brought about a surge in biblical literacy in Bohemia. More and more people could read scripture translated into Czech. They could see how far their clergy had strayed from Christ's call for poverty, charity and humility.

A few outraged clerics were willing to speak up against the church's unseemly greed. Konrad Waldhauser, a radical priest who had come to Prague at Charles IV's invitation, preached to open-air crowds in front of the new Tyn Church on the Old Town Square. Waldhauser tapped into Czech resentment towards the city's German burghers, denouncing them for their greed and love of luxury. His sermons touched a nerve among the noblewomen of Prague, who put aside their gold-trimmed dresses and veils, and adopted more modest attire.

Another cleric named Jan Milic gave up his lucrative position at St Vitus Cathedral to become a wandering preacher. In contrition for his sins, Milic wore a hairshirt, refused to bathe, slept on a plank and subsisted on a bland diet of green vegetables. With the help of some wealthy benefactors, Milic purchased Prague's most famous brothel on Venice Street and transformed it into a refuge he named New Jerusalem, where former prostitutes could earn a living by sewing and copying manuscripts. For Milic, the moral sickness of the church was a harbinger of the apocalypse. Its signs were everywhere. 'Kings are already without mercy,' he proclaimed. 'Judges without justice, prelates are already armed, priests are seducers.'[6] Hearing of a priest who had installed a concealed entrance to his house so that his lovers might come and go discreetly, Milic fired off a letter rebuking him for his poor morality. The priest wrote back, sneeringly accusing Milic of being a 'sodomite'.[7]

*

Five Golden Stars

WENCESLAS IV, MEANWHILE, drifted between bouts of drunken idleness and sudden fits of rage. His father had managed to press the imperial electors into accepting him as king of the Romans, but after Charles's death, Wenceslas's unfitness for the job became so embarrassingly apparent, the electors stripped him of his title. The imperial court abandoned Prague to attend the new emperor-elect, and their patronage of the city's merchants and artisans went with them. Prague's moment of imperial glory was fading.

Charles IV had taken care to keep the church onside as a counterweight to the power of the nobility; Wenceslas, however, was at loggerheads with his archbishop, Jan of Jenstejn, whom he suspected was plotting against him. In March 1393, he summoned the archbishop to a meeting in Mala Strana. When Jenstejn arrived with his entourage, Wenceslas launched into a drunken harangue, then ordered his soldiers to arrest all of them. The archbishop escaped, probably with the help of the sheepish guards, but his three officials were dragged off to a dungeon in the Old Town. There they were tortured by the town hangman, while Wenceslas seethed in a corner. Then the king snatched a burning torch and thrust it into the sides of the wailing prisoners, screaming at them to confess their treason. Suddenly exhausted, Wenceslas dropped the torch and ordered the men to be released. Two of the clergymen were lifted off the rack, but the third one, the archbishop's vicar-general, Jan Nepomuk, was dead. Nepomuk's corpse was carried onto the Charles Bridge and hurled into the river. His body later washed ashore downstream.

THE STORY OF JAN NEPOMUK'S cruel death at the hands of the maniac king later became hopelessly entangled in a Jesuit myth. Nepomuk, so the story goes, had been the queen's confessor, and the king, suspecting her of adultery, had demanded Nepomuk give up her secrets. When the priest bravely refused to break the confessional seal, Wenceslas had him thrown into the Vltava. According to the legend, onlookers had seen a circlet of stars glistening around Nepomuk's head as he floated down the river. The miracle of the stars was cited in support of his canonisation in 1729.

Jan Nepomuk's untimely death is commemorated on the Charles Bridge by a bronze cross with five stars embedded in the parapet wall. It sits beside a dramatic baroque statue of Nepomuk, who clutches a crucifix in one hand and a martyr's palm frond in the other, his head encircled by a nimbus of five golden stars.

Statue of Saint Jan of Nepomuk on the Charles Bridge.

The Burning Books

THE MURDER OF A PRIEST in Bohemia was but a minor disturbance in the larger crisis engulfing the church. The holy institution of the papacy had been rent in two, with one pope based in Italy and a rival pontiff in Avignon, France. Pope and antipope shot accusations and counter-accusations of heresy against each other. If a pope considered himself to be ordained as God's emissary on earth, then a rival pope would, by definition, be a grotesque impostor, an emissary of Satan. It's difficult to overstate how distressing and disorienting this was for the faithful. Could one of the rival popes really be the Antichrist? And if so, which one? Feeling the foundations of the church cracking under them, a council of bishops assembled in Pisa to resolve the crisis. They declared both rival popes deposed, and a new pope was elected. But instead of establishing a single Holy Father, this new election left Christendom with three. Two pontiffs might be regarded as an abomination, but three invited ridicule.

IN EUROPE'S UNIVERSITIES, scholars wondered if it wasn't time to look back at early Christianity in all its primitive innocence. In Oxford, the master of Balliol College, John Wyclif, saw how far the church had wandered from its lean and muscular origins. He called for clergy to divest themselves of their fine robes, their sumptuous palaces and vast property holdings, and rededicate themselves to Christian poverty. Wyclif shocked the curia still further by rejecting the concept of purgatory and the need for clerical celibacy, neither of which, as far as he could see, had any basis in scripture. Wyclif even dared to go so far as to attack the doctrine of transubstantiation – the belief that within the rite of holy communion the bread and wine are literally transmuted into the flesh and blood of Christ. Such thoughts, spoken out loud, led to accusations of heresy, but Wyclif retorted by questioning the very authority of his accusers. Looking back at the early church, he said, he could see no evidence of a pope or a clerical hierarchy. Wyclif wondered if the immense edifice of cardinals, bishops, priests and palaces had become a titanic, even diabolical, imposition on the faithful.

Wyclif was furiously denounced in the highest circles of the church, but his radical essays strongly appealed to Christian idealists within the university. Czech students at Oxford made copies of his work and brought them back to Bohemia. Soon enough, they fell into the hands of a scholar at Prague University named Jan Hus.

JAN HUS WAS AN ABLE student from a poor family in the southern Bohemian town of Husinec ('Goosetown'). He later confessed he'd joined the clergy because it promised him wealth, fine clothes and a respectable position in society. Having earned his master's degree at the university's faculty of arts in 1396, Hus allowed himself some minor pleasures and vanities: feasting with his colleagues, drinking wine, playing chess and swishing about in his master's cloak. But as his relief at having escaped poverty and obscurity faded, he lost his appetite for fine clothes and food, and began to consider more seriously how he should direct his life.

Early on, Hus settled on the principle that he would dedicate himself to truth, and would humbly and happily abandon any notion when he encountered a better, more correct one. Hus was thereby radicalised, not through a wrenching Damascene moment of conversion, but through a series of small hops from one stone to the next, until he realised he had travelled quite some distance from where he'd started. John Wyclif's writings delighted him. 'Wyclif, Wyclif,' he scribbled excitedly in the margins, 'you will unsettle many a man's mind.'[8]

Hus began teaching at the faculty of arts and became a popular figure among his students for his gentle nature and good humour. In 1402, he was appointed as preacher at the new Bethlehem Chapel in the Old Town of Prague.

The monument to Hus that exists today in Prague's Old Town Square portrays him as a gaunt and bony prophet. In reality, Hus was more like Friar Tuck, short and plump with a tonsured haircut. By nature, he was a cheerful optimist, not naturally a rebel, but the church's demand for blind obedience touched a stubbornness in him. His sincere faith in reason and scriptural truth was a fortress he felt he must defend, even if it cost him his life. To do otherwise was to live as though nothing was real or good or true, and to accept that such precious ideals were the playthings of the powerful.

THE BETHLEHEM CHAPEL was the furthest thing from the spidery Gothic cathedral on Hradcany. Worshippers entering St Vitus might imagine they were stepping into a towering stone rocket, poised for launch into the heavens; the Bethlehem Chapel, with its exposed timber cross-beams and pillars, was much less daunting and otherworldly; its uncluttered, open space spoke of community and equality. Paupers congregated there alongside members of the nobility.

Inspired by Wyclif, Hus preached that the rich should give their wealth to the poor, and told his followers they should only recognise the authority of priests who lived in holy simplicity. He criticised the church's extravagant ceremonies as theatrical distractions, and lavish vestments of the curia as vainglorious accoutrements of power. Hus also encouraged women to take on a greater role in public life, reminding them that as creatures made in the image of God, they were the equals of men. Traditional Catholics were horrified, but for Hus it came down to a question of authority: should a Christian remain obedient to the pope, as God's supreme emissary on Earth, even when his commandments were so clearly at odds with the letter and the spirit of holy scripture?

IN THE UNIVERSITY, the new ideas exacerbated resentment and distrust between the Czech- and German-speaking 'nations'. While the Czechs had excitedly welcomed the new thinking, the German-speakers were appalled by Wyclif's attacks on the papacy, and wanted his books suppressed. Religious reform became inextricably bound up with national pride. From this time, Czech nationalists would, rightly or wrongly, uphold egalitarianism and a willingness to stand alone, to speak truth to power as particularly Czech virtues.

Soon enough, the discord in the university caught the attention of the volatile ruler in Prague Castle. Wenceslas IV still had ambitions of reclaiming his imperial title and he wanted Prague University solidly behind him. But of the university's four nations, only the Czechs declared for Wenceslas, while the three German-speaking nations did not. In response, Wenceslas simply flipped the voting rules, awarding the Czechs three votes on the governing council, while the other three nations were allocated a combined vote of one. This prompted a mass walkout of German masters and students, who left Prague to form new universities in Leipzig and elsewhere. At a stroke, Wenceslas had broken the founding ideal of scholarly unity and shrunk his father's university into a narrow nationalist enclave.

JAN HUS WAS ELECTED as rector of the now Czech-dominated university in October 1409. He had, by then, fallen out badly with Prague's Archbishop Zbynek Zajic, who ordered Hus to surrender his copies of Wyclif's books for 'correction'. Hus obediently brought the offending books to the archbishop's palace and brazenly invited him to point out the specific errors within the pages. Zbynek, a former military leader, was not much of a theologian, and was irritated by this challenge to his authority. Zbynek lodged a charge of heresy against Hus, which was helped along with generous bribes handed out to various cardinals, church officials and even the pope himself.[9]

In December 1409, Zbynek decreed that anyone in Prague in possession of John Wyclif's books should surrender them to him for burning. Jan Hus, still believing in the power of sweet reason, audaciously wrote an open letter to the pope, making the case for the necessity of books that are beautiful and true, even if some of their ideas are deemed heretical. If the archbishop of Prague was to have his way, Hus wrote, works by Aristotle would also have to be burnt. Perhaps the books of the Jewish Old Testament would have to go too.

Archbishop Zbynek, undeterred, ordered Wyclif's books to be piled up in his palace courtyard in front of his assembled prelates. The archbishop himself lit the pyre. The satisfied clerics sang a hymn while the books blazed away. The ringing of the bells of St Vitus announced the deed to an infuriated city, sparking protests in churches and in the streets.

THE STRUGGLE BETWEEN Hus and the archbishop had by now become a major headache for Wenceslas IV. With Prague in an uproar, any hope he might have had of persuading the electoral college of his fitness for the imperial crown was shrivelling. The melodramatic charges of heresy against Hus made him look like an incompetent steward of his own domain.

Seeing that popular opinion was largely on Hus's side, Wenceslas stood over the shoulder of his archbishop and forced him to draft a letter to the pope, telling His Holiness it had all been a dreadful mistake, and he should disregard everything he'd said about the existence of heresy in Bohemia. But Zbynek never sent the letter. Fearing for his life, he fled Prague to seek protection in Hungary, but along the way, he fell ill and died. He was replaced as archbishop by Wenceslas's personal physician, who had bid more than anyone else for the job.[10]

Fleas and Flies

JAN HUS MIGHT HAVE held out for years against a badly distracted and divided papacy, so long as he retained the support of the king in Prague. But that support evaporated in 1412, when Pope John XXIII sent emissaries into Bohemia to conduct a mass sale of indulgences to fund a crusade against his rival, Pope Gregory XII.

In Bohemia, the indulgence sale was a particularly egregious spectacle. Coffers were installed in Prague's major churches to collect money, while parish priests brazenly toured the countryside trading indulgences for livestock or even clothing.[11] The whole exercise was so blatantly cynical it sparked a protest march in the city, led by a student dressed as a bare-breasted prostitute, who offered to sell mock indulgences to passers-by.

Jan Hus denounced the indulgence-mongers as crass charlatans. 'What a strange thing!' he told his students. 'They cannot rid themselves of fleas and flies, and yet want to rid others of the torments of hell.'[12]

Hus's speech was greeted with thunderous applause, but it set him up for a confrontation with King Wenceslas, who was in on the indulgence racket and expecting to get his cut. Stirring up opposition to it had made Hus the king's enemy. To his dismay, Hus found many of his fellow academics and friends also edging away from him. The university's theology faculty, which had become wary of the taint of heresy, sided with the king and the pope, and began proceedings against him.

Hus was now the public face of a reform movement that was, in the eyes of the church and castle, spinning out of control. On Sunday, 10 July 1412, the king ordered a crackdown against anti-indulgence protestors. Three young men, known only as Martin, Jan and Stasek, were arrested and thrown into the Old Town prison. Hus led a protest delegation to the town hall, where the councillors assured him that nothing untoward would happen to the men. But when Hus and his supporters dispersed, all three were dragged out in front of the Old Town Hall and beheaded. A horrified crowd formed around the corpses on the bloody cobblestones. The bodies were wrapped in white linen, and carried to the Bethlehem Chapel, where they were buried and commemorated with a special mass. Martin, Jan and Stasek, are remembered today as the first martyrs of the Hussite revolution.

Wenceslas decided to crack down harder. Now acting in concert with the church, he decreed that anyone defending Wyclif's ideas or attacking the sale of indulgences would be exiled. Jan Hus was ex-communicated and the city of Prague was put on notice: no citizen could receive holy communion or be buried in church ground as long as Jan Hus continued to preach in the city.

Hus left Prague and for two years he preached to the nobility and peasantry in the countryside, building up a rebellious groundswell against the degenerate king and clergy. He began to wonder if this might not end well for him. In a letter to a friend, he wrote he now thought it would be better to die than to live badly.[13]

IN HUS'S ABSENCE, the momentum in Prague for reform picked up. Jakoubek of Stribro, a colleague of Hus's, had become deeply troubled by the church's longstanding refusal to give wine to lay people during the mass. The blood of Christ was seen by the church as more precious than the flesh, and the thought that it might be accidentally spilled on the floor by a clumsy layman was simply too horrible to contemplate. The chalice, therefore, was reserved for the clergy.

Jakoubek of Stribro, however, saw absolutely no reason why the common people should be denied the fullness of the Lord's supper. While Hus was ambivalent on the issue, Jakoubek was insistent: the denial of the chalice, to him, was worse than remiss; it was wicked. To the modern secular mind, such nuances might seem astonishingly superstitious, hardly the fuel of revolutionary outrage, but to medieval Praguers, the fear that they might be damned for all time for disobeying a specific instruction, from a loving and all-powerful God was terrifying. What did it say about the church that it should knowingly pervert a holy sacrament?

In no time, the dispensation of both bread *and* wine to lay people became a bedrock, non-negotiable principle of the reformists. They became known as Utraquists, taken from the Latin phrase *sub utraque specie* – 'in both kinds'.

The Death of Jan Hus

WENCESLAS'S HOPES OF becoming Holy Roman Emperor like his father before him came to nothing. Instead, the prize went to his half-brother Sigismund, who was elected king of the Romans by the imperial college. Nicknamed the Ginger Fox, the red-headed Sigismund was a far more energetic and stable figure than Wenceslas. As emperor-elect, his most immediate priority was to repair the schisms in the church, and in 1414, he persuaded Pope John XXIII to convene a grand council of reconciliation. In the autumn of that year, hundreds of cardinals, academics, abbots and bishops from all over Europe converged on the tiny German lakeside town of Constance. Their sacred task was to reunite the church under a single pope; and of bring the Hussite rebels to heel. Sigismund invited Jan Hus to come to Constance and argue his case.

Hus was deeply worried by the invitation. He feared if he left Bohemia he might never return alive, but Sigismund gave him an assurance of safe passage, and so, on 11 October 1414, Hus set out from Prague on horseback, armed with a bundle of tracts he intended to read out to the assembled prelates. As he passed through German towns and cities, people came out of their houses to get a glimpse of the Bohemian troublemaker.

Hus was riding into a trap. While still on the road, the Council of Constance convened and resumed the heresy trial against him. Sigismund's guarantee of safe passage was countermanded, and three weeks after his arrival in Constance Hus was arrested and imprisoned in a cell next to a cesspool, while his accusers prepared their case against him.

EVEN THEN, HUS STILL hoped he would get a fair trial, but at the hearings, he was not permitted to make statements and was ordered to confine himself to answering questions. The proceedings were noisy and chaotic. When Hus tried to explain himself, his accusers shouted at him to give up his legal hair-splitting and to answer a simple yes or no to the charges. Hus was invited to recant his positions, which he said he would do quite happily if the council could produce a better instruction from the scriptures. This provoked mocking laughter and verbal abuse. Hus was then asked to renounce several positions he'd never held in the first place. He refused, saying they should not ask him to perjure himself in the eyes of God.

Hus now gave up all hope of a fair hearing and readied himself to die. Stephen Palec, a former close friend turned enemy, came to see him in his cell one last time. Palec pleaded with Hus not to think so much about the shame of recanting but of the good that might come from it. Hus asked him what *he* would do if he was asked to recant positions he had never held. Palec burst into tears.

HUS WAS FOUND GUILTY of heresy on 6 July 1415 and handed over for ritual degradation. He was dressed in priestly robes, as if for holy mass. Then the chalice was snatched from his hand, and one by one each one of his garments was removed, while a curse was uttered at each stage. His hair was cut off and a tall paper hat was placed on his head with three devils painted on it.

Hus tried to calm himself by singing psalms as the guards led him out to the place of execution next to the Rhine riverbank. On the way, he saw Sigismund and called out to him, 'Is *this* your safe passage?' Sigismund blushed with shame. He would be forever reviled in Bohemia for betraying his word of honour.[14]

Hus was bound to the stake by his wrists, and a rusty chain was tied around his neck. Wood and straw were laid around him up to his chin. When the fire was lit, Hus began to sing again, briefly, but his voice was stifled by the smoke and then he died. He was forty-three years old.

His ashes were scooped up and dumped into the Rhine so that his followers could not venerate his remains.

The First Defenestration of Prague

THE NEWS OF HUS'S EXECUTION detonated a firestorm of protest in Prague and nothing would ever be the same. An angry letter of protest was sent to the Council of Constance, signed by 452 Czech nobles, who pledged themselves to Hus's ideals. Priests loyal to Rome were steadily expelled from the nobles' estates and replaced with Utraquist clergymen willing to serve both bread and wine at holy communion. Wenceslas, not wanting to poke a hornets' nest, looked the other way.

On the morning of 30 July 1419, a radical priest named Jan Zelivsky delivered a fiery sermon at Our Lady of the Snows, taking his text from the apocalyptic book of Revelation. From his pulpit, Zelivsky delivered the electrifying news that the end of human history was at hand, and that they, the righteous poor, would bear the awesome burden of living through the 'night of the Antichrist'.[15] Zelivsky identified Sigismund, whom he called the 'Red Dragon', as the principal instigator of the End of Days. Holding the Eucharist dramatically aloft in both hands, he led his congregation out of the church in a procession through the New Town.

The demonstrators, who had gathered their weapons, marched down to the New Town Hall to demand the release of some Hussite prisoners held in the dungeon. The entry gate was shut. From a high window, the anti-Hussite councillors appointed by Wenceslas shouted down to the crowd. Someone inside threw a rock from the window, which ignited the mob's rage. They smashed down the portal and charged up the stairs. There they found the enemy councillors, picked them up, and hurled them out the open window.

Those who survived the fall were clubbed and stabbed to death as they lay in the street.

THIS FIRST DEFENESTRATION of Prague (there would be more in the centuries to come)* transformed the Bohemian reformists into revolutionaries. For three days, Hussite mobs rampaged through churches and monasteries, helping themselves to the monks' reserves of food, wine and clothes. They attacked the houses of German merchants, driving many of them from the city for good. Brothels in the New Town were invaded, the women expelled and the buildings burnt down. Wenceslas had lost control of his capital. When told of the defenestration, he exploded in rage, then complained of pains in his hand and legs. He expired several days later from a stroke at the age of fifty-eight.

THE DEATH OF THE childless Wenceslas IV cleared the way for his brother Sigismund to succeed him as King of Bohemia, but with most of the Czech nobility in revolt, it wasn't clear how Sigismund would be able to enter the city, let alone find a quorum of barons to formally elect him. In the meantime, Sigismund appointed his brother's widow Queen Sofia as regent of Bohemia.

Fighting broke out between Hussite militias and the loyalist guards posted in the bridge towers. Artillery fire blasted down from the castle into the Hussite strongholds in Mala Strana, while the rebels advanced into the archbishop's palace in Hradcany and ransacked it. The royalists fell back to the castle battlements and Queen Sofia made a hasty departure from the city. On 25 October, a band of Hussite rebels led by a one-eyed former mercenary named Jan Zizka seized the fortress of Vysehrad.

After weeks of fighting, Mala Strana was a rubble-strewn ruin. With winter setting in, the warring parties agreed to an

---

*   'Defenestration' taken from Latin de–fenestra: 'down from the window'.

armistice that would extend until the following spring: the loyalist administrators at the castle agreed to tolerate Hussite worship, so long as the rebels left the churches and monasteries alone. The rebels also agreed to hand back the fortress of Vysehrad, over the furious protests of Jan Zizka.

Nothing Which is Mine or Thine

THE HUSSITES NOW SPLIT into two broad groups: a coalition of moderates from the Old Town of Prague; and a loose group of radicals based in Prague's New Town and the countryside. The moderate Utraquists were ready to accept Sigismund as king, so long as he agreed to practise a live-and-let-live policy towards Hussite forms of worship. But the radicals, full of revolutionary fervour, were ready to go much further: they wanted nothing less than to build a new Jerusalem in the countryside in preparation for the second coming of Christ.

In the spring of 1420, the radicals took over an abandoned castle in southern Bohemia, near a hill they named Mount Tabor, after the biblical mountain where the disciples had witnessed the transfiguration of Christ, wreathed in light. At Tabor, in the bracing fresh air, the radicals established a revolutionary commune, an imitation of the early church, which they believed would light a beacon bright enough to be seen from heaven. Hussite preachers told their flock they could expect to see the final crisis of the earth erupt in the skies any day now. And where else would Christ choose to return if not right here, at Tabor, among the elect?

Heeding the urgent call to salvation, families came to Tabor from all over the Czech lands. The Taborites practised a form of medieval communism that would be remembered centuries later when the socialist republic was established. 'There is nothing which is mine or thine,' they proclaimed. 'Rather, all things in the community shall be held in common for all time.'[16] Social distinctions were cast aside as lords and servants laboured side by side and called each other brother and sister. Peasants, potters, priests, barbers, carpenters, town councillors, cobblers, blacksmiths and cooks laid down their possessions at the feet of Tabor's priests, to be pooled and shared equally among the faithful. The cultish energy of the camp made all things seem possible, but the system fell into crisis when the funds in their community chest ran out. As members of the elect, the Taborites felt entitled to seize whatever they pleased from the enemies of God, which came to include anyone who was not a Taborite. The community rapidly evolved into a military camp, extorting dues from the local peasantry by force. Reports from Kutna Hora that German Catholics were hunting down Hussites and dropping them down mine shafts only accelerated the Taborites' journey from New Testament forgiveness to Old Testament violence.[17]

THE FIRST TARGET OF the Taborites' righteous violence was another millennial cult, the Adamites, who lived in the forests nearby and had adopted an even more primitive form of Christianity. The Adamites claimed they had regained the primeval innocence of the Garden of Eden, and wandered through the towns and forests perfectly naked. They were a throwback to the legendary first Bohemian settlers, who were said to have 'walked about naked in the sunshine' and shared their possessions and lovers alike.[18]

It wasn't all free love. Like the Taborites, the Adamites came to see themselves as avenging angels of the Lord, who should wash their hands in the blood of their enemies. At night, groups of these naked terrorists launched attacks on neighbouring villages, massacring the inhabitants and seizing their goods. This was all too much for the puritan Taborites, who sent a force of 400 soldiers to destroy the Adamite camp. Every one of the Adamites was killed or captured.

Zizka

THE TABORITE LEADER who led the attack on the Adamites was the one-eyed Jan Zizka, who had commanded the Hussite garrison at Vysehrad. After the fortress was handed back to the royalists, Zizka had left Prague in disgust to offer his services to the Taborites.

Zizka was a military leader of genius, the most innovative European commander of his era. Forced to improvise with meagre resources, he invented a fluid new style of warfare that shocked and baffled his enemies for years. A former mercenary, Zizka had already lost an eye in battle and was slowly going blind in the other one. Nonetheless, his mind was able to envision the contours of a field of combat so vividly that he won victory after victory, often against much larger forces.

MEANWHILE, THE CHURCH had roused itself to deal with the uprising in Bohemia. The Council of Constance had repaired the schism in the papacy, deposing the three rival popes and replacing them with a single pontiff, Martin V. In March 1420, Pope Martin called for a crusade against the Hussites. Sigismund summoned warriors from all over Christendom to join forces against the Bohemian heretics. The declaration of the crusade isolated Bohemia from the rest of Europe and intensified the defiant mood in Prague.

At Tabor, Jan Zizka readied his people to fight. Farm tools were remade into weaponry. The flail, a threshing implement with a striking head attached to a pole or rope, was transformed into an effective combat weapon against a knight in armour. Wooden agricultural carts were remade into primitive tanks with slatted walls and hinged flaps; some were designed to hold infantrymen, others to hold lightweight gunpowder cannons.

In most medieval societies, women were brought into combat only in the most desperate circumstances; at Tabor, they were trained to fight as frontline soldiers. A woman, as the crusaders would soon discover, could wield a flail more or less as lethally as a man.[19]

IN PRAGUE, THE HUSSITE authorities hurriedly prepared to defend their city. But when they received reports of the size of Sigismund's approaching armies, their defiance sank into defeatist gloom. An urgent plea for help was sent to the Taborites, and in May 1420 Jan Zizka rode out with his army to save Prague.

Zizka's army was welcomed into the city and offered every hospitality, but the puritan Taborites were offended by the vanity of the townsfolk. They attacked wealthy burghers in the streets, using knives to cut off their foppish moustaches and to slash at the ornate garments of their wives, until Zizka ordered them to desist.[20] He put his troops under strict discipline, holding daily services with militant sermons; 1500 Taborite women set to work digging a deep moat between the New Town and Vysehrad.

Both moderate and radical Hussite barons rallied to sign a common manifesto, the Four Articles of Prague, which declared that people should be free to preach the word of God; that the church should divest itself of all worldly property and secular power; that the Bohemian clergy should be punishable in secular courts for mortal sins; and that both kinds of communion should be granted to lay people.

A set of four captains was elected for each town. Those families unwilling to accept the wine along with the bread were told to leave the city, while the remaining Catholic clergy and town councillors ran to Prague Castle and Vysehrad for protection, hoping Sigismund's crusaders would arrive soon and return control of the city to them.

ZIZKA'S PRIORITY WAS TO prevent a crusader blockade by keeping open a supply line on the eastern road to the city so that Prague could, if necessary, sit tight behind their walls and wait out the crusaders. A steep elevation just outside the city known as Vitkov Hill suddenly became critically important. If it fell to the enemy, the eastern lifeline would be severed. Prague would be completely cut off and forced to choose between starvation and surrender.

With time running out, a garrison of men and women were sent to build earth-and-stone fortifications at the summit of Vitkov Hill. As they hurried to complete their defences, they saw Sigismund's soldiers arriving and slowly spreading out on the far side of the river between Letna Plain and Holesovice. The enemy force, a coalition of Germans, Austrians, Silesians, Hungarians and Czech royalists, covered the whole plain with tents and encampments. Sigismund's troops gathered by the riverbank to taunt the Czech defenders, chanting, 'Ha, Ha! Hus, Hus! Heretic, Heretic!'[21]

VITKOV HILL IS A STEEP, narrow ridge line shaped like a rocky shark's fin. On 14 July, Sigismund's crusaders crossed the river and made their way up the long arc of the hill. They captured a watchtower, then marched up to attack the earth-and-stone breastworks thinly defended by a force of just twenty-eight Taborite men and women armed with guns and flails, and a young girl who threw rocks at the invaders.

Alerted to the danger, Zizka led his main force out from the city walls at a gallop. At the foot of Vitkov Hill, his soldiers began climbing the steep southern slope, their approach concealed by the foliage of the royal vineyards. On reaching the summit, the Hussites surprised the enemy and smashed into their left flank with their flails and pikes. Suddenly, the invaders realised how precariously exposed they were. Attacked by the Hussites to the front and to the side, they were simultaneously being pushed up the hill from behind by the rest of the crusader force. There was nowhere for the invaders to move on the narrow ridge. Several knights shifted over, then tumbled down the side. Men and horses toppled down the rocky slope, crashing into their fellow soldiers, breaking arms, legs and necks. The fight was over in an hour. Despite their overwhelming numerical superiority, the crusaders retreated, leaving nearly 300 of their men broken or dead on the hillside.

Within the city, those who had been bracing themselves for disaster gave thanks to God for their deliverance. The astonishing, unlikely triumph was proof enough to the Hussites that they had become an instrument of divine will. No longer wretched peasants, they were God's warriors, marching towards certain victory.

The triumph also burnished a growing national pride among the Czechs. Somehow, this small nation had tapped into deep reserves of ingenuity, courage and moral rectitude to defeat the forces of a degenerate empire. The proud boast of Czech exceptionalism, personified by the one-eyed hero Jan Zizka, would be both a psychological balm and a torment for centuries to come.

WHILE THE HUSSITES REJOICED, Sigismund reeled in disbelief. The losses at Vitkov Hill only amounted to a small fraction of his army, but crusader morale was sunk. Sigismund dropped his plans for a triumphant coronation at Prague Castle. Instead, he had to be smuggled into the castle on 27 July 1420 by a group of loyalist barons, who crowned him King of Bohemia and then smuggled him out again.

Meanwhile, Sigismund's mercenaries roamed through the woods outside the city walls, murdering Czech civilians, and dumping their bodies on a heap within their camp. The grim satisfaction they gleaned from these atrocities was offset by the stench of the corpses in the summer heat. The unsanitary conditions led to infestations of flies, and then a demoralising outbreak of disease in the crusader camps. Sigismund had been counting on paying his troops with loot from the conquered city. When the money ran out, his coalition partners broke camp and trudged home. The first crusade against the Hussites had ended in complete failure.

NOW THAT THE IMMEDIATE danger had passed, the tensions between the rustic Taborites and the urban Utraquists of Prague flared up again. The moderate Hussites of Prague still dared to hope for reform and eventual reconciliation with Rome, but the radicals in the city and the Taborites wanted a complete break. They demanded that all church properties in Prague be nationalised and that all remaining taverns and brothels be closed. Immodest clothing was to be prohibited. Sins such as fornication, adultery, swearing and consumption of alcohol were to be punished in public. Groups of fanatical Taborites burnt several churches in the New Town, but when they attempted to do the same in the Old Town, they were warned off by members of the butchers' guild who lined up against them with knives and axes.

On 10 August, a party of Taborites marched out of the city walls to the Cistercian monastery of Zbraslav, which held the great tombs of the Premyslid and Luxembourg kings. When they discovered the monastery's wine cellar, all puritan discipline was abandoned and the Taborites drank themselves into a stupor while they ransacked the tombs. The body of Wenceslas IV, only recently laid to rest, was pulled out of its sarcophagus and placed on an altar with a straw crown. The drunken Taborites then poured wine on his rotting head, joking, 'If you'd been alive, you'd be drinking with us anyway.'[22] They returned to Prague later in the day, still drunk, wearing priests' tussocks, parading through the streets with broken paintings and altarpieces.

In September, the rebels put the royalist garrison at Vysehrad to siege. Hearing of this, Sigismund vowed he would 'shit in the faces' of the enemy rather than surrender the fortress,[23] but, as always, he was too slow; by the time his army showed up, the captain of the garrison had already surrendered. Many of the guard went over to the Hussites.

Sigismund's army was then beaten decisively in the village (now suburb) of Pankrac, and more Czech nobles came over to the Hussite cause. In May 1421, the half-starved royalist garrison at Prague Castle gave up hope of being relieved by Sigismund and signed an armistice as well. The seat of Bohemia's kings was now in the hands of the rebels.

POPE MARTIN V, UNFAZED by the collapse of the first crusade, called for a second holy war against the Hussites. In late 1421, Sigismund's army re-entered Bohemia and pinned Zizka's army against the outer walls of Kutna Hora. Zizka escaped by waiting until the middle of the night, then reconfiguring his war wagons into a flying column that punched a hole through Sigismund's lines, scattering his troops with lethal gunfire. Zizka, who was by now totally blind, had been unfazed by the difficulties of fighting in the dark. His feat of improvisation had saved the Taborite army, and along the way he had accidentally invented the world's first mobile artillery unit.

After Zizka's daring escape, the crusaders relaxed their guard and went into winter quarters, but Zizka's blood was up. On 6 January 1422, he wheeled his army around and attacked a regiment of Sigismund's men quartered to the north of Kutna Hora, catching them completely off guard. Sigismund and his remaining forces dropped everything and fled towards the border. At the town of Nemecky Brod, Sigismund ordered his troops to give him cover to escape into Hungary. But Zizka was now a feared, almost mythical figure, and so when the crusaders heard the Hussites' battle trumpets, they panicked and ran again in disarray.

The fleeing crusaders pulled up in confusion at the Sazava River, which had frozen over in the winter cold. Rather than risk their horses on the rickety bridge, the knights elected to ride over the river's icy crust, but when the heavy cavalry gingerly stepped onto the frozen surface, the ice gave way. Soon the river was full of freezing, drowning knights, dragged down by their armour. The second crusade had collapsed even more ignominiously than the first. Bohemia was now completely in the hands of the Hussites.

Zizka's Drum

IN ROME, QUESTIONS WERE asked about Sigismund's competence. A third anti-Hussite crusade was launched, and it too was repelled by the Hussites. But once again, as the external threat to Bohemia receded, tensions between the radical and moderate

Hussites resurfaced. Control of Prague had shifted decisively to the moderate Utraquists, who had become weary of the fanatical Taborites and longed for reconciliation with Rome and Europe. In the brief civil war that broke out between the Hussites, Zizka won battles against the Utraquist forces as decisively as he had against the crusaders. The two factions signed a treaty of peace on 13 September 1424.

One month later, Jan Zizka was dead, a victim of the plague.

AS HE LAY DYING, so the legend goes, Zizka was asked how he wanted to be buried. The general asked that his body be flayed, that a drum be fashioned from his skin, and with this drum, they should go to war. His enemies, he said, would turn and run as soon as they heard its sound.[24]

Zizka died having won every single battle he'd led. Thereafter, his soldiers called themselves 'Orphans', as though they had lost a father. Today Zizka's military genius is commemorated in Prague by a massive equestrian statue at the top of Vitkov Hill, in Zizkov, the suburb that bears his name.

Compactata

THE DEATH OF ZIZKA encouraged the pope to call a fourth crusade against the Hussites. Zizka's successor as Taborite commander, Prokop the Bald, proved to be another gifted military leader, and he dealt out yet more defeats to the crusaders. All of Europe it seemed was ranged against the Czech Hussites, but no one had been found who could defeat them. In France, an angry Joan of Arc fired off a threatening letter to the Bohemian rebels. 'To tell you frankly,' she wrote, 'if I don't find out that you have reformed yourselves I might leave the English behind and go against you ... and relieve you of either your heresy or your life.'[25]

IN AUGUST 1431, a fifth and final crusader army entered Bohemia and yet again, the invaders were utterly routed. War weariness had now set in on both sides, and in October 1431, the Hussites were invited to a church council at Basel to seek a reconciliation. The revolutionary energy of the Hussites was dissipating. The apocalyptic predictions made so confidently at the outset of the rebellion had not come to pass. The world was still there, and they would all have to find a way to live in it.

The radical Taborites, however, wanted no reconciliation. In a bid to undermine peace negotiations, Prokop the Bald's army besieged Pilsen, which was then in Catholic hands. The attack split the Hussites irrevocably. The Czech nobles, both Catholic and Utraquist, closed ranks against the radicals and formed a new military league to keep the peace. In 1434, they defeated the Taborites at Lipany. Prokop the Bald was killed in the fighting and his army was destroyed.

THE BATTLE OF LIPANY brought the Hussite wars to a close. With the radicals defeated, the Utraquists were able to arrive at a compromise with the church, the Compactata of Prague, which was couched in a vague, watered-down form of words that the two sides could live with. The Utraquist form of worship was to be grudgingly tolerated but only in Bohemia and Moravia.

The Compactata opened the way for Sigismund to be accepted at long last as the legitimate King of Bohemia. In August 1436, he declared the war between Christendom and Bohemia to be over and entered Prague unopposed. Sigismund, who was now nearly seventy, had learnt nothing and forgotten nothing. Once on the throne, he indulged in an act of petty vengeance, ordering the last of the Bohemian radicals to be tortured and publicly hanged. People openly wept over the dead and spoke of them as martyrs, and Sigismund was hated more than ever.

Sigismund suffered from painful gout, just as his father had. The day after the executions, one of his feet was suddenly afflicted with fiery pain. His big toe had to be amputated, and then, in stages, the rest of the leg. Praguers concluded the corruption of his soul was eating away at him bodily. On 11 November 1437, the miserable, pain-racked king was carried out of Prague on a stretcher to escape the angry mob. He hoped to reach safety in Hungary, but got as far as Moravia, where Sigismund, the last of the Luxembourg kings of Bohemia, died on 9 December.

Orloj

PRAGUE EMERGED FROM the Hussite wars battered and pockmarked. Artillery fire had levelled whole precincts of the city. Puritan zeal had obliterated countless books, manuscripts, paintings and sculptures. The unity of the church was not restored; the Utraquists governed themselves at a cool distance from the church in Rome, while the remaining Taborites and radicals eventually coalesced into an entirely separate group, the Czech Brethren, who elected laymen and preachers to lead them. The Brethren stressed the primacy of scripture, and preached the gospel of radical equality before God. Unlike their Taborite antecedents, they condemned all forms of violence.

And yet it was during the turbulent fifteenth century that Prague's Old Town Square was endowed with its loveliest jewel, the Astronomical Clock: a masterpiece of art and engineering that, moment by moment, describes the city's position in time and space. The legend of how it came to be is still retold today:

IN THOSE YEARS BEFORE the wars of religion, the proud and wealthy burghers of Prague's Old Town invited a clockmaker named Master Hanus to the city. Their instructions were simple: 'Make us a clock for the tower of our Town Hall,' they said. 'A clock that has no equal anywhere in the world.'

Master Hanus laboured for years, his work concealed by sheets of cloth and timber scaffolding. When the cloth was pulled down, the people of Prague gasped in wonder. The clock was a marvel, a whirling ensemble of golden hoops, numerals, symbols, stars and planets. Its upper dial was ringed with golden numerals to indicate Prague time, Old Czech time, and even ancient Babylonian time. In the centre a disc representing the earth was fixed onto a background of dusky blue and twilight orange. A smaller zodiac ring displayed the paths of the sun and the moon.

Below the clock face was a second dial, a calendar, with a circle of painted medallions representing the twelve months.

Master Hanus invited the dazzled town councillors inside the tower to inspect the clock's engine room: they gaped at the intricate apparatus of interlocking gears, rotated by screw threads attached to weights of various sizes.

The new wonder clock filled the people of Prague with pride. The councillors agreed that Master Hanus had indeed given them the most beautiful clock in the world. They paid him handsomely and invited him to a banquet in his honour at the Town Hall.

That night, Master Hanus was hailed with toast after toast. He drank so much wine he began to feel drowsy. 'Don't worry,' said the mayor, 'we've made a bed for you in the room above the clock.'

Hours later, the drowsy clockmaker was awakened by a noise. In the darkness, he saw a glowing ember floating towards him. As it came closer, he saw it was a piece of hot iron, carried on tongs by the town executioner, who plunged it into both his eyes. His task accomplished, the executioner knelt on one knee and begged Master Hanus's forgiveness.

'It was the only way,' he pleaded. 'We had to be certain you could not make a better clock elsewhere.'

MASTER HANUS, LAY in that room for week after week, pondering his revenge. True, he was blind, but he knew every inch of the tower by touch. And so one night he rose from his bed, felt his way into the clock's engine room, and threw his body into the iron gears, which ground him up and killed him.

THE CLOCK WAS FROZEN at the moment of Master Hanus's death. Not one person in Prague had the skill to repair it. Visitors to Prague dwindled away; no one was interested in seeing a stopped clock. A hundred years passed before the mechanism could be made to run again, and by then all the councillors were dead.

THE FOLK TALE OF Master Hanus is recounted daily to groups of tourists who gather at the Astronomical Clock to watch it chime the hour, but there is no truth to the legend. There was a Master Hanus, but he worked on the clock only after its inception. Its true creator was Mikulas of Kadan, who devised it in 1410 with the aid of an astronomer from the university. Neither man was blinded by the authorities.

The calendar dial was added in 1490, as were the four automated figures that flank the clock on either side. On the left is Vanity, symbolised by an effeminate man with a mirror; he stands next to Greed, represented by a Jew with a moneybag (the statue was altered after the Second World War to make it appear not quite so blatantly anti-Semitic). On the right of the dial is the dreaded Muslim Turk, who turns his back on the fourth and most prominent figure – Death, the skeleton. Every hour, Death's bony arm jerks up and down, ringing the bell, reminding us of our mortality, while the Narcissist, the Moneylender and the Infidel shake their heads foolishly in denial.

The clock's most popular feature, the parade of the twelve Apostles, was installed in the eighteenth century. Every hour, between 9 am and 9 pm, two wooden doors slide open above the dial and a procession of automated wooden statues trundles past, each figure turning momentarily towards the crowd before moving along. St Peter carries a golden key, while St Paul clutches a book and a sword.

THE CLOCK, KNOWN IN Czech as the Orloj, has been stopped several times over the centuries for repairs or restoration. Each time, superstitious Praguers cringe, thanks to another folk legend that attached itself to the clock after the mass execution of twenty-seven Czech rebels in the Old Town Square in 1621. Every year, on the anniversary of their deaths, the ghosts of the Czech martyrs are said to wander up to the Astronomical Clock to see if its hands are still turning. If not, a season of horror and bloodshed will be let loose on the city.

Astronomical Clock, Old Town Square.
From left to right: the Narcissist, the Moneylender,
Death and the Infidel.

The White Lady

THE HUSSITE WARS HAD left Prague an almost entirely Czech city. The Germans who had sided with the church had been forced out, and the Czech language moved from the background to the foreground of public life and was established as the language of religion, education and administration.

In 1458, the Bohemian nobility elected one of their own, George of Podebrady, as their king. George had impeccable Hussite credentials: his father had fought in the battle of Vitkov Hill, and Jan Zizka himself had stood at George's christening as his godfather.

George's rival for the throne was Oldrich II, the Catholic patriarch of the powerful Rozmberk clan, which had dominated southern Bohemia for centuries. The Rozmberks' vast landholdings included twenty-two castles, six towns and close to five hundred villages and hamlets.[26] As a young man, Oldrich had been a Hussite sympathiser, but when war broke out he joined the royalist cause.

Oldrich had hoped to be elected king by the Bohemian estates, but George outfoxed him by cutting a deal with Oldrich's eldest son, Jan, to waive a major family debt in return for his support. Oldrich could only seethe helplessly as Jan rode alongside the new king on his coronation procession through the streets of Prague. Liberated from the crushing debt, Jan was now free to resolve a scandal that had weighed on the Rozmberk family's conscience for years: the plight of his sister Perchta.

PERCHTA OF ROZMBERK had been married off at a young age to a powerful Moravian landholder, John of Lichtenstein. But the union was based on a terrible misunderstanding: Oldrich believed his future son-in-law was wealthy enough not to require full payment of the bridal dowry. John, however, had spent freely on banquets and tournaments, and was relying on Perchta's dowry to clear his debts. When the money was not forthcoming, he beat Perchta, refused to spend any money on her, and forced her to sell her jewellery. Perchta sent plaintive letters to her father: 'When you gave me in marriage,' she wrote, 'it would have been better had you buried me in the ground.'[27] Oldrich, however, was unwilling to encroach on a fundamental tenet of male-dominated society: the rule of a husband over his wife. All he could do was to write back, lamely asking his daughter to be of good cheer.

Perchta's miserable situation became a scandal among the nobility, until her brother's deal with King George made full payment of the dowry possible.

After her husband's death, Perchta returned to the family estate at Cesky Krumlov. She lived long enough to see every one of her children die from various causes before she succumbed to the plague in 1476. Thereafter, the castle servants reported seeing a pale female apparition in the chambers and corridors, wearing a simple white dress with keys bound to her sash. Naturally, the ghostly figure was believed to be the restless spirit of Perchta, who had been cursed by her husband on his deathbed when she refused to forgive his cruelty.

Perchta made repeated visits to the family nursery at Cesky Krumlov. One night in 1539, the nurse caring for the infant Peter Vok Rozmberk fell asleep in her chair. When she awoke, she saw the White Lady looking over the baby's crib. In her terror, she shouted at the apparition to leave. The White Lady obediently passed through the wall and was never seen again.

THE TALE OF PERCHTA'S GHOST is just one of many white-lady stories told all over the world. The legends are nearly always attached to the tale of a woman who was badly wronged in life. In Mexico, La Llorona weeps as she goes about looking for children to drown. In Guatemala, La Siguanaba lures unfaithful men to a cliff's edge, where they fall to their deaths in fright. In Ireland, the White Lady of Kinsale is known to push soldiers down stairs in revenge for the death of her husband. In Japan, ghostly *yurei*, clad in white burial kimonos, are seen walking through Japanese villages at night. Kuchisake-onna, a beautiful woman whose face was slashed from ear to ear by her samurai husband, wanders the streets, asking villagers, 'Am I pretty?'

Evolutionary psychologists refer to these apparitions as 'sensed presences', which tend to appear in isolated or stressful environments. Coldness also seems to be a factor.[28] But the broad cross-cultural similarities of these women in white suggests some kind of universal archetype, a projection that answers to a universal human need or fear. Perhaps Perchta and her weird sisters are some kind of psychotic manifestation of guilt for the mistreatment of women.

THE BOHEMIANS HAVE another folk tale of a malevolent woman in white – the Polednice or Noonday Witch, who can be spied in the hot summer months, gliding eerily through the tall fields of wheat in a billowing white dress, looking for children.

In the nineteenth century, Karel Jaromir Erben, a young scholar at Prague's National Museum, travelled around Bohemia, gathering up old Bohemian folk tales and reworking them into fabulously macabre poems. His book *A Bouquet*, was an instant classic, read by adults and children ever since. In Erben's 'Noonday Witch', an overworked mother becomes so exasperated by her little boy's temper tantrum that she cries out for the witch to take him.

> *Come for him, you Noonday Witch, then!*
> *Come and take this pest for me!'*
> *In the door into the kitchen,*
> *Someone softly turns the key.*[29]

And suddenly the Noonday Witch is there, advancing towards her in the airless room. The terrified mother clenches her little boy ever more tightly, as the witch slowly extends her hand. Then the clock strikes midday, the woman's husband strides in from the fields for his lunch and sees that his wife has squeezed their son to death.

Ich bin ein Hussite

GEORGE OF PODEBRADY SUCCEEDED in stabilising Bohemia, but his bid for reconciliation with Rome was a lost cause. Pope Pius II scorned all his diplomatic overtures, demanding that he renounce the Utraquist heresy and enforce strict Catholic orthodoxy in his kingdom. When George refused, he was ex-communicated. To George's mind, it was a poor time for the pope to be picking a fight with his fellow Christians. Europe was still reeling from the conquest of Constantinople by the Muslim Ottoman Turks in 1453, and now Mehmed the Conqueror's fearsome Janissaries were marching further into eastern Europe.

To contain the common threat to Christendom, George tried to work around the intransigent pope. He wrote to the various Christian kings and princes of Europe with a radical proposition, a 'League of Princes' that would bring together the major European powers to coordinate a common military response to the Turkish threat. Differences between the powers, he suggested, could be settled peacefully by a pan-European assembly that would move between the major cities every five years.

The courts of Europe mulled over George's proposal, and then rejected it for fear of antagonising the pope, but his idea is today widely recognised as the first iteration of an idea that would come to fruition five centuries later as the modern European Union.[30]

GEORGE WAS TO BE THE very last Czech to wear the crown of Saint Wenceslas. After his death in 1471, the Bohemian estates offered the crown to the eldest son of the King of Poland. The Polish Jagiellonian kings, pre-occupied by battles elsewhere, were absentee monarchs, and for five decades, the country was effectively run by the Czech nobility; the powers of the royal central government were worn down to a nub.

Ludvik, the last Jagiellonian King of Bohemia died in 1526, falling off his horse in a battle against the Ottoman Empire. With the throne vacant and no obvious successor in sight, Archduke Ferdinand of Austria put himself forward as a candidate.

THE TWENTY-FOUR-YEAR-OLD Ferdinand was a Habsburg, and the younger brother of the Holy Roman Emperor Charles V. Ferdinand was militantly Catholic, but he readily agreed to confirm the privileges and religious liberties of the Utraquists and to move his court to Prague Castle.

Ferdinand's election as king was to have momentous unforeseen consequences. The nobles expected their new ruler would be heavily preoccupied defending Austria and Hungary against the Ottoman Turks, leaving control of Bohemia in their hands. Ferdinand, however, was an unusually adroit politician, and his tenure saw a sharp shift of power from the estates back to the monarchy.

Ferdinand's reign began just as the Protestant Reformation was underway in Germany and Switzerland. The German Lutherans discovered they had natural affinities with the Czech Hussites. At Leipzig, in the debate which preceded his ex-communication, Martin Luther himself had happily declared, *'Ja, Ich bin ein Hussite!'*[31]

The Utraquist doctrine of dispensing both the bread and the wine to congregations was adopted by nearly all the reformed churches, and with that the Czech Utraquists, the pariahs of Catholic Europe, were no longer isolated; the Protestant revolt plugged them into a dynamic continental movement. The evangelical New Utraquists moved towards the Lutherans, while the conservative Old Utraquists slowly drifted back towards the safety of the Catholic church. The Czech Brethren naturally gravitated towards the more puritanical Swiss Calvinists.

The Belvedere

KING FERDINAND WAS careful not to tread on the prerogatives of the Bohemian nobles so long as he needed their financial support in the war against the Turks. It was only in 1545, after a truce was concluded with the sultan, that Ferdinand felt strong enough to sharply curtail their power. When he requested they supply him with troops to support his campaign against the Protestant German princes, the Bohemians balked and raised a small army to assist their co-religionists. Ferdinand easily defeated the German rebels without their help, and the feeble revolt of the Czech Utraquists collapsed.

On his return to Prague, Ferdinand ordered the public execution of four rebel barons. He placed the town councils under the firm control of the castle, and, in a decision that would have enormous consequences down the track, the power of the Bohemian estates to elect their king was revoked, leaving them only the right to 'confirm' the Habsburg candidate presented to them. Bohemia was to be slowly absorbed into the Habsburg's Austrian Empire.

HAVING BOXED IN THE Bohemian estates, Ferdinand was ready to re-assert Catholic power in Prague. The church had changed since Jan Hus's time: it had rid itself of its more corrupt elements and recovered much of its confidence. Ferdinand invited the Jesuits to Prague and gave them the use of a Dominican monastery in the Old Town, the Clementium, where they established a college to compete with the Utraquist-dominated university. The Clementium attracted the sons of the Catholic nobles and wealthy burghers, giving Ferdinand a reliable pool of talent for his administration.

The Jesuits established a dazzling library at the Clementium, which claims, with some justification, to be the most beautiful in the world, with its twisting baroque pillars, ornately carved shelves and a luminous ceiling fresco. In his short story 'The Secret Miracle', the Argentinian novelist Jorge Luis Borges imagined that God himself was hiding in the Clementium Library inside a single letter printed in one of its thousands of volumes.

*

FERDINAND WAS A COLD-BLOODED political operator but he had a sentimental side. He was deeply devoted to his wife, Anne, and in 1531 he conceived of creating a pleasure palace for her in the new Italian style on the northern bank of the stag moat, which would be crossed by a covered wooden bridge.

The summer palace, known as the Belvedere, was a spacious and light-filled Renaissance palazzo, surrounded with an airy open arcade and decorated with dozens of classical murals, including an image of Ferdinand presenting Queen Anne with a flower. Along the ridge, Ferdinand established an orangery of aromatic trees bearing figs, almonds, apricots, oranges and lemons.

The airy palace looked like nothing else in Prague. On a warm summer afternoon, it must have seemed like a floating dream, compared to the stony Gothic castle across the moat.

THE SUMMER PALACE WAS completed in 1564, but Queen Anne had long since died after giving birth to her fifteenth child. Today, the pleasure palace created for her is regarded as the loveliest example of Renaissance architecture north of the Alps.

During the Hussite rebellion, artists, architects and craftsmen had avoided revolutionary Prague rather than risk having their work destroyed by riots, cannon fire or Puritan vandalism. That was all set to change. With the Belvedere, Prague had glimpsed the first rays of a new dawn of art, science and magic, which was to be presided over by the strangest human being ever to dwell in Prague Castle.

=== CHAPTER FOUR ===
THE GREAT WORK

1550–1619

Holy Roman Emperor Rudolf II as 'Autumn',
by Giuseppe Arcimboldo.

JUNE 1600: A THOUSAND excited spectators gathered in the open-air courtyard of Recek College. The crowd, an assortment of medical students, dignitaries and fashionable Praguers, looked on as the freshly hanged corpse of a man was carried into the courtyard and brought to the waiting figure of Dr Jan Jesenius. The doctor produced a scalpel, then slid it across the lower trunk of the dead man's body, carefully exposing the subcutaneous layer of flesh and then the abdominal muscles.

The public autopsy unfolded over five days, as Jesenius methodically dissected the inner workings of the hanged man's body, exposing the intestines and stomach, then the kidneys, liver and gall bladder, the reproductive organs, the chest, lungs, and heart and finally the skull, brain, eyes and ears. The surgeon was thankful, he said, for the unusually cool summer weather, which allowed him to proceed without being overly bothered by the stench.

Dr Jesenius, born in Breslau, educated at three universities – Wittenberg, Leipzig and Padua – was a surgeon and anatomist with a lively and wide-ranging intellect; by his mid-thirties he had already written several treatises on philosophy, politics and medicine: *On the Immortality of the Human Soul*, *For the Defense Against Tyrants* and *On the Place of Putrefying Bile in Acquired Malaria*.

Jesenius came to Prague at the invitation of the famous astronomer Tycho Brahe, who had just accepted the position of the emperor's imperial mathematician. Jesenius was enchanted by Prague and was moved to praise it as 'probably the richest city, worldwide'. His public autopsy created a sensation, and his published notes from the dissection, sprinkled with fables and quotes from the bible, earnt gushing praise from fellow physicians. 'On this way you will stay on the summit' one of them wrote. 'Your name will flare into the coming eras.'[1]

A Chamber of Wonders

PRAGUE, AT THE END of the sixteenth century, had entered a golden age of art and science. The ideals of the Renaissance – the pursuit of knowledge, a rejection of dogma, a rediscovery of the genius of the classical world – had spread north from Italy slowly and haltingly, but the new spirit transformed the Bohemian capital into a cosmopolitan city of 60,000 souls, the largest in central Europe. Rudolf II, Holy Roman Emperor and grandson of Ferdinand I, had shifted his court from Vienna to Prague, reviving the city's status as a political and cultural centre. Elegant new palaces, built by Italian architects and stonemasons, took their place on Prague's dramatic skyline.

The Italian artisans were soon followed by astronomers, artists, inventors and alchemists, who came to Prague, intent on the discovery of new knowledge, or the recovery of secrets they believed had been lost to the world since ancient times. Just as Jesenius used his scalpel to reveal the organic machinery under the skin of the human animal, others deployed mathematics, observations of the natural world and magic rites to uncover the secret workings of the cosmos.

Many of these Renaissance scholars shared an underlying assumption that everything in the world had a secret unity. They believed there was a hidden network of correspondences between all things, created by God, who endowed humans with perception and reason so we might figure it out. Most people perceived the cosmos the same way a cat might observe a Shakespeare play, noticing the shouting and the movement, without comprehending the larger coherent narrative. It required exceptional minds to investigate the clues that God had left littered around the earth to understand his workings.

THE CENTRAL FIGURE OF this glittering era was the strange, reclusive emperor in the castle on the hill. Rudolf II, in his portraits, looks at us impassively with large round eyes framed by quizzical gingery eyebrows. His sensitive mouth, set in his bulging Habsburg jaw, neither smiles nor grimaces. His demeanour betrays nothing of his state of mind; Rudolf would rather observe than be observed.

Foreign visitors to the imperial court in Prague were fascinated by the inscrutable emperor. The English diplomat Sir Philip Sidney sketched him as 'few of wordes, sullein of disposition, very secrete and resolute ... extremely Spaniolated'.[2] 'Spaniolated' meant overly stiff and formal, steeped in the customs of the gloomy court in Madrid, where Rudolf had received his education. But the emperor's neutral expression was carefully cultivated. He was a man caught between his responsibilities, his secret obsessions and his painfully introverted nature.

As emperor, Rudolf was invested with great power and dignity, but the exercise of those powers was constrained by the hardening divisions within his realm, particularly in Bohemia. Friendly relations between families withered as both Protestants and Catholics found common cause with their co-religionists beyond the kingdom's borders. Protestant noblemen travelled to universities at Wittenberg and Geneva, where the flame of the Reformation still burnt brightly, while Catholic nobles urged the Vatican to set up forward bases in Prague for a *reconquista* of the souls of the wayward Bohemians. Their efforts were fervently supported by the increasingly militant Habsburgs, who now dominated central Europe from their German branch in Vienna, while a Spanish branch of the family ruled from Madrid.

The Bohemians, overwhelmingly Protestant, remained stubbornly resistant to re-Catholicisation, but they were still divided between the establishment Utraquists, who behaved as a kind of church-in-exile within the Catholic mainstream, and the radical anti-clerical Czech Brethren. Each group deemed the other too unreasonable or too ungodly.

Rudolf, bored and irritated by this Christian infighting, strove to keep a lofty distance above it all. He resented Catholic pressure from his family, the papal nuncio and the Jesuits as much as he disdained the Protestant squabbling over petty points of dogma. His refusal to come down hard on one side or the other kept the peace for a long time, but it won him few friends.

BELEAGUERED BY THE entrenched religious hatreds and wearied by the bureaucratic grind, the emperor retreated into the inner world of his private obsessions. Within the walls of his enormous palace at Hradcany, Rudolf became a hoarder on a stupendous scale, surrounding himself with beautiful, weird and wondrous things: wildly erotic paintings, intricately engraved gems, clockwork robotic devices, and esoteric books. He installed these fantastic treasures in his own private Kunstkammer, a chamber of curiosities within Prague Castle, where he would lose himself for hours, alone.

Rudolf's Kunstkammer became famous throughout Europe but was seen by only a few visitors. Carlo Manfredi, ambassador for the Duke of Savoy, arrived at Hradcany in late 1604 and spent nine frustrating months waiting around for the emperor to grant him an audience. When Rudolf finally consented to receive him, Manfredi solemnly presented him with an Indian dagger, a rhino horn studded with rubies, a large silver model of a ship containing half an Indian coconut and a crown, and three bezoars – hard stones that grow in the stomachs of animals made from compacted hair and indigestible material that were thought to neutralise poison.

Rudolf was delighted with the gifts and he shyly invited Manfredi to take a tour of the Kunstkammer. The ambassador passed from room to room in amazement, gazing at the numbered cabinets, cases and chests. Mounted on the walls he saw a stuffed loris, a sloth and a red-billed toucan. In the middle of one room stood a long green table laden with mechanical devices: a clock with an astrolabe and rotating planets, a robotic metal peacock that could walk and fan its feathers, and a small harpsichord made of glass.[3] Manfredi was most impressed, however, by a large bowl carved from a single chunk of agate, whose natural veining spelt out the word 'CHRIST'.[4]

OUTSIDE THE STILLNESS of the Kunstkammer, Rudolf kept a menagerie of living wonders within the castle grounds: birds of paradise, crocodiles, a cassowary from New Guinea, a dodo from Mauritius, and a special enclosure full of big cats – lions, tigers and leopards. Exotic creatures from distant climates were unlikely to last long at Prague Castle, but such concerns failed to move the compulsive collector in the castle. 'What he knows,' wrote Archduchess Maria of Styria, 'he feels obliged to have.'[5] Rudolf was particularly fond of one lion named Mohamed, given to him by the Turkish sultan (in one of the brief interludes of peace between them), which he treated like a domestic pet and allowed to prowl the castle grounds and corridors. Mohamed would sometimes curl up and sleep at the emperor's feet, which would have been a fine way to keep court business brisk and to the point. But Rudolf often lacked the funds to feed the big cats properly; court records show several compensation payments made to various servants who had been mauled, some of them fatally.[6]

Of all these wonders, natural and artificial, the treasures most precious to Rudolf were a six-foot-long unicorn horn (most likely from a narwhal) and a jewelled chalice from Constantinople, which he believed to be the Holy Grail – the cup that caught the blood of Christ as it spilled from the cross. In moments of anxiety, Rudolf would sometimes perform a rite of protection with these two magical objects; drawing a circle with the tip of a sword, then retreating into the circle with the grail and the long horn, to pray and meditate.

Prima Materia

RUDOLF II, HOLY ROMAN EMPEROR, King of Hungary, Croatia and Bohemia, Archduke of Austria, was born in Vienna in 1552. His parents, Maximilian of Austria and Maria of Spain were first cousins who had sixteen children together, six of whom died before reaching their second birthday.

Rudolf emerged from his mother's womb sickly and small. To sustain his feeble heartbeat, the newborn was inserted into the warm carcase of a freshly killed lamb. Having survived this ordeal, he became the oldest living male issue of Maximilian and Maria. Hoping for great things, they had the French seer Nostradamus cast a horoscope for their infant son. The astrologer predicted Rudolf would, 'attain a great exaltation of reign and empire'.[7]

At the age of eleven, Rudolf and his younger brother Ernest were packed off to Madrid to be placed in the care of his uncle, King Philip II of Spain, a black-clad militant Catholic who personally supervised their religious education. He insisted the boys accompany him to an *auto-da-fé* in Toledo where he witnessed the burning of a band of Lutheran heretics at the stake. Philip relished this kind of ghastly spectacle, but it surely must have traumatised the brothers. Like so many of Philip's ventures, the lesson proved counterproductive: Rudolf recoiled from his uncle's fanaticism, and as a ruler he showed no interest in persecuting the Protestants and Jews of his realm.

If Philip had failed to make a religious zealot of his sensitive nephew, he did succeed in kindling a fascination for the weirder realms of art and science. While wandering the vast and gloomy corridors of Philip's El Escorial palace, the teenaged Rudolf was exposed to his uncle's collection of alchemical and astronomical books and paraphernalia, as well as Hieronymus Bosch's feverish triptych: *The Garden of Earthly Delights*, with its dream-like landscapes of heaven and hell.

IN 1571, NINETEEN-YEAR-OLD Rudolf was at last permitted to return to his parents in Vienna. His father, a warm-hearted man, was delighted to welcome his sons home but was dismayed by their 'Spaniolated' manners ingrained by their uncle Philip.

Maximilian was now Holy Roman Emperor and Rudolf heir apparent. His father prepared him for the imperial throne by awarding him the various crowns and titles of the Habsburg realms, and in 1575, Rudolf was brought to Prague, to be crowned King of Bohemia, and King of the Romans. The Italian portraitist Giuseppe Arcimboldo sketched Rudolf at his coronation, but his bejewelled crown looks too large for his head, and weighs down on him.

Maximilian died a year later, and Rudolf duly succeeded him as Holy Roman Emperor. He was twenty-four years old. His family and their Jesuit confessors watched him closely to see if he would turn out to be a steadfast ally of the church or a backslider like his father, who had become so worn down by Catholic dogmatism, he refused the last rites on his deathbed.

Drawing of Rudolf II receiving the crown of St Wenceslas,
by Giuseppe Arcimboldo, 1575.

The Glory of the Whole World

THE RUDOLFINE ERA was ill-starred from its inception: in 1577, within the first year of Rudolf's reign, a comet streaked across the skies of Europe. Court astrologers linked it to Saturn and Mars, a disastrous combination, a sign of God's displeasure with the mortal realm and, perhaps, its new ruler.

Rudolf was intelligent, curious and tolerant, but in all other respects he was tragically unsuited for the role of emperor. He lacked resolve and was a poor judge of character. He was too shy to impress his will upon people and succumbed to long bouts of mental illness. Problems were left to fester in the hope someone else might sort them out. When he did rouse himself into action, it was often too late and the matter would blow up in his face, making him appear even more hapless.

In Vienna, where he began his reign, Rudolf soon became morose and indifferent to his responsibilities. His mother tried to arrange a marriage with Philip's daughter Isabel – which would have been yet another marriage of first cousins – but Rudolf dragged his feet and nothing came of it. Rudolf would go on to father several children with his favourite mistress, but all were born out of wedlock and ineligible to succeed him.

At first, the young emperor tried to participate in the rounds of balls and court dinners in Vienna, but he soon became ill and severely depressed. He remained in his bed for months. Courtiers began to wonder if he'd inherited the same strain of Habsburg madness that had afflicted his great-grandmother Joanna the Mad, who had refused to allow her husband's body to be buried in case he should be resurrected from the dead.

The months of illness and inactivity passed into years, until 1580, when Rudolf recovered enough strength to undertake several trips to Prague, which offered him a degree of peace and isolation, compared to the busy, noisy court in Vienna. On the castle grounds, he supervised the construction of handsome new Renaissance palaces that lifted some of the stony Gothic gloom from the precinct, and Rudolf's spirits rose along with them.

In 1583, he took the bold step of moving the imperial seat from Vienna to Prague, shifting the Holy Roman Empire's centre of gravity. The move was justified by military considerations as much as personal preference; Vienna was too close to the frontier with the Ottoman Turks. Prague, located 200 miles to the northwest, was safer and more defensible. Perched high on the bluff at Hradcany, the castle was close to the city and yet detached from it. Here he hoped he could hold his meddlesome family at bay, live on his own terms and follow his own star.

PRAGUE AT THE TIME of Rudolf's coronation was still a conglomeration of five contiguous towns, each ringed with walls and gates, a mix of grand stone houses, Gothic churches and medieval slums.

In 1591, a young English traveller named Fynes Moryson came to the city as part of his grand tour of Europe and liked it well enough to stay for two months. At a distance, Prague appeared magical. But up close, the city offended Moryson's nose: the handsome squares were piled with horse dung, and the open sewers created a stench that he thought would repel a Turkish invasion far more effectively than the city's rundown fortifications.[8] Moryson was also offended by the sight of men shamelessly pissing in the streets, and by the Bohemian women, who thought nothing of going unaccompanied to a tavern and drinking alongside the men.[9]

This unseemliness in no way stopped Moryson from having a fine old time among the Praguers. He drank wine and ate pickled oysters in a pub. He hiked up to Hradcany to witness a funeral at St Vitus Cathedral, and to inspect the outer walls of Rudolf's palace. Peering over the moat wall into the emperor's garden, he spotted a dozen camels, a yak and two leopards.[10]

The Golden Monkey

NO PART OF PRAGUE intrigued Fynes Moryson so much as the city's labyrinthine Jewish quarter – 'the little City of the Jewes' – where he observed a religious service, a funeral and a circumcision in the synagogue.[11]

In Rudolf's time, the ghetto held close to ten thousand souls, living within a tight huddle of cramped streets, fetid canals and slanted patchwork buildings of timber and stone. Still, the conditions of Jewish life had improved in recent decades, and Prague's reputation as an enlightened, tolerant city attracted talented Jewish scholars from all over Europe.

*The Old Jewish quarter of Prague,
photographed in the nineteenth century.*

Throughout the sixteenth century, new synagogues, public buildings and houses sprung up in the ghetto, bringing a sense of pride and possibility to the inhabitants. A private family oratory on the edge of the Jewish cemetery was converted into a new temple, the Pinkas Synagogue, with a mix of late Gothic and Renaissance features. It was founded by Aaron Meshulam Horowitz, a prominent member of the community, and named after his grandson, Rabbi Pinkas Horowitz, but in Jewish folk memory, the man who gave his name to the synagogue is remembered as a poor rag seller:

PINKAS WAS A GOOD and pious man, but he had no money, and every day he walked the streets of the Prague ghetto with a sack of old clothes that he sold to provide for his family. At the end of each day, he would hand over his few coins to his wife, eat some bread and then study the Torah.

A wealthy Bohemian count from the Old Town took pity on this honest man, and so each year he gave Pinkas a gold coin to pay for the Passover Feast. When he received this generous gift, Pinkas would thank Yahweh, the god of the Hebrews, for his good fortune. This irritated the count, who thought he deserved at least some thanks for his charity. So, when the holiday of Pesach came, the count told Pinkas, 'It seems you have no need of my gold. God, who is good to you, will surely provide for you, since you always thank him so nicely.'

When Pinkas returned to his small home, his wife asked him how much the count had given him; he pulled out two pieces of dust from his pockets.

'How can we observe our duty to God and our family,' she asked, 'if we cannot buy food for the feast?'

At that moment, something smashed through the window and landed at their feet in a heap of broken glass.

It was a dead monkey.

Pinkas and his wife looked over the strange creature in horror and saw it had died in great pain.

'What is the meaning of this?' he gasped. 'And who threw it in here?'

'We must get rid of it,' said his wife, 'or the rich man who owns it will think we stole it and killed it.'

'Yes. We must burn it,' he said.

But when Pinkas lifted up the dead monkey, gold coins fell from its open mouth. Pinkas then cut open the animal's belly and more coins spilled from its gut. It was more gold than he had ever seen in his life. More than enough to hold the Passover feast.

Pinkas and his wife thanked God for this miracle.

THE FOLLOWING MORNING they went to the market and purchased flour to make the matzos, chicken bones for the soup, bitter herbs, and some wine. The children were given new clothes.

The count was surprised to hear that Pinkas and his family had somehow managed to set a very fine table without his donation, and so he came to visit him in the Jewish quarter.

'But how could you afford all this?' asked the count.

'I must tell you the truth,' said Pinkas. 'Someone threw a dead monkey through my window. Its mouth and belly were full of gold coins.'

The count asked to see the animal. He recognised the red collar around its neck.

'But that monkey belonged to me,' he said. 'It died just yesterday.'

The count thought for a moment. 'I thought the monkey had been ill, but now I know what happened,' he said slowly. 'I am in the habit of testing gold coins by biting them. The wretched animal must have thought I was eating them, and done the same. It swallowed too many coins and that's what killed it.'

The count looked at Pinkas with a dawning understanding. 'And my servants ... when they found it dead, they must have wanted to play a trick on you. That's why they flung it through your window.'

He picked up his hat and cloak and made his way to the door. 'And now I no longer have any doubt that God helps you, Pinkas,' he said. 'You should keep the money and enjoy it.'

In gratitude for this unlikely fortune, Pinkas built the synagogue in Prague that bears his name.

*

AFTER THE NAZIS WERE expelled from Prague in 1945, the Pinkas Synagogue was remade as a memorial for the Czech Jewish people murdered in the Holocaust. The names of all 77,297 victims were inscribed in simple letters on the walls. Drawings made by the child inmates of Terezin concentration camp were put on display in glass cases.

In 1968, the communist authorities closed the memorial, citing damage caused by humidity and damp. The regime lost interest in renovating the building and the names of the dead were destroyed or damaged through neglect. After the Velvet Revolution, President Vaclav Havel made the restoration of the memorial a priority, and from 1992 to 1996 the names of the victims were carefully re-inscribed on the walls.

THE WEALTHIEST JEW in Rudolfine Prague was the financier Mordechai Maisel, who made himself indispensable to the emperor by advancing him substantial loans for his wars against the Ottoman Turks.

Maisel also put his money to work beautifying the ghetto. In 1586, he financed the construction of a handsome Jewish Town Hall, to be built in the Italian Renaissance style next to the Old-New Synagogue. The most curious feature of Maisel's town hall is its two clocks: the tower is crowned with a conventional timepiece with Roman numerals, but just below on a scooped panel there is a Jewish clock ringed with Hebrew letters. Just as Hebrew text runs from right to left, the arms of the Jewish clock run anti-clockwise. The two clocks are said to symbolise the tensions in Jewish life between the sacred and the secular, the particular and universal, the need to be distinctive and the longing to fit in.[12]

Mordechai Maisel had no children to inherit his wealth. By law, this meant that on his death, his money and property could be confiscated by the king. Rudolf, however, granted Maisel the right to dispose of his wealth as he saw fit. Maisel accordingly wrote a will naming his relatives as beneficiaries, but when he died in 1601, Rudolf reneged on his promise. Maisel's family were shocked by the emperor's betrayal, but could do nothing as bailiffs carted off barrowloads of Maisel's gems, gold coins, silver candelabras and fine fabrics from his house in the ghetto. The starry-eyed obsessions of the emperor had made a thief of him.

Maisel was buried in the Jewish cemetery and it was rumoured that his wife, Frumet, stashed a portion of her husband's treasure inside the stone memorial behind his headstone.

MaHaRal

CLOSE TO MAISEL'S TOMB is a pinkish gravestone crowned with a lion and a cluster of grapes, the symbol of a full, prosperous life. Here lies the body of Rabbi Judah ben Loew.

Rabbi Loew was one of the great scholars of the Rudolfine era who wrote many books on philosophy, ethics and Jewish mysticism. For all his wisdom, he was at odds with the new spirit of the age. Far from being impressed by the recent advances in mathematics, astronomy and physiology, Loew was convinced that the sum total of human knowledge had actually degenerated since the time of the ancient Jewish sages, and that the font of wisdom was slowly draining from the world.

Rabbi Loew was spoken of as a *zaddik*, a righteous scholar with special insights into the secrets of the cosmos. He was a master of the Jewish Kabbalah, the poetic system of thought that maps the correspondences between God and mortal beings. The rabbi's awe-struck disciples named him the Maharal of Prague (a contraction of the Hebrew *Morenu Ha-Rav Loew* into *MaHaRal*: Our Teacher Rabbi Loew).

At some point, the occult-obsessed emperor in the castle became aware that the world's most admired Kabbalist scholar was living just across the river, and so, on 23 February 1592, he summoned Rabbi Loew so they might speak in his private residence. Neither man chose to reveal the substance of their conversation.

The Maharal's deep understanding of the mysteries of the Torah and the Zohar, the book of Kabbalistic knowledge, gave credence to rumours of his magical powers. There was a story that the rabbi had stunned Rudolf by stopping his carriage on the Charles Bridge merely by raising his hand to it. When Christians tried to stone him, it was said he transmuted their rocks into butterflies.

THE MAGICAL DEED MOST famously attributed to the Maharal is the creation of the golem of Prague, an animated humanoid made from slops of mud scooped up from the banks of the Vltava.

The word 'golem' appears only once in the Torah, where it denotes an unfinished human, something raw and crude. Adam, the first man, is the original golem, created from mud and kneaded into a shapeless husk.[13]

Golem legends were popular among Jewish communities in the Middle Ages, but the classic tale of the Prague golem does not originate in sixteenth-century Bohemia, but in the romantic German folk tales of the nineteenth century. The name of the famous magic rabbi, the Maharal, served well enough for the necromancer of the story.

According to the legend, Rabbi Loew decided to create the golem as a guardian to protect the Jews of Prague from a pogrom. One night he and his two disciples wrapped themselves in white linen and carried their lanterns down to the banks of the Vltava. The Maharal (representing air), and his followers (fire and water), scooped up handfuls of river mud and sculpted it into a golem (which was earth). The men uttered prayers while circling the creature. Then the Maharal reached up and carved the word 'EMET' – the Hebrew word for truth – on its forehead. Into its mouth, he placed a shem, a scrap of parchment with one of the seven sacred names of God written upon it, and with that, the golem was brought to life.

Rabbi Loew led the monster back to his house. By day it served as a tireless domestic servant and by night it patrolled the ghetto, keeping the Jews safe from malicious gentiles. But the rabbi's wife, Pearl, disliked it. She was troubled by its clay eyes and its dark face, which shone as though it had been greased with butter. And each day, she noticed, the golem grew a little taller.

EVERY FRIDAY, ON THE eve of the sabbath, the Maharal took care to remove the *shem* from the golem's mouth to render it inert. But one week, the rabbi forgot, and the golem ran wild through the Jewish quarter, tearing down houses, pulling up trees and thrashing about on the ground like a monstrous child.

When the Maharal found the creature, he commanded it to be still, then ordered it to take off his boots. As the golem bent down, the rabbi erased the first letter of 'EMET' from its forehead, leaving the word 'MET', which means death, and the creature collapsed into a pile of mud.

The sludge was shovelled into a trunk and carried up to the attic of the Old-New Synagogue, where it was ordered never to be disturbed. The attic was sealed up and the uppermost stairs removed.

IN 1920, THE JEWISH reporter Egon Kisch, who had grown up with the golem legend, decided to see if there really was a chest of mud stashed inside the roof. One morning, before dawn, he brought his mountain-climbing gear to the Old-New Synagogue. Seeing no one was around, he scaled the walls, removed a few roof tiles and lowered himself into the attic. In the semi-darkness, he groped his way through the jagged ceiling arches. A bat crashed into his face, but otherwise he discovered nothing.

Kisch, who was both a communist and an atheist, declared his mission to be a success; but in publishing the story in the Prague press, he accepted he had unwittingly brought it back to life. The golem was popularised in the early twentieth century by Gustav Meyrink's fever-dream of a novel, and by Paul Wegener's classic silent film, where the director played the title role himself.

In 1938, as the Nazi threat loomed over Prague, Kisch wished he could summon the golem to protect the city: 'I too would give the command: *Arise and go! Our enemies are closing in on my Prague!*'[14]

Paul Wegener as the Golem in his 1915 silent film of the same name.

The Name of the Lady

JUST AS KABBALISM THRIVED in the Jewish quarter, a similar occult movement took hold in Rudolf's castle; a discipline whose ideals were expressed in the pages of a strange and baffling book titled *The Chymical Wedding of Christian Rosenkreuz*. The author was unknown.

The book told the tale of a German knight, Christian Rosenkreuz, who receives a mysterious invitation to assist at the wedding of a king and queen. At the royal castle, he and an assortment of other guests are subject to a set of punishing ordeals to test their fitness to attend the ceremony. Presiding over these tests is an otherworldly woman in a majestic red velvet dress, with a white ribbon around her waist. Her head is crowned with a green laurel wreath.

On the evening of the third day at the castle, after a fine dinner, Christian is emboldened to ask the woman in the red dress for her name. She answers with a riddle:

> *My name contains five-and-fifty, yet only has eight letters. The third is a third part of the fifth; if it is added to the sixth, they make a number whose root exceeds the first letter by as much as the third itself, and is half of the fourth. The fifth and seventh are equal, and the last is equal to the first, and these make as much with the second as the sixth, which is just four more than thrice the third. Now tell me, Sir, what is my name?*

Christian turns her riddle over in his mind but is hopelessly caught in its intricacies. He can see it's a simple code, A = 1, B = 2, and so on, but the riddle is sealed inside itself, and cannot yield an answer. So he politely asks the lady if she will provide him with a single clue. She smiles graciously and agrees. He asks for the value of the seventh letter and she replies, 'As many as the gentlemen here.' Having counted nine gentlemen, Christian is soon able to correctly decipher the lady's name.

✳

The Chymical Wedding of Christian Rosenkreuz was both an allegorical romance and a manifesto of an occult art that was the great passion of the age. Its name was concealed in the lady's riddle: ALCHIMIA.

Alchemy offered its practitioners nothing less than the means to transmute base metals into gold and to attain everlasting youth. Rudolf II, endlessly curious, always short of gold and terrified of death, found the glitter of this 'noble art' irresistible, and he refitted the Powder Tower on the north wall of the castle as an alchemical workshop. The emperor was most likely introduced to alchemy by his personal physician, Dr Tadeas Hajek, a brilliant polymath who lived in the House at the Green Mound on Bethlehem Square. Hajek's workshop was an alchemist's dream: its walls richly decorated with gold inscriptions, hieroglyphs and pictures of birds, flowers and fruits.

Hajek and his fellow alchemists spent years attempting to process metals like mercury and lead through a multi-staged ordeal of heating, cooling, mixing and distillation, so as to bring their essential qualities into play with each other. The ultimate goal was to create a primordial substance known as the philosopher's stone: the transformative agent that could transmute base substances into the noble metals of gold and silver, and could act as an elixir of life. The quest for the philosopher's stone was known as the *magnum opus*, the great work.

It was, of course, a frustratingly futile endeavour, but the struggle itself was meaningful; the working of metals was supposed to mirror a process of inner transformation, a distillation of the gold of the human soul. Humility and imagination were essential ingredients. Would-be adepts could never find their way by sticking to the straight line of deductive reasoning. Instead they had to enter a labyrinth that confounded linear logic, and which called upon intuition and humility, the golden thread of Ariadne, to reveal the true path. Christian Rosenkreuz was wise to humbly ask the lady for a clue, because arrogant logic was not enough to decypher her riddle: a gift of grace was required to unlock it.

THE MONTH AFTER I LEFT post-revolutionary Prague, I found an edition of sixteenth-century alchemical drawings in a second-hand bookshop on London's Charing Cross Road. The images were weirdly beautiful, and clearly allegorical, but they thwarted my attempts to unpick their meaning. On one page, I saw a gigantic glass vessel floating upon a body of water. Inside the flask, a naked man and woman embraced, as the sun and moon looked on from the rocks nearby. In the neck of the flask, a child (or was it a cherub?) floated above the couple, and a nine-branched tree sprouted up from the child's head above the rim. I knew well enough that there might be some correspondence between man/woman and sun/moon, and that the glass flask obviously denoted some kind of chemical process, but otherwise I was clueless as to its meaning, if it had one. The images seemed to burn with the need to communicate something important but inexplicable. Eventually I saw that these enigmatic diagrams are intended to function as a kind of mandala, a graphic device designed to pin down rational thought and allow the subconscious mind to come forth and throw out flashes of creative insight that might later be identified as intuition or divine revelation.

ALCHEMY TRACES ITS ORIGINS to fourth century Alexandria, where goldsmiths and metal workers became proficient in dyeing metal alloys to make them look like gold. What began as a marketplace hustle inspired a whole body of mystical thought that suddenly made grand claims for its vast antiquity. In Alexandria it was said that the secrets of alchemy had been brought to earth by fallen angels, who had passed them on to their earthly wives.

Such ambitious work had to be undertaken in great secrecy. 'Mysteries made public become cheap, and things profaned lose their grace', warned the narrator of *The Chymical Wedding*. The master alchemists therefore encoded their work in densely symbolic language to keep them safe from the greedy, the unimaginative and the impatient. But sincere practitioners of the art were inevitably frustrated in their attempts at transmutation. The secretive culture of the alchemists concealed their failures.

THE RENAISSANCE OBSESSION with alchemy is now widely regarded as an embarrassing dead end, a stumbling block of medieval obscurantism that delayed the arrival of genuine science. Scholars would have to wait until the Enlightenment before the invisible college of arcane knowledge would finally give way to the open academy, the scientific method and evidence-based chemistry.

In Rudolf's time, sincere alchemists were outnumbered by charlatans, known as 'puffers', who came to Prague hoping to win the emperor's patronage. One such puffer, a Greek Cypriot named Mamugna of Famagusta, strode through the streets of the Old Town with a pair of black mastiffs, brandishing nuggets of gold that he claimed to have made himself. Another named Geronimo Scotta made a spectacular entry into Prague with three red velvet carriages drawn by forty horses, but he soon lost his money and reputation, and ended up selling potions from a booth in the Old Town Square.[15]

THE DEEPEST AND HOLIEST dream of alchemy was the chemical wedding itself: the refinement of the soul through the sacred marriage of opposites: male and female, sun and moon, sulphur and mercury. The wedding releases the better self, the uncommon gold, *aurum non vulgi*, that lies within. It's a demanding process, as Christian Rosenkreuz discovers; one that chimes with F. Scott Fitzgerald's famous test of a first-rate intelligence – the ability to hold two opposed ideas in mind at the same time and still retain the ability to function.[16]

The chemical wedding of equal opposites.

Magus

FOR RUDOLF'S DOMESTIC SERVANTS, the chilly castle must have been an unsettling place to work, with sulphurous smoke trailing from the Powder Tower, portraits of naked women hanging from the walls, and hungry lions padding through the hallways. Scientists and alchemists came to and from the palace. What purpose did all this strangeness signify? Was their master in league with the devil?

In early August 1584, word spread through the city that the famous English magus Dr John Dee had come to Prague along with his companion, the Irish seer and alchemist Edward Kelley. Tadeas Hajek, who had long corresponded with Dee, invited them to lodge with him in his House at the Green Mound and offered them the use of his alchemical workshop.

Dee was a genuine scholar, highly regarded across Europe for his work as a mathematician and a geographer. But his current work with Kelley made such pursuits seem mundane. The two men, for some years now, had been communicating with angels.

JOHN DEE WAS BORN in London, and educated at Cambridge University, where arithmetic had led him to numerology; astronomy to astrology; and the natural sciences to alchemy. His reputation as a master magician was established at Trinity College, where he engineered a stunning stage effect for a production of an Aristophanes play by creating a gigantic winged scarab beetle that flew around the auditorium. The audience was astonished, and afterwards he was denounced as a sorcerer. Dee insisted the effect was arrived at 'Naturally, Mathematically and Mechanically', hinting at the use of 'wheles' and pulleys.[17]

After establishing his reputation as a mathematician on the continent, Dee returned to his home at Mortlake in Surrey, where he established a library that was said to be the largest repository of books on the natural sciences and the occult in England.

As one of the most learned scholars in the realm, Dee was called upon to give cartographic advice for an expedition to find a northwest passage across the Americas to Europe. Elizabeth I invited him to cast the royal horoscope and to advise her on the most auspicious day for her coronation. Dee's reputation in London was such that Shakespeare modelled his character Prospero from *The Tempest* on him.

IN THE 1580s, Dee concluded that no man or book could bring him the wisdom he longed for, so he looked for shortcuts to knowledge through his occult research. Like other scholars of the time, Dee believed that God had imbued all things with the radiant light of creation, and that such rays could be gathered and focused in polished crystals. These 'show stones' required a sensitive medium, or 'scryer', to summon otherworldly visions from their depths. There was no sin in this: scrying, he believed, was a form of 'natural magic', wholly different from diabolical magic proffered by powerful demons. Indeed, with his show stone, he hoped to redeem all of humanity from its alienation from God.

Dee thought that the expulsion of Adam and Eve from the Garden of Eden had resulted in a breakdown of communication with heaven. Since then, humans had only been able to understand the Creator dimly and imperfectly. By communing with angels through his crystal show stone, Dee hoped to recover this sublime lost language and resume the broken conversation between God and his creation.

Dee's first scryers had proved unsatisfactory, but in 1582, a stranger arrived at his door offering his services. The visitor introduced himself as Edward Talbot, but afterwards revealed his true name, Edward Kelley.

EDWARD KELLEY, thirty years Dee's junior, was a charismatic and imaginative charlatan. Very little is known of his early life. At some point both his ears had been lopped off by the authorities for forgery, a disfigurement he tried to conceal by wearing a cap with long side-flaps.

Kelley took little time to deduce the secret desire within John Dee's heart. He read Dee's diary and tantalised him by feeding parts of it back to him through the visions he reported in the crystal show stone. Kelley's first contact was with the archangel Uriel, which greatly excited Dee; Uriel, he believed, had given the language of creation to Noah's ancestor Enoch.

The two men settled into a routine of regular scrying: Kelley would describe the lurid visions and voices he perceived, and Dee would put questions to the angels who appeared in the crystal. The rich imagery Kelley conjured up – a book with text written in blood on golden pages, an angel eating red fruit from a flourishing tree – persuaded Dee that his seer was genuine. Dee kept a detailed account of these sessions in his occult diary, later published as *A True and Faithful Relation of What Passed for Many Years Between Dr. John Dee and Some Spirits*.

Word of Dee and Kelley's sensational breakthrough soon spread throughout Europe. In 1583, Count Albert Laski of Poland, a patron of alchemists and seers, invited the two men to come with him to his estate in Cracow and to bring their families. Dee, who feared he was out of favour with Elizabeth and her court, was only too happy to accept.

On 21 September, the two families slipped out of Mortlake under cover of darkness and boarded a ship bound for the continent. After passing through Rotterdam and Bremen, they made their way into Cracow.

The sojourn in Poland was a disappointment all round. Kelley, who had presented himself to Laski as a master alchemist, failed to produce the elixir of life as he had promised, and the count was running out of money. At the same time, the angels in the show stone were telling Dee he must go to Prague to warn Rudolf to renounce his sinfulness, lest the angels pull him down from his throne. The prospect was terrifying – who was Dee to say such a thing to the Holy Roman Emperor? But the angels were insistent, and so, on 1 August 1584, he and Kelley set out on the long carriage ride to Prague.

AT THEIR FIRST SÉANCE in the House at the Green Mound, Kelley saw a gaping furnace mouth blasting out smoke and a seething lake of black pitch. Then he saw an angel named Madimi, appearing in the shape of a girl in a green and red gown, who uttered a litany of warnings: 'Woe be to women great with child, for they shall bring forth monsters. Woe be unto the Kings of the Earth, for they shall be beaten in a Mortar.'[18]

Once again Dee was told he must confront the emperor and rebuke him for his sins, but this time Madimi raised the stakes; she told Dee that the Son of Darkness would kill his children and drive his wife to suicide if he didn't comply. Kelley's motives here are unclear: it's impossible to know whether the angels' apocalyptic warnings came from a psychotic state of mind, or from a desire to torment his partner, or if he simply enjoyed engineering such confrontations to see what would come of them. In any case, at the angels' insistence, Dee penned a letter to Rudolf, asking for an audience, and on 3 September, a message arrived at the House at the Green Mound, telling him to come to the palace at two o'clock that afternoon.

DEE ARRIVED AT PRAGUE Castle without Kelley, who had drunk too much wine the night before and was nursing wounds from a fist fight. Dee got lost wandering though the castle labyrinth until Rudolf's chamberlain found him and brought him into the emperor's offices. Dee found Rudolf sitting impassively at a table, with a copy of his book *Monas Hieroglyphica*, which he had donated to Rudolf's father decades earlier. After introductory formalities, Rudolf came right to the point and said he believed that Dee had a message to communicate to him.

'So I have,' said the Englishman, who looked around, and seeing they were alone, took a deep breath and told Rudolf that the Angel of the Lord had ordered him to rebuke the emperor for his sins: 'The Angel of the Lord hath appeared to me, and rebuketh you for your sins. If you will hear me, and believe me, you shall triumph. If you will not hear me, the Lord, the God that made heaven and earth (under whom you breathe and have your spirit) putteth his foot against your breast, and will throw you headlong down from your seat.'

However, Dee said, if the emperor was ready to forsake his 'wickedness', then the Lord would make him great, and deliver him victory against the Great Turk.

If the emperor was offended by Dee's audacity, he did not show it. Speaking softly, he told Dee he believed him, and offered a vague promise that he would take him into his care. Rudolf indicated the audience was concluded, and Dee respectfully made his exit.

AFTER DEE LEFT THE CASTLE, a suspicious Rudolf sent a courtier, Jakob Kurz, to call on Dee at the House at the Green Mound. Kurz spoke with Dee for six hours on the nature of his research, while Kelley sulked in his bedroom. The courtier was unimpressed, and after he delivered his report, the emperor let it be known there would be no more invitations to the castle. Rudolf's Catholic advisors feared that

Dee was consorting with evil spirits, and suspected he might be acting as an English spy on behalf of Queen Elizabeth's principal secretary, Sir Francis Walsingham.

Dee and Kelley decamped to Trebon, south of Prague, to the castle of Vilem of Rozmberk, who offered them use of his alchemical laboratory. At Trebon, relations between Dee and Kelley deteriorated. Dee was beginning to suspect his sidekick was a charlatan, but the old man had come so far down the road of angelology with him, it was unthinkable to admit their years of work amounted to nothing more than fantasy.

Three months after their arrival at Trebon, Kelley announced he had produced a tiny granular speck of the philosopher's stone. Soon afterwards, he told Dee he had used the granule to transmute a small amount of mercury into an ounce of gold. Rumours of his 'achievement' spread quickly and suddenly Kelley, not Dee, was the star magus and alchemist of Europe.

SPIRITUAL GURUS, as they ascend ever closer to the godhead, all too often come back down the mountain with a holy writ to reorder the sex lives of their followers. In April 1587, Edward Kelley told Dee that the angel Madimi had appeared in the show stone and had shocked him by parting her cloak to reveal her nakedness. Then, Kelley said, she had commanded both men to 'cross-match' with each other's wives. Dee, who loved his young wife, Jane, dearly, became distressed and begged Jesus and the Holy Spirit for help, but Madimi rebuked him for his insolence and told him that all things are permitted to the godly. That night, as he went to bed, Dee told Jane mournfully that he 'could see no other remedy' other than to submit to the angel's demand. Jane wept and trembled, but agreed to do as she was asked.

Dee drafted a covenant that expressed everyone's willingness to put aside their bewilderment and to bow to 'this most new and strange doctrine', which he said was 'above human reason'.

Two weeks later, Dee wrote a terse entry in his diary: *Pactum factum* – 'Pact fulfilled'.[19]

FORTY WEEKS AFTER THE covenant was concluded, Jane gave birth to a son. Dee agreed to raise the boy as his own, and said nothing more about the matter. Kelley tried to raise his spirits by producing a liquid he called 'divine water', but it failed to act as promised. Nonetheless, the reputation of Kelley the alchemist and angel interlocutor continued to grow as Dee's began to fade. In January 1589, Vilem of Rozmberk made it clear that Dee had outstayed his welcome at Trebon. Dee and his family returned to England, where he was appointed warden of Manchester College.

Kelley, now very much in demand, was warmly welcomed back to Prague by Rudolf, who gave him the use of the workshop in the Powder Tower. The English ambassador observed Kelley at work and was completely convinced the Irishman had cracked the secret of transmutation. He claimed he'd seen Kelley produce 'perfect gold' from base metal, which 'came forth in great projection'.[20] The delighted emperor made Kelley a baron of Bohemia and awarded him with several estates. Rudolf now awaited a stream of gold to flow from Kelley's workshop, but when it failed to materialise, he concluded he'd been duped, and threw Kelley into prison.

Kelley was released two years later, but was arrested again after a fight with a rival alchemist. The circumstances of his subsequent death are unknown. There were rumours he'd faked his own suicide, or that he'd fallen from a tower window trying to escape. In any case, there are no further reports of him after 1598. Rudolf turned to other alchemists in hope of finding the elusive philosopher's stone, and to his astronomers to decode the mysteries of the heavens.

The Empire of the Stars

THE MOST CELEBRATED astronomer in Europe was the Danish aristocrat Tycho Brahe. Tycho was a man of striking appearance, with closely cropped red hair, small black eyes and a long walrus moustache. As a younger man, he had fought a duel and come away with the foremost part of his nose sliced off. He concealed this disfigurement with a prosthetic nose made from an amalgam of silver and gold, which he attached daily to his face with a dab of adhesive.

Tycho had been educated in the ancient traditions of astronomy, which assumed that the earth sat at the centre of an unchanging cosmos, and that the planets rotated across the sky inside vast, transparent spheres. The outermost sphere contained the sparkling stars. Astronomers were taught that the heavens were not open and spacious, but glassy and solid. The concept was poetic, but it cramped the imagination; the crystalline spheres kept the Earth encased within a crystal orb, like a cosmic snowdome.

Tycho's meticulous observations of the night sky put a major crack in the heavenly spheres. In 1572, he spotted a new star in the Cassiopeia constellation where none had existed before, an event that should have been impossible according to the ancient wisdom. This was a supernova, a dying star, blowing out gargantuan amounts of gas, light and heat. Although more than 7500 million light years from earth, it shone more brightly in the sky than our neighbouring planet Venus. Tycho published his detailed observations in a book, *De nova stella*, which overturned the ancient consensus of an unchanging universe and opened the skies. There was a dawning awareness that our world is not fixed inside a rotating crystal mechanism, but positioned in open space that humans might conceivably pass through one day on their way to other worlds. A contemporary said of Tycho: 'He subdued with his rare spirit the empire of the stars.'[21]

THE DRAMATIC APPEARANCE of this new star made it clear that a new model of the cosmos was required, using better and more accurate instruments to record its movements. To that end, the Danish king, Frederick II, gave Tycho an island in the strait between Denmark and Sweden, where Tycho built the world's most advanced observatory, named Uraniborg, after Urania, the muse of astronomy. Tycho ruled his island like a medieval potentate, entertaining his guests with riotous, drunken banquets attended by Jepp, his dwarf jester, whom he believed could see into the future, and his beer-drinking pet moose. But after Frederick's death, Tycho fell out with the new king, Christian IV, and in 1597, he was obliged to abandon Uraniborg.

Tycho and his entourage wandered through Europe until Tadeas Hajek urged Rudolf to invite him to Prague. Rudolf wrote a flattering letter to Tycho, offering to appoint him imperial mathematician, with a castle of his choice and a salary much higher than any palace courtier. Sorely in need of a new patron, Tycho set out in 1599 with his two sons to pay a visit to the emperor.

On arriving at Prague Castle, Tycho was given the honour of meeting the emperor alone. The two conversed in Latin, but Rudolf spoke so softly, Tycho had difficulty at times picking up what he said. Tycho then presented three books of his astronomical observations to Rudolf, which delighted the emperor.

For his new observatory, Tycho selected a mansion on a huge

estate thirty-six kilometres northeast of Prague named Benatky. He invited students to live there and assist him in his work, which included supplying the emperor with regularly updated horoscopes. At the time, astronomy and astrology were firmly bonded fields of study; astronomy focused on celestial mechanics, while astrology was concerned with the meaning of those mechanics and the influence of the heavens on the course of human events.

TYCHO WAS ONE OF the last great astronomers to make his observations without a telescope, and among the last to hold fast to the dying idea that the earth sat fixed at the centre of the cosmos. He knew of Copernicus's new model which established the sun at the centre, but he chose not to fully accept it. Instead he came up with a dizzyingly complicated hybrid theory that had all the *other* planets revolving around the sun, but with the sun and everything else still orbiting around the earth, which remained fixed in the divinely ordained centre of things.

Although Tycho's model was hopelessly wrong, the body of data he'd gathered over twenty years on the motion of heavenly bodies was invaluable for its volume and its precision. His oversized sextants and quadrants identified the positions of the stars to within an arc minute, which allowed him to measure planetary movements with an accuracy never previously attempted. But his stubborn loyalty to his flawed cosmological model left him unable to do anything much with his mountain of data. Tycho's achievements were to be outshone by the man he invited to join him at Benatky: a pockmarked German astronomer with poor eyesight named Johannes Kepler.

JOHANNES KEPLER, despite his various ailments and afflictions, was buoyed all his life by an indestructible optimism that carried him through his travails and the numerous dead ends of his scientific research. He saw the world as a labyrinth of puzzles, created by God, who had happily endowed him with the intellect to solve them. For Kepler, human curiosity was as natural and as beautiful as birdsong. 'We do not ask for what useful purpose the birds do sing,' he wrote, 'for song is their pleasure since they were created for singing. Similarly, we ought not to ask why the human mind troubles to fathom the secrets of the heavens ...'[22]

Kepler was born in the German town of Weil der Stadt, on the edge of the Black Forest, in 1571. His father, whom he barely knew, was a mercenary, and his mother a healer and herbalist, who was rumoured to be a witch.

The young Kepler astonished his elders with his easy grasp of complex mathematical concepts. Putting aside his ambition to become a Lutheran minister, he took up a teaching job in the Austrian city of Graz, where he pondered the movement of the planets.

Unlike, Tycho, Kepler was an early and enthusiastic convert to Copernicus's heliocentric model, but he wasn't satisfied to merely annotate the position of heavenly bodies. The clockwork motion of the planets appeared to suggest a grand design, a hidden set of principles. What is it that determines the spaces between the planets? And why do they move at different speeds?

One day, while in the classroom, Kepler was struck by a powerful idea. He suddenly imagined that the spaces between the orbits of the planets might be represented by a set of five perfectly symmetrical solid shapes – the triangular pyramid, the cube, the octahedron, the dodecahedron and the icosahedron – nested inside each other like a set of Russian dolls. This, he was sure, explained why there were six planets, with five spaces between them (Uranus and Neptune were yet to be identified as the seventh and eighth planets).

His excitement doubled when he realised that when placed within a sphere, every point of these perfect solids, would touch the inside surface of the sphere simultaneously. This implied an essential relationship between these perfect shapes and spherical planetary motion. 'It is amazing!' he wrote, giddily. 'Within a few days everything fell into its place.'[23]

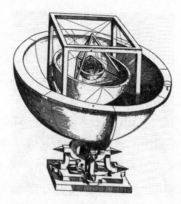

Kepler's model of the solar system,
from his work Mysterium Cosmographicum *(1596).*

KEPLER'S SPLENDID MODEL of the architecture of the cosmos was poetic but entirely wrong. Nonetheless, he spent years attempting to shoehorn the observational data into it. The flash of inspiration had been so galvanising, it seemed to Kepler to have been seared into his mind by God himself, a notion that carried him through all the troubling inconsistencies that were to follow.

Kepler presented his model in his first book, *Mysterium Cosmographicum*, which he published at the age of twenty-five. He sent a copy to Tycho Brahe, and the two began a lively correspondence. Tycho told Kepler he would be welcome if he chose to come and work with him.

In 1598, Archduke Ferdinand of Styria decreed that all Protestant teachers were to be banished from Graz. Taking Tycho Brahe at his word, Kepler, along with his wife and children, made their way to Prague. When Tycho Brahe heard of Kepler's arrival, he sent a message at once, inviting him to live and work with him at Benatky. 'You will come not so much as a guest,' he wrote, 'than as a very welcome friend and colleague in the contemplation of the skies.'[24]

KEPLER DULY ARRIVED at Benatky a few weeks later, but the grandiose Dane soon clashed with the touchy schoolmaster. Tycho was more standoffish than his letter implied, and his assistants treated Kepler like a domestic servant.

Tycho asked Kepler to study the orbit of Mars, a task that both excited and maddened him. Mars's trajectory across the sky seemed perverse: the planet would sail along, then slow down, come to a halt, retrace its steps and then resume its former course. He knew that Tycho's storehouse of thousands of sturdy little data bricks would allow him to construct a better, more truthful model of planetary motion than Tycho's absurd and convoluted theory, if only he could be allowed full access to them. But Tycho peevishly hoarded his data, and passed it out in dribs and drabs.

The shabby treatment wore away at Kepler's self-esteem until he could bear it no longer and he presented Tycho with a list of demands. He wanted a substantial regular salary and a separate apartment where he could work undisturbed by Tycho's raucous dinner parties. Tycho was ready to reach a settlement, but at dinner Kepler drank too much and insulted his host. Tycho became indignant, and Kepler stormed off to Prague the next morning.

A week later, having calmed down, Kepler sent Tycho an abject apology via Jesenius the anatomist, who had become his close friend. 'What shall I mention first?' Kepler wrote. 'My lack of self-control, which I can only remember with the greatest pain, or your benefactions, noblest Tycho, which can neither be enumerated nor valued according to merit?'[25]

With a weary sigh, Tycho came to Prague and in a fatherly manner, offered Kepler a ride back to Benatky in his coach. He promised Kepler he would pay him a proper salary. The two men had come to accept that they needed each other, and would both have to try harder to get along.

TYCHO HAD HOPED THAT the distance between Benatky and Prague would keep Rudolf from interrupting his work, but the anxious emperor had come to depend on his astrological forecasts and he ordered Tycho to relocate to Prague to be close at hand. Tycho, with the greatest reluctance, assented and installed his instruments on the terrace of the Belvedere in the royal gardens.

Tycho's dyspeptic mood might have influenced the bleak horoscope he delivered to Rudolf in early 1600. The stars, he bluntly told the emperor, indicated he would likely be assassinated within a few years. Rudolf, shocked to the core, became even more isolated, hardly venturing beyond the Kunstkammer and his private quarters, clutching at his treasured unicorn horn and holy grail.

MORE MINDFUL NOW of his sensitive deputy, Tycho brought Kepler to Prague Castle in October 1601 to introduce him to the emperor and inform him they had begun a new great work: a comprehensive tabulation of the position of the stars and planets, that they wished to dedicate to him. The proposal pleased Rudolf and lifted his gloom somewhat.

Two weeks later, Tycho Brahe was dead.

THE ACCOUNT OF TYCHO'S strange death was recorded in Kepler's diary. Both men had been invited to a supper at Peter Vok of Rozmberk's mansion in Hradcany. Rozmberk was a generous, gregarious host and Tycho drank heavily. According to Kepler, Tycho needed to relieve his aching bladder, but the rules of etiquette required him to stay at his place at the table until the host had risen:

> *Holding his urine longer than was his habit, Brahe remained seated. Although he drank a little overgenerously, and experienced pressure on his bladder, he felt less concern for his state of health than for the demands of courtesy. By the time Brahe returned home, he could not urinate any more … He spent five days without sleep. Finally, with the most excruciating pain he barely passed some urine, and yet it was blocked. Uninterrupted insomnia followed; intestinal fever; and little by little, delirium.*[26]

As he lay on his deathbed, Tycho begged Kepler repeatedly, 'Please, let me not have lived in vain.' He wanted Kepler to confirm his hybrid planetary model, a request Kepler couldn't possibly accede to in good faith. On 24 October, the delirium subsided momentarily, then Tycho expired.*

Rudolf was devastated by the loss of his imperial mathematician and arranged a grand funeral at the Tyn Church. Tycho's remains were encased in a red marble tomb in the church's nave, where they lie today.

---

* For centuries, Kepler was suspected of having poisoned Tycho, but modern forensic investigations revealed the probable cause of death was uremic poisoning caused by a damaged kidney.

Two days later, the emperor named Kepler as his new imperial mathematician, entrusting him with the responsibility of completing the Rudolfine Tables. The salary was a fraction of the sum granted to Tycho, but it allowed Kepler to move his family into a fine house in the New Town.

KEPLER NOW EMBARKED on the most fruitful period of his career. In between devising horoscopes for his emperor, Kepler kept puzzling over the question of the maddeningly eccentric passage of Mars. If the heavens were open and airy, Kepler wondered, what force was governing their orbits? Perhaps, he thought, the planets were living entities with 'world souls', whizzing through the heavens like spaceships. If so, how did they chart their course without clear markers to guide them?

Kepler reasoned that the sun must be emanating some kind of invisible force at a distance, like magnetism, holding the planets in their orbits and sweeping them along. But here he ran into a problem with Copernicus's new model. To make his computations work, Copernicus had done something odd: he had placed the focal point of planetary motion not in the heart of the sun, but at the centre of the earth's orbit, which, intriguingly, was offset from the sun's position. How could this be possible, if the earth's orbit was managed by the invisible exertions of the sun? Was there a second force at work?

Step by step, Kepler pulled out all the flawed assumptions of ancient astronomy and arrived at last at a transformative idea: that the shape of planetary motion is driven, not by one, but by two dynamic forces: one based in the Sun, and the other within the planet itself. He imagined that these dynamic forces create dual focal points at the centre of the solar system, which shape the orbits of the planets not as a perfect circle, but as an ellipse, a slightly elongated circle.

Kepler tested this elliptical model with Tycho's observational data and was overjoyed when they fitted together perfectly. 'I felt as if I had been awakened from a sleep,' he wrote later.[27]

∗

HAVING BEEN DIGNIFIED with the title of imperial mathematician, Kepler's social status in Prague rose accordingly and he took to wearing fine, black silk and ruffled collars. He was pleased to be invited into the mansions of several noble families, although he was too embarrassed by his relatively modest home to return their hospitality. Still, he was dogged by petty troubles: his health was poor and his salary was paid only intermittently, forcing him to petition the imperial authorities, who came to regard him as a nuisance. He wrangled for years with Tycho's estate for access to his astronomical data, and he argued constantly with his wife, who refused to touch a penny of her dowry when money ran short.

In 1608, he was ready to publish his magnum opus on planetary motion, *Astronomia Nova*, 'The New Astronomy', but he was so short of funds, he had to forfeit the entire first edition to the printer to cover the costs. Putting aside any resentment he may have had over his unpaid salary, Kepler dedicated the book to Rudolf and generously paid tribute to Tycho's work in the title:

A NEW ASTRONOMY *Based on Causation*
or A PHYSICS OF THE SKY
derived from Investigations of the
MOTIONS OF THE STAR MARS
Founded on Observations of THE NOBLE TYCHO BRAHE.[28]

In the *New Astronomy* Kepler set out his first two laws of planetary motion, which are (put very simply):

1. The planets travel around the sun in elliptical orbits, with the sun located at one of the two focal points.
2. Planets travel more quickly the nearer they are to the sun.

Later, he arrived at his third principle, the one that pleased him most: a mathematical formula that relates the orbital period of the planets to their distances from the sun. Armed with these three principles, an astronomer could accurately predict where a planet would be at any time in the future. It was the greatest scientific achievement of the Rudolfine era. Of all the brilliant minds that came to Rudolf's Prague, it was the awkward schoolmaster whose mind travelled furthest into the heavens.

IN 1608 KEPLER ACHIEVED another breakthrough of sorts, by creating the world's first work of science fiction, a short story titled 'Somnium', or 'The Dream'. 'Somnium' tells the tale of a young man from Iceland, the son of a witch, who studies astronomy in Denmark under the great Tycho Brahe. When he returns to Iceland, his mother introduces him to a daemon who tells him of his regular flights to the moon and of the bizarre creatures that live on its surface.

Kepler wrote 'Somnium' to shift the imagination of his readers towards the Copernican system; he wanted them to appreciate that if the earth could be seen from the moon, it would appear to be moving through space like the other planets. But the most wonderful aspect of his story is its joyful description of space flight. Humans would have to wait another 360 years before astronauts could behold an 'earth-rise' from the lunar surface, but it was Kepler who imagined the possibility of such a moment in the first place.

✳

I Know that I am Dead and Damned

BY 1608, WHEN KEPLER was writing 'Somnium', his emperor had become a lonely, embattled figure. He had tried to allay Christian infighting by calling on all Christendom to unite in the common struggle against the Ottoman sultan, who had resumed hostilities against him in 1593. But the war was dragging on, leaving large tracts of Hungary and Transylvania ravaged and lawless.

Rudolf, remembering Tycho's prediction, feared assassination, not at the hands of Protestants, but from Catholic hardliners who suspected he'd become a Protestant sympathiser like his father. The English diplomat Henry Wotton reported to London that a Flemish priest had been discovered in the emperor's privy chamber, with a crossbow hidden in his wide sleeve.

'I know that I am dead and damned,' Rudolf told his valet. 'I am a man possessed by the devil.'[29] This confession was duly passed on to the papal nuncio and to Rudolf's family in Vienna and Madrid.[30] Stoking his paranoia, they persuaded him to sack several long-serving Protestant counsellors and replace them with militant Catholics.

In 1606, a riot in the Protestant city of Donauworth provoked Rudolf into purging the local council and replacing its members with reliable Catholics. In response, the Protestant principalities within the empire formed the Evangelical Union, a military alliance against Catholic aggression. The empire's Catholic princes, led by Maximilian of Bavaria, then felt obliged to set up their own Catholic League. The Evangelical Union looked to France for support, the

Catholic League looked to Spain. It was Rudolf's job to hold this collection of princes together under the umbrella of the Holy Roman Empire, but the only firm point of agreement between them now was that he should go.

In 1606, Rudolf's scheming younger brother Matthias convened a meeting of the Habsburg archdukes to 'tear from him the sceptre and the crown'.[31] They were particularly offended by Rudolf's obsession with the occult, denouncing him in a letter they all signed:

> *His majesty is interested only in wizards, alchemists, Kabbalists and the like, sparing no expense to find all kinds of treasures, learn secrets and use scandalous ways of harming his enemies ... He also has a whole library of magic books. He strives all the time to eliminate God completely so that he may in future serve a different master.[32]*

The rebellious archdukes named Matthias as the new head of the Habsburg family and called for the emperor to name him as his successor. Rudolf bowed to their wishes and appointed Matthias governor of Hungary. The Hungarians were in a state of armed revolt against the empire, and Rudolf probably hoped to entangle his brother in an intractable mess. But Matthias quickly forged a settlement with the Hungarian rebels and the Ottoman empire by the simple expedient of granting them everything they asked for, and then leaving his older brother to find the money to pay for it. Rudolf was ready to overrule him, but he had made too many enemies. In March 1608, the Moravian estates declared their support for Matthias, as did the estates of Hungary and Austria. On 3 May, Matthias arrived at the Bohemian border at the head of a 20,000-strong army, ready to depose his brother and take his place.

Rudolf summoned an assembly of the Bohemian estates to ask for their support. The emperor, now fifty-five, stepped into the chamber stooped and downcast. In his thin, small voice, he apologised for being too ill to preside over the session and then shuffled back out of the room.

The price of peace with his brother was to surrender most of his empire to him: Matthias was to be awarded Austria, Hungary and Moravia, while Rudolf was permitted to retain Bohemia, Silesia, Lusatia and the imperial crown.

THE BOHEMIAN ESTATES used this moment to exploit Rudolf's weakness by extracting a guarantee of religious freedom in return for their support. Rudolf had no alternative but to concede, and on 9 July 1609 he signed a Letter of Majesty – a charter of rights – which allowed Protestants to open churches and schools as they wished. Protestants rejoiced, believing they had secured their liberties, but Rudolf resented having his arm twisted in this manner. With his enemies closing in, he resolved on a last desperate gamble, and reached out to his nephew Leopold, the Bishop of Passau in neighbouring Bavaria.

LEOPOLD, WHO WAS more of a reckless adventurer than a holy man, had an army of 10,000 mercenaries at his disposal across the border. In 1610 Leopold wrote to Rudolf, asking permission to bring them into Bohemia for the winter. Waving aside all advice to the contrary, Rudolf enthusiastically consented, hoping the presence of his nephew's troops would make it easier to stare down his enemies.

In early 1611, with Rudolf's blessing, Leopold and his Passauer army crossed the border into southern Bohemia and made their way towards Prague. The Passauers, underpaid and poorly disciplined, plundered every town they passed through. Prague's civic leaders pleaded with the emperor to order the Passauers to turn back. Rudolf, who preferred to wave his sword around rather than strike with it, consented, but the mercenaries were now off the leash and refusing to be restrained.

ON 13 FEBRUARY, sentries at Prague Castle spotted the approaching Passauer army. In the Old Town, the Tyn Church bells sounded the alarm, creating panic in the streets. Groups of men and women gathered stones and carts to set up a barricade at the bridge tower.

The Passauers pulled up outside the western ramparts of the city. That night they blasted through the walls with a concentrated burst of artillery fire and streamed into Mala Strana and Hradcany, pillaging one house after another. By ten o'clock the next morning, Mala Strana was a burning wreck. Dead bodies littered the streets.

From their high point on Hradcany, the Passauer artillery fired a barrage of cannonballs across the river into the Old Town. Leopold's mercenaries regrouped to cross the Vltava, but as they funnelled onto the bridge, they came under heavy fire from the tower and barricades on the far side. Still, they pressed forward. A Passauer cavalryman charged ahead though the barricade and galloped into the streets of the Old Town, waving a pistol. But, seeing he was alone, he panicked, and took off for the New Town, where he was pulled from his horse and killed.

While the local militias held the line at the bridge, a Protestant mob ran wild in the Old Town, looting the treasures of the Benedictine cloisters. Another mob invaded the cloister of Our Lady of the Snows and murdered any monks they could find. The church was ransacked and the altar destroyed. Then the Jewish quarter was attacked and pillaged.

Fearing the whole town was tipping into bloody anarchy, the Protestant nobles took control, ordering the mob leaders to be arrested and imprisoned, and with that, the plundering came to a halt. The next morning, Protestant militias brought their artillery pieces forward to strengthen the Old Town's bridge defences. Unwilling to risk cannon fire, the mercenaries retreated into their positions on the other side of the river and refused to leave unless they were paid huge sums of silver.

THE BLAME FOR THE disaster was of course sheeted home to Rudolf. The papal nuncio and the Spanish ambassador left Prague in disgust, and went over to Matthias's camp. Peter Vok of Rozmberk, who had once been close to Rudolf, also switched his support to Matthias and agreed to pay off the mercenaries to be rid of them. Leopold and his Passauer army took the money and slunk out of Prague, leaving Rudolf's golden city streaked with blood.

A FORTNIGHT AFTER the departure of Leopold's mercenaries, Matthias and his army marched into Prague unopposed. The Protestant nobles and burghers voted to support him as king of Bohemia so long as he agreed to recognise the Letter of Majesty confirming their rights, which he did willingly. Rudolf was forced to abdicate the Bohemian throne, but allowed to retain his imperial title and his occupancy of Prague Castle. He was still an emperor, but his tiny empire went no further than the walls of Hradcany. Legend has it that a shattered Rudolf stood at his window and uttered a terrible curse on the city:

Prague, ungrateful Prague, I have made you famous but now you are driving me, your benefactor, out. Let revenge come upon you and damnation befall you and all the Czechs! [33]

Alone and powerless, Rudolf was assailed with persistent bronchitis, and his legs became swollen with oedema. He tried to treat his ailments by drinking an elixir containing amber and finely ground bezoar stones, but the magic potion did nothing for him and his legs became gangrenous.

In January 1612, his servant brought him the awful news that his favourite lion, Mohamed, was dead. Rudolf remembered a horoscope given to him years earlier that predicted he would share the lion's fate, and he died three days later on 20 January. His sarcophagus – garishly plastered with cherubs and crests – lies today in the vault of St Vitus Cathedral.

The Second Defenestration of Prague

MATTHIAS, THE NEW Holy Roman Emperor, had no great love for Prague. In 1612, he moved the imperial court back to Vienna, a decision that deeply offended Bohemians, who feared they were being downgraded to an Austrian outpost. The sudden departure of imperial counsellors, bureaucrats and foreign ambassadors from Hradcany left Praguers feeling cut adrift from the wider world once more.

Matthias, who had connived for decades to replace his older brother, soon discovered he had won a hollow triumph. In Vienna, he realised he was seen by his family as a mere placeholder for a younger, more militant generation of Habsburgs waiting in the wings. The leader of this group was Archduke Ferdinand of Styria, a softly spoken, burning-eyed fanatic. As ruler of his southern Austrian domain, Ferdinand had moved from one town to the next, pulling down Protestant churches, making a bonfire of their hymnal books. He went so far as to dig up graves and strew the roads with Protestant corpses. It was he who had ordered the Protestant expulsions that had driven Kepler out of Graz. 'Better a desert,' he had proclaimed, 'than a country full of heretics.'[34]

Ferdinand bore a strong physical resemblance to Rudolf – the swollen Habsburg jaw, the sandy hair, the protruding lower lip – but Rudolf had been the figurehead of an open and tolerant age that was receding; Ferdinand, narrow and doctrinaire, was coming in on the new tide, ready to give the empire's unsteady framework of religious tolerance a good hard kicking. Ferdinand saw this as a form of tough love. 'Non-Catholics consider me unfeeling in my prohibition of heresy,' he once told his Jesuit confessor. 'I do not hate them but love them; unless I loved them free from any concern, I would leave them in their error.'[35]

When Matthias nominated Ferdinand as King of Bohemia, it put the Czech barons in a bind. Technically, it was they who were supposed to elect their king, but under the Habsburgs this had become a mere formality, and they were gulled into accepting the obnoxious Ferdinand, even though he was known to be utterly hostile to their religious beliefs.

Although Ferdinand had agreed to uphold the Letter of Majesty, once safely installed on the throne he began to chip away at the Protestants' liberties. Freedom of speech was curtailed and non-Catholics were again banned from high office. Discontent turned to outrage when Ferdinand's deputies in Prague ordered a Lutheran church in the town of Hroby to be torn down, and then jailed a local Protestant leader for speaking out against it. In May 1618, a group of radicalised Protestant nobles sent a list of grievances to the castle, but the letter was condescendingly dismissed by Ferdinand's Catholic deputies.

ON THE MORNING OF 23 May, a delegation of Protestant nobles marched up to Hradcany at the head of an angry crowd to confront the arrogant officials. The procession, led by a Protestant nobleman and war veteran named Jindrich Thurn, entered the palace and barged into the small council chamber room, where they found the two most hated Catholic deputies, Vilem Slavata and Jaroslav Borita, seated at their desks. As the mob poured into the room, Slavata and Borita were pushed into a corner. Furious argument broke out as the deputies tried to defend themselves against a flurry of accusations. Then the mood turned murderous.

The two Catholic deputies were seized by the arms and legs. At first, they thought they were being arrested, but when they were dragged towards the window, they understood their fate. Borita cried, 'Jesu Maria! Help!' then he was hoisted up and flung out the window. Slavata was also pushed out, but he clung on desperately to the sill. A rebel pounded his fingers with the hilt of a dagger and the deputy released his grip, falling twenty metres to the ground below. The court scribe was thrown out the window too, for good measure.

All three were injured, but alive. The broken men limped and crawled away to safety while the triumphant mob jeered and fired pistol shots from the window. Afterwards, the Catholics claimed the Madonna had interceded on the deputies' behalf by catching them and carrying them to the ground. The Protestants retorted that the men had only survived by landing in the huge heap of mouldering dung that sat at the foot of the window.

*

THE DEFENESTRATION of the deputies was, of course, premeditated; Thurn and his followers were consciously re-enacting the Hussite rebellion of two centuries earlier. The potent symbolism of Protestant defiance was irresistible.

Just as Thurn intended, this Second Defenestration of Prague radicalised the participants and forced people to take sides. The Protestant nobles at once formed a Bohemian provisional government, which voted to raise an army of 16,000 men, to be led by Jindrich Thurn.

In Vienna, Ferdinand demanded that the emperor launch a crusade against the rebels in Prague, but an increasingly ill Matthias tried negotiation instead. In the months that followed, letters shot back and forth fruitlessly between Prague and Vienna, while both sides reached out for external support and prepared for war. The Habsburgs could count on military assistance from their cousins in Spain, as well as from the Catholic leaders of Bavaria and Poland. The estates could only hope that Protestant rulers in Germany, England and Holland would come to the aid of their co-religionists.

Emperor Matthias went to his grave on 20 March 1619, predicting terrible things would happen after his death. The Habsburgs, unwilling to concede an inch to the empire's Protestants, put forward Ferdinand to succeed Matthias as Holy Roman Emperor.

Realising that compromise was now impossible, the Bohemian rebel barons took the fateful step of deposing Ferdinand as their king, and offered the vacant throne to a young Protestant prince, Frederick V of the Palatinate of the Rhine. They hoped both he and his glamorous Scottish bride, Elizabeth, would rally all of Protestant Europe to their cause.

*

JOHANNES KEPLER HAD LEFT Prague in despair after Rudolf's death and taken up a position in Linz as a schoolteacher. He completed the great star catalogue, the Rudolfine Tables, in 1623, but the Rudolfine moment, an era that had prized inquiry, contemplation and knowledge, died with its great patron in Prague Castle. The dream of spiritual unity was passing. The men of action were about to have their day and the turmoil in Prague was about to drag all of Europe into an abyss.

Kepler died in Regensburg on 15 November 1630, but the city's cemetery was later destroyed by marauding soldiers and his bones were scattered. All we have left of his grave are the words he wrote for the inscription. It serves well enough as an epitaph for the whole Rudolfine era:

I measured the skies, now the shadows I measure.
Skybound was the mind, earthbound the body rests.[36]

CHAPTER FIVE

A BOHEMIA OF THE SOUL

1620–1815

Frederick and Elizabeth, the Winter King and Queen.
Painted by Michiel Janszoon van Mierevelt and Robert Peake, respectively.

Two Phoenixes

FREDERICK, PRINCE-ELECTOR of the Palatinate of the Rhine, and his glamorous wife, Elizabeth, entered the rebel city of Prague on 31 October 1619. They were welcomed with an honour guard, cheering crowds and streets decked out in blue and silver banners. Elizabeth made a good first impression on her new subjects by her eagerness to meet them despite her advanced stage of pregnancy, but eyebrows were raised at her elaborate hairdo and plunging neckline.

The couple were carried up to St Vitus Cathedral, where they were crowned separately and solemnly as King and Queen of Bohemia. As the royal couple left the cathedral, they tossed newly minted silver coins to the crowd. Street parties broke out across Prague and the fountains were filled with wine.

Elizabeth was the daughter of King James I of England and Scotland. Her life up until this point had been like an enchanted dream. When her father had become king, she had been placed in the care of the doting Lord Harington of Warwickshire, who created a miniature wooden village for her on his estate with an aviary and a menagerie stocked with the tiniest breeds of cattle from the British Isles. Elizabeth called this little zoo 'her fairy farm' and she appointed a family of peasants to be the keepers of her birds and beasts. The cost of the fairy farm nearly bankrupted Harington.

As Princess Elizabeth entered her teens, several royal suitors came forward to ask for her hand. Eventually her family settled on Frederick, Prince Palatine of the Rhine, who was close to Elizabeth in age and religion. The couple met for the first time at Whitehall Palace in October 1612 and were instantly delighted with each other. They were both sixteen, good looking and earnestly Protestant, although they worshipped at different churches: he was a Calvinist, while she had been raised in the established Church of England.

The wedding at Whitehall on St Valentine's Day 1613 was an extravagant affair. Elizabeth's bridesmaids were adorned with so many jewels that their passage through the chapel was said to resemble the milky way. Despite the solemnity, Elizabeth was unable to stifle her giggling during the nuptial vows, which charmed the guests. The poet John Donne likened the young married couple, to 'two phoenixes, whose joined breasts, are unto one another mutual nests'.[1]

THE HAPPY COUPLE settled in at Frederick's palace in Heidelberg. They were by now deeply in love. Frederick constructed an elaborate Italian garden on the estate for her and a house for her pet monkeys. When he was obliged to leave on business, they corresponded constantly, expressing their yearning to be reunited as soon as possible. Elizabeth would give birth to thirteen children and was almost constantly pregnant throughout the course of their marriage. Their years in Heidelberg were to be the happiest of their lives.

Frederick's sweet, sad eyes and affectionate nature endeared him to people, but he failed to inspire fear or command respect. The most one could expect of him, his teacher had remarked, was that he would duly follow honest advice.[2] When the Bohemian estates terminated Habsburg rule and offered him their crown, Frederick was torn. His mother and his council of advisors emphatically urged him to refuse, as did the other German prince-electors, fearing acceptance would ignite a religious war. His father-in-law, King James, was opposed to the idea as well.

That might have been the end of the matter, but Frederick's ambitious chancellor, Christian of Anhalt, advised his prince to seize the day and accept his destiny as the saviour of Protestant Europe. Anhalt told Frederick he had in his hands 'the means of overturning the world'.[3] By that he meant the Holy Roman Empire: the Bohemian crown would give Frederick a double vote in the electoral college, handing the Protestants a 4–3 majority and, with it, the power to elect a non-Habsburg Protestant emperor. Publicly, Elizabeth proclaimed her neutrality, but privately she urged Frederick to make a queen of her. 'I would rather eat sauerkraut with a king,' she said, 'than roast meat with an elector.'[4]

Frederick agonised for weeks. Nothing in his young life had prepared him for such a momentous decision. After searching his conscience, he wrote to the Bohemians on 28 September to tell them he would be their king.

FREDERICK'S ACCEPTANCE of the Bohemian crown triggered a war of stupefying scale and intensity, which took three decades to run its course and left central Europe a burnt-out ruin. In terms of human destruction, there would be nothing like it until the First World War. Between 1618 and 1648, eight million people would die from violence, hunger and disease, mostly in the German lands. The populations of some regions of the Holy Roman Empire declined by seventy-five per cent.[5]

This cataclysm, known as the Thirty Years' War, was really a series of interconnected conflicts. It began as a civil war within the Holy Roman Empire, then pulled in Spain, the Netherlands, Denmark, Sweden and France. It was so complex and multifarious, with so many moving parts and conflicting allegiances, that it defies any attempt to make sense of it. British historian Veronica Wedgwood nonetheless summed up the horrifying pointlessness of it all: 'Morally subversive, economically destructive, socially degrading, confused in its causes, devious in its course, futile in its results, it is the outstanding example in European history of meaningless conflict.'[6]

The mystery of the Thirty Years' War is that the conflict was so harrowing and lasted so long, and yet, at the outset, so few entered the fight with any real enthusiasm. But such was the foul feeling between people that no one could summon the energy to stop it. The kings and princes who entered the war cited different justifications at different times, depending on who they were talking to. It was one of the many paradoxes of the war that it should have been triggered by such a mild, well-meaning prince.

*

AS FREDERICK AND ELIZABETH settled into their new lives at Prague Castle, the outlook for the Bohemian rebellion appeared to brighten. The noble estates of Austria, Moravia and Hungary declared their support; Denmark and Sweden and the Dutch republic expressed their willingness to recognise Frederick as the legitimate king. Militarily, the rebels were on the offensive: Frederick's Hungarian allies took the city of Pressburg,* and then joined forces with Jindrich Thurn's Bohemians to lay siege to Vienna.

For a dizzying moment, it seemed that the Bohemian rebels might prevail, until Ferdinand, now Holy Roman Emperor, turned it all around. The emperor reached out to Maximilian, the powerful Catholic Prince of Bavaria. In return for his support, Ferdinand proposed that Maximilian could keep any part of Frederick's Palatinate that he could take, and Frederick's electoral title along with it. Then, on 22 November, the siege of Vienna had to be called off when the Hungarians rode off to defend their homeland against an invading army of Cossacks.

By the end of the year, Frederick was looking like the leader of a lost cause. His natural allies began to edge away from him. In December, he called a meeting of the Protestant military alliance, the Evangelical Union, but hardly anyone bothered to show up. And despite Elizabeth's pleading, her father, King James of England, flatly refused to get involved. 'There are some princes in Germany,' he told Frederick's ambassador, 'who wish for war in order that they may aggrandise themselves. Your master is young and I am old. Let him follow my example.'[7]

---

* Modern-day Bratislava.

At the same time, Frederick and Elizabeth's popularity in Prague was plummeting. The Bohemians had hoped the couple would bring in great and powerful friends to aid their cause, but so far, they had delivered nothing. Elizabeth's flamboyant clothes and behaviour alienated her from her subjects, and the royal couple scandalised onlookers when Frederick bathed naked in the Vltava for the amusement of Elizabeth and her ladies-in-waiting.

Frederick had stumped up his own gold to pay for soldiers, but when he asked the Prague burghers to do the same, they refused, forcing the unpaid Bohemian army to pillage the countryside to feed itself. Frederick's enemies mocked him, nicknaming him the Winter King and Elizabeth the Winter Queen, because they were not expected to hold onto their crowns beyond a single season.

FREDERICK'S SHORT REIGN in Prague entered its terminal phase when Ferdinand turned his fellow Protestant electors against him. John George, the prince-elector of Saxony, a cynical, hard-drinking Lutheran, saw Frederick as a gormless fool who had disturbed the peace. On 20 March, John George allied himself with Ferdinand and the Catholic League. An ultimatum was delivered to Frederick, ordering him to leave Bohemia by the first day of June. Frederick's final lifeline snapped when the Evangelical Union, of which he was nominally the head, declared their neutrality in the conflict. Abandoned by the princes and kings they thought they could rely upon, and unloved by their subjects, Frederick and Elizabeth awaited the final hammer blow.

White Mountain

ON 26 SEPTEMBER 1620, the combined armies of Ferdinand's Catholic League and Maximilian's Bavarians crossed the Austrian

border into Bohemia, led by Ferdinand's general Count Johann Tilly.*
They overran western Bohemia without much difficulty, passing
through a bleak landscape of empty villages and burnt-out farmhouses.
Tilly's troops were hungry and exhausted, but Maximilian insisted
they press on through the wet and cold towards Prague.

Meanwhile, King Frederick's Protestant mercenaries, unpaid and
on the verge of mutiny, prepared to defend the capital. Frederick's
chancellor-turned-general, Christian of Anhalt, ordered his men to
set up camp on a headland just outside Prague known as Bila Hora
– White Mountain.

'THE BATTLE OF WHITE Mountain' conjures an image of an
epic alpine fight to the death, but a visit to the battle site, a thirty-
minute tram ride from Prague Castle, brings it down to size. White
Mountain is no snowy peak, but a flat open field atop a long low
hill, surrounded by suburban houses. It takes its name from its
chalky soil.

On the night of 7 November 1620, Anhalt's unhappy Bohemian
army barely bothered to throw up rudimentary breastworks along
the ridge line. Anhalt was aware the enemy was nearby, but assumed
they were as exhausted as his men, and he told Frederick he did not
expect an attack the following day. Frederick left the camp to return
to his pregnant wife and family in Prague.

The Bohemians awoke on 8 November to a damp and misty
morning. In the early dawn, Christian of Anhalt saw the Catholic
armies advancing through the fog towards the slope of the hill.
He ordered his forces to spread out along the ridge line, with
infantry and artillery in the centre and cavalry at the flanks. The
20,000-strong Catholic forces outnumbered the 15,000 defenders,

---

* Among Tilly's troops was the mathematician and philosopher René Descartes.

but the Protestants held the high ground and could fire down on their enemies at the base of the hill.

Nothing much happened for the rest of the morning as Maximilian of Bavaria argued with his generals. Meanwhile, the imperial soldiers attended an open-air mass. A wild-eyed Carmelite priest, Padre Domenico, brandished a painting of the Nativity that he claimed had been desecrated by the Bohemian heretics. Stirred by this outrage, they looked up at the enemy on the ridge line. Beyond them lay Prague and all its riches.

AT MIDDAY, TWELVE CANNONS boomed out from the imperial lines, signalling the Catholic infantry to advance up the hill. But instead of digging in and picking off the attackers from the high ground, Anhalt sent his cavalry charging down the slope. The Bohemian infantry was ordered into the fray, but seeing the bloody fighting, they stopped, fired a single volley of shots from a distance, then broke and ran from the field.

Anhalt ordered a counterattack from a cavalry unit, which cut into the advancing Catholic line and pushed it back down the hill. Tilly held his nerve and sent in his own cavalry veterans, led by Padre Domenico on horseback, who appeared through the smoke, holding aloft a crucifix and the vandalised Nativity scene. Tilly's horsemen attacked the weak Bohemian centre. The line broke and the defenders retreated in a wild panic. A single Dutch Protestant unit in the centre stood its ground until every one of them was cut down. By two o'clock, the Bohemian army was totally vanquished.

AFTER A PLEASANT LUNCH at Prague Castle, the Winter King was shocked to see his soldiers staggering through the city gates, covered in blood and mud. Christian of Anhalt arrived at the castle and breathlessly told the royal family their army had been destroyed and they must flee the city at once. Frederick and Elizabeth packed up the children and the crown jewels in a fluster, but in the confusion, they piled into their carriage without their young baby, which had to be retrieved and handed to them through the window. The short, inglorious reign of the Winter King and Queen was over. Neither would ever see Prague again.

THE REBEL LEADERS IN Prague tearfully surrendered to Maximilian of Bavaria, whose army entered the city unopposed. The imperial soldiers broke into the castle and helped themselves to the scattered silks, jewellery and firearms. Rudolf's Letter of Majesty guaranteeing Protestant liberties was discovered and sent to Vienna, where Ferdinand scornfully cut it to shreds. The emperor appointed new administrators in Prague, who drew up a list of enemies to be tried and condemned. When the death sentences were sent to Ferdinand for his approval, he blanched and fled the room, but the following morning, after a night of anguished prayer, he signed the documents.[8]

Temno

TO THE NORTHWEST OF PRAGUE, nestled in the fold of the St Joachim Valley, lies the little spa town of Jachymov. In 1516, a Protestant noble, Count Stefan Schlick, was given a licence to mine silver there and to mint coins. The silver coin became known as the Joachimsthaler, which was simplified to *thaler*, and the name caught on. The Dutch minted their own silver pieces called *daalders* and brought them to North America, where they eventually gave their name to the world's benchmark currency, the United States dollar.

The silver from the St Joachim Valley made the Schlick family exceptionally wealthy and politically influential. Stefan's descendant Count Andreas Schlick had been among the Protestant nobles present when the Catholic regents were thrown from the castle window. After the defeat at White Mountain, his name was placed at the head of the list of men to be executed.

ON 21 JUNE 1621, the condemned rebels were brought under guard into the Old Town Square and led up to the scaffold. The square was packed with observers and guarded by hundreds of soldiers, swords at the ready in case of a riot.

The platform, erected next to the Astronomical Clock, was draped in black, with a three-metre-high crucifix positioned in front of the executioner's wooden block to ensure it would be the last thing the condemned would see before lowering their heads. Drummers pounded out a tattoo to drown out any cries for mercy or shouts of defiance, while the executioner, wearing a red hood, stood by with four sharpened swords.

Schlick, the first of the condemned, stepped up onto the platform, knelt at the block and put down his head. Then the edge of the blade was upon his neck and it was all over for him.

The second man to come forward was Dr Jan Jesenius. In the years since he had performed that public autopsy in Recek College, Jesenius had published several books on anatomy and medicine, and in 1616 he had been elected rector of Prague University. As a distinguished Protestant scholar, he had undertaken several diplomatic missions on behalf of the Bohemian estates and had delivered a speech welcoming the Winter King and Queen to Prague. For that offence, his tongue was cut out before he was decapitated. Jesenius's body was quartered and his severed head impaled on a spike on the eastern tower of the Charles Bridge, along with the heads of other offenders. The doctor had been dismembered for talking too much only a few blocks from where he once conducted a dissection in the spirit of free inquiry.

Twelve nobles, knights and burghers were beheaded that morning. Another fifteen rebels were hanged. The executed men are commemorated today by twenty-seven white crosses embedded in the paving stones in front of the Old Town Hall, next to the Astronomical Clock.

THE MASS EXECUTIONS IN the Old Town Square amounted to a decapitation of Czech society, ushering in an era that Czech nationalists call *temno* – the 'darkness' – as Ferdinand scourged Bohemia of its heresy and remade Prague as a showcase city of the Counter-Reformation. Protestant clergy were banished, and their chapels destroyed. Czech culture would also have to take a back seat. From now on, the German language would occupy the commanding heights of government and bureaucracy, while Czech became the language of peasants and urban poor. Prague University was placed under Jesuit control and later merged with the Clementium to form the Charles-Ferdinand University. Prague's population dropped like a stone, from 60,000 to 40,000 and then 20,000.

Ferdinand gave the remaining Protestant nobles a simple choice: accept the Catholic confession or go into exile. Flocks of Czech Brethren slipped over the border into Germany rather than accept Catholicism in bad faith.

John Amos Comenius, the author of *The Labyrinth of the World and the Paradise of the Heart*, travelled to the Netherlands, where he became famous for his rational and compassionate teaching theories. Comenius was invited to become president of the newly founded Harvard University in the colony of Massachusetts, but settled in Sweden instead. His exile felt like a chronic ache, just as it would for later generations of writers and intellectuals forced to leave Prague to escape a foreign despotism. Those who fled after the 1968 Soviet invasion saw the obvious parallels between themselves and the exiles of 1620. Locked out of their own country, living in faraway nations, they cultivated an inner garden of language, landscape and memory that author Josef Skvorecky called a 'Bohemia of the Soul'.[9]

Generalissimo

FERDINAND'S NEW administrators in Prague established a special commission to confiscate the Protestants' landholdings and to parcel them out to their friends and accomplices at cut-rate prices. In the two years following White Mountain, more than half of Bohemia's total land area changed hands. It was the largest transfer of private property in Europe until the communist era.[10]

The sudden glut of empty expropriated houses caused property prices in Prague to crash. At the same time, the local mint began issuing low-grade thalers debased with copper, so the property market was suddenly flooded with buyers willing to pay for land, but with the rubbishy new coins, which Ferdinand was obliged to accept at face value. The chief beneficiary of this windfall was not the emperor, but his military commandant in Prague, Albrecht z Valdstejna, better known by his German name of Wallenstein.

Portrait of Albrecht von Wallenstein,
painted by Anthony van Dyck, 1629.

WALLENSTEIN WAS BORN INTO a Czech Protestant family, but as a young man he abandoned the Lutheran church to become a Catholic and Habsburg loyalist. He served in the court of Emperor Matthias, and when war broke out he brought a regiment of Moravian cavalry over to the emperor's side. The victory of the Catholic armies at White Mountain carried Wallenstein right into the centre of Bohemia's new ruling class, and the land confiscations allowed him to pick up nearly sixty estates at half price or less.

With this newfound wealth, Wallenstein was able to fund his own loyalist army and to build a stupendous new residence in Prague. In 1623, he bought a long swathe of land just below the castle. Twenty-six houses, six gardens and two brickworks were razed to make way for the Wallenstein Palace, one of the city's great baroque treasures. Here the general and his guests could look out from its triple-arched loggia onto an Italianate garden filled with statues, bubbling fountains and manicured lawns with scratching peacocks. In the evenings, Prague's new elite could gather for concerts in the main hall under a gigantic ceiling fresco of the general depicted as Mars, the god of war. Even the stables were lavish: each one of Wallenstein's thirty-seven horses had its own painted portrait hanging in its box.*

Wallenstein spent little time in this oasis of peace, as he was constantly away at war, winning crushing victories against the Protestant armies. A grateful Ferdinand made him the duke of Friedland and appointed him supreme generalissimo of his armed forces. In less than a decade, Wallenstein had risen from obscurity to command the largest army seen in Europe since the fall of the Roman Empire.[11]

Wallenstein's contemporaries were in awe of his skill as a commander; his superstitious soldiers noticed that those around him always seemed to walk away from battle unwounded, and concluded that he carried some kind of mysterious protective aura around with him.

Fighting had now broken out on several fronts. In 1624, the Protestant Netherlands entered the conflict, closely followed by Catholic Spain. A year later, Protestant Denmark came to the rescue of their fellow Lutherans in northern Germany, supported by English and Scottish troops. When Wallenstein knocked the Danes out of the war in 1629, the emperor elevated him once again, making him duke of Mecklenburg and general of the Oceanic and Baltic seas.

Wallenstein, standing at the head of a 100,000-strong army, was now a continental power in his own right, inspiring fear and dread in the empire's German prince-electors. For years the princes had suffered the upstart general marching through their lands, and now

---

* Today the Wallenstein Palace is the home of the Czech Senate.

that he had served his purpose and brought them close to victory, they pressed the emperor to dismiss him.

In September 1630, Ferdinand bowed to their demands and sacked his most successful general, but his timing was disastrous. Thinking the end of the war was at hand, the overconfident emperor had issued a harsh new measure, an Edict of Restitution, which decreed that all lands taken over by Protestants since the Reformation be confiscated and restored to Catholic ownership. The edict alienated his few Protestant allies and goaded Sweden into joining the war, led by its warrior-king Gustavus Adolphus, thereby prolonging the continental conflict for another nineteen years. A furious Prince John George of Saxony defected from the imperial coalition, and in November 1631, his Saxon army invaded Bohemia and seized Prague. Ferdinand's administrators barely escaped the city in time. The Saxons expelled the Jesuits once again and took down the skulls of Jesenius and the other rebels from the bridge tower where they had sat for the past decade.

IN DESPERATION, FERDINAND turned to the man he'd raised up and then cast aside, but Wallenstein extorted an extraordinary price for his return: he demanded Ferdinand grant him power to negotiate with the enemy as he saw fit. The emperor, pushed into a corner, had no choice but to hand over a prerogative that put his Czech general at the same diplomatic level as him.

In a matter of months Wallenstein raised a new 100,000-man army, and pushed the Saxon army out of Prague. He fought the Swedes to a standstill at the bloody Battle of Lutzen in 1632, but then retreated with his army into Bohemia and sat out the winter in his opulent palace in Prague. Wallenstein had become sick of Ferdinand and weary of endless war, and he refused to pursue the enemy or lend assistance to his Bavarian allies. Instead, he entered into negotiations with Jindrich Thurn, the Bohemian exile who had instigated the second defenestration, who was now serving as a Swedish general. Thurn told him the Swedes had given up all hope of doing business with the fanatical Ferdinand, but, he suggested slyly, if a pragmatist like Wallenstein were to take the crown of Bohemia for himself, then the prospects for peace would be much better.

In Vienna, the emperor and his court were deeply troubled by Wallenstein's refusal to move. Suspecting treachery, the emperor resolved to get rid of his dangerous general once and for all. In February 1634 Wallenstein was charged with high treason; five days later, his officers kicked in his bedroom door and gutted him with their halberds.

The Fury of the Goths and the Vandals

AS THE WAR RAGED on, more states were drawn into the fighting. The mercenary armies fanned out across central Europe like locusts. First, they devoured the farmers' food and fodder, then the seed corn and breeding animals, leaving towns, villages and farms to starve. Rumours of cannibalism circulated through the countryside. Plague broke out, leaving some towns and villages completely depopulated. A German chronicler observed:

> How miserable is now the state of the large cities! Where in former times there were a thousand lanes, today there are no more than a hundred. How wretched is the state of the small and open market towns! There they lie, burnt, decayed, destroyed, so that you see neither roofs nor rafters, doors or windows ... You travel ten, twenty or forty miles without seeing a single human being.[12]

IN 1635, AFTER SEVENTEEN years of war, starvation and plague, Ferdinand reached the painful conclusion that he could not re-impose Catholicism by force of arms and he reluctantly signed a peace treaty with the Saxons at Prague Castle. The other Protestant German states signed up later, bringing the civil war within the empire to a close, but the Habsburgs' wider war dragged on. The French entered the conflict in the same year, not on the side of their Catholic co-religionists, but in coalition with the Habsburgs' Protestant enemies. The religious dimension of the conflict lost any meaning it may have had as the war became a naked struggle between the French and the Habsburgs for European supremacy. Ferdinand II did not live long enough to see the end of the conflict. He died in 1637, leaving his burnt husk of an empire in the hands of his son, Ferdinand III.

In the final phase of the war, the Swedish army twice invaded Bohemia, but the arrival of a Protestant force failed to spark much enthusiasm. 'I had not thought to find the kingdom of Bohemia so lean, wasted and spoiled,' wrote a Swedish commander, 'for between Prague and Vienna all is razed to the ground and hardly a living soul is to be seen in the land.'[13]

IN 1648, REPRESENTATIVES of the warring nations, having fought each other to a standstill, gathered at last in Westphalia, Germany, to bring the Thirty Years' War to a close. As peace negotiations got underway, a Swedish army raced towards Prague, hoping to plunder what remained of its wealth before an armistice could be declared. The war's final act would be played out in the same city where it had begun three decades earlier.

The Swedish invaders took Mala Strana and Hradcany almost without a fight, and went from house to house, seizing whatever they could find and murdering the inhabitants. Had they arrived thirty years earlier, the Protestant Swedes might have been greeted as liberators. Instead, citizens, burghers and students barricaded the eastern end of the bridge to keep the mercenaries out of the Old Town. The Swedes launched an artillery bombardment from the castle, while the Praguers hung on for three months, waiting for news of the peace settlement that would oblige the invaders to pack up and go home.

Unable to cross the river, the frustrated Swedes had to settle for ransacking the castle palaces. Rudolf II's incomparable collection of paintings, statues and objets d'art were crated up and sent down the river in barges to be shipped off to Stockholm, where many of them remain to this day.

THE FINAL SIGNATURES on the Peace of Westphalia were penned on 24 October 1648. In terms of religious boundaries, the signatories agreed on a return to the year 1624, not 1620 as the Czech Protestants would have dearly wished. Prague was to remain fixed as a Catholic city under tight Habsburg control. Those who had fled after White Mountain would remain in exile.

Nine days later, news of the peace reached Prague, and the Swedes, laden with booty, made their way home.

TODAY ON THE CHARLES BRIDGE, a commemorative plate, written in Latin, asks passers-by to take a moment to remember the defiant Praguers of 1648:

Rest here, walker, and be happy.
You can stop here willing.
But here unwilling was stopped
The fury of the Goths and the Vandals.[14]

Irregular Pearls

A STILLNESS FELL UPON Prague with the signing of the peace of 1648. Some houses had been smashed by Swedish cannon fire, but the city's battered face had otherwise not changed very much in thirty years. The drastic population losses had left streets quietened and houses emptied.

The new emperor, Ferdinand III, decided to express his gratitude to Prague's citizens for their heroic stand against the Swedes by erecting a fourteen-metre column topped with a statue of the Virgin Mary (the Marian Column) in the middle of the Old Town Square. While those who venerated the Mother of Christ were touched by the gesture, others saw the towering column as an act of propaganda, a massive Habsburg victory flag planted into the heart of the city.

In Mala Strana, the new Catholic administrators moved into the vacant mansions and set about remodelling them in the new style from Italy known as baroque. The word came from the Portuguese *barroco*, a jeweller's term used to describe an irregular, teardrop pearl.[15]

The new style was melodramatic and fussy, full of implied motion and tension. The baroque, which appears so dramatic in the bright light and hard-raking shadows of Rome and Madrid, takes on a different tone in Prague. The pearlescent northern European light softens the hard edges; the gradients between light and shade are smoother. The style would become so prevalent in Prague, that today all the other architectural forms seem to point to it or lead away from it.

Prague's new baroque buildings, monuments and churches were a world away from the elegant Renaissance structures of the previous era – the golden Schwarzenberg Palace on Hradcany Square, the dreamy Belvedere in the Royal Gardens, or the charming House at the Minute on the Old Town Square, covered in classical *sgraffito*.

Under the Habsburgs, the new baroque style became an instrument of propaganda and power. The liquid writhing curlicues, the gilded edges, the arrayed statues gasping in agony and ecstasy were designed to impress and intimidate as much as to inspire delight. There was no escaping it: from 1683, some thirty stone and bronze saints sprouted up along the balustrades of the Charles Bridge like weird stone plants. Today, the bridge's avenue of saints is one of the glories of Prague, but in their time, those imposing stone sentinels must have struck an intimidating, even oppressive note for Praguers as they hurried across the Vltava.

Black Soup

THE ITALIAN ARCHITECTS and stonemasons who brought the baroque to Prague were followed by Italian merchants, who introduced the city to the pleasures of tailored clothing, fine food and clothes, red wine, olives and coffee.

Coffee, or 'black soup', as it was sometimes called, was sold to the rich as a luxury item until a drop in prices made it an everyday pleasure. As public demand increased, an exotic figure in a hooded Arabic cloak could be seen wandering the streets of Mala Strana, selling coffee heated on a portable brazier. He kept the sugar in his pockets.

Giorgio Diodato was born in Damascus into an Assyrian Christian family. He'd come to Prague via Cairo and Rome, where he'd discovered a passion for coffee and for Western Roman Catholicism, which he embraced with all the zeal of a convert. In 1714, after several years selling coffee in the street, he established Prague's first coffeehouse in the House of the Golden Snake near the Charles Bridge.*

Diodato's coffeehouse sold a range of exotic goods besides coffee: oranges, lemons, cinnamon, cloves, bergamot, chocolate and angelica water – a sweet-scented liquor believed to be an antidote to the plague. Many of his customers were Jewish, so he littered the café with books and Catholic pamphlets he'd written to helpfully direct them towards the true Christian faith. Diodato wanted his customers to be in no doubt as to his loyalties; in 1716, to celebrate the birth of a son and heir to the emperor, he redecorated the coffeehouse into a Habsburg fantasia. He hung portraits of the royal family in the windows, along with a smaller portrait of himself prostrate at their feet. Lest anyone question his religious allegiances, Diodato put up a picture of the Turkish sultan cringing helplessly beneath the Habsburg eagle, crying out, 'Oh Muhammad! Help me!'[16]

ONE DAY IN 1713, a foreign visitor came into Diodato's café, looking for help. Jacob Simon Toff was a Jewish businessman from Constantinople; he said he had come all the way to Prague to be reimbursed for his efforts on behalf of the beleaguered Jews of Jerusalem. In the Holy Land, he explained, the impoverished Jewish community was being squeezed by the Ottoman governor to pay

---

* The snake emblem can still be seen on the corner of the building.

a *jizya*, a special tax, that applied only to non-Muslims, but the Jews there had no money. Several rabbis had been arrested and the authorities were threatening to burn down their synagogues unless they paid up. The desperate rabbis had sent emissaries to the Jewish diaspora and Toff had come to the rescue. He had paid the steep ransom, 300 gold ducats, in exchange for a promissory note, signed by sixteen Jerusalem rabbis, that guaranteed him full repayment of his gold from the most exalted rabbi in the world, the Prince of Israel, who happened to be living in Prague.

DAVID OPPENHEIM WAS Prague's chief rabbi, the leader of the largest Jewish community in Europe. On taking up the post in 1702, he was elected *nasi' b'erets yisra'el* – Prince of the Land of Israel – an honorific that made him responsible for collecting funds to support the oppressed communities in the Holy Land. Oppenheim was a wealthy man and a great scholar. By the time he came to Prague, he had amassed the largest collection of Jewish books and manuscripts in the world, but the strict censorship regime in Bohemia made it impossible to bring the library with him to Prague, so he had left it in Hanover, in the care of his son Joseph.

When Jacob Simon Toff came to see him in Prague, Oppenheim readily repaid the 300 gold ducats, but the rabbis' note also stipulated that Toff would be entitled to a further payment of 1200 florins for his expenses. Oppenheim gave him lodgings and a weekly stipend, but he short-changed Toff on his expenses, offering him only 844 florins for his trouble.

Toff, incensed by Oppenheim's meanness, found his way to Giorgio Diodato's coffeehouse to ask for advice from a fellow easterner. The coffee-master at once agreed to act as intermediary and interpreter when Toff decided to pursue the full amount owed to him through the courts in Prague.

AN OUTBREAK OF THE plague delayed proceedings for four years. In the meantime, Toff declared he wanted to be baptised as a Christian. Diodato was overjoyed and only too happy to be of assistance. Toff's conversion brought with it a shift in legal strategy: he and Diodato now argued that Oppenheim's payment of the sultan's *jizya* had tipped a large sum of money from the Habsburg lands into the Ottoman treasury, a charge that amounted to treason. Toff produced his own promissory note in evidence to the magistrate's court. The case bumped along for three more years until the court found in favour of Oppenheim and the rabbi was cleared of all charges.

Toff and Diodato launched a series of appeals, which eventually came to the attention of the imperial court in Vienna. A special investigation into the affair led to a decree: all collections on behalf of the Jews of Israel were now expressly forbidden. Furthermore, no one in the empire was permitted to hold the blasphemous title of Prince of Israel. The court gave thanks to Diodato for his role in exposing the 'Jewish intrigues', but his request for compensation was dismissed.[17]

THE OPPENHEIM TRIAL ruined Giorgio Diodato. He was required to pay court costs and damages that cost him his home and his coffeehouse. His wife, Maria, cast him out of the marital bed: 'I no longer desire you,' she said. 'You have totally ruined us for the sake of imperial interests, so go to the Emperor and let *him* help you.'

Diodato tried to escape his debtors by absconding to Germany and Austria, but he still owed money to Toff, and the two now became bitter enemies.

After Toff's death, Diodato returned to Prague and threw himself on the mercy of the Old Town council, who agreed to award him some money to help him set up another café. The councillors expressed their hope that the money might restore the happiness of the Diodato marriage, but it was not to be. Maria berated her husband in the coffeehouse as a fool. She refused to let him eat at the family table, forcing him to take his meals at the local orphanage. Diodato died in poverty and was buried at the Church of St Thomas in Mala Strana. David Oppenheim died a revered member of his community. On his tombstone in the Jewish cemetery, he is remembered, not as the Prince of Israel, which was now forbidden, but simply as a 'man among men'. His vast repository of books and manuscripts was purchased by Oxford's Bodleian Library, where it remains to this day.

Giorgio Diodato of Damascus, pamphlet, 1714.

The Impossible Empress

PRAGUE, ONCE THE CAPITAL of the empire, had become a Habsburg outpost, governed from a special chancellery in Vienna that issued decrees to its obedient governor in the castle. The Bohemian Diet, the assembly of the estates, was a relic of a bygone age that met only to ratify decisions already taken by the imperial court, which in turn served at the pleasure of the emperor in Vienna, the morose and ponderous Charles VI.

In an age of absolutism, so much rested on the character of the monarch, but Charles, grandson of Ferdinand III, was among the feeblest of the Habsburg emperors. Charles had no sons and he exhausted what little energy he had trying to persuade the other monarchs of Europe to accept his eldest daughter, Maria Theresa, as his legitimate successor. Charles's untimely death in 1740, after consuming a meal of death cap mushrooms cooked in oil, put Maria Theresa in the hot seat.

MARIA THERESA WAS twenty-three years old when the sun, moon and stars landed on her head. Her father had bequeathed her an empire lumbered with debt and an antiquated military. Despite Charles's efforts to secure her as his successor, he had not bothered in any way to prepare her for such a role. Her education was perfunctory and she had never been invited to attend the councils of state. Maria Theresa was understandably terrified but had no choice but to press on. She later wrote, 'I found myself without money, without credit, without army, without experience and knowledge of my own and finally, also without any counsel, because each one of them at first wanted to wait and see how things would develop.'[18]

Maria Theresa was obliged to follow the advice of the mediocre ministers she inherited. But although unschooled in statecraft, she was pragmatic, a good judge of character and she learnt on the job quickly. Diarists recorded her emotional nature, but it seems Maria Theresa deployed these outbursts quite deliberately to confound her opponents. As her self-assurance grew, she proved herself capable of swiftly adjusting to radically changed circumstances, and became, arguably, the greatest ruler the Habsburg clan ever produced. When she received the crown of Bohemia, she became the one and only woman, other than the legendary Libussa, ever to rule Bohemia.

Maria Theresa was a strikingly charismatic figure in an otherwise dreary court. The Prussian Ambassador was dazzled by her. 'Her gait is free,' he wrote in a letter to Berlin, 'her bearing majestic, her figure large, her face round and full, and her voice clear and pleasant … there is no denying that Maria Theresa is a most charming and delightful woman.'[19]

She was exceptionally fond of her flighty and adulterous husband, Francis Stephen, the Duke of Lorraine. Until the burden of office had fallen on her, the two had enjoyed staying up late, dancing and gambling at cards, sleeping in, then lounging around in the afternoon in loose dressing gowns. They had sixteen children together, including the unfortunate Marie Antoinette of France. When a friend of Francis's suggested he sleep in a separate bedroom from her, Maria Theresa launched into a tirade and mocked the miscreant at court for the rest of his unhappy life.

Within months of her father's death, the kings and princes of Europe began to circle Maria Theresa's empire like wolves, intending to pull off parts of it for themselves. The most dangerous of these predators was King Frederick II of Prussia, later known as Frederick the Great.

FREDERICK OF PRUSSIA had been drilled in the military arts throughout a hideously cruel boyhood. When his father realised his son was homosexual, he tried to 'cure' Frederick by forcing him to watch the beheading of his young lover Hermann von Katte. Frederick was obliged to marry, but he had no children and his social circle was almost exclusively male. After a rare military defeat, he wrote to a friend, 'Fortune has it in for me; she is a woman, and I am not that way inclined.'[20]

Frederick spoke French rather than German, which he thought was a vulgar language. He composed symphonies and sonatas for the flute, an instrument he played exceptionally well for guests at his pleasure palace outside Berlin, named *Sans Souci* – Without a Care.

Although he aspired to be a philosopher-king, Frederick was addicted to war and the martial values that surround it: courage, audacity and male comradeship, while not particularly minding the horrors it inflicted on lesser beings. Battlefield glory was everything: 'Dogs!' he once shouted at his guards when they hesitated. 'Do you wish to live forever?'[21]

In December 1740, citing a flimsy legal pretext, Frederick seized the mineral-rich province of Silesia from Maria Theresa. In April the following year, his Prussian army defeated her Austrians at the Battle of Mollwitz. Frederick's aggression affronted Maria Theresa and stiffened her resolve to fight back. She came to think of him as demonic, and often referred to him as 'that evil man', Frederick, equally appalled, simply described her as 'impossible'.[22]

FREDERICK'S EASY VICTORY fed a suspicion that the Habsburg dominions, led by a woman, were incapable of defending themselves. In September 1741, the French army, allied with Duke Charles Albert of Bavaria, invaded Austria, sparking the War of the Austrian

Succession. Desperate for troops, Maria Theresa made a dramatic appearance before the Hungarian Diet in a gold-embroidered ethnic Hungarian dress. Shrewdly playing the part of a damsel in distress, she lifted up her infant son, Joseph, to the assembly and tearfully reminded them of the vows of loyalty they had made at her coronation. Her appeal moved the nobles to cheer and vow, 'We consecrate our lives and our blood to you.'[23]

The French and Bavarian armies surged towards Vienna, then changed course and swung into Bohemia. As the invaders approached Prague, Maria Theresa sent a 36,000-strong army, led by her husband, to come to the city's aid. But Francis Stephen had no experience of military command and his army moved slowly, pausing frequently to allow him to go hunting with his officers.

The invaders arrived at the walls of Prague and prepared for a siege, but the garrison protecting the city was well provisioned and confident they could hold out until Francis Stephen's meandering army showed up. With time running out, the French commander, Maurice de Saxe, crept out one night to personally look for weak points in Prague's fortifications. Just after midnight, he ordered the Saxon cavalry to launch a diversionary attack on the Strahov Gate. At the same time, he led a party of grenadiers further along the moat to the poorly defended Bruska Gate, where they found a high bastion next to a ledge of rubble. The grenadiers scaled their ladders in a tense silence. The sentries, firing down on the Saxon cavalry, failed to see the grenadiers slipping up behind them with their sharp bayonets. The grenadiers dropped the drawbridge at the gate, and the French dragoons galloped into the conquered city.

CHARLES ALBERT OF BAVARIA was presented with the sword of St Wenceslas and proclaimed King of Bohemia on 7 December 1741.

Maria Theresa burst into tears when she heard the news in Vienna. Once again, her outrage fed her resolve. 'My mind is made up,' she told her Bohemian chancellor, Count Kinsky. 'We must put everything at stake to save Bohemia.'[24] First she had to swallow her hatred and make peace with Frederick of Prussia by ceding most of Silesia to him. The deal freed up her troops to wheel around and retake Prague from the invaders on 2 January 1743.

Charles Albert escaped Prague and rode on to Frankfurt, where he was elected Holy Roman Emperor, the first non-Habsburg to wear the crown in three centuries. Maria Theresa promptly cut the ground from under him: her Austrian troops invaded Bavaria and took his capital Munich, forcing Charles Albert to languish in Frankfurt for three years, exiled from his own dominion.

MARIA THERESA WAS BY now very much in command of her empire. Her father's hacks had been replaced with competent advisors. In April 1743, she entered re-conquered Prague to be crowned as the legitimate queen of Bohemia. It should have been a gratifying moment of triumph, but she arrived in Prague in a foul mood, still furious with the Czech nobles for giving 'her' crown to the Bavarian duke. After a chilly ceremony at St Vitus Cathedral, she went straight back to Vienna. In a letter, she dismissed the bejewelled crown of St Wenceslas as a *Narrenhäubl* – a fool's cap.[25]

MARIA THERESA BARELY had time to catch her breath. In the new year, Frederick resumed their duel. The Prussian king was unnerved by her military successes. Knowing how badly she wanted to recover Silesia, Frederick decided to act pre-emptively: he renewed his alliance with France and invaded Bohemia.

On 11 September 1744, Frederick put the people of Prague to siege yet again. These were miserable years for Prague's inhabitants, living through weeks of shattering cannon-fire, food shortages, disease and the dread of marauding soldiers. After a week of bombardment, the garrison surrendered, and Frederick rode with his generals into the battered city.

Frederick stayed a single night in Prague, before moving on. He left behind 5000 troops, who looted the city's mansions. Frederick took the rest of Bohemia with little difficulty, but when his French allies failed to come to his aid, the advancing Austrians forced him to retreat. His garrison was ordered to abandon Prague in a hurry, grabbing the last of the treasury's cash on their way out the door. Frederick later reflected, 'My experience has shown that Bohemia is easily conquered, but difficult to dominate.'[26]

PRAGUE WAS ONCE AGAIN in Habsburg hands, but there were rumours that the Jews of the city had been secretly collaborating with the Prussians all along. The rumours eventually reached the ears of Maria Theresa, and in December 1744 she decreed that every single Jewish person in Prague, all 10,000 of them, were to be gone from the city by the end of January. They were to be banished from Bohemia altogether by the end of June.

Prague's rabbis sent out a distress signal to other communities in Europe. 'What shall we poor souls do?' they wrote. 'The children, women, infirm and aged are not in a condition to walk, especially at this juncture, being cold and frosty weather.'[27] Nonetheless, Prague's Jews, who made up a quarter of the city's population, obediently left their homes and found lodgings as best they could in the outlying villages of Holesovice and Karlin (now suburbs of Prague).

The call for help brought together an extraordinary international coalition in opposition to Maria Theresa's decree. The pope, the

Turkish sultan, the English and Danish ambassadors all petitioned her to rescind the merciless edict. The Bohemian chancellery in Vienna told her they feared the economic consequences of tearing out the empire's financial arteries. For once, the stubborn empress reversed her decision. Jews would be permitted to re-enter Prague, once they had paid a 'toleration tax' of 300,000 gold pieces.[28]

THE HAPLESS CHARLES ALBERT was an emperor in name only. When he died in January 1745, Maria Theresa claimed the title of Holy Roman Emperor for her husband, who became Francis I of the new house of Habsburg-Lorraine. The new emperor posed for his imperial portrait in a suit with so many ruffles he appears to be encased in coral, but real power remained in his wife's hands. Francis was happy to serve as her lieutenant and devoted himself to successfully rebuilding the imperial finances, as the War of the Austrian Succession wound down.

Maria Theresa now had a free hand to pursue far-reaching reforms to her empire based on Enlightenment principles. Secular schools were established throughout Bohemia and attendance at the elementary level was made compulsory for boys and girls. To encourage inoculation against smallpox, she hosted a dinner for sixty-five newly inoculated children at the Schonbrunn palace and served them at the table herself.[29] Determined to extinguish superstition in her realm, she sent her personal physician, Gerard van Swieten of the Netherlands, to investigate the existence of vampires in Serbia and Bosnia; he came back damning the vampire myth as 'a barbarism of ignorance'.[30]

WHEN FRANCIS DIED IN 1765, the imperial crown was passed on to their eldest son, who became Emperor Joseph II. Maria Theresa had taken care to give Joseph the education she never had, but she remained jealous of her prerogatives and continually stepped on his initiatives. His zeal for new thinking frightened her.

In her final years, Maria Theresa, like Queen Victoria, became a devotee of the cult of her dead husband. She converted his private study in Schonbrunn Palace into an absurdly ornate shrine, panelled with portraits of Francis and their sons. On her deathbed, she wore Francis's dressing gown. After her funeral, a slip of paper was discovered in her prayer book on which she had scribbled her calculations of the exact duration of their marriage down to the hour: '29 years, 6 months, 6 days; that makes 29 years, 335 months, 1540 weeks, 10,781 days, 258,744 hours.'[31]

＊

WHEN EMPEROR JOSEPH II looked across the Habsburg lands, he saw irrationality, superstition and medieval malpractice everywhere. He made his first visit to Prague during a terrible famine. As he peeped out from his carriage window, he was distressed by the spectral figures in the streets, and angered by the church's apparent indifference. 'In this city,' he wrote, 'where there is a rich Archbishop, a large cathedral chapter, so many abbeys and three Jesuit palaces ... there is not a single proven case where any of these took in even one of the miserable wretches who were lying in front of their doors.'[32]

From 1780, Joseph issued a flood of social, legal and religious reforms that shook the pillars of the old social order. Religious toleration was extended to Lutherans, Calvinists and Orthodox Christians, who were allowed their own houses of worship, so long as the entrance was hidden from the street. Children under nine were forbidden to work; civil marriage and divorce were permitted; torture and capital punishment were abolished.

The Bohemian crown was now only the third-most important trinket in the Habsburg jewel box, after the imperial crown and Hungary's holy crown of St Stephen. Joseph had not even bothered to come to Prague for his coronation. Still, he intended to beautify Prague and rationalise its administration. He brought down the walls and borders between the four independent towns – Hradcany, Mala Strana, the Old and New towns – and united them into a single city. The old moats between the fortification walls of the Old and New towns were filled in and covered over with a tree-lined boulevard – today's Narodni Trida, or Avenue of the Nation.

JOSEPH TRANSFORMED JEWISH life in Prague by lifting the social burdens and legal constraints imposed on them for centuries. Jewish people were no longer required to wear a yellow star on their clothes. They were permitted to attend the theatre and enter the university, and encouraged to open factories and businesses. Jews were even allowed to leave their homes on Sundays, an activity previously forbidden on the grounds that the sight of Christ's murderers on the street was too provocative on the sabbath.

These humane reforms were driven not so much by compassion, but a desire for greater efficiency and homogeneity within the empire. By making life freer for Jews, Joseph hoped to draw them out of the ghetto and to integrate them into society as loyal servants of the crown. 'Everything exists for the state,' he'd written, troublingly, in 1763, 'so all who live in it should come together to promote its interests.'[33]

In his own way, Joseph was as determined as Ferdinand II to impose a flat uniformity on the untidy mosaic of peoples and cultures he ruled. To that end, he made German the sole official language of government and higher education, which kept the Czech language outside the forums of power. Jews, in turn, were required to adopt German names and forbidden to keep business records in Yiddish or Hebrew.

Joseph's reforms lifted educational standards and opened opportunities across the board, but the improvements only made Czechs and Jews more conscious of their relative disadvantage, more aware of their history, and better able to articulate their unhappiness with the state of things. There was a sad awareness that something had been lost, or taken from them. Bit by bit, Czech scholars began to locate and pick up the fragments of their national identity, broken up and scattered after the Battle of White Mountain.

In the 1780s, Czech began to revive as a literary language among a small group of devotees. Karel Tham published a *Defense of the Czech Language*, along with several Czech dictionaries and translations of Shakespeare. A Czech-language theatre, the Bouda, opened in the Horse Market in 1786. In the same year, the first modern Czech play, *Bretislav and Jitka*, was staged at the handsome new Estates Theatre in the Old Town.

The Rake's Reward

IN 1786, THE ESTATES THEATRE staged a new opera, *The Marriage of Figaro*, by the famous composer and prodigy Wolfgang Amadeus Mozart. *Figaro* had received a cool response at its premiere in Vienna, but in Prague the playful opera was received rapturously.

One critic described it as a masterpiece. When Mozart's admirers in Prague invited him to visit, the young composer was only too pleased to accept.

On 11 January 1787, two coaches rolled into Prague carrying Mozart, his wife, Constanze, an entourage of musicians and the Mozarts' pet dog. Mozart soon realised everything he'd heard about Prague was true: 'I saw with the greatest of pleasure,' he wrote to a friend, 'all these people flying about with such delight to the music of my *Figaro*, for here nothing is talked about but *Figaro*; nothing played but *Figaro*, nothing whistled or sung but *Figaro*.'[34] The Mozarts were feted at parties across the city. They ate fine food, slept in each day and basked in the adulation of the city's music lovers.

On 19 January, Mozart's Symphony No. 38 premiered in Prague and was thereafter known as the Prague Symphony. The composer capped the evening's entertainment by gleefully improvising variations on an aria from *Figaro* at the piano. Afterwards, he said he counted the day as one of the happiest of his life.[35] Mozart's wildly popular reception led to a commission to create another opera to be premiered at the Estates Theatre later in the year.

Back in Vienna, Mozart decided to collaborate once more with his librettist Lorenzo da Ponte on a reworking of the tale of Don Juan, the fabled seducer of women. They toyed with several titles, 'The Guest of Stone' and 'The Rake's Reward', before settling on the Italian version of the great lover's name: *Don Giovanni*.

MOZART RETURNED TO PRAGUE in October and stayed at the luxurious Villa Bertramka, where he worked frantically to complete the score in time for its scheduled premiere. Da Ponte arrived soon after, still scratching away at his libretto. Despite the looming deadline, da Ponte found time in Prague to catch up with an old friend and fellow Venetian, who had once been Europe's most notorious womaniser, Giacomo Casanova.

After an exciting life as an adventurer, musician, cleric, spy, Kabbalist and con artist, the 62-year-old Casanova had run out of puff and had accepted employment as a librarian at the Castle Duchkov in the mountains of northwest Bohemia. Casanova was glad to have an income, but the job was boring and, at times, humiliating. It was quite a comedown for a man who had once socialised with Voltaire and Catherine the Great. By the time he caught up with da Ponte, the ageing *roué* was in poor health and contemplating suicide.

When he heard da Ponte was working on an operatic version of *Don Giovanni*, the great lover's curiosity was piqued, and he reportedly dropped in on a rehearsal. Mozart was in the theatre, still busily scribbling away at the score. The frustrated singers, tired of receiving their parts in dribs and drabs, had locked Mozart in a room, refusing to let him out until he'd completed the opera. It was Casanova, allegedly, who persuaded them to release the composer and then offered to help with the libretto. On opening night, copies of the score of the overture were handed out to the orchestra with the ink still wet on the page.[36]

MOZART STEPPED UP TO the conductor's podium at the Estates Theatre to cheers at 7 pm on 29 October 1787. From the thunderous opening chords to the melodramatic climax, where the wicked Don Giovanni is dragged down to hell, the audience was completely enthralled. Mozart and the cast received a standing ovation, while Casanova watched from a box seat. When asked later if he'd seen *Don Giovanni*, Casanova laughed and said, 'Seen it? I practically lived it.'[37] He began writing his entertaining memoirs soon afterwards.

The evidence that Casanova assisted with the libretto to *Don Giovanni* is circumstantial, not conclusive. But in the 1990s, a draft of a scene from Act II of the opera, written in his distinctive looping handwriting, was discovered among his papers at Castle Duchkov. It was the scene where Don Giovanni swaps clothes with his servant Leporello as a ruse to seduce the maid of Donna Elvira.

Mozart's opera achieved far greater fame than Casanova's *The Story of My Life*, but it was his name, rather than that of the fictional Don Giovanni, that became the byword for a legendary lover.

CHAPTER SIX

SLEEPING ON A VOLCANO

1815–1935

Everyday Art Nouveau in Prague.
Entrance to a language school on Vojtesska Street, in the New Town.

THE NAPOLEONIC WARS of the early nineteenth century overturned the European order. Prague sent soldiers to fight on behalf of the emperor in his disastrous campaigns against the French, but the city was, for once, largely unmolested by the continental conflict swirling around it. Napoleon's frequent incursions into the

German provinces, and his stunning victory at the Battle of Austerlitz in neighbouring Moravia, shattered the Holy Roman Empire's rickety medieval framework, forcing Joseph's nephew and successor, Francis II, to accept a downgrade in status and become Francis I of the newly minted Austrian Empire.

After Napoleon's defeat at Waterloo in 1815, representatives of the major European powers assembled in Vienna to establish a new balance of power for the continent. In the new dispensation, Francis was to preside over a new German Confederation, a conglomeration of thirty-eight states and cities, with the two most powerful member states, Austria and Prussia, also ruling over large swathes of territory outside the confederation. It was somewhat simpler than the system that had preceded it, but not by much. Bohemia was still a Habsburg possession and Prague was to remain a provincial capital.

At the end of the congress, the conservative Austrian foreign minister, Prince Klemens von Metternich, was satisfied he had set the world to rights and had re-established the natural order of things. But the system of absolute monarchy so dear to his heart presupposed the existence of a capable, business-like monarch, and his emperor Francis I was not that man. Francis was a micro-manager and a procrastinator, averse to any change or disruption for fear of the little demons of revolution climbing up through the cracks. When Metternich handed him a proposal to carefully devolve power from Vienna to the empire's various principalities, Francis promised he would look at it, but then put the proposal in a desk drawer where it stayed for eighteen years.[1]

Centuries of intermarriage caught up with the Habsburg dynasty at this time. Francis had heedlessly married his double first cousin, and their eldest son, Ferdinand, was born with hydrocephaly, giving him a swollen cranium, intellectual disabilities and constant epileptic seizures, as many as twenty a day. Francis believed that taking his son out of the line of succession would damage the institution of the monarchy, so he set up a special council of regents that he hoped would govern on Ferdinand's behalf when he was no longer around.

THE DREAD OF REVOLUTION, with its upheavals and royal decapitations, haunted the emperor and his chancellor Metternich, who tried to monitor and suppress the dissemination of radical ideas through the mail and printing press.

Bohemia's reputation as a nation of malcontents and trouble-makers brought it under particularly tight official scrutiny. In Prague, networks of police spies wormed their way into public gatherings, bookshops and other potential nests of subversion.

Charles Sealsfield, a Czech-American writer, described the stultifying climate of suspicion and bad faith created by Metternich's legions of police informers in Prague. 'Every footman in a public-house is a salaried spy,' he wrote. 'There are spies paid to visit the taverns and hotels, who take their dinners at the high table. Others will be seen in the imperial library for the same purpose, or in the bookseller's shop, to inquire into the purchases made by the different persons.' Sealsfield concluded that Bohemia was, 'without doubt, the most oppressed and least favoured of all the provinces and kingdoms of the Austrian empire'.[2] No one could be sure who was secretly working on behalf of the police and the bonds of trust began to fray.

Bohemia was politically inert. Sealsfield witnessed a dismal session of the once fiercely independent Bohemian Diet at Prague Castle. After some perfunctory introductions, the Habsburg commissioners put forward a taxation proposal, which was accepted by the Bohemians 'in silence with a long bow'. The speaker then asked the assembly if they had any matters to propose. Another moment of deep silence passed. Then the speaker thanked everyone for their attendance and the session broke up. Despite this dismal spectacle, Sealsfield thought Bohemia's rebellious spirit was merely sleeping, and that a new Jan Zizka, 'in the present gloom, would scarcely fail to find at least a million of adherents'.[3]

THAT WAS SURELY AN exaggeration, but national awareness was slowly stirring among the Czechs. The publication in 1809 of a comprehensive guide to Czech grammar extended and formalised the language, making it the preferred means of printed communication for a new generation of professional teachers, writers, dramatists, journalists, doctors and lawyers. In 1818, a group of scientists and scholars founded a Bohemian Museum in Prague. A young historian named Frantisek Palacky suggested the institution publish separate journals in German and Czech. The German version soon petered out, but the Czech language *Journal of the Historical Museum* found a large, enthusiastic readership.

Czech nationalism began as a cultural project, but the realisation of a distinctive Czech political entity was always going to be difficult in a nation where the everyday lives of Czechs, Jews and German Bohemians were so intertwined. Nonetheless, Praguers, who once would have described themselves as Bohemians, Catholics, Protestants or subjects of a king, duke or emperor, were increasingly asked to identify themselves as Czechs or Germans.

Old patterns of life, held together for centuries by webs of tradition and familiarity, were pulled apart by new economic forces and the migration of people to the urban centres, where the society was rootless and restless, and the work was often repetitive and meaningless. A person's identity and station in life, once taken for granted, suddenly fell into question. There was nostalgia for the traditional seasonal pace of life, portrayed so lovingly in a popular Czech novella titled *Babicka* – 'The Grandmother'.

BOZENA NEMCOVA, the author of *Babicka*, was nothing like the wise and steady grandmother she portrayed so fondly in her book. She was the very prototype of the nineteenth-century urban 'bohemian' woman: brilliant, impulsive, unconventional and intellectually emancipated. Her depiction of rural life was drawn from happy memories of her childhood in a small Bohemian village, where she grew up as the daughter of a coachman and a laundry woman. At seventeen, she was forced into an arranged marriage to Josef Nemec, a soldier almost twice her age. They had four children together, and settled in Prague in 1841. Nemec, an aggressive and occasionally violent Czech patriot, encouraged Bozena to put aside her German romances and read Czech literature instead.

Nemcova's first published work was a patriotic poem, 'To the Bohemian Women', which brought her to the attention of a circle of writers and intellectuals in Prague, who were enthralled by 'her charming directness and her marvellous mind'. She was strikingly lovely. Vlasta Pittnerova, a younger Czech writer, recalled an encounter with the dazzlingly beautiful Nemcova on a country lane: 'with field flowers in her hands, in her waist and in her hair'. The radical priest Frantisek Klacel fell in love with her and invited her to become part of a utopian community of brothers and sisters. He called her 'the greatest treasure of my miserable life'. When she slept with another of the 'brothers', Father Klacel wept tears of jealous agony and the group broke up acrimoniously. [4]

BY THE 1850s, the family was running out of money. Her husband's politics had brought him under official suspicion, and he was demoted to a minor customs job in Slovakia. In November that year their eldest son died of tuberculosis. Nemcova sent begging letters to friends asking for coins or even 'a few potatoes'.

The family returned to Prague, where she and her husband were put under close police surveillance. She continued to see her lovers, but her feelings towards her unemployed husband veered between revulsion and pity. 'If I was as emancipated as people think,' she wrote, 'I would have fewer worries.'[5]

When *Babicka* was published in 1855, it was quickly recognised as a classic and became the foundational work of modern Czech literature, but it did nothing to pull Nemcova out of poverty and illness. Her friends despaired at her inability to manage what little money she had. A group of admirers, appalled at her situation, collected a sum of money for her, but were irritated when she immediately gave most of it away to a friend to pay his debts, then spent the rest on a lavish dinner party.

Her husband's unrequited love curdled into bitterness and hatred. One afternoon, Josef came home to find her putting together her collection of folk tales for publication. He grabbed the pages and began to tear them up. She tried to snatch them back, but he wouldn't let go, so she bit his hand hard enough to draw blood. Josef raised his hand to hit her, but their son intervened. Josef stormed out of the house and spent the evening loudly cursing his wife's name in the taverns of Prague.

ONE OF THE FOLK tales in that collection, 'The Little Stars of Gold', tells the story of a poor girl named Bozena, who sets out on the long walk to her aunt's house through the snow. Along the way she gives her last piece of bread to a beggar, her shawl to a shirtless child, and then her skirt to another shivering little orphan. Bozena is warmed by the thought that she has brought comfort to people even worse off than herself. As night falls, a shower of little golden stars rains down into the forest and lights her way. She gathers the stars in her apron and falls asleep. When she wakes up, a stream of gold coins spills out of the apron. It was a poignant rescue fantasy from a woman who thought she deserved some reward for having given away so much of herself to other people.

Bozena Nemcova died in poverty at the age of forty-one. Her funeral was a great pageant of Czech nationalism, attended by huge crowds. Her hearse was decorated with garlands of flowers, followed by a procession of young girls holding candles. Today, her image is printed on the Czech Republic's five-hundred crown note.

Two Congresses

THE PUBLIC APPETITE for the nostalgic comforts of Bohemian folklore was, in part, a reaction to the shocks of economic modernisation. The predominantly German areas of northern and western Bohemia, close to deposits of coal and iron, were the first to industrialise. In 1815, a chemical works was established in Prague's Old Town, followed by a paper factory. Prague's first steamer, *Bohemia*, chugged its way down the Vltava in 1830. A rail line connecting Prague and Vienna opened in 1845. Gas street lights were introduced in 1847, illuminating the night-time city in a rich golden hue. Cotton-processing plants sprang up in the new industrial suburbs of Smichov and Karlin. The staggering profits from these enterprises lifted their Jewish owners from the ghetto into the upper ranks of the imperial bourgeoisie.

The new factories made Bohemia an industrial dynamo, the most economically advanced province in the Austrian Empire, but artisans whose work had once accorded them a degree of dignity and satisfaction found their livelihoods made redundant by the flood of cheap mass-produced goods. The population drift from the countryside into the city emboldened employers to cut workers' wages again and again, while demanding longer working hours. In 1844, the announcement of a wage cut at a mill yard sparked a revolt. Striking workers smashed the newly installed cotton-printing machines in factories across the city, then attacked Jewish businesses in the Old Town, breaking windows and scattering goods, before they were dispersed by imperial troops.

Frustrated expectations and social anxiety festered among the status-conscious educated middle classes. The Carolinum and Clementium, now merged as the Charles-Ferdinand University, turned out graduates who competed for scarce jobs in the imperial civil service. Those who scrambled onto the first rung of the ladder found themselves toiling for years at menial clerical jobs on subsistence pay. By the 1840s, Prague's social mix of hungry and exhausted workers, educated Czech nationalists and thwarted brooding intellectuals could only be held down by Metternich's secret police for so long.

Revolutionary pressure was building not just in Bohemia, but all over Europe. Harvest failures in the 1840s led to rising food prices across the continent. The gap between the wealth, rights and privileges of those who owned property and those who didn't widened even further. On 29 January 1848, Alexis de Tocqueville stood up in the French Chamber of Deputies and warned the assembly, 'I believe that we are, at this moment, sleeping on a volcano.'[6]

THE ERUPTION CAME SOONER than de Tocqueville expected. On the night of 29 February, a masked ball was held in Prague. In the course of the evening, letters arrived bearing news that the monarchy in France had fallen again, and a new republic had been proclaimed. The news was whispered excitedly from guest to guest, to avoid attracting the attention of the police in the room. Friends gathered in small groups and quietly toasted the revolution.[7]

After decades of political inertia, events began to move with astonishing rapidity. A week after the Paris uprising, posters appeared in Prague calling for citizens to attend a public meeting. On Saturday evening, 11 March, several thousand discontented workers, artisans, students and young intellectuals showed up at the St Wenceslas Baths and voted resoundingly for the introduction of a constitution with a genuinely representative Bohemian assembly, as well as for free speech, trial by jury, and for the 'organisation of work and wages'. A leadership group dubbed the St Wenceslas Committee was commissioned to flesh out their demands into a petition to be presented to the emperor in Vienna.

After four days, and some wrangling, the petition was ready to be delivered to the imperial authorities, but then amazing news came in on the evening train from Vienna: breathless travellers reported that a bloody uprising of workers and students in the Austrian capital had overthrown the government. Metternich had fled Vienna and was on his way into exile. Ferdinand, the good-natured but mentally disabled emperor, had been persuaded to appoint a new, more liberal administration.

The news emboldened the St Wenceslas Committee to sharpen the language of their petition, but when their delegation brought it to Vienna, they were fobbed off with a patronising, evasive response from the emperor's ministers. On returning to Prague, the committee sent the delegates straight back again, this time with a more stiffly worded document, but by the time they arrived, everything had changed. Other imperial cities – Budapest, Venice and Milan – had also risen in violent revolt against Habsburg rule, and the imperial administration was now ready to make significant concessions, agreeing to a new, somewhat democratic Bohemian assembly and to the establishment of Czech as an equal language. On 1 April, the St Wenceslas Committee was folded into a new Prague National Committee which instantly became a *de facto* local government.

It was at this point that the Czechs and Bohemian Germans began to pull in sharply different directions. Demands for greater political rights for the Czech majority had no appeal for the German radicals in Prague, who were drawn instead to the dream of a single pan-German state which was being excitedly promulgated in Berlin and Vienna.

THAT SAME MONTH, the distinguished Czech historian Frantisek Palacky received a letter from the convenors of a pan-German national assembly that was to be held in Frankfurt. The assembly's task was to create a constitution for a democratic parliament to represent all the German lands, from the Rhine to the Alps to the Baltic Sea. The convenors assumed that Bohemia, as one of the ancient kingdoms of the Holy Roman Empire, would naturally want to join a greater German state, and they invited Palacky to attend as a delegate.

Palacky wrote back, frostily thanking the convenors for their kind invitation, but stating that he could not possibly join their German assembly. 'I am a Czech of Slavonic origin,' he wrote proudly, 'and with all the little I possess and all the little I can do, I have devoted myself for all time to the service of my nation. That nation is a small one, it is true, but from time immemorial it has been a nation of itself and based upon its own strength.'

Moreover, he told the convenors they were making a terrible mistake. A greater German republic, he wrote, would be inherently unstable, and would crack open the protective shell of the Habsburgs' empire, exposing the nations of eastern and central Europe to the insatiable 'Asiatic' Russians. A strong, multinational Austrian Empire was needed as a bulwark against the Czar's colonial ambitions. If Austria didn't already exist, he wrote, it would be necessary to invent it. [8]

PALACKY'S LETTER CREATED A sensation in Prague; thousands of copies were printed and distributed. The Prague National Committee endorsed the letter, while in Vienna, the pro-Austrian sentiments were warmly received by the new imperial government, which offered Palacky the position of minister for education. Palacky turned them down, and continued to press for Czech autonomy within the empire's boundaries.

Many German Bohemians, however, were offended by Palacky's rebuke to their hopes of Bohemia's inclusion into a greater Germany. Heated claims and counterclaims were advanced to prove that Bohemia was 'innately' Czech or 'innately' German. Long-burning Czech resentment contended with German fears of becoming second-class citizens in their own homes.

German-speaking liberals and radicals began to walk away from the Prague National Committee. On 3 May, a German nationalist meeting was broken up by furious Czechs. Both groups fought for control of Prague's National Guard. On the streets, Czechs sang the chorus of a provocative popular song, 'Forward against the German, forward against the murderer, against Frankfurt.'[9]

Only a handful of people bothered to vote in the elections for the German national assembly, suggesting that the great majority of German Bohemians preferred to continue under Habsburg rule. The radical German nationalists sent their own representatives to Frankfurt anyway. An Austrian delegate told the assembly: 'I believe that since Bohemia cannot be held in the German Confederation by conviction, she must be bound to Germany by the sword's edge.'[10] Both groups had travelled a very long way from the happy solidarity they'd enjoyed just two months earlier.

AS A COUNTERWEIGHT to the pan-German movement, Frantisek Palacky announced that Prague would host its own pan-Slavic congress in June. Palacky intended the gathering to be an in-house affair, confined to Slavic groups within the Austrian Empire, but when the delegates streamed into Prague on 2 June 1848, they were joined by Slavic representatives from the Russian and Ottoman empires.

The authorities in Vienna, badly rattled by multiple popular uprisings across the empire, feared the subversive potential of Palacky's gathering and sent a monarchist hardliner, Field Marshal Alfred von Windischgratz, to Prague as its military governor. Whippet-thin, with a manicured moustache and a fixed expression of icy disdain, the reactionary field marshal drew no distinctions between liberals, radicals and nationalists; to him, they were all part of the same anti-monarchist rabble.

Many German Bohemians welcomed his appointment, but Czechs saw Windischgratz's arrival as a dangerous provocation, and a sign that Vienna no longer thought it had to make concessions to their nationalist hopes and was intent on smacking them back into line.

Upon taking up his post, the field marshal went looking for a fight; he enlarged the imperial garrison in Prague and paraded his men ostentatiously through the working-class areas of the city. As delegates began to arrive in Prague for the pan-Slavic congress, Windischgratz placed his artillery on the hills overlooking the city, ready to fire at the first sign of trouble.

VIENNA'S FEARS OF SUBVERSION were unfounded; the pan-Slavic congress had no clear agenda and talk of political unification went nowhere. No two groups had the same perspective: Czechs fretted about being absorbed into a greater Germany; Serbs, Croats and Slovaks were more concerned about Hungarian power; while the Poles saw a strong Hungary as their best potential ally against the domineering Russians and Prussians.

Unable to make much political headway, Palacky drafted a manifesto that romantically portrayed the Slavs as a liberty-loving people, who had suffered since ancient times at the hands of the imperialistic Romans and Germans.[11] The manifesto called for the Austrian Empire to be reconfigured as a federation of nations enjoying equal rights under the Habsburg crown. But then the whole congress had to be shuttered, because gunfire had broken out in the streets.

The Prague Uprising

STILL CONVINCED THE CONGRESS was an anti-Habsburg conspiracy, Windischgratz had sent his troops into the taverns of Prague on the night of 11 June, looking for Slav delegates to arrest and expel from the city.

The next morning, after mass, a crowd of angry Czechs marched to the field marshal's headquarters on Celetna Street to demand his resignation. As they approached the building, they encountered a delegation of German Bohemians who had come to offer the field marshal their full support. Shouting broke out between the groups, then shoving and fighting. A squadron of grenadiers, bayonets fixed, rushed into the street, and was soon met by armed Czech and German National Guard units. The untrained Czech and German militias shot wildly at each other. Windischgratz's wife, Eleonore, was watching the fighting from a window, standing between her two sisters, when a stray bullet fired from across the street shattered the glass and killed her.

The radicals retreated into the narrow streets and lanes, where they erected barricades and called for the people of Prague to rise up against the foreign troops. But there was no plan, and no central leadership. Liberals and nationalists like Palacky refused to support them. Within a day, Windischgratz's troops easily cleared the main traffic arteries, allowing the field marshal to deploy his men and materiel as he pleased.

On the morning of 15 June, rebels camped on the barricades in the Old Town woke up to discover Windischgratz's troops had disappeared from the skirmish lines. Then from the hills, the field marshal's artillery opened fire on the Old Town. The flour and wheat mills next to the Charles Bridge were set ablaze by the shelling. After two days, the insurgents surrendered. Around fifty workers and students had been killed in the fighting.

Windischgratz declared martial law and sent in columns of troops to occupy the Old and New towns. He dissolved the Prague National Committee and sent all the remaining Slavic congress delegates back home. The plans for an elected Bohemian assembly were thrown out.

Windischgratz set up an official inquiry into the uprising and pushed it to 'discover' evidence of a pan-Slavic conspiracy. His final report accused Czech liberals and nationalists of treason, which Palacky and others decried as absurd, when for months they had been declaring their desire to remain inside the empire as free and equal citizens.

THE FORCEFUL SUPPRESSION of the Prague uprising went some way towards restoring Habsburg confidence after five perilous months of humiliating backdowns and concessions. Windischgratz was brought back to Vienna, where he crushed another bloody uprising in that city. The counter-revolutionaries now held the upper hand and moved to put the monarchy on a firmer footing. On 2 December 1848, Emperor Ferdinand was persuaded to abdicate in favour of his eighteen-year-old nephew, who became Franz Joseph I.

The new emperor was awarded the crown of Bohemia, but never bothered to come to Prague for a coronation ceremony. Czech nationalists like Palacky could be forgiven for thinking that it was they who appreciated the idea of a dynastic multi-ethnic empire better than the Habsburgs.

Former emperor Ferdinand I in retirement at Prague Castle.

Smetana's Brain

IN RETIREMENT, FERDINAND MOVED to Prague, where he took up residence in the castle. The former emperor was delighted to find his adopted city full of music, and he regularly made his way down from Hradcany to attend piano concerts by the gifted Czech composer and pianist Bedrich Smetana. Like Mozart, Smetana had been a child prodigy, performing concerts at the age of six. As a young man, he had struggled to support his family as a piano teacher and concert pianist, but in 1850, Ferdinand offered him a post as his court composer, which enabled him to complete several orchestral works.

Smetana and his wife, Katerina, had four daughters together, but three were lost to tuberculosis and scarlet fever. He dedicated his achingly sad Piano Trio in G Minor to the eldest, Bedriska, a work that was praised by Franz Liszt but received poorly by the Prague critics. Feeling unappreciated, Smetana relocated to Sweden, but the cold climate exacerbated his wife's illnesses and she too succumbed to tuberculosis. 'She died gently,' he wrote, 'without our knowing anything until the quiet drew my attention to her.'[12]

A mournful Smetana returned to Prague in 1862 and gave two concerts that were sparsely attended. Stung by critics who derided his work as 'too German', he composed an opera, *The Bartered Bride*, which incorporated traditional Bohemian folk dances. This too was indifferently received, but over the course of four years Smetana rewrote it, adding some livelier tunes and making it more distinctly Czech. When the reworked version of *The Bartered Bride* was staged in 1870 it was a smashing international success and made Smetana a national hero.

Smetana now set to work on a new opera, *Libussa*, based on the story of the legendary princess. It was completed in 1872, but withheld from performance until the construction of a new National Theatre could be completed.

PRAGUE'S NATIONAL THEATRE was the brainchild of Frantisek Palacky, who established a society to raise funds for its construction. In 1852, the perfect location was found: a site on the corner of the Vltava embankment and Narodni Street, with a view to the castle across the river. Construction proceeded in fits and starts, and the magnificent neo-Renaissance building was completed in 1881 to sighs of satisfaction; the theatre's grandeur brought dignity and a sense of permanence to Czech culture.

On opening night, 11 June 1881, Smetana's *Libussa* finally received its premiere, after a nine-year wait. The semicircular auditorium with its four balconies was filled with 1700 excited Praguers. Smetana had not been offered tickets and had to watch the premiere from the director's box. *Libussa* was received with thunderous applause and the composer was called to the stage to take a bow.

IN THE 1870s, SMETANA composed a romantic cycle of six symphonic poems, which he titled *Ma Vlast* – My Country. The second poem in the cycle, 'Vltava', was written to evoke the sound of the mighty river as its tributaries converge into a rolling torrent. The tune is a crowd pleaser wherever it's played; the slow, lilting rhythm induces audiences to sway dreamily from side to side as they hum along.

Bedrich Smetana was now widely loved as the founder of a distinctively Czech national music, but in the early 1880s he told friends he feared the onset of madness. The creeping symptoms of syphilis, contracted in his youth, brought on a constant ringing in his ears and then rendered him completely deaf. In 1884, a birthday banquet in his honour was held in Prague, but he was too ill to attend. He was removed to a lunatic asylum, where he died several months later.

SMETANA'S DISEASE-RAVAGED BRAIN was taken to a medical institute, where it was preserved in a large glass jar. In the late 1940s, the bottle was given to a Professor Ladislav Haskovec, the personal physician to the first communist president, Klement Gottwald. When Gottwald fell ill, Haskovec was arrested by the secret police, who raided his home. Not knowing what to make of a spongy pickled object in a jar, they flushed Smetana's brain down the toilet.

Blood Libel

THE NINETEENTH CENTURY changed Prague's Jewish quarter almost beyond recognition. In 1850, the quarter was renamed Josefov, in honour of the emancipator emperor Joseph II. Joseph's reforms had, however, emptied the quarter of much of its Jewish population, since they were now free to live elsewhere in the city, and Josefov had degenerated into a crime-ridden slum. In 1893, the quarter was deemed to be dangerous and unsanitary, and was progressively demolished, leaving only the medieval synagogues, the cemetery and Mordechai Maisel's Jewish Town Hall standing. The ramshackle tenements were replaced by spacious apartment blocks designed in the Paris Beaux-Arts style.

Prague's emancipated Jews had followed Joseph's advice to assimilate and prosper, but many were torn between the rootless freedom of modern urban life and nostalgia for the ancient ways of the ghetto. Many were left somewhat stranded between the Czech-speaking majority and the ever-shrinking German-speaking minority. Most Jews spoke German as their first language, making them doubly foreign to Czech nationalists. And coursing under the skin of Bohemia like a persistent infection were residual strains of medieval anti-Semitism.

ON 1 APRIL 1899, the day before Easter Sunday, the body of a nineteen-year-old woman named Anezka Hruzova was found in a forest near her village of Polna. Her throat had been cut and her head was wrapped in her torn blouse. Some rope was found near the body, indicating she had been dragged some distance.

The police report commented on the surprisingly small amount of blood discovered at the scene, given the gruesome nature of the murder. This, and the timing of the death being so close to Passover, led to speculation that Anezka had been the victim of a Jewish ritual murder.

A 23-year-old itinerant Jewish shoemaker named Leopold Hilsner was arrested and tried at Kutna Hora on 12 September. The evidence against him was so thin as to be almost non-existent, and rested heavily on the old blood libel, the theory that the victim's Christian blood had been harvested by a Jew to make the Passover bread. The press reported the case sensationally, resorting to the crudest anti-Semitic tropes.

Despite the absence of evidence, Leopold Hilsner was found guilty and sentenced to death. Hilsner's legal counsel lodged an appeal, but it seemed hopeless until an academic at Charles University spoke up against the conviction.

TOMAS MASARYK, A PHILOSOPHY professor, had studied the trial proceedings carefully, visited the scene of the crime and published a pamphlet, in which he coolly dissected the numerous legal errors, obfuscations and instances of prejudicial conduct. Masaryk declared that the bigotry surrounding the case was perverse and unworthy of the Czech people. 'People who pretend to save the Czech nation,' he wrote, 'actually poison it with base, incongruent lies and ignorance.'[13]

Masaryk's objections were widely publicised, making him a figure of hate among Czech anti-Semites. Protestors invaded his lectures and shouted abuse at him, but Masaryk stood his ground. 'To make certain the demonstrators did not think I was afraid of them,' he later recalled, 'I walked all around the lecture hall, challenging them to argue their points; no one dared.' Prague's Social Democrats offered Masaryk their cautious support, but the university, cowed by the demonstrations, suspended his lectures for a fortnight. He was disappointed by colleagues who looked the other way when he passed them in the corridor. Masaryk considered migrating to the United States, but his American wife, Charlotte, urged him to stay and fight. When angry demonstrators appeared outside the Masaryk house, Charlotte came out and spoke to them until they dispersed.

IT WASN'T THE FIRST time the polite professor with the trim beard had drawn fire from ultra-nationalists. Years earlier, Masaryk had carefully examined a set of epic medieval poems dear to the hearts of Czech chauvinists, then published an article debunking them as modern forgeries. For that he was denounced in a newspaper as a 'loathsome traitor' and 'a ghastly ulcer'.[14] Their indignation fed his indignation. 'What made me angry,' he recalled, 'was to see people defending the manuscripts when they did not believe in them but were afraid to admit it.'[15]

Masaryk's attack on the integrity of the Hilsner trial sealed his reputation in the minds of Czech chauvinists as a traitor and a corrupter of the minds of Czech youth. He fought back, declaring, 'I will not allow myself to be violated by anybody, and I will not retreat in the face of lies and misunderstood slogans.'[16]

Masaryk's doggedly rational arguments weakened public confidence in the Hilsner trial verdict. An official medical review delivered a scathing attack on the standards of evidence, particularly on the claim of a mysterious absence of blood. A second trial was held, with a second murder charge attached to it, and again Hilsner was found guilty, but the sentence was commuted to life imprisonment. Leopold Hilsner would have to endure eighteen years in an Austrian prison before he was pardoned, but his defender, the bespectacled philosophy professor, would become the greatest Czech leader since Charles IV.

TOMAS GARRIGUE MASARYK was born the son of an illiterate Slovak coachman and a Czech cook who worked at one of the Habsburgs' Moravian estates. His father laboured like a serf on the property, and Masaryk was stung by the sight of that hardworking man doffing his cap to the pampered aristocrats who rode to and from the royal estate. Masaryk only began his formal education at eleven, once his father had obtained permission from his superiors to do so. Masaryk thrived at school and was eventually admitted to the University of Vienna. His doctoral thesis on the social phenomenon of suicide identified the loss of religious certainty as the cause of modern despair.

While studying in Leipzig, Masaryk fell in love with an American student, Charlotte Garrigue, and they married a year later in the United States. Under Charlotte's influence, he became a firm supporter of universal suffrage and equal rights for women, and to make his point he took Charlotte's surname as his middle name, an unusual gesture for the time. In 1881, he and Charlotte moved to Prague, where he took up his appointment as professor of philosophy at Charles-Ferdinand University.

Masaryk's mind was wonderfully wide ranging: he was one part fifteenth-century Hussite; another part straitlaced Victorian; and yet another part seemed to live curiously in the future. In 1929, when talking pictures first appeared, Masaryk was bold enough to envisage wireless transmission of video images. 'Just imagine,' he said in his jaunty English, 'you could observe from your place, say in the sitting room, the jungles of Africa and what the beasts are doing there. You could see and listen to the jungles of our society! Every man then would be forced to be honest, and there would be no secret plotting anymore … Wonderful, no?'[17]

Masaryk wrote essays on Jan Hus, hypnotism, prostitution, alcoholism and the perils of zero-sum nationalism. He travelled to Czarist Russia in its final years, where he enjoyed long conversations with Tolstoy, but came home convinced that his people should turn to the democratic west, and away from the embrace of their autocratic Slavic cousins.

MASARYK ENTERED politics unobtrusively in 1891. In Austria's imperial parliament he led the tiny Czech Realist Party, but he was attracting a growing legion of admirers in Britain and the United States. Over time, these friends took up senior posts in the British foreign office, *The Times* of London, and the White House. Masaryk, who was half-Slovak, also reached out to Slovakia's up-and-coming intellectuals and students.

He took some time to arrive at a political philosophy; although attracted to socialist principles of equality, he eventually rejected Marxist ideology, which he saw as too prescriptive and materialistic.

Above all, Masaryk considered himself a democrat, believing that democratic systems naturally guided their citizens towards reasonableness and tolerance, and went some way to smoothing the harsher edges of modern capitalism.

Shadowgraph

IN 1887, WHILE MASARYK was lecturing in the university's philosophy department, in another building a physicist named Ernst Mach was experimenting with a loaded gun.

Mach, the university's professor of experimental physics, wanted to show how a bullet travelling faster than the speed of sound compresses the air in front of it, creating a ballistic shock wave. Shock waves are invisible, but the rippling of the air creates a momentary shadow that he captured with an ingenious photographic technique called a shadowgraph. When the bullet was fired, it crossed two trip wires (the two vertical lines in the photo below), which triggered the camera. The snapshot captured the shadow of a strong shock wave bowing at the nose of the projectile, a weaker shock wave at the rear and the rippling wake of the bullet behind it.

Ernst Mach's historic shadowgraph of a bow shock wave
around a supersonic bullet.

ERNST MACH, like his colleague Masaryk, brought his forensic curiosity to bear on a whole range of subjects. He was the first scientist to understand how the speed of air flow over a body affects its aerodynamic behaviour. The increments of air speed in supersonic jet aviation (Mach 1, Mach 2 and so on) were later named in his honour.

The American philosopher William James, who came to visit him in Prague, was in awe of his intellect. 'I don't think anyone ever gave me so strong an impression of pure intellectual genius,' he wrote.[18] Over time, Mach developed a Buddhist-like theory on the acquisition of knowledge through the senses. His ability to straddle the worlds of science and philosophy led him to intuit a subtle truth that had eluded other scientists – an explanation for the phenomenon of inertia, which would eventually lead to a radical new understanding of the nature of the universe. It was the first major challenge to Isaac Newton's work in more than two centuries. Mach summed up his inertia theory neatly to one of his students: 'When the subway train jerks, it's the fixed stars that throw you down.'[19]

Mach began with a thought experiment. He wondered what would happen if it were somehow possible for a human to spin around in an otherwise perfectly empty universe, with no planets, stars or galaxies to provide a point of reference. Mach thought that under those circumstances it wouldn't *feel* like you were spinning at all – your arms would not lift up and pull away as they normally do. This, he thought, implied some kind of mysterious interaction between everything in the universe. Mach's theory was compelling, but he could not explain the reason for the interaction; *how* the distant stars could somehow pull up the arms of a person twirling around under normal circumstances on earth.

MACH'S IDEAS CAUGHT the attention of a young physicist named Albert Einstein, who came to Prague in 1911 to take up a professorship at the university – Mach had long since left to take up a post in Vienna.

Prague, at the time of Einstein's arrival, was rapidly modernising. Electric trams had begun coursing through the city's traffic arteries. A second river crossing, the granite Palacky Bridge, had opened in 1876, followed by the Legion Bridge in 1901 and the iron Cechuv Bridge in 1908; the Manes Bridge, connecting the New Town with Smichov, was under construction. Einstein took some months to warm to his new home. In letters to friends he complained about the difficulty of the Czech language, the bedbugs and the quality of the drinking water. As a German-speaking Jew, he felt unwelcome at a time of surging Czech nationalism.

Einstein had already published his Special Theory of Relativity, which established the speed of light as the cosmic speed limit. Like Mach, he had broken with Isaac Newton's concept of space and time being 'always similar and immovable' and was ready to travel a great distance further.

He found himself taking long solitary walks along the Vltava, during which his General Theory of Relativity began to slowly cohere in his mind, and with it the revolutionary understanding that the universe is not fixed and absolute, but curved and elastic. His new theory of gravity was expressed concisely as 'space tells matter how to move; matter tells space how to curve'.[20] Mass, he realised, warps the spacetime around it like a bowling ball on a rubber sheet, and affects the motion of other masses nearby. Einstein revealed that reality was far weirder than the universe of straight lines and absolute measurement described by Newton.

*

EINSTEIN, WHO LOVED music and debate, soon found his way to a weekly salon for Jewish intellectuals, hosted by the brilliant Berta Fanta in her apartment on the Old Town Square. In May 1911, she invited Einstein to give a lecture at the salon on special relativity. Max Brod came along and brought his close friend Franz Kafka.

At that stage, the 27-year-old Kafka had published several short stories but was yet to write any of his major works. Disappointingly, although Einstein and Kafka moved in similar social circles in Prague, there's no evidence the two ever spoke. Einstein's talk on relativity at Berta's salon probably left Kafka baffled and bored; he wrote nothing of it in his diary or letters.

FRANZ KAFKA HAD LIVED in Prague all his life; he drank coffee at the Café Louvre and the Arco, worked diligently throughout the day for an industrial insurance company, and by night he visited the Red Peacock brothel, discreetly located on a hidden laneway off the Old Town Square. Kafka often complained of feeling suffocated by Prague. His Hebrew teacher Friedrich Thieberger recalled standing with him one day at the window of the Kafka family apartment on the Old Town Square. As they looked down, Kafka pointed at the various buildings and said, 'This was my high school, the university was over there, in the building facing us, my office a bit further to the left.' Kafka's finger drew a few small circles in the air: 'This narrow circle encompasses my entire life.'[21]

Although Prague is never mentioned by name in Kafka's fiction, it's difficult to imagine *The Trial* taking place anywhere else. Prague, in the pages of *The Trial*, exists on the threshold between the waking world and an anxiety dream. The opening sentence seems to anticipate the totalitarian horrors to come:

Someone must have been telling lies about Josef K., he knew he had done nothing wrong but, one morning, he was arrested.

THE OUTBREAK OF the First World War came as lightning from a clear blue sky for intellectuals like Kafka's friend Max Brod. 'War to us,' he wrote, 'was simply a crazy idea, of a piece with, say, the perpetual motion machine or the fountain of youth.'[22]

The international crisis, sparked by the assassination of a Habsburg archduke in Sarajevo, pitted the central powers of Austria-Hungary and Germany against Russia, France and the British Empire. Frightened and appalled by the stampede to war, Max Brod and his circle of friends resolved to visit the wisest man they knew, Tomas Garrigue Masaryk, to ask him to do something to halt the looming catastrophe. Masaryk received them politely in his office, but had no words of consolation to offer.

Shortly after the meeting with Brod and his friends, Masaryk slipped out of Prague and reappeared months later in Paris, as leader of the Czech liberation movement in exile.

GERMAN BOHEMIANS CHEERED the declaration of war, as did many Jews, who enlisted to fight for the empire. Fruit-sellers in the New Town collected apples, pears and plums to hand out to soldiers at the train stations. Legions of Czech volunteers answered the call to mobilise, but they were watched closely for the first signs of sedition and the city was placed under tight military control. Newspapers were shut down; real and potential subversives were arrested. German propaganda, summoning people to the struggle against the Slav menace, was counterproductive in Prague. Some Czech soldiers were seen carrying a banner:

> *Red-coloured handkerchief, wave through the sky,*
> *We fight the Russians, though we don't know why.*[23]

Be Like Svejk

JAROSLAV KOVARICEK HANDS me coffee in the living room of his home on the New South Wales north coast. Jaroslav is a retired radio broadcaster and musicologist, who migrated to Australia from Prague after the 1968 Soviet invasion. 'To understand the Czech nature,' he advises me, 'you should know two authors: Hasek and Kafka. Kafka shows all the absurdity and mystery. Hasek was, in a way cynical, but we Czechs were masters in using the Svejk techniques.'

He's talking about Jaroslav Hasek's *The Good Soldier Svejk*, the classic tale of the Bohemian soldier who survives the First World War by playing the buffoon. Svejk acts like he's enthusiastic to get to the front, but he makes a nuisance of himself and spends his time playing cards, getting drunk and being dragged in and out of jail. The whole novel smells like beer. When Svejk's commanding officer gravely informs him of their imminent departure for the front, Svejk expresses his deep joy: 'Humbly report, sir, I'm awfully happy. It'll be really marvellous when we both fall dead together for His Imperial Majesty and the Royal Family.'[24]

SVEJK'S ADVENTURES ARE based on those of his creator, who was himself a spectacular buffoon and prankster. Jaroslav Hasek came from a miserable home, scarred by poverty, illness and suicide. After finishing his studies he briefly held down several jobs before slipping into a more congenial life in Prague as a writer, vagrant and drinker.

In 1906, Hasek fell in love with Jarmila Mayer and tried to clean up his act to win her parents' permission to marry her. He became a journalist of sorts; in 1910, he was appointed editor of *Animal World* magazine, but was sacked when it was discovered he'd written articles about non-existent animals he'd made up.

Despite his uncertain prospects, Hasek married Jarmila on 23 May 1910. A year later, he attempted to jump off the Charles Bridge, right at the spot where Jan Nepomuk was thrown to his death centuries earlier. It's not clear if this was a prank or a genuine suicide attempt. In any case, he was pulled off the parapet by a passing hairdresser and incarcerated in a mental institute.

On his release, Hasek reunited with Jarmila and founded the Cynological Institute of Prague, a pretentious name for his dog-fancier's salon, where he made a living picking up stray mongrels, dyeing their fur and selling them off as thoroughbreds with exquisite pedigrees. He founded a political party with his drinking friends called the Party of Mild Progress within the Limits of the Austro-Hungarian Law.

In 1912, he and Jarmila had a son, Richard, but she left him soon afterwards and took the boy with her. At this point Hasek abandoned respectable society entirely and took up his old bohemian life, drinking all day and sleeping on friends' couches. For a while he stayed with the cartoonist Josef Lada, who would later provide the illustrations for *Svejk*. He hung out a professional shingle on Lada's door that read:

Jaroslav Hasek: Imperial-Royal Writer,
Father of the Poor in Spirit and Certified Parisian Clairvoyant.[25]

WHEN WAR BROKE OUT IN 1914, Hasek could not resist provoking the authorities. He checked into a hotel brothel under a Russian name, and in the guest book he stated that his reason for visiting Prague was to 'look into' the activities of the Austrian military high command. The building was soon surrounded by police, who were mortified when they realised the military spy hiding in the brothel was, in fact, that idiot Hasek. Someone noticed that Hasek's fake Russian-sounding name, when spelt backwards, became 'kiss my arse' in Czech. In his defence, he insisted he'd been trying to help the war effort by testing police vigilance, but they jailed him anyway for five days.

IN 1915, HASEK ENLISTED with the Austrian army and was sent to fight the Russians in Galicia. He was captured and sent east, to central Asia, to a bleak prisoner-of-war camp near Kazakhstan. When he heard a special Czechoslovak Legion was to be formed to fight the Austrians, he joined at once, but after the Bolshevik takeover in Russia, he defected again to join the Red Army. The Czechoslovak Legion denounced him as a traitor.

In Moscow, Hasek threw his lot in with Lenin's Bolsheviks and was sent back to central Asia for propaganda work. In 1920, he went further east, to Irkutsk on the Mongolian border. For two years in Irkutsk, he served as a sober and ruthless communist apparatchik. He survived a bout of typhoid and also, allegedly, an assassination attempt.

AFTER THE WAR, HASEK showed up in Prague again, accompanied by his new Siberian wife, Shura, whom he had married bigamously. Shunned as a traitor to everyone and every cause, Hasek retreated to a cottage in the countryside with Shura, where he began to draw on his adventures to write *Svejk*. By now he was morbidly obese and drinking heavily. He published three volumes of stories, but died in 1923 before he could finish his fourth. He was a few months shy of forty. Hasek's obituary was published but hardly anyone believed it, and so only a couple of old friends and his eleven-year-old son, Richard, showed up at his funeral.

HASEK'S BOOK BECAME the most translated Czech novel of all time. In the 1920s, a conservative Czech critic worried the popularity of *Svejk* might present a threat to national security, encouraging soldiers towards sloth and cynicism in the face of German aggression.[26] But the Nazi invaders were equally infuriated by the Svejkian behaviour of the Czechs under occupation, which one observer defined as 'a baffling willingness to comply with any and all demands, and an equally baffling ability to execute them in such a way that the effect is quite different from that contemplated by those who did the commanding'.[27] Nazi ideologues saw danger in laughter. 'The Reich will not to be mocked,' snapped Reinhard Heydrich, the Butcher of Prague.[28] After Heydrich's assassination, a quisling minister berated his fellow countrymen for their 'national peculiarity, which culminates in the disgusting figure of a calculating sloth and titular idiot Svejk'.[29]

I ASK JAROSLAV KOVARICEK if he ever tried playing Svejk with the communist authorities. 'Of course!' he says, brightly. 'We all did. There was the day when I had a political indoctrination session. The party leader was talking about the advantages of a planned economy under communism, unlike capitalism, he said, which was always falling into crisis.

'"So, comrade," I asked, "please explain this to me: why do we always give awards to those traitors, the *uderniks*?" The *uderniks* were the heroes of socialist labour, who received medals from the party for overfulfilling the economic plan by 120 percent.

'I said, "These *uderniks* are in the service of the Western imperialists! They want to destroy the economy!" The communist asked me to explain myself, and I said, "Well, if everything is planned to 100, and someone is making 120 … then that means they are *wasting material*."

'I said all that with an absolute innocent expression on my face.

'I was like Svejk.'

The Good Soldier Svejk.
Illustration by Josef Lada.

IN JANUARY 1916, a year and a half into the fighting, the US consul noted that life in Prague seemed oddly normal. 'The streets are crowded with well-dressed people … coffee-houses, cinematographs, theatres, and cabarets are going full blast.'[30] But as 1916 rolled on, the mounting casualties, combined with food and coal shortages, shook Praguers out of their indifference. Hungry women and children clustered outside official buildings demanding food, only to hear district officers nervously assure them that everything that could be done was being done. In the suburb of Holesovice, a group of women ambushed a bread shop owner on her doorstep. They seized her loaves, but then thrust their money into her pockets. 'Madam, we don't cheat you of anything,' one of them insisted. 'We are hungry, we give you money!'[31]

FRUSTRATED BY HIS noisy room in the Old Town, Franz Kafka asked his sister Ottla to help him find a more suitable place to write. She found him a dwelling in the castle district among the row of tiny fairy-tale houses known as the Golden Lane. The little houses, no bigger than twenty square metres each, had been constructed in the sixteenth century to accommodate Rudolf II's castle fusiliers, and were later occupied by goldsmiths and castle servants. The Golden Lane was not then the picturesque tourist attraction it is today, and Kafka had no interest in working in such a dilapidated environment, but Ottla set to work making it clean and cosy. 'In the beginning, it had many shortcomings,' he wrote to his on-again, off-again fiancée Felice Bauer. 'Now it suits me perfectly.'[32] Each evening he would carry his supper up the hill, write in the deep silence until midnight, and then walk back down to the Old Town through the snow.

While Kafka burrowed deeper into his 'dreamlike inner life', the city outside his tiny castle sanctuary was running out of food and fuel. The trams had stopped running and the theatres were closed. In April 1917, the announcement of a further tightening of rations sparked riots. Hungry mobs raided restaurants and hotels, searching for food. The imperial government's authority was withering away.

AS THE AUSTRIAN EMPIRE limped on through the war towards defeat, Tomas Garrigue Masaryk hopped between the Allied capitals, using his network of contacts to lobby anyone who might help the cause of Czech independence. In Paris, he joined forces with the Slovak leader Milan Stefanik to coordinate a campaign for a united Czech and Slovak nation. All the while, Masaryk kept in touch with a group in Prague known as the Czech *maffie*, who were covertly working towards national independence from within.

Masaryk persuaded the Russians to support a Czechoslovak Legion to fight against the Germans and Austrians. The Legion grew into a force of more than 100,000 soldiers, who fought against the central powers on the eastern front, against the Bolsheviks in the subsequent Russian Civil War, and at one point, seized control of the Trans-Siberian Railway from Samara to Irkutsk. The effectiveness of the Legion impressed the Allied leaders and helped convince them of the viability and desirability of a post-war Czechoslovak state.

THE FINAL YEAR OF the war, 1918, opened with Germany and Austria launching a last great offensive, which ended with their forces in full retreat. The empire's Czech, Polish and Hungarian regiments mutinied and decided to go home.

On 6 January 1918, a group of Czech parliamentarians met at Prague's Municipal House to issue a declaration demanding independence, which was recognised by the French on 29 June; the British on 8 August; and the Americans on 2 September.

The war came to a close, as Winston Churchill quipped, with a drizzle of empires falling through the air.[33] Karl I, the last Habsburg emperor and King of Bohemia, never actually abdicated; he simply became the ruler of nothing at all as the empire's constituent nationalities made their bids for independent nationhood.

The Czechoslovak National Council declared itself a provisional government on 18 October, with Masaryk as prime minister and his protégé Edvard Benes as foreign minister. Following the American model, they issued a 'Declaration of Independence of the Czechoslovak Nation', which declared the resolve of its people to be free of the 'denationalising oppression which we have suffered for the past three hundred years' – in other words, since the Battle of White Mountain. The new Czechoslovak democracy would guarantee freedom of speech, religion, assembly, the separation of church and state, universal suffrage and rights for women, 'who shall be placed on an equal footing with men, politically, socially, and culturally'. The declaration ended on a triumphant, optimistic note: 'Democracy is victorious … The forces of darkness have served the victory of light – the longed-for age of humanity is dawning.'[34]

NEWS OF THE DECLARATION was greeted excitedly by Czechs and Slovaks, but with deep disquiet among German Bohemians. In late October, the Czechoslovak National Council drew up plans for their post-war government. Masaryk was to be president of the new republic, while Karel Kramar, who had been arrested at the start of the war, was to be prime minister. Benes was to stay in the job of foreign minister, and Masaryk's Slovak ally Milan Stefanik would be defence minister. Only one cabinet position without portfolio was set aside for a German Bohemian.

Masaryk's failure to fully embrace the Germans, at the outset, as equal partners in the new nation, was a severe misjudgment. Fearing they would soon be strangers in their own lands, the German Bohemian deputies in Vienna moved quickly to declare their own autonomous German-Austrian state, as four separate islands on the borders of Bohemia and Moravia. But they received no international support, and when Czech troops took control of the Germanic borderlands on Armistice Day, they met almost no resistance from the local populace.

*

The Martyr and the Mother of God

ON THE NIGHT OF 7 November 1918, a crowd of several hundred Praguers drifted into the Old Town Square after attending a commemoration of the Battle of White Mountain. The crowd was in high spirits as they gathered around the two rival monuments in the square: one dedicated to the martyr Jan Hus, the other to the Virgin Mary.

The monument to Hus had been placed there three years earlier to commemorate the 500th anniversary of his death. The sculpture was melodramatic and magnificent. It looked like a mad stone-and-bronze birthday cake, with the upright figure of Hus at the apex surrounded by his followers. Inscribed on the base was his famous quote: *Pravda Vitezi* – Truth Prevails.

But that night, the revellers were more interested in the other monument, a tall baroque column capped with a statue of Mary, mother of God. The Marian Column had been planted in the square centuries earlier by the Habsburgs as an act of thanksgiving for the Virgin's assistance in the fight against the Swedish marauders of 1648.

Many Czechs, however, had come to see it as a totem of Habsburg dominance and a symbol of the slow strangulation of their language and culture. Now that the Habsburgs had been toppled, it seemed their column should come down too.

A group of firefighters climbed the Marian Column with their ladders and lashed their ropes around the Virgin's neck. A few horrified Catholics tried to defend the monument but were held back by the cheering crowd as the firemen turned their winches. Then, above the shouting, there was a sudden wrenching crack and the Marian Column came crashing down onto the paving stones.

Czech nationalists rejoiced while deeply distressed Catholics denounced the act as mob vandalism. For the Czechs, the toppling of the column was a symbolic act of banishment. The Habsburgs were gone for good. But departing with them was the fragile inter-ethnic comity that had been kept in place by a shared allegiance to the monarch. The new nation of Czechoslovakia would have to find some other unifying principle to hold its various nationalities together. Tomas Masaryk hoped that, given enough time, they might all become good democrats. In the meantime, he would have to serve as the focal point of shared allegiances.

TOMAS GARRIGUE MASARYK, once reviled as a traitor to the Czechs, returned to Prague in December 1918 as the hero of the new nation he had done so much to create. Stepping off the train, he was given the traditional homespun offering of bread and salt, and was reunited with his family. The ordeal of the war years had taken their toll on his wife, Charlotte, who had remained in Bohemia while her husband was away. The death of their son

Herbert from typhus had left her depressed and anxious. Their younger son, Jan, however, had survived the war and would follow his father into government, first as a diplomat, then as foreign minister of Czechoslovakia.

OUTSIDE THE TRAIN STATION, Masaryk was led towards a flower-covered imperial carriage drawn by two white horses, but he chose to travel less ostentatiously to Prague Castle in an open-top car. Bells rang out across the city as crowds cheered their president through the streets.

Masaryk was conscious of the need to carry himself with the utmost dignity as head of state and took care to mask his feelings in public. When Edvard Benes returned to Prague, Masaryk was so worried he'd be overcome by emotion, he received Benes in private at the castle rather than publicly at the railway station. With tender affection, he put his arms around the man he'd come to regard as a son.

The First Republic

MASARYK'S FIRST NIGHT in Prague Castle was a sleepless one. Once the public euphoria died down, bitter antagonisms surfaced, exacerbated by the continuing food shortages. Prague was in almost constant turmoil throughout 1919 and 1920, riven with inter-ethnic violence and industrial protests.

The presence of Masaryk, in these turbulent years was critical in holding the country together, socially and ethnically. The Czechoslovak Republic had thirteen million citizens; of these, half were Czech, a quarter German, roughly a sixth were Slovak, in addition to smaller populations of Ruthenians and Hungarians.[35] Masaryk was a realist about inter-ethnic harmony, proclaiming, 'You don't necessarily have to love one another in order to live together in peace.'[36]

The republican constitution divided power between a bicameral parliament, a cabinet of ministers and a president who was head of state. But no other figure enjoyed anything like Masaryk's prestige, and so the office of the presidency began to accrue enormous informal power. The first parliamentary elections in 1920 produced a mix of conservative agrarian parties, Social Democrats, Catholic Christian Democrats and a few German nationalists.

In the mid-1920s, the economy began to take off. Czechoslovakia had inherited a stunning sixty to seventy per cent of the former empire's industrial potential, most of which lay in the German-populated border areas. Czechoslovakia's relatively cheap labour, combined with its sophisticated production base and excellent education system, lifted the country into tenth position among the world's industrialised powers. The five towns of Prague's historic centre were merged with the surrounding suburbs to form Greater Prague, a city of 676,000 souls.

The Friday Men

ON 25 JANUARY 1921, a new play titled *R.U.R.* opened at Prague's National Theatre. In the opening scene, a manager is giving dictation to his secretary, when a visitor, Lady Helen, arrives and asks the secretary where she's from.

'Here, from this factory ...' she replies. 'I was manufactured here.'

The secretary is an artificial human: obedient, efficient and emotionless, a mechanical golem, one of many mass-produced at the factory. Karel Capek, the author of *R.U.R.*, called his humanoid machines 'robots', taken from the Czech word *robota*, meaning 'forced labour'. In the course of the play, the idle humans hand over more and more responsibility to the robots, until they rise up to kill their human masters.

In the century following the premiere of *R.U.R.*, the troubling thought that humans might unwittingly build machines that would replace us became a well-worn trope of science fiction, but in 1922 Capek's vision was shocking and provocative. The play was translated into many languages and Capek's robots appeared on stage in London's West End and on Broadway, where a young Spencer Tracy played one of the automatons.

IN 1926, KAREL CAPEK met Masaryk at a reception at Prague Castle, and thereafter he and the president became close friends. Capek had taken little interest in politics before the war, but Masaryk's feat of creating an enlightened democratic state from the crude materials of Czech nationalism struck him as miraculous, and worth defending, particularly among his friends, who were of the revolutionary left.

Capek invited the president to the regular salon he held in his cramped Vinohrady apartment on Friday nights. The Friday Men, as they called themselves, were a raucous group of intellectuals, journalists, writers and politicians, who addressed each other with mock formality, while Capek, coffeepot in hand and half a cigarette jutting out of his mouth, played host.[37]

The group was politically diverse but socially narrow: no women, Germans or Slovaks were ever invited. Capek encouraged good-humoured conversational combat, but his deeper hope was to forge a degree of friendship between prominent liberals, communists and conservative Catholics, and a shared loyalty to Czechoslovak democracy.

President Masaryk's occasional visits had a sobering effect on the normally garrulous Friday Men; alcohol was taken off the table and the conversation lurched in fits and starts. Younger members were intimidated by the president's bearing and dignity while communists tried to bait him with good-humoured barbs, which Masaryk seemed to enjoy more than flattery.

President T. G. Masaryk,
sketched by fellow Friday Man Adolf Hoffmeister, 1934.

'I TRY TO KEEP MY eye on everything,' Masaryk told Capek.[38] The castle's intelligence network was closely monitoring Russian-directed communist activity, but Masaryk was more troubled by the rise of a Mussolini-inspired movement calling itself the Czech

National Fascist Community. The Czech fascists, who had infiltrated elements of the armed forces and the right-wing parliamentary parties, were pan-Slavist, anti-German and anti-Jewish. Masaryk denounced them as 'pathological scum'.[39]

In 1926, the president invited the Friday Men to join him at his summer residence in Lany, outside Prague. After dinner, he read out a newspaper report speculating that he was contemplating a temporary presidential coup to forestall a fascist military takeover.

'What do you say to that?' he asked.

No one spoke.

Masaryk warned the group that the Czech fascist leader, General Radola Gajda, might use the forthcoming Sokol gymnastic congress in Prague to launch a fascist putsch, and he asked them to speak up for parliamentary democracy. 'We must not fear the fascists,' he said. 'But we must counter their heckling with our arguments.'[40]

Masaryk was prepared to use more than argument to defeat them. On 2 July, General Radola Gajda was arrested on spurious espionage charges and stripped of his rank. Czech fascists continued to indulge in street fights and violent attacks on left-wing party meetings, but Masaryk suppressed their activities with a mix of legal and extra-legal methods. In parliamentary elections, the Czech fascists never won more than two per cent of the national vote.

THE ASCENT OF Adolf Hitler in Germany dramatically altered Czechoslovakia's outlook. Most of Britain's conservative establishment disregarded the Nazi leader's rantings as theatrical bluster, but Masaryk and his foreign minister, Edvard Benes, entertained no such delusions.

Madeleine Albright, who would one day become the first woman to serve as US secretary of state, was born in Prague in the interwar years. Her father, Josef Korbel, worked in the Czechoslovak foreign ministry and in 1936 he was asked to accompany a delegation of Yugoslav scholars to visit Masaryk at his home.

Masaryk had suffered a stroke that had impaired his speech somewhat, but Korbel was struck by the old man's tall, dignified bearing, with his high-starched collars, wire-rimmed spectacles and trim Van Dyke beard. As Masaryk spoke with the Yugoslavs, Korbel's gaze roamed around the modestly furnished room, sweeping past the leather-bound volumes on the shelves, the roses on the mantlepiece, and then lit upon Masaryk's desk, where he saw two books: *Faust*, by Goethe, and Adolf Hitler's *Mein Kampf*.[41]

CHAPTER SEVEN

THE BLACK CROW

1935–1939

Nazi propaganda postcard 1938, showing the shaded
Sudeten German regions of Czechoslovakia.

The Second President

TOMAS MASARYK LIVED long enough to see his most cherished hopes for his country realised. Edvard Benes, the man who succeeded him as president, had to watch all those hopes burn to the ground.

The disaster was all the more shocking when Praguers later contemplated the breathtaking heights from which they'd fallen. In the first decades of the twentieth century, the symbols of modern

Prague had been the Skoda automobile, the Art Nouveau café, the Barrandov movie studios and the electric tram. The totems of the next era would be the tank, the cramped deportation train, the propaganda broadcast and the unmarked secret-police car.

DEDICATED, HUMOURLESS and utterly incorruptible, Edvard Benes (pronounced 'Ben-esh') was described by another diplomat as 'a cool realist, whose only serious consideration was what was good for his country'.[1] Like his mentor Masaryk, hard work and ambition had carried him from his poor rural childhood into the presidency. He neither drank nor smoked, and his wife, Hana, had to teach him how to talk and behave in polite society. As foreign minister, Benes was well briefed and dogged; in debates, he often prevailed by wearing his opponents down, explaining his lines of reasoning at length in his high-pitched voice.

When advancing age finally forced Masaryk to relinquish the presidency, Benes was the obvious successor. Those who raised concerns about his shortcomings to Masaryk were silenced by the old man's rejoinder: 'Gentlemen, if not Benes, then who?'[2] Benes was elected president by the National Assembly on 18 December 1935, just as a shadow had fallen on Czechoslovakia.

BENES AND MASARYK had always seen democratic France and Britain, as natural allies, which they hoped would buttress Czechoslovakia against an unstable Germany to its west, a radicalised Hungary to its south and a chaotic Russia to its east. The foundation stone of Czechoslovakia's national security was a Treaty of Mutual Assistance signed with France in 1925. There was no corresponding pact with London, but Benes fully expected that if France went to war on Czechoslovakia's behalf, then Britain would inevitably be drawn into the fight – a powerful deterrent for any would-be invader. But everything depended on France maintaining its resolve to contain Germany.

ADOLF HITLER INTENDED to test that resolve. The new German chancellor longed to seize the Czech lands and incorporate them by force into the Third Reich. Geographically, this had a certain logic to it: on the map, the Czech lands looked like a fish entering the mouth of a German shark. Just before his ascent to power, Hitler had told a confidant that Germany must have 'a steel-hard power centre' to ensure a decisive ascendancy over European nations. The Bohemian-Moravian basin would be colonised by German farmers, and the Czechs expelled from Central Europe.[3]

Hitler was eventually able to force his way into the Czech lands through the Sudetenland, the crescent of borderlands populated predominantly by German-speaking Bohemians and Moravians who had lived there for centuries. Although these areas had never been part of Germany, the three-million-strong Sudetendeutsche spoke German at home and at work, read German books and newspapers, and sent their children to German schools. For centuries, they had been ruled by a German-speaking monarchy in Vienna, until they woke up one day in 1918 to find themselves a minority in a new nation, governed from Prague by Czechs.

FOR MASARYK AND BENES, the question of how these millions of ethnic Germans might fit into their republic was an awkward one. National self-determination had been the fundamental moral principle behind the emergence of Czechoslovakia after the First World War. But if the compelling moral claim was to create a homeland for the Czech and Slovak peoples, did that not give the

Sudeten Germans the right to make similar claims for themselves? At Versailles, Benes tried to skate over the issue, giving vague assurances to the Allies that Czechoslovakia would be a kind of Switzerland of central Europe, a confederation of self-governing ethnic cantons, but that's not what happened.

Given that the Sudetenland held a quarter of Czechoslovakia's population and most of its industrial strength, Prague should have expended every effort to reach out warmly to the Sudeten Germans and make them feel at home in the new multi-ethnic republic. But Masaryk, in his inaugural address as president, uncharacteristically blundered, referring to the Sudetendeutsche patronisingly as 'our Germans', and describing them as a people 'who originally entered the country as immigrants and colonists'.

After that poor start, Masaryk vowed to do better to win over their loyalty. But the Prague government failed to make its ethnic German citizens feel and act like full participants in the state. The glad, triumphal language of the Czechs, and the loss of German primacy could not be ignored. 'The Czech landlord was friendly and tolerant,' noted historian Igor Lukes, 'but he made sure his Sudeten tenants knew who owned the house.'[4]

Some progress at integration was made in the 1920s: ethnic Germans served in the Czechoslovak cabinet, and the booming economy boosted confidence in the central government. A leading ethnic German politician of the time went so far as to declare, 'We have lived with the Czechs for a thousand years, and through economic, social, cultural and even racial ties, we are so closely connected with them that we really form one people. To use a homely metaphor: we form different strands in the same carpet.'[5]

But the carpet began to fray and tear under the stresses of the economic crisis of the early 1930s. The global depression hit the manufacturing industries in the Sudetenland particularly hard, leading to mass unemployment across the region, which was inevitably blamed on the government in Prague.

THE GREAT DEPRESSION also created mayhem across the border in Germany, radicalising voters and propelling the Nazis into power in 1933. Hitler wasted no time jump-starting the German economy with massive re-armament and public-works programs, funded by a complex shell game of deficit finance, which anticipated future returns from the plunder of conquered nations.

Germany's economic recovery, celebrated with nationalistic language and Nazi pageantry, could not help but make a powerful impression on their cousins over the border in the Sudetenland. Admiration for Hitler among the Sudeten Germans was by no means universal, and many Germans stood ready to defend Masaryk's democracy, but Prague appeared indifferent towards them. Public-works projects created to relieve unemployment appeared to favour Czech workers over ethnic Germans, and the new Czechoslovak Radio service broadcast almost entirely in Czech, leaving the Sudetenland areas receptive to blasts of Nazi propaganda from across the border.

THE DISGRUNTLED GERMAN minority in Czechoslovakia found its voice in a somewhat mousy former gymnastics instructor named Konrad Henlein. In October 1933, Henlein formed a movement that became the dominant political force in the region: the Sudeten German Party (SdP). Henlein was careful at first to declare his loyalty to Prague; his stated wish was not for integration with the German Reich, but for greater autonomy within the republic, a reasonable demand on the face of it. Henlein made frequent visits to London where he cultivated the good opinion of Britain's elites in a conservative suit, but at home, he took to addressing public rallies in the style of a Fuhrer, with banners and uniformed supporters.

THE TROUBLES IN THE Sudetenland worried Benes, who was at the same time receiving a stream of military intelligence on Germany's re-militarisation. In 1935, he took out a second insurance policy by signing a treaty with the Soviet Union. Benes had no illusions about the Soviet leader, Josef Stalin, whom he saw as a vicious medieval throwback to Ivan the Terrible. He also knew an alliance with Moscow would further alienate the Sudeten Germans and appal the British, but these considerations were trumped by the need to create a powerful double-edged deterrent against a German attack. An alliance with Stalin would deliver domestic benefits to Benes as well, forcing the local communists to abandon their subversive activities and rally behind his government.

Fingers of Fire and Hail

THE CZECHOSLOVAK Communist Party had emerged in 1921 from a revolutionary faction of the Social Democrats and was closely allied with the Soviet Union. Support for the party had climbed through the 1920s, but Stalin's erratic policy shifts and his murderous suppression of dissent were becoming ever more difficult to defend. In Prague, the party's slavish adherence to the Moscow line made it appear unpatriotic, and despite the crisis in world capitalism party membership fell dramatically in the five years after the Wall Street Crash, from a high of 155,000 members to just 55,000.[6] In its weakened state, the party's operations required a substantial monthly subsidy from the Soviet Union to stay afloat.[7]

The party's leader in Prague was a squat square-headed former carpenter named Klement Gottwald, who prevailed over his rivals by following the Stalinist line, no matter how wildly the Great Helmsman tacked and changed course. Accused in the National Assembly of being Moscow's stooge, Gottwald snarled, 'We go to Moscow to learn from the Russian Bolsheviks how to wring your necks. And you know that the Russian Bolsheviks are masters in this.'[8]

But after the treaty with Stalin was signed, Gottwald had to change his tune, and he suddenly became a Czech patriot and a strong supporter of Benes's foreign policy. He spoke up for the nation's territorial integrity and called on citizens to remember the legacy of Jan Hus. Prague's proletarian revolution would have to wait.

Prague's communists were a mix of party functionaries, factory workers and intellectuals. Much of the movement's appeal lay in its claims to scientific rigour and historical inevitability. Like Taborites awaiting the second coming, Prague's communists awaited the apocalyptic final agonies of capitalism, and the bright new dawn that would follow.

IT WAS THIS PROMISE of a heroic future, in which art, technology and ideology would converge to produce a new kind of human, that made Marxist thought irresistible to a new generation of artists and writers coming of age in the fast-moving twentieth century.

In 1920, a group of avant-garde Prague artists and poets formed a movement, Devetsil, that carried the banner for cultural and political progress. The Devetsil artists were excited by the new forms of popular culture, film and jazz, and were influenced by the competing modernisms of the early twentieth century: Cubism, Russian Constructivism, Italian Futurism and the German Bauhaus. But the Praguers were most powerfully drawn to French Surrealism, which encouraged them to explore the dreamlike realms under their city's skin.

SURREALISM AND PRAGUE were always a natural fit, and in early 1935 the city's writers and painters felt a flutter of excitement when word spread through bars and cafés that the founders of French surrealism, André Breton and Paul Eluard, were coming to town.

On 27 March, Breton, with his thick black hair and his long leather coat, stepped onto the platform of Prague's Wilson Station, accompanied by his new wife, Jacqueline, and Eluard, dressed more conservatively in a coat and tie. They were met by the Czech surrealist poet Vitezslav Nezval, who walked the visitors all over the city, through the Old Town, across the Charles Bridge and up to the castle.

Everywhere they looked, the French surrealists encountered strange and beautiful things: the stone saints on the bridge; the enigmatic symbols above the doors on Nerudova Street; the backwards clock in Josefov. Breton was particularly intrigued by the Golden Lane at Hradcany, and its reputation as an alchemists' ghetto.

Nezval introduced the Frenchmen to other Devetsil surrealists: writer-artists Karel Teige, Jindrich Styrsky and the painter Toyen. Born as Marie Cerminova, the androgynous Toyen would easily fit the contemporary gender description of 'non-binary'. Toyen's phantasmagoric work, which often featured sexually explicit images broken up into chaotic and absurd collages, was wild, even by today's standards.

For both the Czech and French surrealists, it was an intoxicating encounter. Breton gave lectures to packed halls and was interviewed by the local press and Czechoslovak radio. On his return to Paris, Breton wrote to Nezval to tell him that Prague had given him one of the most beautiful memories of his life.

THE CZECH AND FRENCH surrealists were aligned not just artistically, but politically as well. Their twin prophets were Karl Marx and Sigmund Freud, the pioneering psychoanalyst who had revealed the erotic and irrational currents running beneath the surface of polite society. Thomas Edison was greatly admired too, as a magician who had harnessed the power of electricity to bathe modern cities in dazzling light. Surrealism, science and socialism, they believed, were outgrowths of the same revolutionary spirit that would expose hidden and compelling truths and transfigure the modern human. They pinned their hopes on the Soviet Union as the harbinger of world revolution.

But although the surrealists in Prague and Paris were ready to put themselves in the service of the movement, it wasn't clear that the revolution would have them. Moscow had decreed that any art that strayed beyond the bounds of socialist realism was to be condemned. To Breton's dismay, the French Communist Party obediently followed Stalin's line and denounced surrealism as 'bourgeois formalism', a not particularly apt description of the sublimely weird work spilling onto the surrealists' canvases.

Breton had been a strong Communist Party supporter, but by the time of his arrival in Prague he was ready to acknowledge that the union between revolutionary art and politics was cracking. At a public lecture at Prague's City Library, he warned that Stalin's oppressive cultural decrees presented artists with a terrible choice:

'either they must give up interpreting and expressing the world in the ways that each of them finds the secret of within himself and himself alone … or they must give up collaborating on the practical plan of action for changing this world'.[9]

Breton published a tract denouncing Stalin. His co-signatories included Max Ernst, Salvador Dali, Dora Maar, René Magritte and Man Ray. Nezval and the other Czech surrealists refused to add their names to the letter, but most were, like Breton, ready to break with Stalin. Vitezslav Nezval, however, remained a party loyalist. A hastily convened meeting of the Prague Surrealist Group in March 1938 broke down with ugly accusations and counter-accusations, and the following day, Nezval announced the group had been dissolved, but they reconfigured the next day without him. Nezval, who had so beautifully described the city in his hallucinatory poem 'Prague with Fingers of Rain', walked away from surrealism forever, and became an obedient socialist-realist, composing hymns to Stalin.

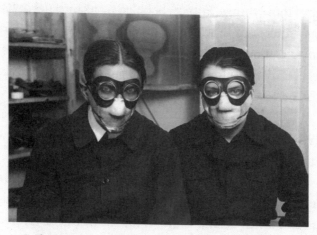

Jindrich Styrsky and Toyen with painters' masks, 1929.

*

We Will Remain Faithful

ONE OF THE MOST significant factors attracting Prague's avant-garde to international Marxism was its clear-cut hostility to fascism in general and Nazi revanchism in particular. The feeble response of the democracies to fascist aggression earnt their contempt.

In March 1936, Hitler violated the Treaty of Versailles provisions by sending his newly expanded Wehrmacht into the demilitarised Rhineland between France and Germany. The French army was still, on paper, the most powerful military force on the continent, but the French General Staff were mired in pessimism and warned the civilian leaders that an intervention would lead them straight back into the misery of prolonged trench warfare.

The terrible flaw in Benes's strategy was now exposed. The whole edifice of Czechoslovakia's national security rested on a stable and resolute France, but the French republic in the mid-1930s was neither of those things. France, hobbled by its internal divisions, was no longer interested in striking a punitive blow against Germany for its treaty violations, and had assumed a defensive posture. The treaty had deluded Benes into thinking his country was safer than it really was, and in the end proved to be worse than useless.

BENES'S EXPECTATION THAT Britain might stand with him against a newly militant Germany was also ill-founded. Although there was no defence pact between the two nations, Benes, the indomitable optimist, expected that in the event of a German attack, the Anglo–French relationship would work like a string, tugging Britain along to defend Czechoslovakia. But he had it exactly backwards: it would instead act as a leash that the British would pull on to restrain France from drawing the both of them into a new war with Germany.

Although Benes might have seen Britain as a natural ally in the club of European democracies, the sentiment was not widely reciprocated in Britain's Foreign Office, which regarded Czechoslovakia with a cool, unsympathetic eye, suspecting, quite correctly, that the president was trying to manipulate Britain into doing his bidding. Benes, irritating and unsociable, was widely disliked in Whitehall, even by opponents of German appeasement, one of whom described Benes as 'a blind little bat, who has done a lot of flapping in his night'.[10]

Benes's ambassador to London was Jan Masaryk, son of the republic's founder. Masaryk the younger was charming and spoke English fluently, but he soon realised Britain was unlikely to go to war on behalf of an oddly named foreign nation in faraway central Europe. Walking past No. 10 Downing Street one day, Masaryk pointed at the black door and told his companion, 'I spend most of my official time in there, explaining to the gentleman inside that Czechoslovakia is a country and not a contagious disease.'[11]

Winston Churchill was one of the few parliamentarians to speak in support of the Czechoslovak Republic. Churchill – a mangler of foreign languages, who referred to Benes as 'Herr Beans' – praised Masaryk and Benes from the backbench for having 're-founded an ancient nation … on the broad basis of Social Democracy and anti-Communism'.[12] But Churchill was on the backbench and was widely seen as an erratic old man whose time had passed.

ALARMED BY GERMAN AGGRESSION, Benes ordered the construction of a chain of concrete blockhouses reinforced with layers of boulders and debris along the northern and western borders of Bohemia, where the mountainous terrain offered excellent natural defences against an invading army. Between the blockhouses, rows of spiked anti-tank barricades nicknamed 'Czech hedgehogs' were laid alongside reams of barbed wire, which would ensnare an invading force and expose it to heavy artillery and machine-gun fire.

The catch was that most of these defensive emplacements ran through the mutinous Sudeten borderlands, and Prague's preparedness to fight Germany was interpreted as an act of hostility by the local German population. When the government, citing national security reasons, replaced local German postmasters and police officers with Czech officials, the clamour for tribal loyalty grew louder. German democrats who remained loyal to the republic were subjected to enormous social pressure to support Konrad Henlein's separatist SdP. In the May 1935 parliamentary elections, the SdP had won fifteen per cent of the national vote, giving them more seats than any other party. Ominously, some of the new SdP deputies appeared in parliament in jackboots.

Noting the increasingly radical mood of his followers, Henlein wrote a confidential letter to Berlin, offering to do what he could to place all the Bohemian lands in the hands of the Fuhrer.

THE HEALTH OF THE seemingly immortal Tomas Masaryk declined steeply after he left office, and on 14 September 1937 he died peacefully at his home. Under a cool, clear sky, President Benes and the Masaryk family followed the flag-draped coffin in its procession from the castle to Wenceslas Square. A million citizens lined the route. There had been nothing like it since the death of Charles IV.

At the funeral, Benes delivered an uncharacteristically emotional eulogy, calling for every citizen to work towards Masaryk's dream of a 'just, staunch, unconquered, developing, humanitarian democracy'. Looking up to the ghost of Masaryk he vowed, 'President-Liberator, to the bequest which you placed in our hands, we will remain faithful!'[13]

Great and Simple at the Same Time

DESPITE THE DARKENING international situation, Prague was in an upbeat mood in the summer of 1937. After years of stagnation, the economy had picked up and unemployment was falling. Prague's theatres were full, and its concert-hall season was oversubscribed. Shoppers bought fruit, flowers and toys beneath the coloured umbrellas of the Old Town markets. Fashion designer Hana Podolska, hailed as the Czech Coco Chanel, supervised the fitting of exquisite evening gowns on movie stars and socialites in her luxurious salon in the Lucerna Arcade. Praguers argued about politics and art in the city's famous cafés, while late-night revellers descended into Prague's cave-like nightclubs, 'where silhouettes floated past on a tide of cigarette smoke'.[14] Cinema-goers at the Kino Lucerna laughed at the rollicking anti-fascist satire *The World Belongs to Us*, starring the comedy duo George Voskovec and Jan Werich, who accidentally foil a fascist plot led by a former carnival barker.*

ANOTHER FILM LIGHTING up the screens in Prague that summer was the drama *People on the Floating Ice*, co-starring Lida Baarova, the most popular Czech film actress of her time. Lida, twenty-

---

* The negatives of this film were destroyed during the subsequent Nazi occupation.

four years old, was a star in Prague and Berlin. On screen she was enigmatic and reserved, like Greta Garbo. Her luminous presence attracted Hollywood talent spotters, who offered her a contract to make four films a year in the United States. Lida considered the offer but turned it down because her private life was in turmoil; she was embroiled in a dangerous love affair with one of the leading figures of the Third Reich.

Lida Baarova.

LIDA BAAROVA HAD BEGUN her movie career at Prague's Barrandov Studios. In 1934, she was cast in the German film *Barcarole* as Giacinta, the most beautiful woman in Venice. Her co-star was Gustav Frohlich, the handsome star of the classic science-fiction film *Metropolis*. They became engaged and moved in together.

One day in Berlin, production on the set of *Barcarole* came to a halt when the new chancellor of Germany, Adolf Hitler, visited the studio. Hitler fixed his gaze on Lida, which unnerved her. Afterwards, she received an invitation to join the Fuhrer for tea in his office in the Chancellery building. As the star and the dictator sipped from their teacups, Hitler asked her if she would like to stop being a Czech and become a German. She politely refused. Then Hitler shyly confessed that she reminded him of another woman who had once been very important to him.

'When I saw you at the studio,' he said, 'I was stunned. The photograph that stands always on my desk came to life.' It was, she later discovered, a picture of Hitler's niece and former lover Geli Raubal, who had found his obsessive attention suffocating and had apparently shot herself in the heart.

After an awkward silence, Lida said, 'I'm extremely sorry.' Then she left.[15]

AS PROMINENT FILM STARS, Lida and her lover, Frohlich, attended extravagant parties hosted by Joseph Goebbels, Hitler's propaganda minister. Goebbels was fascinated by Lida's cool beauty, her almond eyes and high cheekbones, and the two became secret lovers. Lida claimed she was undone by his penetrating voice: 'I felt a light tingling in my back, as if his words were trying to stroke my body.'

Hoping to impress her with his mastery over an audience, Goebbels invited her to watch him deliver an important party speech. He promised that every time he touched his lips with his handkerchief, he would be thinking of her. The next day, Goebbels thundered from the podium, 'The Jew is a parasite! A destroyer of culture!' Then he pulled the handkerchief from his suit pocket and gently dabbed his lips.[16]

GOEBBELS BEGAN TO FANTASISE about abandoning his wife and children and starting a new life with Lida in Tokyo as the Reich's ambassador to Japan. When he put this to his wife, Magda, she went straight to the Chancellery to complain to Hitler. The Fuhrer was aghast. The unmarried, childless Fuhrer enjoyed the easy comfort of being able to step in and out of the Goebbels' family life as he pleased. More than that, Nazi propaganda had held up the Goebbels family as a role model. Magda had given birth to four children, with a fifth on the way, and had been awarded the Nazi Order of Motherhood. A breakup of their marriage would be a public scandal.

After Magda left, Hitler hauled in his propaganda minister. It was an uncomfortable meeting for both men; their relationship was that of cult leader to an adoring acolyte. 'Adolf Hitler,' Goebbels had once declared in his diary, 'I love you because you are both great and simple at the same time. What one calls a genius.'[17] Now he was torn between his idol and his lover. He begged to be released from his post and be allowed to divorce his wife, but Hitler pounded his fist on the desk and snapped, 'He who creates history has no right to a personal life!'[18]

Goebbels mournfully bowed to his leader's demand and left the room. 'And now a new life is beginning,' he wrote in his diary that night. 'A hard, tough life, dedicated to nothing but duty. My youth is over.'[19]

WHEN LIDA WAS TOLD of Hitler's demand, she became frantic and threatened to kill herself. 'My wife is a devil,' Goebbels told her over the phone, helplessly.

Lida was advised by the police to leave Germany for her own safety. She hurried home to Prague, to the family home: an airy Art Deco mansion paid for by her earnings as a movie star. Milos Havel, the founder of Barrandov Studios (and Vaclav's uncle) welcomed her back, but she was snubbed by her former friends and colleagues, who had heard of her affair with the fascist Goebbels.

Lida now regretted turning Hollywood down. She came to believe that if she'd gone to America, she could have been as famous as Marlene Dietrich. Dietrich, however, had impeccable anti-Nazi credentials and Lida did not.

The Dark Year

IN EARLY NOVEMBER 1937, Hitler told his general staff he was ready to create that 'steel-hard power centre' in central Europe, by engulfing Austria and Czechoslovakia. He told his generals he believed the British were ready to give up on the Czechs. The generals were sceptical, until Lord Halifax arrived from London two weeks later and confirmed it.

Halifax, a close confidant of British prime minister Neville Chamberlain, had flown to Berlin and caught the train up to Berchtesgaden, where he told Hitler that a variation in national boundaries would be acceptable to Britain, provided it was not based on force. This represented a major change in British foreign policy and amounted to giving Hitler a free hand to pursue territorial gains in central Europe.

On the train out of Berchtesgaden, Halifax penned an optimistic assessment of the meeting for Chamberlain. He felt sure, he wrote, that Hitler was sincere when he said he did not want war.[20] Several months later, Halifax was promoted to foreign secretary.

ON 20 FEBRUARY 1938, Hitler declared to the Reichstag that over ten million Germans in Austria and Czechoslovakia were suffering

intolerable persecution, and asserted his right to 'defend' those Germans, regardless of where they lived. His homeland of Austria was his first target.

On 11 March, the chancellor in Vienna was overthrown and the Austrian Nazi leader Arthur Seyss-Inquart issued a 'request' for German military assistance. At 5.30 am the next day, the Wehrmacht crossed the border, and Austria was incorporated into the German Reich.

The same day, a small, unmarked plane flew over the Czech border and dropped a shower of leaflets with the message: *Sagen Sie in Prag, Hitler lasst Sie grussen* – 'Tell them in Prague, Hitler sends his greetings'.[21]

JAN MASARYK CAME at once to see Halifax, but the British foreign secretary saw no reason for alarm. He told the ambassador he had received private assurances from Hitler's people that the absorption of the German Austrians had been a 'family affair'. But the Czechs were a different people and of no interest to them. Halifax asked Masaryk for his opinion of Hitler's assurances. 'Even a boa constrictor needs a few weeks of rest after it has filled its belly,' he replied.

'What would you do if Germany attacked?' Halifax asked.

'We'll shoot,' said Masaryk.[22]

BENES STILL HAD FAITH the French would stand with them against Germany, if it came to that. France's prime minister, Leon Blum, had only recently given Prague several rock-solid assurances they would honour their treaty, no matter what. Blum's government, however, fell two weeks later. The new prime minister, Edouard Daladier, and foreign minister, Georges Bonnet, were defeatists who saw the alliance with Prague as a painful liability that risked dragging them into a war that neither the French nor the British wanted to fight. Benes was increasingly portrayed in the French press as a dangerous fool, ready to risk a European war over tiny scraps of land.

Chamberlain and Daladier jointly pressed Benes to make major concessions to the Sudeten Germans, in order to secure the peace, but this would prove an impossibility. On 28 March, Konrad Henlein had been summoned to Berlin, where Hitler promised him the Sudeten problem would be settled 'in the not too distant future'. In the meantime, he said that Henlein should inflame tensions, by making unacceptable demands of Prague.

'So we must always demand so much that we can never be satisfied?' Henlein asked. Hitler indicated his agreement.[23]

THE NAZI PROPAGANDA machine now bombarded the international press with concocted stories of Czech atrocities against ethnic Germans. Throughout March, Henlein held mass rallies in the Sudetenland attended by crowds chanting, *Ein Volk, ein Reich, ein Führer!*[24] On 27 April, he demanded that Prague grant complete autonomy for ethnic Germans wherever they might live, in the Sudetenland, Prague or elsewhere, and official tolerance for National Socialism: an impossible demand.

Benes felt himself being pushed into a corner. Under pressure from France and Britain, he let Henlein know he was open to negotiations, although how a patchwork of Nazi enclaves was to exist within a democratic Czechoslovakia was unclear. Benes was playing for more time to re-arm. He consoled himself with the expectation that if Hitler attacked, the Czechoslovak forces, dug into their Sudeten defences, could hold the invaders at bay for several weeks, by which time the French and the Soviets would surely come to their aid.

May Crisis

ON THE AFTERNOON of 20 May, Prague's high command received reports that German tanks and troops were assembling at various points along the border. Benes ordered a partial mobilisation of the armed forces, and within hours, 200,000 trained reservists accompanied by battalions of mechanised infantry were on their way to their mountain fortifications. Foreign observers noted the Czechoslovak military's 'clock-like precision'.[25]

Czechoslovakia now had thirty equipped and trained army divisions, backed by armoured units and a modernised air force of more than 1200 planes.[26] The message was clear: Czechoslovakians would not fling open their gates to Hitler as Austria had done. They would dig in and fight.

Daladier was roused to warn Germany that France would stand by its treaty obligations to Czechoslovakia. Even Halifax thought it necessary to state that Britain might well become involved too. Hitler's foreign minister, Joachim von Ribbentrop, issued a furious denial that any invasion was imminent and was doubly angered when the denials were treated with scepticism.

FOR ONCE, BERLIN WAS speaking the truth. There were no German plans to invade that weekend. The jumpy Czechs had overreacted to a collision of several erroneous intelligence reports and some vague threats embedded in a piece of anti-Czech propaganda. Even though nothing happened, the impression that the Nazis had been poised to attack couldn't be erased from world opinion.

For Germany, the non-event was a propaganda disaster: the world was given the impression that the Nazi bullies had been thwarted by Benes standing shoulder to shoulder with the Western democracies.

Hitler sank into a black mood for days, brooding on the

embarrassment. On 28 May, he summoned his generals and told them that preparations for an invasion must be completed by no later than 1 October. 'I am utterly determined,' he said, 'that Czechoslovakia should disappear from the map.'[27]

PRESIDENT BENES SAW the dummy crisis of May as a successful dress rehearsal for a real German attack. The élan shown by his own well-trained forces, combined with the solid backing he'd received from France and Britain, bolstered his confidence that his country could stare Hitler down.

But it was all an illusion. Without the solid support of the British, the French would look for excuses to back away from their obligations to Prague. And British support would not be forthcoming. Prime Minister Neville Chamberlain had concluded that Czechoslovakia's situation was hopeless. In a candid letter to his sister, he wrote:

> You have only to look at the map to see that nothing that France or we could do could possibly save Czecho-Slovakia from being over-run by the Germans if they wanted to do it. The Austrian frontier is practically open; the great Skoda munition works are within easy bombing distance of the German aerodromes, the railways all pass through German territory, Russia is 100 miles away. Therefore, we could not help Czecho-Slovakia – she would simply be a pretext for going to war with Germany.[28]

Moreover, the distasteful treaty Benes had signed with the Soviet Union lost much of its value after a paranoid Stalin purged his Red Army command, ordering its most talented senior officers to be shot or beaten to death. The terrorised Soviet military would take years to rebuild. In any case, there was no shared border with the Soviet

Union. A military rescue force would have to enter the country through Poland, a move the Poles would never consent to.

✳

The Hangman with His Little Bag

BRITAIN'S LEADERSHIP HAD now formed a settled view that Benes was an intransigent nationalist and a threat to world peace. On 20 July, in an effort to push Benes along, the British ambassador to Prague, Sir Basil Newton, suggested that an 'independent' mediator be brought in to negotiate a solution between Benes and Henlein's SdP.

Benes, visibly upset, told Newton the British proposal was unacceptable, but when Newton threatened to publicise the offer of mediation alongside Prague's rejection of it, Benes backed down. Chamberlain promptly announced the mission to the House of Commons, but claimed falsely that it was Britain that had generously agreed to provide a mediator at *Prague's* request. It was one of many acts of British cynicism and treachery that Benes would remember after the war.

The mediator chosen by the British, Lord Runciman of Doxford, was an aristocrat in a winged collar and a top hat, who undertook his mission in a fog of ignorance, arrogance and naïveté. He and his entourage arrived at Wilson Station on 3 August, and were greeted on the platform by the Mayor of Prague, President Benes's chief of staff, and a delegation from the SdP, invited by Newton. When the correspondent for London's *Daily Telegraph* glimpsed Runciman, he muttered a line from Oscar Wilde's 'The Ballad of Reading Gaol': 'The hangman with his little bag came creeping through the gloom.'[29]

Runciman held several meetings with Benes and other government leaders at Prague Castle, described as 'brief and distinctly cool',[30] then settled in for a lengthy conversation with the SdP representatives at the Hotel Alcron. SdP deputy Karl Hermann Frank complained that the crisis was entirely of Prague's making, and no concessions from Benes would ever be acceptable.[31] Frank's statement should have made it clear to Runciman that mediation was impossible but still he pressed on.

A desperate Benes decided to call the SdP's bluff by offering them everything they wanted short of secession. On 24 August, he put forward a plan to divide the country into self-governing territories, three of which would be German. This flummoxed the SdP, which was still under instructions to demand so much they could never be satisfied. 'My God,' gasped Frank, 'they have given us everything!'[32]

Henlein and Frank rushed to Berlin for further instructions and were told to quickly find a pretext to break off negotiations. They put forward a story that one of their representatives had been hit by a Czech police officer, which meant further talks were out of the question. On 15 September, Chamberlain called Runciman and told him to come home.

RUNCIMAN'S REPORT, delivered A week later, ignored Benes's latest offer to the SdP. The viscount instead expressed his sympathy for the 'Sudeten case', and condemned Benes's government for failing to address the Germans' grievances. Disregarding the fact that under Czechoslovak law even an ethnic minority like the Sudetendeutsche enjoyed rights and protections unavailable in the Third Reich, Runciman recommended that the frontier districts be handed over to Germany, 'promptly and without procrastination'.[33]

*

WAR NOW SEEMED CLOSE, and the strain was felt across the capital. Gas masks were distributed. Jewish families crowded the train stations and the airport, desperately trying to get out.

Benes delivered a radio speech on 10 September, calling for calm and goodwill. 'Let us be prepared,' he concluded, 'for every sacrifice, but let us also be optimists through the darkest days.'[34]

A British journalist, W. Robinson, heard the speech in a hushed café, listening along with the other patrons to the broadcast. Afterwards, the café-goers broke out into anxious discussions, and Robinson stepped outside. In the rainy darkness, he saw a long, trailing procession of clerics, nuns and church-goers, filing along the street. The priests held aloft a precious black-and-gold statue of the Madonna and Child known as the Palladium of Bohemia. The icon was said to have been a gift from St Methodius, and to have been worn by St Wenceslas on the day of his murder, a thousand years earlier.

Like its ancient Trojan namesake, the Bohemian palladium was revered as a sacred protective totem of the city. Robinson was moved by the longing of the marchers to be delivered into a state of peace and safety. The parade was, he thought, 'a national act of intercession by a people in deadly peril'.[35]

A Faraway Country

ON 12 SEPTEMBER, Adolf Hitler addressed the Nazi Party rally in Nuremberg, promising he would soon have to do something about the anti-German 'terror' in Czechoslovakia. The speech was the cue for an uprising in the Sudeten territories. Thousands of SdP paramilitaries took to the streets, killing Czech policemen and attacking railway stations and post offices. The government in

Prague declared a state of emergency and sent in thousands of police officers. Henlein and the other SdP leaders evaded arrest by fleeing over the border into Germany.

Now that the SdP leaders were gone, their hold on the territory began to evaporate. Many Sudeten Germans were relieved to see the back of Henlein and his henchmen, and there was talk of forming a new moderate German party to negotiate with Benes.

AND YET, DESPITE THE improving prospects for peace, Neville Chamberlain concluded at this moment the situation was hopeless and required his dramatic intervention to save the day. Chamberlain decided to press the button on a secret plan he'd been holding in reserve – to fly to Germany to meet Hitler personally and resolve the Sudeten crisis man to man. Hitler quickly agreed, and Chamberlain flew out the next day.

There were three meetings in total between Hitler and Chamberlain in Germany, culminating in the infamous document known as the Munich Agreement, a debacle neatly summarised by historian Norman Davies: 'under pressure from the ruthless, the clueless combined with the spineless to achieve the worthless'.[36]

Chamberlain, confident that he could 'handle' Hitler, met the Fuhrer alone for their first meeting at Berchtesgaden on 15 September. Hitler complained that the question of the Sudeten Germans 'was like a spearhead' in his side. 'I am willing to risk a world war,' he said, 'than to allow this to drag on.'

Chamberlain coolly admitted he personally didn't care one way or the other about the separation of the Sudetenland from the rest of Czechoslovakia, but he needed to think through the practicalities, and he would have to consult his cabinet colleagues and the French government.

He flew back to London, and the next day invited Daladier and Bonnet to Downing Street to persuade them to accept a German takeover of the Sudetenland. It never occurred to him to consult Prague as well. After a half-hearted protest, Daladier relented. Both governments would lean on Benes to comply with Hitler's demands. Meanwhile, Jan Masaryk was frantically calling everyone he knew in the British government, trying to find out what was going on. 'They're talking about us without us,' he told his secretary.[37]

BASIL NEWTON AND Victor de Lacroix, the British and French ambassadors in Prague, were sent to the castle with a note for Benes, telling him he must surrender the Sudeten territories to Germany. Both governments would magnanimously offer to guarantee the new borders of Czechoslovakia if he did. Benes, aghast, immediately contacted the Soviet legation to ask if they would meet their treaty obligations and stand with his country. The Soviets gave no clear answer other than to suggest that if Czechoslovakia lacked French support, it should make its case to the League of Nations. Furious with his worse than worthless 'allies', Benes fired off a reply to London and Paris rejecting their proposal and went off to bed.

The president was woken an hour later by a staff member with news that the envoys were on their way back to the castle. Newton and Lacroix entered his study at 2 am to tell him his rejection of their proposal was unacceptable. Newton said that war was imminent and the clock was ticking. They wanted Prague to surrender the Sudetenland on these 'friendly' terms, before Hitler simply went in and took it for himself. Ambassador Lacroix wept with shame. When pressed, he was forced to admit that if Germany attacked Czechoslovakia, France would not come to her aid, no matter what their treaty said. Benes warned the envoys their policy would have grave consequences for all of Europe and then dismissed them. Lacroix was still weeping as he left.

BENES'S CABINET DEBATED the ultimatum all morning. At noon, Newton and Lacroix were back once again at the castle, demanding an answer. The mood of the envoys had shifted from embarrassment to impatience. Benes was deeply offended by Newton, who stood in the door of his library, arrogantly wondering aloud what kind of government could take so long to make up its mind.

At 5 pm, Benes told the envoys the Czechoslovak government would 'sadly accept' the French and British ultimatum, with two crucial provisos: both nations must thereafter guarantee the survival of what was left of Czechoslovakia, and the Prague government would need to sign off on the details of the handover.

On hearing the news of this capitulation, outraged Praguers gathered at the castle gates, singing the national anthem, chanting, 'Give us weapons! Give us weapons!'[38] After midnight, the state police were called in to clear the demonstrators from the castle precinct. Benes, completely spent, slept through the whole uproar.

On awakening, the president appointed a new prime minister, General Jan Syrovy, a well-known war hero who wore an eye-patch. The news was greeted with scenes of jubilation in the streets by demonstrators who saw Syrovy's appointment as an indication that the government was now willing to fight.

CHAMBERLAIN, MEANWHILE, was back in Germany with Benes's capitulation in his pocket. Chamberlain expected Hitler to be pleased with the prize he had just handed to him but, to his shock, the Fuhrer said these arrangements would no longer work and everything had to be resolved within the next few days.

Czechoslovakia, he said, was an unnatural state that had no right to exist. He would simply go ahead and take the Sudetenland without their assistance. 'The Czechs,' he said, 'must be annihilated.'[39]

Chamberlain protested he had given Hitler everything he'd asked for at considerable political cost to himself, but Hitler was adamant. The prime minister flew back to London deeply depressed.

CHAMBERLAIN WAS READY to resign rather than lead the country into war, but his cabinet was at last moving towards taking a stand. Several ministers wondered if Hitler had somehow mesmerised their prime minister.

In Prague, the mood had also shifted decisively. Benes was now ready to defy Hitler, alone if necessary. Jan Masaryk handed a letter to Halifax, proclaiming, 'Against these new and cruel demands my government feel bound to make their utmost resistance and we shall do so, God helping. The nation of St Wenceslas, Jan Hus and Tomas Masaryk will not be a nation of slaves.'[40]

Halifax, using a diplomatic double negative, told Masaryk that the British government would no longer oppose a general mobilisation of the Czech military. France's Foreign Ministry also encouraged Benes to mobilise.

Benes grasped at these messages of support from London and Paris like a drowning man handed a lifeline. 'When he read the message', his private secretary recalled, 'he stood motionless for a while and looked at it intently ... Then he put the note on a desk, said "yes", and started pacing up and down the room. Then he returned to the desk, picked up the note, and again said "yes, yes" several times, and started walking. I noticed that he was excited as never before.' The president then said, 'This means war! The English have advised us to mobilise!'[41]

Tanks and trainloads of troops were again sent directly to the border, and the city observed a blackout in anticipation of a possible German bomber attack.

At midnight, government ministers left Prague Castle and saw, for the first time, a completely dark city at their feet. Beyond the bluff of Hradcany there was only an eerie void.

BRITAIN TOO WAS READYING for war with Germany, but the prime minister confessed to Halifax, 'I'm wobbling all over the place.' That night, on 27 September, Chamberlain famously expressed his anguish in a BBC radio broadcast: 'How horrible, fantastic, incredible it is that we should be digging trenches and trying on gas masks here because of a quarrel in a faraway country between people of whom we know nothing.'[42]

Entirely Alone

ON THE EVENING OF 28 September, President Benes was in the midst of frantic war preparations, when he learnt that Chamberlain and Daladier were on their way to Germany to meet with Hitler and the Italian dictator Benito Mussolini, in a last-ditch effort to rescue the peace.

Chamberlain had received a new message from Hitler that had given him fresh hope. Germany, it said, was now prepared to accept the British proposal and was offering a free plebiscite vote in the Sudeten regions. Hitler was even prepared to guarantee the borders of the new Czechoslovakia. It was 'the last tuft of grass on the very verge of the precipice', as Chamberlain later put it, and he snatched at it.[43] The leaders were to meet in the Bavarian city of Munich. Benes was not invited.

The worried president sent two of his emissaries from Prague to Munich. They arrived late in the afternoon and were not admitted to the conference building. Instead they waited in their hotel room for news, closely watched over by Hitler's Gestapo.

At 7 pm, a British diplomat stopped by to warn the Czechs that the outcome of the talks was likely to be worse for them than expected. Then, at ten o'clock, Chamberlain's senior advisor, Sir Horace Wilson, arrived to outline the agreement forged by the four leaders: the Sudeten territory was to be entirely surrendered to Germany; no plebiscite was to be held; some 800,000 Czechs were to be absorbed into the Reich along with the German population; and the elaborate frontier emplacements in the Sudetenland were to be surrendered to Germany.

The Czechs raised their voices in objection, but Wilson's offsider scolded them: 'Should you reject this plan you'll be dealing with Germany completely on your own. The French will put it to you more elegantly,' he scoffed, 'but believe me, they are in complete agreement with us.'[44]

At 1.30 am, Chamberlain invited the Czech envoys into his hotel suite. The British prime minister was tired, he said, but 'pleasantly tired'. He yawned repeatedly and told them it was the best possible deal he could get for them. Daladier, deeply ashamed, stared at his fingernails.

BENES WAS TAKING HIS bath at the castle when he was given the news: the Germans would enter the Sudeten territories at midnight. The cabinet held an emergency meeting where a distressed Prime

Minister Syrovy told the ministers that the Allies had given them a choice between being murdered and committing suicide.

At this critical moment, Benes's generals urged him to fight, arguing that if they did so, the French and British people would eventually force their governments to come to their aid. But Benes, sick at heart, tormented by weeks and months of unrelenting pressure and disappointment, gave way.

Yes, he said, Czechoslovakia could defy all of Europe and fight alone, but the result would be the destruction of the nation. All he could do was recommend they accept the Munich ultimatum.

PRIME MINISTER SYROVY delivered an agonised broadcast at five o'clock that afternoon. People openly wept as they heard the old warrior's speech through the public-address system in Wenceslas Square:

> *I am passing through the saddest moment of my life, for I am fulfilling a most painful duty, a duty which for me is worse than death … We were confronted with a choice between desperate and hopeless defence … and acceptance of the conditions imposed on us under pressure and without war, which in their mercilessness are unexampled in history. We were abandoned. We stood entirely alone.*[45]

THAT NIGHT, THE CZECHOSLOVAK army began its withdrawal from the mountain fortresses in the Sudetenland. At 2 pm the next day, Hitler's Wehrmacht rolled across the border to be welcomed by a sea of swastika flags. Thousands of Sudeten Jews, Czechs and

German democrats dropped everything and ran towards Prague. But Czechoslovakia was now a shrunken remnant of its former self, economically weak and militarily defenceless. The road to Prague lay open.

Nazi Germany enters the Sudetenland, 1938.

MUSSOLINI HAD TOLD DALADIER he would be applauded on his return to Paris, but the French premier was ashamed for having betrayed an ally. He was shocked to hear the crowds at Le Bourget airport chanting '*Vive Daladier! Vive la paix!*' 'The blind fools,' he muttered.[46]

In London, the cheers were thunderous. Chamberlain let himself get so carried away, he leant out his Downing Street window and told the ecstatic crowd he had secured 'peace for our time', a lapse he soon regretted.[47]

A grim Winston Churchill ruined the festive atmosphere in the House of Commons, declaring, 'We have sustained a total and unmitigated defeat ... Silent, mournful, abandoned, broken, Czechoslovakia recedes into the darkness.'[48]

✳

BENES'S SURRENDER TO the Munich ultimatum struck a deep wound upon the Czech psyche that lingers even today. Philosopher Jan Patocka, who lived through the crisis, was unforgiving in his assessment of Benes. 'The general staff told him that we would be defeated if we fought alone, but that nevertheless we must dare it against all. For all that, he gave it up. He broke the moral backbone of the society, which was prepared to fight.'[49]

Winston Churchill also thought Benes was wrong to surrender. 'Once fighting had begun,' he wrote, 'France would have moved to his aid in a surge of national passion, and Britain would have rallied to France almost immediately.'[50] But the Allies had repeatedly declined to check Hitler's aggression; Benes can surely be forgiven for not placing his hopes on a sudden recovery of French and British valour. And to heap responsibility onto the shoulders of Benes, a man forced into an impossible dilemma, is to blame the victim and not the true criminals.

Czechs still torment themselves playing the 'what if ...?' game: what might have happened if Benes had flung the Munich Agreement back in the faces of its authors and ordered his divisions to dig in and fight to the death? Former US secretary of state Madeleine Albright, who was an infant in Prague at the time of the Munich Agreement, tried to game out the likely consequences in her memoir *Prague Winter*. She thought the German Wehrmacht would have prevailed eventually, but not before being badly mauled by a well-entrenched Czechoslovak army that had everything to fight for.

Albright concluded that although the country would have endured untold suffering, its ethos would have emerged unscathed, which might have seemed like thin compensation for the dead and their families, and for the likely destruction of Prague. Her father the diplomat lamented that 'in her hour of crisis, Czechoslovakia had as her president not a leader, but a negotiator'.[51]

The Second Republic

FOUR DAYS AFTER NAZI Germany occupied the Sudetenland Benes resigned the presidency and on 22 October flew to London, where he and Hana moved into a spacious villa in Putney. In the company of friends, Benes raged at his treacherous allies and neighbours, and predicted they would be the next to suffer. 'Poland will be the first to be hit. France will suffer terribly for having betrayed us, wait for that … Chamberlain will live to see the consequences of his appeasement … Hitler will attack them all, the West and Russia as well, and finally America will come in.'[52]

Benes's replacement at Prague Castle, Dr Emil Hacha, was a retired Supreme Court justice who neither wanted the presidency nor was capable of offering any resistance to Nazi demands. Praguers joked that if Hacha was handed the menu at a dinner with Goering, he would ask, 'Where do I sign?'

After taking up residence at the castle, the new president consoled himself with the thought that the city and the nation had avoided destruction. He wrote to a friend, 'Still, as you know, [the statue of] Saint Wenceslas is still standing in its place, Charles Bridge is still standing, too, the castle district was not blown "into the air" and hundreds of thousands of our young people are still breathing and living.'[53]

The new government, made up mostly of Catholic reactionaries, did everything in its power to appease Hitler. Elements in Czech society that had always felt a sneaking affinity with fascism and anti-Semitism came to the fore. State censorship was introduced along with an enabling act that allowed the government to rule by decree. The Czechoslovak Communist Party was banned and Klement Gottwald fled to the Soviet Union. Masaryk's vision of a tolerant, democratic Czechoslovakia was as dead as he was. 'Every feature of liberalism and democracy,' wrote US diplomat George Kennan, 'is hopelessly and irretrievably discredited.'[54]

Attempting to keep on Hitler's good side, Hacha's government dismissed its Jewish civil servants. 'Non-Aryans' in business and the professions were pushed out of their jobs, even though there was no official definition of what constituted an 'Aryan'. A law was passed to establish two labour camps to intern the Czech Roma people, who were characterised as 'nomadic vagabonds who avoid work'.[55] Only one in twenty would survive the coming cataclysm.

As the nightmare year of 1938 came to a close, Jewish Praguers succumbed to despair. Some Jewish industrialists chose to simply drop everything and get out. Rudolf Thomas, the editor of the liberal newspaper *Prager Tagblatt*, lost all hope and swallowed a lethal dose of sleeping pills alongside his wife.[56]

JUST BEFORE CHRISTMAS, a young English stockbroker named Nicholas Winton was invited to Prague and shown around the city's refugee camps populated by those forced to flee from the Nazi-occupied Sudetenland.

Winton became deeply worried about the Jewish children in the camps, and what might happen to them should they fall into the grasp of the Nazis. Fearing he was running out of time, Winton took a room at the Grand Hotel Evropa, where he and several colleagues frantically lobbied democratic governments to take in the refugee children.

The United States, Australia and New Zealand refused, so Winton turned to the British government, citing a new law that permitted the entry of refugee children. Each child would require a foster parent and a fifty-pound guarantee.

Hearing of the heroic 'Englishman of Wenceslas Square', desperate parents came to the hotel to beg him to include their children in the migration plan, known as the Czech Kindertransport. But of the 6000 or so names on his list, only 669 would escape.

THE SECOND CZECHO-SLOVAK Republic had included a hyphen in its name to appeal to the Slovak population, which was nonetheless drifting further away from Prague. In March 1939, Hitler summoned the Slovak leader Josef Tiso to Berlin and advised him to declare independence and to ask for the protection of the German Reich. Otherwise, Hitler said, he would simply hand Slovakia over to the Hungarians. Tiso readily agreed.

With his country falling apart, President Hacha asked to meet with Hitler to clarify the situation. He and his entourage arrived in Berlin at 10 pm on 14 March, and were kept waiting at the Hotel Adlon for hours while Hitler watched a movie in the Chancellery. Hacha was finally received by Hitler at 1.15 am and bluntly informed that Bohemia and Moravia had to be entirely incorporated into the Reich and that the German army would invade at dawn. His colour rising, the Fuhrer shrieked that if Hacha didn't want Czech blood to be spilt, he should order his army to stand down at once. Hacha collapsed into an armchair, as grey as a stone. Hermann Goering smiled, took the old man by the hand and said softly that Prague was a beautiful city and it would be a shame if the Luftwaffe had to flatten it just to make a point.

With that, Hacha trembled and passed out. Fearing the Czech president had suffered a heart attack, and that he would be accused of murder, Goering called in Hitler's private physician, Theodor Morell, who injected Hacha with a methamphetamine cocktail. When Hacha revived, he was handed a telephone and told to call his ministers in Prague to advise surrender. After a second injection from Morell, Hacha signed the document thrust in front of him, placing his country entirely in the hands of Adolf Hitler.

IN PRAGUE, THE CHIEF of military intelligence, Frantisek Moravec, received a telephone call from the Czech military attaché in Berlin, warning him of the imminent German invasion. Moravec, a Benes loyalist, had been preparing for this day. Putting down the phone, he convened his most trusted staff members and asked them to gather as many intelligence documents as they could carry. That night, he and his ten colleagues flew to London, where they handed over the precious cargo of agents' files, technical equipment, codes and cyphers to Britain's Secret Intelligence Service.

HITLER'S ARMY ENTERED Prague in the early hours of that morning, in the midst of a snowstorm. At daybreak, columns of motorised infantry, motorcycles and armoured vehicles clattered through the icy slush of the streets, while Goering's Luftwaffe roared across the sky. US diplomat George Kennan saw Czech women walking through the snow, weeping into their handkerchiefs.

That morning, a Jewish friend pounded on Kennan's door, asking for asylum. The United States was still a neutral power so Kennan had to refuse, but said his friend could stay at least until the authorities demanded he be handed over. Kennan watched his terrified friend pace from room to room, chain smoking, unable to eat; his brother and sister-in-law had already killed themselves and he wondered out loud whether he should do the same.[57]

At mid-morning, German forces rolled into Wenceslas Square. The spectacle was reported live to air from a balcony of the Grand Hotel Evropa by radio broadcaster Frantisek Kocourek. To him, it seemed an avatar of death had cast a shadow over the city.

From somewhere far away, a huge, black crow has flown into Prague. I have seen it spread its wings and sweep down above the square over the searchlights and listening devices being paraded here by the German army.[58]

Horrified Czechs mostly remained indoors. Photos of those who came out to watch the motorised units roaring through the cobblestoned streets show a range of responses: Bohemian Germans hail the invaders with the Nazi salute. Other faces in the crowd are contorted in grief, fists raised in helpless protest.

At Prague's Wilson Station, the last Kindertransport train was preparing to leave with a contingent of 250 Jewish children, but after the announcement of the invasion the train disappeared. Nicholas Winton later recalled, 'We had 250 families waiting at Liverpool Street [in London] that day in vain. If the train had been a day earlier, it would have come through. Not a single one of those children was heard of again.'[59]

IN THE LATE AFTERNOON, Hitler's motorcade entered Prague and carried him up to the castle in triumph. Placing both hands on the sill of an open window, like a draftsman at his table, he surveyed the conquered city. Hitler, the thwarted architect, was displeased by the sight of the mini-Eiffel Tower on Petrin Hill. 'The lookout tower on that hill has to go,' he ordered. 'It spoils the overall effect.'[60] *

Hitler at Prague Castle, 1939.

---

* The tower on Petrin Hill remains there to this day.

THAT NIGHT, HITLER slept in the great keep of the kings of Bohemia, the former home of St Wenceslas and Tomas Masaryk. The next morning, with the German swastika fluttering over the castle, he proclaimed the Czech lands would be incorporated into Greater Germany as the Reich Protectorate of Bohemia and Moravia.

Czechoslovakia had ceased to exist.

CHAPTER EIGHT

FROM DARKNESS INTO DARKNESS

1939–1948

The Czernin Palace.

The Black Palace

THE CZERNIN PALACE is a hulking beast of a building, the single biggest chunk of baroque architecture in Prague, and the home of the Czech Republic's Ministry of Foreign Affairs. Inside the lobby I shoot off a text to Marek Toman, who works here, and has offered to give me a tour. Marek is a prolific Czech author and poet, and I enjoy his company very much. We have become fast friends since I arrived in Prague a month ago. Marek has written an ingenious fictional memoir, *In Praise of Opportunism*, with the Czernin Palace itself as its central character.

The building, Marek tells me, was built by a nobleman named Humprecht Jan Czernin, who returned to Prague in the 1660s after serving as the Habsburgs' ambassador to Venice. Czernin expected to be given an important position at court, but was snubbed by Emperor Leopold I. The count avenged himself by building this gigantic pile at a slightly higher elevation than Prague Castle, so he could look down on the emperor from his window. The end result was every bit as imposing as Czernin had hoped, but he died before it could be completed.

In the palace vestibule, Marek points to a paved courtyard. 'That is the spot,' he says, 'where Jan Masaryk fell to his death from his bathroom window above.'

I look up to the third floor. It's a fifteen-metre drop to a hard landing. 'What do you think, Marek? Did he jump or was he pushed?'

'No one has ever been able to know for sure. For me, I think he was murdered.'

'How long was he lying there, before his body was discovered?'

'Maybe four or five hours. They found him in his pyjamas.'

UPSTAIRS, MAREK LEADS me through the elegant state rooms, used mostly today for diplomatic events and media conferences. We finish the tour in Jan Masaryk's former apartment. The drawing room is spacious and light-filled. Medieval tapestries hang from the walls and Turkish rugs stretch out across the floor. In the far corner is a grand piano. 'Masaryk was a charming man,' Marek tells me. 'He used to play this piano and sing with his friends and guests.'

The piano faces a huge window that looks over the whole of the castle district. I see the black spires of St Vitus poking up in the distance, and the pale-yellow walls of Our Lady of the Angels.

In his novel, Marek imagines the arrogant Czernin Palace falling in love with the modest church of Saint Loreta across the square. Little flecks of snow are blowing past the window and, for a moment, I really do feel the searing tragedy of Masaryk's lost republic.

'I'm trying to understand, Marek, what it means to live in a small nation that becomes the plaything of great and terrible neighbours.'

'It means,' he said, 'that every situation seems temporary. When things are good, you feel it can't last for too long.'

'And yet,' I reply looking out at the rooftops of Hradcany, 'the Bohemians built this city like it was going to be here forever, to be enjoyed forever.'

'Yes,' he said. 'It's hard to explain.'

Jan Masaryk at his piano in the Czernin Palace.

*

Protectorate

IN 1939, THE CZERNIN PALACE became the headquarters of the Nazi SS and the German Reichsprotektor. Hitler permitted the feeble Dr Hacha to remain as a nominal president of a puppet Czech administration, but the real power lay with the Reichsprotektor. As a sop to outraged world opinion, Hitler gave the job to his former foreign minister Konstantin von Neurath, an aristocrat widely seen as a 'moderate' in the Nazi hierarchy.

Reichsprotektor Neurath arrived in Prague on 5 April 1939 and was welcomed ceremonially with a motorcade and a torchlit military parade in Wenceslas Square, but only a scattering of loyal Germans showed up. The silver-haired Neurath was a pragmatist; deferential to the Fuhrer, but not a believer in his mystic destiny. His brief was to pacify the population while siphoning off the nation's wealth and industrial resources.

Neurath's comparatively mild approach put him at loggerheads with his ambitious deputy, Karl Hermann Frank, the former SdP deputy who was now the ranking SS senior officer in Prague. Thin and bird-like in appearance, Frank was a pan-German fanatic who had pushed past Konrad Henlein to become the most powerful Bohemian German in the new regime. All monuments to Masaryk's republic were dismantled. Road traffic was shifted from the left- to the right-hand side of the road, while the black-and-gold German-language street signs replaced the red-and-white Czech placards. The Gestapo, Hitler's secret police, set up headquarters across town in the Petschek Palace, a former bank, equipped with windowless concrete vaults, suitable for the detention and torture of enemies of the Reich.

Meanwhile Nazi propaganda told a story of a grateful nation, happy to be liberated from fumbling Czech democrats. German aid agencies rolled into Prague with truckloads of free meals for 'starving' families, but the only takers were hungry and frightened Czech refugees from the Sudetenland. Struggling to find camera-worthy subjects, Nazi photographers found a group of local children and asked them to demonstrate how they said their prayers. Pictures of urchins with uplifted arms were then presented to the world with the headline: 'Prague children beg for food'.[1]

Czechs found ways to thwart the authorities. German officials frequently found their telephone lines cut dead or the fuel tanks of their cars mysteriously empty. In the cinemas, projectionists played Nazi newsreels at high speed or blurred the picture, while crowds jeered in the darkness. A performance of Smetana's *Ma Vlast* at the National Theatre was given a raucous fifteen-minute standing ovation while the conductor kissed the score and held it up to the audience.

THE LESSONS OF *The Good Soldier Svejk* had not been forgotten. One evening in a Prague beer garden, a group of students who had been drinking heavily took up a mocking cry, calling for *Lebensraum* – living space – for the Czech people. The joke appealed to the other pub-goers, who joined in, chanting: 'We want colonies! Colonies for the Czechs!' Two visiting Germans sitting nearby missed the irony and were deeply impressed; they reported the incident to the Nazi news service, as evidence of Czech enthusiasm for the benefits that would surely come as members of a German empire with overseas colonies.[2]

IN BETWEEN THESE OUTBREAKS of defiance and humour, a degree of gloomy listlessness set in that summer. Electrical storms crackled in the sky. The US consul noted a 'strange lethargy, almost a paralysis' in Prague. 'People prefer to sit through the summer evenings in the beer gardens or the little parks along the rivers ... to wait with involuntary patience for the approach of something which none of them could quite describe but which they are all convinced must come and must affect all their lives profoundly.' He noted, sadly, that the Czechs were one of the few people in the world who longed for war; it was the only thing offering any hope of liberation.[3]

EDVARD BENES, WHO HAD relocated from London to Chicago, had arrived at the same conclusion. In America, Benes felt the old energy and ambition stirring within him once more. Although his reputation had been badly dented by his decision not to fight the Munich ultimatum, he believed he was the obvious man to lead a Czechoslovak government-in-exile. There was still no good answer to his late mentor's question, 'If not Benes, then who?' Although the United States was officially neutral, there was widespread sympathy in America for the Czech people. Benes was granted a meeting with President Roosevelt, who offered him private encouragement. 'I still consider you to be the president,' Roosevelt told Benes, 'though I don't say so in public.'[4]

BENES RETURNED TO LONDON on 12 July 1939 to find that Hitler's invasion of Czechoslovakia had pulled down the whole rotten edifice of British appeasement. Winston Churchill invited Benes to a lunch at his home in Kent. Churchill, who was soon to re-enter the ministry after ten years in the political wilderness, rose to his feet and paid tribute to his guest: 'I don't know how things will develop,' he said emotionally, 'and I cannot say whether Great Britain will go to war on Czechoslovakia's behalf. I only know that the peace, which will be made in the future, will not be made without Czechoslovakia.' Benes was moved to see tears running down Churchill's cheeks.[5]

Pact of Steel

BY MARCH 1939, the British cabinet was at last ready to swallow hard and seek an Anglo–Soviet alliance, but they had let things go on for too long and were too late. On the night of 21 August, Berlin and Moscow announced a German–Soviet Non-Aggression Pact. Following Stalin's lead, the Czechoslovak Communist Party in exile instantly dropped its hostility to Hitler and declared itself in favour of peace.

The world was agog. How had the Nazis and the Bolsheviks, who had traded insults for years, managed to hold hands and come together? But both sides stood to make enormous gains, and there were longstanding secret links between the Red Army and the German Wehrmacht, which had been conducting clandestine joint military exercises in the Russian hinterland since the 1920s.

The insults between Nazi Germany and the Soviet Union had obscured deep underlying similarities. Both regimes were totalitarian cults armed with state power. It was Mussolini who gave the most concise formulation of their totalitarian ethos: 'Nothing outside the state. Everything within the state. Nothing against the state.'[6] To that he might have added, 'Everything through the state': both regimes had created party institutions to replace civic organisations, from the boy scouts to gymnastic clubs to motherhood groups. The party – Nazi or Communist – saturated itself into the entire fabric of everyday life like an inky dye.

Despite their distinctly different characters, Hitler and Stalin had similar histories: both had come from the provinces to the metropolis; both had been redeemed from their youthful ignominy and transfigured into god-like emperors. Most significantly, both men had arrived at the same sociopathic worldview: that life was, at heart, a brutal Darwinian contest of strength, and that compassion was either madness or hypocrisy. It was Prague's tragedy that it lay within the grasp of both these men in the same century.

THE NAZI–SOVIET PACT contained a secret protocol, that drew a line down the middle of Poland and divided it between them. In his invasion notes, Hitler gathered his senior staff and told them, 'War is better now.' In his notes he had scribbled: 'No pity – brutal attitude –might is right – greatest severity.'[7]

In September, Germany's invasion of Poland triggered the Second World War that Chamberlain had dreaded and sacrificed Czechoslovakia to avoid. But when the Soviets, in accordance with the secret protocol, seized the eastern portion of Poland for themselves, the Allies chose to look the other way rather than be drawn into a wider war.

EVEN UNDER THE WATCHFUL eyes of the Gestapo, Praguers found ways to test the limits of official tolerance. Jews were now required to wear a yellow star on their coats, but some non-Jewish Praguers wore them too in solidarity with their Jewish friends. On 28 October 1939, Czechoslovak Independence Day, a group of Czech medical students passed out handbills, calling for Praguers to resist the occupation. When protestors gathered in Wenceslas Square, chanting, 'We want freedom!' and 'Long live Benes!', German provocateurs waded into the crowd and a melee broke out. Protestors threw stones at German shops. Shots were fired by police, and one of the medical students, Jan Opletal, later died in hospital of a bullet wound. He became another Czech martyr, murdered by the servants of foreign fanatics.

On the day of Opletal's funeral, thousands of Czechs came into the city centre to follow the hearse to the train station. The crowd then marched down to Charles Square, singing the national anthem. Czech police, under German orders, broke up the protestors, but the students regrouped and marched down Narodni Street.

SS leader Karl Hermann Frank left the Czernin Palace to inspect the disturbances. On Narodni Street, protestors brought his car to a halt and punched his driver in the face, breaking his nose. More police and SS men were ordered onto the streets, and by midday, the city had sunk into angry silence again.

The next day, Reichsprotektor Neurath announced the closure of the Czech universities. Nine student leaders were dragged from their homes and shot by the Gestapo. Another 1200 students were sent to Sachsenhausen concentration camp.

Various resistance groups now formed across the new protectorate, coordinating their activities through a Committee of Home Resistance, but unlike the Polish resistance, the Czech underground lacked military weapons and had to confine its activities mostly to intelligence gathering. Bureaucrats, bookkeepers and telephone operators within the protectorate passed on information to London via railway workers or through hidden radio transmitters.

IN LONDON, EDVARD BENES'S relationship with the British government improved markedly after the wretched Neville Chamberlain stood down and was replaced as prime minister by Winston Churchill. Chamberlain, who was dying from bowel cancer, spent the final six months of his life angrily defending his record against his critics, who accused him of leaving Britain helpless and friendless against Nazi Germany.

Benes formed a Czechoslovak government-in-exile, naming Jan Masaryk as foreign minister, while Frantisek Moravec, his intelligence chief, maintained contact with the British intelligence services and the Czech underground. When France and the Netherlands fell to Hitler's Wehrmacht, Benes urged Czech and Slovak soldiers and airmen to do everything they could to escape to England. Soon enough, 4000 soldiers somehow found their way across the Channel, ready to form the nucleus of an Allied Czechoslovak legion. Czech airmen joined the RAF and were to play a significant role in the coming Battle of Britain.

The Blond Beast

ON 22 JUNE 1941, when Hitler tore up his pact with Stalin and invaded the Soviet Union, the Czechoslovak communists were obliged to perform yet another *volte face*. The party dropped its anti-war stance and made common cause with the resistance in Prague.

In the occupied Czech lands, underground communist cells initiated an effective sabotage campaign, destroying railway carriages and cutting telephone lines. Strikes and work-slow campaigns led to an eighteen per cent drop in industrial production, threatening the Nazi war effort.[8] Reichsprotektor Neurath was sent home and replaced by the deputy SS leader, Reinhard Heydrich.

HEYDRICH, NICKNAMED 'The Blond Beast' by his colleagues, was a particularly cold-blooded operator in an exceptionally vicious regime. Tall, fair-haired, with an elongated nose and tiny icy-blue eyes, Heydrich looked every bit the Aryan in a regime led by men who otherwise resembled toads or hairless cats. Hitler, who described him admiringly as 'the man with the iron heart', particularly valued his ability to bring fuzzy 'problems' for the Reich into sharp focus, and then to briskly implement a radical solution. It was Heydrich who would chair the meeting at Wannsee that arrived at the Final Solution to the Jewish problem.

On his arrival in Prague, Heydrich instantly proclaimed martial law. More than a thousand suspected enemies of the Reich were arrested and brought in for interrogation. Red-typed posters were plastered all over the city announcing the names of those sentenced to death. Among them was Hacha's prime minister, Alois Elias, who had been feeding information to the resistance. Elias's 'confession' was published in the major newspapers and he was executed on a shooting range in northern Prague.

Heydrich lost no time in implementing a new set of racial policies for the protectorate. On 2 October, he summoned senior officials to the reception hall of the Czernin Palace to announce the Reich's plans for the Czech lands: Bohemia and Moravia, he said, must be entirely Germanised to create living space. Racially acceptable Czechs could become Germans, but those hostile to the Reich would be 'stood up to the wall'. Racially inferior, but well-intentioned Czechs must consent to be sterilised. The rest would eventually be expelled from the greater German heartland into Russia's Arctic wastes, where, he said, 'they must serve us as slaves'.[9] In the meantime, Czech workers in vital defence industries would be mollified with better rations, higher wages and more days off. 'The Czech worker must be given fodder,' he said, 'so that he can fulfil his tasks.'[10]

SS bureaucrats embarked on a racial inventory of the protectorate's entire population under the pretext of a health check-up, which fooled no one. Heydrich insisted on taking a 'scientific' approach, but definitions of what constituted a German, a Slav or a Jew were slippery and subjective. A person's 'racial essence' might be defined by their ancestry, their name, their body type, their overall bearing and even the orderliness of the house they lived in. People who had once happily existed as 'amphibians', as conversant in German as they were in Czech, were required to choose one side or the other.

HEYDRICH URGED HIS STAFF to maintain 'correct social conduct' in their dealings with Czechs, but to never let them forget who was in charge. Reaching back a thousand years into Bohemian history, the Reichsprotektor seized on the precedent set by St Wenceslas, as a Czech ruler who had bent the knee to a German overlord.

Heydrich now demanded his own rite of obeisance from the Czechs; in November, he was welcomed into the crypt of St Vitus by President Hacha, who presented him with the seven keys to the crown jewels of Bohemia on an embroidered velvet cushion. Heydrich politely returned three of the keys as an act of goodwill.

The gleaming crown jewels of Bohemia were arrayed before the Reichsprotektor, who touched the sceptre with his gloveless hand. There is no evidence that Heydrich placed the jewel-studded crown of St Wenceslas on his head, and such a gesture, even for him, seems unlikely. But nonetheless a rumour spread through Prague that Heydrich hadn't been able to resist a self-coronation, thereby setting in train an old curse: that he who wears Wenceslas's crown wrongfully will die within the year.

Anthropoid

THREE DAYS BEFORE CHRISTMAS 1941, a twin-engine British Halifax flew out of southern England, flying low across occupied

France and Germany to avoid detection. On board were nine Czech and Slovak paratroopers, all trained by Britain's Special Operations Executive. Each was kitted out with Czech-made suits, underwear, shoes, cigarettes, matches and forged identity papers.

Among the passengers were two best friends: Jozef Gabcik, a Slovak, and Jan Kubis, a Czech. No one else on board was aware of the dangerous mission entrusted to them by Czechoslovakia's government-in-exile, and neither man expected to survive it.

The British and Soviet governments had for some time been pressuring Benes to contribute more to the war effort, but resistance activity in the protectorate had been smothered by Heydrich's campaign of terror. Benes, embarrassed by the apparent passivity of his people, broadcast messages to Prague from London, calling for more action, but many Czechs elected to accept the shame of captivity rather than risk a futile death at the hands of the Gestapo.

With his people's reputation sinking among the Allies, Benes approved a dramatic scheme that would erase the stigma of Czech passivity: they would drop Czechoslovak paratroopers into Prague to assassinate Reinhard Heydrich.

The plan was wildly dangerous. No senior Nazi had ever been assassinated before. Benes's spy chief, Frantisek Moravec, warned that retaliation from Hitler would be murderous. Nonetheless, Benes gave the order to proceed with the mission, which was code-named Operation Anthropoid.

Gabcik and Kubis were personally selected by Moravec, and given special commando training in Scotland, then dropped along with the seven other paratroopers into the Bohemian countryside. Gabcik and Kubis made their way through the snow to Prague, where they were billeted with several families working with the resistance.

FOR MONTHS GABCIK and Kubis monitored Heydrich's daily routine, looking for the ideal time and place to strike. Then, on 23 May 1942, a crucial piece of intelligence fell into their laps. Josef Novotny, a Czech watchmaker, had been called into Heydrich's office to repair an antique clock. As he set to work, he noticed the Reichsprotektor's itinerary on the desk. Thinking quickly, Novotny screwed the document up and put it in the wastepaper basket. He repaired the clock and left the office. A sympathetic cleaner collected the precious document, and within hours it was in Kubis's and Gabcik's hands.

The itinerary revealed Heydrich would be leaving Prague in four days' time, possibly for good, to take up a new post elsewhere in the Reich. After months of preparation, the assassins now had just four days to complete their mission. By now, members of the Prague underground and their fellow paratroopers had figured out Gabcik and Kubis's mission, and they fired off a protest to London, warning that the killing of Heydrich would cost thousands of lives. The reply from London was adamant: they were to proceed with the mission regardless of the consequences.

Gabcik and Kubis had accepted they were likely to be killed and made their farewells to their hosts. Gabcik had fallen in love with Libena Fafkova, the daughter of one of the families, and the two celebrated their engagement joyfully and quietly in her Prague apartment.

ON THE MORNING OF 27 MAY, Reinhard Heydrich left his mansion, fourteen kilometres to the north of Prague, in an open-topped Mercedes Cabriolet chauffeured by an oversized SS officer named Klein. Security was almost non-existent; Heydrich believed he had nothing to fear from the cowed people of Prague.

The car passed through the northeastern suburbs on its way to Hradcany. As the driver rounded a hairpin turn, Gabcik strode out from behind a tram and stopped in front of the car, forcing the driver to brake hard. Gabcik flung aside his folded coat, revealing a Sten submachine gun.

At this critical moment, the gun jammed.

The driver froze. An amazed Heydrich stood up from his seat and pulled out his pistol. As Heydrich took aim at the fleeing Gabcik, Kubis ran up from behind and lobbed a home-made anti-tank grenade at the back of the Mercedes, which detonated under its rear fender. The explosion rocked the car, blasting shrapnel through the car seat into Heydrich's lower back.

Full of fury, the wounded Heydrich staggered out of the car and chased after Kubis, who took off downhill on his bicycle. After twenty steps, Heydrich collapsed from shock and blood loss.

Lying on the ground, he ordered Klein, his driver, to go after the assassin. Pistol now in hand, Gabcik ducked into a butcher's shop. As Klein entered the shop, Gabcik, shot him twice in the leg and made his escape, leaving the bodyguard groaning on the ground. Both he and Kubis slipped into the streets and met at their rendezvous point, believing they had failed in their mission.

HEYDRICH, MEANWHILE, was still lying in the street, bleeding heavily. A woman helped him into a Tatra delivery van and ordered the driver to take him to a nearby hospital. An X-ray revealed that Heydrich had suffered major damage to his spleen, one lung and his diaphragm. But his wounds were treatable and he was expected to recover.

NO ONE IN PRAGUE could fail to notice that something momentous had happened that morning. Within the hour, an apoplectic Adolf Hitler was on the phone to SS leader Karl Hermann Frank, demanding he execute as many as 10,000 Czechs in retaliation for the attack. Prague was completely sealed off. SS squads fanned out throughout the city looking for the culprits. The Gestapo raided thousands of buildings, conducting house-to-house searches, but discovered nothing. Germany offered a reward of a million Reichsmarks for information on the assassins. Hacha's government doubled it.

IN HOSPITAL, HEYDRICH'S condition stabilised, but two days after the attack, he became feverish as sepsis set in. Fragments of horsehair from the car's upholstery implanted in his abdomen had poisoned his blood. He needed penicillin, but there was none to be had in the German Reich.

Himmler rushed from Berlin to the bedside of his dying lieutenant, who was resigned to his fate; he quoted a line from an opera written by his father, who had been a composer:

The world is just a barrel-organ which the Lord God turns Himself.
We all have to dance to the tune which is already on the drum.[11]

Then Heydrich fell into a coma and died. Bernhard Wehner, the detective sent from Berlin to investigate the assassination, thought Heydrich's face in death possessed 'deceptive features of uncanny spirituality and entirely perverted beauty, like a renaissance Cardinal'.[12]

Heydrich's death mask, on a 1943 commemorative stamp.

THE DEATH IN PRAGUE of the Blond Beast made front-page news across the world. President Hacha condemned the assassination and urged members of the public to come forward to help the police investigation. Benes's people in London denounced Hacha as a traitor and a quisling.

The procession of Heydrich's silver and gunmetal coffin from the castle to the Old Town was hailed with Nazi salutes from onlookers. Newsreel footage shows crowds crammed into the Old Town Square, with people climbing all over the Jan Hus monument to get a good look. In a close-up, one woman, presumably a German, is dabbing her eyes, while another's face is screwed up with grim satisfaction.

The coffin was carried by special train to Berlin, where the entire Nazi leadership, led by an emotional Adolf Hitler, gave their fallen Siegfried a hero's funeral. Heydrich was raised to the pantheon of the regime's exalted dead. Hitler swore to take revenge upon the assassins and to conduct mass reprisals against the Czech people.

AFTER WEEKS OF house-to-house searches, the investigation had failed to identify, let alone locate the culprits. False intelligence surfaced, linking the assassins to the village of Lidice, fourteen miles northwest of Prague.

On the morning following Heydrich's funeral, uniformed police and intelligence officers sealed off the village. Under Hitler's orders, 173 men from Lidice were taken to a farm and shot in groups of ten, while the village's houses were looted and burnt to the ground. The process took hours. Every woman in Lidice was deported to a concentration camp. The few children found to be worthy of Germanisation were handed over to SS families; the rest died in the gas chambers with their mothers. The burnt-out remains of the village were bulldozed or blown up with explosives. Lidice was literally obliterated.

Unlike other Nazi atrocities, the massacre at Lidice was proudly trumpeted by German propaganda, and the world recoiled in horror. The massacre gave the war a deeper moral dimension in the eyes of people who had not yet been fully aware of the depths of Nazi depravity. Towns in Brazil, Mexico, the United States and Panama renamed themselves Lidice in sympathy. A settled view took hold in the Allied nations that a negotiated peace with the Nazis was impossible; the regime that destroyed Lidice must itself be destroyed.

IN PRAGUE, THE PROTECTORATE authorities warned of harsher measures if Heydrich's killers were not handed over by 18 June. Rumours coursed through the city that the Germans intended to execute one in every ten citizens until the assassins were identified.

On 16 June, a young man named Karel Curda walked into the Petschek Palace and told the Gestapo he could help them with their manhunt. Curda was one of the Czech paratroopers dropped along with Gabcik and Kubis. Whether he was motivated by a desire to forestall a larger civilian massacre is unclear, but he admitted after the war that the large reward was a factor. He told the Gestapo he did not know the hiding place of Gabcik and Kubis, but he could direct them to several resistance safe houses connected to them, including the home of Alois and Marie Moravec in Zizkov.

The Gestapo stormed into the Moravec family apartment before dawn. Marie Moravec managed to bite down on a cyanide capsule, which killed her within minutes. Alois and their son, Ata, were hauled into the cells of the Petschek Palace for interrogation. After hours of torture, the seventeen-year-old Ata was force-fed whisky to make him talk. There is a story that Ata's spirit was broken when one of the interrogators presented him with his mother's severed head inside a fishtank. Ata gave his torturers the name of Gabcik and Kubis's hiding place: the Church of Cyril and Methodius in the New Town.

IN THE PRE-DAWN DARKNESS, trucks carrying 800 SS men converged on the Orthodox church, between the river and Charles Square. When the Germans burst through the door, Kubis and two of his fellow parachutists were in the gallery over the nave, armed with colt revolvers. They opened fire, shooting down every SS soldier that charged in. The three men held their ground for nearly two hours against grenades, guns and automatic weapon fire until Kubis, severely wounded, put his gun to his head.

The Germans prepared to leave, but then the discovery of some extraneous items of clothing in the church indicated there were more resistance fighters hidden elsewhere. A carpet was pulled back, revealing a trapdoor to the crypt, where Gabcik was hiding with three well-armed comrades, Valcik, Hruby and Svarc. The SS foot soldiers pulled up the trapdoor, but each one who tried to descend the narrow, winding staircase got his legs shot to pieces and had to be pulled out. A priest was ordered to shout down to them that they had nothing to fear and they should give themselves up. 'Never! Never!' was the famous reply from the crypt. 'We are Czechs! We will never surrender, do you hear us? Never!'

By now, SS leader Karl Hermann Frank had arrived at the church and was screaming at his underlings to finish the job. They dragged a firehose up to the ventilation window to flood the crypt, but the parachutists easily knocked it out with a ladder. The traitor Curda was brought up to the window to assure the men they would be well-treated if they gave up. The response was another burst of gunfire.

At noon, eight hours into the siege, the stone floor was dynamited to create an opening into the crypt, but by then Gabcik and his friends had exhausted their ammunition and used their last bullets on themselves.

THE DEATH OF HEYDRICH'S assassins was followed by another wave of reprisals. The families of the paratroopers and the priests who had given them sanctuary were murdered. Alois and Ata Moravec, were deported to Mauthausen concentration camp where they were executed. Hoping to avoid further reprisals against his church, the Orthodox Bishop of Prague took responsibility for the decision to hide the men and his life too was forfeited. Bishop Gorazd was recognised as a martyr by the church. The traitorous Karel Curda identified an underground radio group in the village of Lezaky, and that town too was utterly destroyed.

EDVARD BENES NEVER allowed himself to doubt that Hitler's bloody revenge had been a price worth paying. He believed Lidice had given him a galvanising symbol of German wickedness and

Czech martyrdom. The Czechs could now be portrayed as fellow sufferers rather than supine collaborators. 'What the Germans are doing is horrible,' he told the Prague resistance, 'but from a political point of view they gave us one certainty: under no circumstances can anyone doubt Czechoslovakia's national integrity and her right to independence.'[13]

BY 1943, NAZI GERMANY was in retreat on several fronts. The massive Soviet counterattack after the Battle of Stalingrad was pushing the Wehrmacht back across its conquered territory in the east. Nazi propaganda no longer spoke of *Lebensraum*, but of a life-and-death struggle against Bolshevism for the soul of Europe. The possibility of defeat brought cold fear into the hearts of Hitler's quislings in Prague. With Heydrich dead, the Sudeten-born K. H. Frank became the real power in the land. Frank cancelled Heydrich's expensive and disruptive racial inventory in order to muster the protectorate's energies towards total war on behalf of the Third Reich. Resistance activity dropped to negligible levels again. Seeing no way of expressing opposition, Czech people seethed with resentment. They had seen the Jews of Prague being rounded up and taken away and wondered if the same fate lay ahead for them. They awaited the day, not so distant now, when they might exact some revenge against the vicious, strutting Germans.

Carousel

ON THIS FEBRUARY MORNING, outside Prague's Holesovice train station, I collect some hot coffee from a vending machine and then walk through the sleety rain to the bus platforms. The destination signs are not clearly marked, so I check the placard bolted onto a pole and see 'Terezin' printed with a neat list of departure times underneath.

After an hour-long journey through the Bohemian countryside, the bus drops me at a stop on the banks of the Ohre River. Up ahead I see Terezin's tall slanted walls surrounded by a gaping, empty moat with just a thin streak of slushy water at the bottom.

Terezin was built as a fortress in 1780 by the Habsburgs to secure Bohemia's borders against a Prussian attack. They named it Theresienstadt, after Empress Maria Theresa, but now it goes by its infamous Czech name.

The town is neatly laid out in a grid, with derelict Habsburg-era buildings that seem to be mostly uninhabited. It's mid-morning on a Saturday but there's no one around, only the occasional passing car.

The shabbiness of Terezin reminds me sharply of the communist era, in a way that Prague no longer does. The window of a discount clothes shop displays a single dress on a dusty headless mannequin. Around the corner, a pawn shop opens its doors momentarily and a couple emerge with an old portable TV set. The shopkeeper bids them farewell then bolts the door shut.

In 2001, a former Australian prime minister, Paul Keating, delivered a speech in Berlin at the newly rebuilt Potsdamer Platz. Keating, a lover of German music and culture, shocked his hosts by saying he thought the reconstruction of Berlin after the war was a colossal mistake. He said the ruined city should have been left as an immense open-air museum, as a monument to 'false notions of glory, to nationalism, to idolatry, to racism, to political criminality'. Berlin was, he said, 'what people in Australia might call, with reference to Aboriginality, an un-sacred site. A site made sacred by its un-sacredness.'[14]

This place, Terezin, is such a ruin. It is a truly awful place, a town too airless to feel haunted.

IN OCTOBER 1941, TEREZIN fortress was requisitioned by Reinhard Heydrich to be refitted as a concentration camp for Czech Jews, who would be held there until they could be transported to the death camps in Poland. Heydrich decreed that Terezin would also take in prominent Jewish people from the Reich whose disappearance would be noticed by the outside world: decorated veterans of the Great War, scholars, artists and musicians. The SS brazenly advertised Terezin as a spa town, fit for a comfortable retirement. Many Jews in central Europe willingly handed over their life savings in exchange for the promise of well-furnished private rooms with a lakeside view.

There was no lake. Of the 141,000 Jews sent to Theresienstadt, 33,000 would die of overwork, malnourishment and disease. Another 88,000 would be shipped east to extermination camps like Auschwitz. The camp's population fluctuated wildly, depending on the timing of the transports. Zuzana Justman, a child prisoner, remembers the streets of Terezin were so jammed at times she found it difficult to walk without bumping into anyone.[15] But then a consignment of prisoners would be sent to an unknown destination in Poland, never to return, and the streets would thin out again.

BETWEEN 1941 AND THE FINAL transports of 1944, a kind of desperate cultural miracle unfolded here, as the influx of musicians, actors and scholars made the Jewish ghetto at Terezin, briefly, one of the richest cultural centres in Europe. The commandant Karl Rahm initially refused to allow prisoners to pursue cultural activities, but relented when he realised that art and entertainment might make the prisoners more docile and less likely to panic when herded onto a transport.

Soon there were public poetry performances in Czech and German; a distinguished rabbi delivered philosophy lectures to hundreds of inmates in a cramped garret. The actress Vlasta Shonova directed a production of Cocteau's *La Voix Humaine*, while Prague's Puppet Theatre staged performances for children. An opera, *The Emperor of Atlantis*, was rehearsed but never performed due to the systematic removal of performers on the transports to Auschwitz.

AS NEWLY ARRIVED INMATES lined up for their daily rations, some were amazed to find themselves standing in the queue behind a famous movie star. Kurt Gerron was a moon-faced German Jewish actor and cabaret performer who had starred alongside Marlene Dietrich in *The Blue Angel*. He had begun his career in Berlin's interwar cabaret scene, and was the first man ever to perform 'Mack the Knife' at the 1928 premiere of Brecht and Weill's *Threepenny Opera*. He made the jaunty murder ballad his signature tune.

Gerron's charismatic presence and his huge roly-poly figure had made him one of the most popular screen stars in Germany, an instantly recognisable presence. In the early 1930s, he became a successful film director, which brought him wealth and power.

Gerron had refused to take warnings about the Nazis seriously. His friend Peter Lorre, who had become a Hollywood star in *Casablanca*, tried to bring him to America, but Gerron declined when he was told that first-class transport was not available. He fled to Paris with his family, and then to Amsterdam, where he was arrested in 1943. A year later he was sent to Terezin.

IN RECOGNITION OF HIS ABILITIES, Gerron was invited by commandant Karl Rahm to mount a show at Terezin. He devised a cabaret named *Carousel,* and was rewarded with superior food rations, private quarters and a promise of immunity from the transports. Gerron often took to the stage himself, performing songs that obliquely touched on life in Terezin and the black hole that they might disappear into at any moment. The theme song to *Carousel* described life in the camp as a 'strange voyage, a journey without a destination'.[16] *Carousel* held more than fifty performances, but the production was controversial among the prisoners: some saw it as a form of collaboration – aiding the Nazis by distracting the inmates. Others insisted the cabarets were a consolation amidst the terror.

TROUBLED BY REPORTS of the mass disappearance of Jews within the Nazi-occupied lands, the International Red Cross demanded an opportunity to inspect one of the Reich's 're-settlement camps'. Himmler saw an opening for a propaganda coup and scheduled a Red Cross inspection of Terezin for late June 1944.

Commandant Karl Rahm ordered a beautification campaign: gardens were planted; buildings were given a coat of paint; prisoners constructed fake shops, a fake bank, a fake school and a playground to give an illusion of normalcy. The problem of visible overcrowding was solved by the deportation of 7503 elderly ghetto inhabitants to Auschwitz.

The Red Cross delegation arrived at Terezin on 23 June, headed by Maurice Rossel, a 28-year-old Swiss doctor, who was led around the Potemkin village by Rahm. The medicos observed a soccer game in the town square and a production of the children's opera *Brundibar.*

Children were served a hearty meal, with cucumber salad and a chocolate dessert – treats no one had ever seen before in Terezin.[17]

Paul Eppstein, the Jewish 'mayor' of Terezin, delivered a speech, written for him by the SS. Eppstein, who had a black eye from a beating administered to him by Karl Rahm, likened the camp to a pleasant country town. Despite the evidence of violence, and the eerie, glazed expressions on the faces of the silent 'villagers', Rossel noticed nothing amiss and he delivered an upbeat report. Life in the town, he wrote, was 'almost normal'. After Rossel's departure, most of the children photographed in the report were transported to Auschwitz.[18]

THE SUCCESS OF THE ruse at Terezin emboldened the SS to attempt an even more grotesque deception. Kurt Gerron was called to Rahm's office and commissioned to direct a short film about the idyllic conditions at Terezin. The presentation was to be called *The Fuhrer Gives the Jews a City*, and would be shown in neutral nations to allay their concern about the treatment of Jews in the Third Reich. Gerron agreed, on the understanding his life would be spared. Mortified inmates were once again conscripted to appear as joyful villagers.

Only fragments of the film survive. Terezin appears as a model town: young men play soccer in the sunshine; women create pottery while an artist moulds a fountain sculpture; a children's choir sings an oratorio by Mendelssohn. Inmates dressed in fine clothes watch a performance of *Carousel*, but under the close supervision of SS guards standing just outside the frame.

Gerron's direction achieved uneven results. He confided to his cameraman, 'I can direct the scene, but I cannot erase the horror from people's eyes.'[19] An inmate remembered Gerron pleading with his actors to laugh and smile, despite the presence of the SS:

Bathed in sweat, Gerron urged us, implored us, begged for discipline, for us to follow orders absolutely. He cracked jokes and made despairing efforts. 'Please, no incidents, don't provoke any use of force!' He begged us urgently: 'Do what I show you, when I laugh, laugh with me!' And he began a contagious, irresistible laugh, during which he wobbled his fat belly, so that we really had to laugh, even though the situation for him and for us was anything but laughable. Laugh, Pagliacci![20]

AS SOON AS FILMING was complete, the transports to Auschwitz resumed. Kurt Gerron and his wife were among the deportees. Gerron was seen on the train platform, rigid and helpless, 'like a pillar of stone. He had to be helped into the wagon.'[21]

On arrival at Auschwitz, Gerron was sent immediately to the gas chambers. The next day, with the Red Army approaching, Himmler ordered the gas chambers to be closed.

No Angels

IN FEBRUARY 1945, the 'Big Three' Allied leaders met at Yalta on the Black Sea coast to discuss their plans for the post-war world. Churchill and Roosevelt were profoundly exhausted and far from their best. Stalin, for his part, made it clear that after the war, he wanted to establish a protective buffer between the USSR and the rest of Europe, a swathe of friendly states that he said must be 'free of fascist and reactionary elements'.[22] All three leaders understood this buffer would likely include Czechoslovakia; it would be up to Stalin to define what he meant by 'fascist and reactionary'.

Edvard Benes had already concluded a mutual non-aggression treaty with Stalin. With the Red Army in control of eastern Europe, he knew the scope of Czechoslovakia's post-war independence would lie in the hands of the Soviet dictator. Benes reasoned he should secure Soviet patronage sooner rather than later, otherwise Stalin might simply install someone like the communist leader Klement Gottwald as leader of post-war Czechoslovakia.

Benes, who had been so quick to grasp the true ambitions of Adolf Hitler, disastrously misjudged Stalin at this critical time. He persuaded himself that the war had tempered the Soviet dictator and made him more amenable to cooperation and co-existence with the West. Reaching out to Stalin, he hoped, might secure his generosity and allow Czechoslovakia to follow its own course after the war.

IN EARLY 1945, with Nazi rule collapsing all over Europe, Benes was ready to come home, but he would make his triumphant return from the east. He arrived in Moscow on 17 March, along with Jan Masaryk and the other members of his government-in-exile.

Benes believed the Soviet Union would offer his country the best protection against a revived Germany down the track. As a down payment, he would have to accept the loss of the easternmost point of the old Czechoslovakia, a sliver of territory known as Carpathian Ruthenia, to the Soviet Union. This would give the USSR a shared border with the new Czechoslovakia.

In Moscow, representatives of the Czech political parties sat down with Klement Gottwald's communists and the Slovak National Council to discuss the shape of the new Czechoslovakia. Benes wanted to stand above the fray, so he unwisely excused himself from their deliberations. This meant that Gottwald, not Benes, chaired the meeting.

The communists had arrived with an agenda, unlike Benes's people who hadn't bothered to draft a program of their own. They were faint-hearted democrats at best, preoccupied by the need to punish the German 'traitors' in their country to ensure that Germany could never again pose an existential threat to a Czechoslovak state. The desire for retribution kept Benes's men looking backwards, while the communists kept their eyes on the future, so when Gottwald proposed a whole raft of radical economic and political proposals they were waved through.

Gottwald's communists got everything they wanted: nationalisation of the economy, the banning of the right-wing Agrarian Party and control of the key ministries that would eventually allow them to introduce a police state. Jan Masaryk was to have the post of foreign minister, but a Slovak communist, Vlado Clementis, would shadow him as a junior minister. Benes expressed some vague misgivings about the provisional government cabinet but, keen to observe the proprieties, he accepted their recommendations.

THAT EVENING, Stalin hosted a farewell dinner in the Kremlin. In one of several toasts, he tried to prepare them for the arrival of the Red Army in their country. 'Do not judge them too harshly,' he said; 'they are tired by a long war and have become a little uncontrolled. Anyway, Red Army men are no angels.'[23]

Red Army soldiers were young men, often from rural backwaters, who had been fed propaganda that told them the Soviet Union was the most economically advanced society in the world. As they entered the towns and cities of Poland, Germany and Czechoslovakia, they were dumbfounded by the prosperous farms with modern equipment, the urban centres with handsome buildings and indoor plumbing. They stole cars, rugs, bicycles, crockery and above all wristwatches, which became a portable status symbol; some Russian soldiers were seen with five or six strapped to their wrists.

The Russian troops treated women, particularly German women, in the newly 'liberated' territories as spoils of war. Their campaign of mass rape was the largest inflicted on Europe since the attack of the Mongol Golden Horde in the thirteenth century and constitutes one of the worst war crimes of the modern era. Soviet officers were either indifferent to such attacks or encouraged them. The consequences were predictable: women committed suicide, many contracted venereal diseases or required abortions. The lingering effect of that campaign on the survivors and their families can hardly be imagined.

BENES ARRIVED IN THE east Slovakian city of Kosice on 4 April, where he swore in his new provisional government. Never a particularly charismatic figure, Benes tried to rally the anguished and divided Czechs by appealing to their one shared passion – hatred for the Germans. Moving on to Brno, he delivered a speech asking for the nation's help to 'liquidate in its entirety the German problem'.[24] Benes's advisor Prokop Drtina told a crowd of cheering Czechs that the ethnic Germans were 'a foreign ulcer in our body', which could no longer be tolerated. 'We must begin to expel the Germans from our land at once, immediately, by all methods.'[25] *Rude Pravo*, the communist party newspaper, described the Germans as 'animals ... without morality, without human feelings'.[26]

Uprising

THE FINAL DAYS of the war reminded Heda Margolius of a passage through a long train tunnel. 'From far away you could see the light ahead,' she recalled, 'a gleam that kept growing, and its brilliance seemed ever more dazzling to you huddled there in the dark the longer it took to reach it. But when at last the train burst out into the glorious sunshine, all you saw was a wasteland full of weeds and stones, and a heap of garbage.'[27]

Heda was a Jewish woman who had survived Auschwitz, and escaped while on a forced march to another camp. She had made her way home to Prague, but found many of her pre-war friends were too frightened to take her in. Standing on the thresholds of their apartments, she could see how ashamed they were of their fear. A friend who had once promised to be her 'anchor', was tormented by her sudden appearance. 'He wanted not to know me, to know nothing about me and live. Live in peace and quiet in the middle of death and desperation. Still, I believe that while he was talking to me he realized that his calm was gone for good. Even if he were never to hear from me again, his life would not be the same.'[28] Heda, exhausted and terrified, made her way from house to house. At one point she considered suicide, Eventually, she was put in touch with the resistance, who found her an empty apartment in the affluent suburb of Dejvice, behind the castle. She waited out the final weeks of the war there, while resistance fighters came and went, stashing weapons and bringing in wounded partisans.

ON 30 APRIL, ADOLF HITLER shot himself in his Berlin bunker, but Prague remained under Nazi occupation. Four days later, word spread through the city that the Red Army had entered the country from the east and the Americans were coming in from the west. The city readied itself for an uprising. Post office and railway workers tore down German signs and posters. Tram conductors refused to give change in Reichsmarks.

The Nazi authorities stepped up security at the Czechoslovak Radio building in Vinohrady, placing machine guns and coils of barbed wire at the entrance. SS reinforcements were sent in, but the staff had torn down the German signs and the SS men got lost in the corridors. They were unaware that for months the staff had been moving equipment out of the building to set up secret transmitters in preparation for the uprising.

THE NEXT MORNING, on 5 May, Praguers woke up to see the national flag flying from public buildings. Switching on their radios, they heard the announcer speaking provocatively in Czech, not German. A contingent of loyal Czech police protected the radio staff as they secretly entered the broadcasting building from the back entrance or from the adjacent rooftops.

At midday, the German-appointed radio director arrived at the building with troops to find that the staff had barricaded themselves inside. Czechoslovak and American flags were flying from the roof. SS troops exchanged gunfire with Czech partisans.

At 12.33 pm, the announcer broadcast an emergency message to the city: 'Calling all Czechs! Come and defend Czech Radio! The SS are murdering Czech people here. Come and help us!'[29] Listeners could hear the sounds of combat in the background.

The broadcast was heard across Prague as the signal for a general uprising. From her apartment window, Heda Margolius saw civilians with rifles running down the street. Weapons caches hidden years before were dug up from under basements and garden beds. Secret depots in warehouses and factories were cracked open and guns passed around.

The resistance sent bands of armed civilians to the radio building to support the embattled Czech police units. The SS troops were driven into the building's courtyard and basement, which was then flooded with fire brigade hoses. By mid-afternoon, the resistance had captured the telephone exchange, the post office and the main train station. The fighting had spread all over Prague, but weapons were in short supply.

HEDA MARGOLIUS LEFT her bolthole in Dejvice to volunteer at a makeshift resistance centre in the basement of a cinema. She and another woman were entrusted with a dangerous mission: to pick up a cache of weapons that had been stashed under the railway station six years earlier.

Dressed as nurses, the two women made their way from doorway to doorway, avoiding gunfire. At the station, they spotted a large laundry basket with a red cross on it. They grabbed a handle each and hauled the heavy basket away. Once out of sight, they peeked under the sheet and saw a layer of bandages and medical supplies, and further down a pile of guns.

Rounding the corner, they were stopped by an armed German soldier. Heda's companion dropped her handle in fright, and the basket hit the ground with a tell-tale metallic clank. Thinking quickly, she lifted the sheet and pulled out some bandages. Speaking German, she offered them to the soldier who politely accepted them and the women continued on their way with the basket.

THE END OF THE WAR was just days away, but a million or so German army troops led by Field Marshal Ferdinand Schorner remained encircled within Bohemia and Moravia. Schorner ordered the Waffen-SS units still in Prague to hold the city at all costs; his army needed the city's bridges to retreat to the west, where they hoped to surrender to the Americans, rather than suffer the vengeance of the advancing Red Army. But the Prague SS garrison found itself pinned down by resistance fighters, who tore up cobblestones and constructed barricades with overturned trams, trucks, carts, mattresses and timber beams.

The resistance fighters were joined by rogue Russian units led by General Andrey Vlasov, who had earlier defected to fight with the Germans, but now switched sides once again, and supported the resistance with heavy weaponry. Confusingly, Vlasov's troops attacked German positions from German tanks, inscribed with 'DEATH TO HITLER' and 'DEATH TO STALIN'. Artillery fire pounded through the city. Czech civilians lay dead in the streets. With just two days of the war left to run, the fighting had finally come to Prague.

IN THE EARLY HOURS of 6 May, four columns of Wehrmacht and SS troops from outlying districts arrived in central Prague. At dawn, gun battles broke out in suburban streets. Several armoured vehicles rolled into Vinohrady to take back the radio building but were held at bay by the Czech militia.

At the radio building, Czech partisans and police exchanged shots with SS units until late afternoon when two Messerschmitt fighter-bombers dropped a 250-kilogram bomb on the building. The explosion knocked out the radio transmitter, but the resistance was able to resume broadcasting eighty minutes later from a new transmitter in Strasnice.

As the fighting intensified across the city, an excited announcer broadcast a newsflash: The US army had entered the country. 'Pilsen is occupied! British and American tanks are advancing towards Prague!'[30]

THE AMERICANS HAD HEARD Prague's cry for help but could do nothing. US General George Patton's 3rd Army had been given orders to halt at Pilsen, just eighty kilometres west of Prague. At Yalta, the Allies had agreed that the Red Army would drive the Germans from Czechoslovakia, but Patton's tanks and troops had advanced more rapidly than expected and the general wanted to push on to Prague. The British high command repeatedly urged the Americans to let Patton's army liberate the capital rather than leave the job to the Soviets. Churchill pressed President Truman to act: 'There is little doubt that the liberation of Prague ... by your forces might make the whole difference to the post-war situation.'[31]

The question was put in the lap of the Allied commander General Dwight Eisenhower, who was advised, misleadingly, that the Red Army was close to Prague, and didn't want their men killed in friendly fire. Eisenhower, who wanted to preserve American lives, decided he wouldn't sacrifice his troops for 'purely political purposes' and confirmed the order to stay put in Pilsen.

Patton still strained at the leash. Three of his soldiers were sent into Prague to report on the state of the uprising. Dodging sniper fire, the Americans raced their jeep through the city, right up to the resistance headquarters in Bartolomejska Street, and brought one of the leaders, Captain Jaromir Nechansky, back to Pilsen. Patton was moved by their report of the courage of the Czech fighters, and pleaded with his superiors one more time to be allowed to liberate Prague. General Omar Bradley telephoned him to reinforce Eisenhower's decision: 'You hear me, George?' Bradley said, 'Goddammit, *halt.*'[32]

THE NEXT DAY, 7 May, Hitler's successors surrendered unconditionally to the Allied powers. Even so, General Schorner ordered his troops in Prague to keep fighting until his army could make its escape to the American lines in western Bohemia.

Meanwhile, the siege at the radio headquarters intensified; resistance fighters coming and going from the building came under murderous fire from SS machine gun positions, set up on the first floor of a nearby school. Within the radio building, a band of fighters volunteered to take out the nest of Nazi machine guns. The Czech partisans were joined by two British soldiers, Private William Greig and Thomas Vokes, who had escaped from a nearby prisoner-of-war camp.

The band of volunteers made their way towards the school through a network of underground cellars and surfaced in an apartment block opposite the Nazi stronghold. Climbing to the top floor, they fired into the school windows across the road, but the Germans refused to surrender and returned fire. The resistance fighters were badly outgunned and several of their men were shot. There was talk of abandoning their mission, but then Thomas Vokes came up with a new plan. Knowing the Germans were desperate to avoid falling into the Red Army's hands, he suggested they bluff them into surrendering to the British army instead.

In a nearby house, a Czech woman cleaned and pressed their uniforms into a near pristine state. Then, accompanied by two Czech commanders, the sharply kitted out British soldiers approached the school under the cover of a white flag, striding forward with as much coolness and authority as they could manage.

Inside the building, Greig informed the SS commanding officer that a British parachute division had already entered the city, and that a combined invasion force was just hours away. Vokes warned the SS commander that unless he surrendered right now, he and his men would be completely destroyed. The commander signed the surrender document at 11.40 am, agreeing to abandon the school. In addition, he handed over a carload of *Panzerfaust* anti-tank weapons, guns and ammunition to the Czech fighters.[33]

ELSEWHERE IN THE CITY, panicked SS men ran wild, shooting groups of civilians and plundering their houses. Waffen-SS units used Czech civilians as human shields for their tanks. Czech guerrillas retaliated with random killings of anyone they deemed to be German, or a German sympathiser.

SS armoured units set up positions in the Old Town Square to shell a resistance cell operating from the ancient catacombs of the Town Hall. The tanks opened fire on the medieval building, shattering the north and east wings and setting the Astronomical Clock ablaze, along with its painted calendar dial and wooden statues. Thick black smoke floated up past the Tyn Church spires. By the following morning, the clock was a blackened ruin.

ON 8 MAY, THE PRAGUE uprising entered its third day, as the Germans resumed bombarding resistance positions around Prague. The desperate Czech partisans were running out of ammunition. The Red Army had not yet arrived, the Americans weren't coming. Prague's historic centre was in danger of being blown apart by German artillery and aerial bombardment.

GENERAL RUDOLF TOUSSAINT, THE last German military commander of Prague, was desperate too, and ready to cut a deal with the Czech resistance. At 10 am, he was picked up in Mala Strana by three Czech partisans, blindfolded with a tattered piece of a swastika flag and driven to resistance headquarters.

Toussaint made his offer to the resistance leaders: he would surrender the city if they would allow his soldiers to depart unharmed the following morning. After hours of negotiation, Toussaint signed the surrender.

'Who am I now?' Toussaint muttered. 'A general without an army. All I can do is go home and sit in the ditch and look at the blue sky.'

The Germans had lost another war.

'We deserved it,' Toussaint told his hosts.[34]

Wounded German officer, Prague uprising. Zdenek Tmej.

THE NEXT MORNING, 9 May, a convoy of German armoured vehicles and trucks roared out of Prague. The city at last fell into silence, broken only by the occasional crack of gunfire from a few isolated pockets of SS men. More than 1600 Czechs had died in the uprising, with thousands more injured.

THAT AFTERNOON, A COLUMN of Soviet tanks was spotted on the outskirts of Prague. A radio reporter went out to ride alongside the liberators. 'We are coming down the winding hill from the castle,' he told his listeners excitedly. 'On the left is Klarov, on the right Hradcany, and before us a city is spreading out whose joy reaches the stars. At this moment, the Red Army has liberated Prague!'[35]

Heda Margolius came out to witness the entry of the Soviet troops: 'People streamed into the streets to cheer, to welcome, to embrace their liberators, asking them into their homes, offering them every good thing they had. Pretty girls covered the tanks with flowers and climbed onto the armoured trucks. The Russians laughed good-naturedly and took out their accordions. The world was full of fragrance and music and joy.' At sunset, she walked through Mala Strana to the Klarov Bridge and looked out at the peaceful city spread out before her. There was no one around. At the entrance to the bridge, Heda saw the corpse of a uniformed SS man, lying on the cobblestones in a pool of black blood. She looked down at the now harmless creature and thought to herself: 'Now, at this moment and on this spot, the war is over, because he is dead and I am alive.'[36]

Edvard Benes returns to Prague.

Wild Transfer

PRESIDENT BENES and his wife, Hana, made their triumphant return to Prague on 16 May 1945. In this season of liberation, dazzling spring weather broke out over the city. The cherry trees on Petrin Hill and Letna Park came into blossom; the theatres, concert halls and the university opened their doors once more.

From a high window at the castle, Benes took a moment to survey his still-intact capital with satisfaction. 'Is it not beautiful?' he said. 'The only central European city not destroyed. And it was all my doing.'[37] He had convinced himself he had done the right thing after all in surrendering to the Munich ultimatum.

Czech filmmakers produced a propaganda documentary with the help of the British and Soviet authorities titled *We Shall Keep Faith*. The film opened with a sunlit view of T. G. Masaryk's study, followed by footage of Benes at his funeral in 1937, pledging to remain true to the great man's vision for the nation. The film offered a comforting narrative of restoration, but a return to the *status quo ante bellum* was impossible. The founder's dream of a tolerant multi-ethnic republic was gone for good. The war had carried the Czech people too far from his values and there was no way back. Premysl Pitter, a Christian pacifist observed, 'The waters have receded, but the earth remains covered with dirt.'[38]

IN THE WEST, PEOPLE had taken comfort in the thought that democracy and human decency had prevailed over Nazi wickedness. The Americans and the British could reassure themselves that some mysterious process of cosmic justice had lent strength to their armies. But a great many Czechs had arrived at the opposite conclusion: they had seen their democratic values, their humanism, overpowered by the Nazi juggernaut. Czechs now knew, in their bones, the cynical truth of Lenin's famous maxim *kto kovo*, literally 'who, whom': the whole question of politics and power is – who will prevail over whom?[39]

Benes's aide Prokop Drtina had absorbed this logic of might-makes-right when he proclaimed it was now the turn of the Czechs to prevail over the Germans: 'One of us must leave,' he said, 'either the Germans or us – and since this is a Czech country and we are the winners, they are the ones to go!'[40] Hitler had poisoned the well of co-existence, and he had been cheered on by too many local Germans. Czech self-righteousness justified the seizing of property that didn't belong to them, and deflected attention from their own collaboration with the Nazi authorities.

THE NEW GOVERNMENT resolved that the local Germans be divided into three categories: those guilty of crimes against the republic were to be expelled or put on trial; Germans who had actively opposed the Nazis could stay; and the rest would need to reapply for citizenship.

It would have taken a statesman of exceptional ability and moral authority to reconcile the two peoples and guide the republic back to a peaceful, if uneasy, form of co-existence. But Benes, never an inspiring leader, wasn't up to the job and didn't want to do it anyway. In Brno, he had called on his people to avenge themselves. 'The German people,' he said 'ceased to be human in this war … and behaved like a monster. Their nation must pay for this with a severe punishment … We must liquidate the German problem definitively,' an act, he hinted darkly, that would require, 'the combined strength of everyone'.[41]

Heeding this incitement to violence, Czechs took matters into their own hands in a three-month outbreak of ethnic cleansing, a period known as the 'wild transfer'. In this lawless environment, the Bohemian Germans faced a terrible and final nemesis, as the vengeful Czechs held them responsible, collectively, for the crimes of the Nazis.

In Prague on 9 May, thousands of German residents were ordered to pack a suitcase and assemble in Strossmayer Square, where men with buckets of paint daubed swastikas on their coats and luggage. From there they were led into a nearby cinema and held captive for several days. Soviet soldiers made repeated visits in the darkness of the cinema, selecting women by torchlight to be raped, helping themselves to watches and jewellery. Dr Friedrich Korkisch, a law academic, was at home with his wife when two Czech partisans came to their apartment and ordered them to leave at gunpoint. A truck was waiting outside for them. The couple were told they could take with them only what they could carry. They were both elderly, so a Czech neighbour carried an extra suitcase for them. Outside their door, a jeering crowd had assembled. The cry went up that Czechs should not be bag-carriers for Germans, so the helper went back inside with the suitcase. Someone punched the doctor in the head.

Korkisch and his wife were sent to Tynice, near Cesky Brod, to a camp where Germans were routinely worked to death as farm labourers. Nearly every prisoner suffered typhus or malnutrition. Korkisch estimated the death rate for the year at forty to fifty per cent. Despite their advanced age, he and his wife survived, and after two years at the camp, were expelled into the American-occupation zone of Germany. They never saw their apartment in Prague again.[42]

THE HUMANITARIAN CRISIS created by the wild transfer was raised at the Allies' Potsdam Conference in mid-July. Churchill expressed his grave concern, while US president Harry Truman wondered how all the ethnic Germans could be accommodated in a devastated Germany. The leaders accepted the deportations would go ahead but should be temporarily suspended while the Allies prepared their respective zones of occupation in Germany to receive the refugees.

By the end of 1946, nearly three million ethnic Germans, mostly from the Sudetenland, had been expelled into the American and Soviet occupation zones. The estimated death toll of the transfers varies wildly. Early estimates placed it at around 270,000 people. More recent research puts the figure much lower, at between 24,000 and 40,000, which includes suicides and unexplained deaths.[43] Stripped of their property and most of their possessions, the survivors would have to restart their lives in a defeated country struggling with food and housing shortages.

German women paving the streets in Prague, 1945.

The Soft Bitterness of Life

NAZI WAR CRIMINALS and collaborators now faced a grim future or no future at all. SS commandant K. H. Frank was picked up by the US army in western Bohemia. Eight thousand spectators gathered in the courtyard of Pankrac Prison to witness his hanging; among them were relatives of those killed at Lidice.

Konrad Henlein surrendered to Patton's army in Pilsen, where he took his own life by slashing his wrists with a concealed razor blade. Karel Curda, the Czech paratrooper who had betrayed Heydrich's assassins, was tried and convicted of high treason. Asked by the judge how he could have betrayed his friends, he replied, 'I think you would do the same for a million marks, your honour.'[44] He too was executed in Pankrac Prison on 29 April 1947.

LIDA BAAROVA, at war's end, was taken into custody and sentenced to two years' prison for collaboration. Her affair with Goebbels destroyed her family. Her mother died of a heart attack under interrogation by Czech police. Her sister, Zorka Janu, also an actress, was blacklisted from the theatre. Deeply depressed, she jumped from a window to her death.

On her release from prison, Lida married a young actor, Jan Kopecky, and the couple slipped across the border into Austria. In Salzburg, she found work as a barmaid at the Café Mozart, where she received high tips from customers astonished to be served by a movie star.

Lida resumed her film career in the 1950s, acting in several Spanish and Italian films, including Fellini's *I Vitelloni*. She took on stage work, but the odium of her Nazi past still clung to her. At the Graz Theatre, she was met with egg-throwing protestors. She wrote one memoir, *Escapes*, and then another, *The Soft Bitterness of Life*, which contradicted several of the claims in the earlier one.

Lida kept no memorabilia of her time with Goebbels. 'I've torn up all my pictures of us,' she said irritably in her later years. 'Thanks to him I fell into the depths of hell.' At other times she claimed to be unrepentant about the affair. When asked to reflect on Nazi war crimes, she just shrugged, 'I feel indifferent. I just want to forget the whole episode.'[45]

Interregnum

POST-WAR CZECHOSLOVAKIA had become, as Benes hoped, a much more homogenous nation. The Czechs and Slovaks now had a nation to themselves, almost entirely free of Germans, ethnic Hungarians and Ruthenians. Before the war, Germans had comprised 29 per cent of the population of Bohemia and Moravia. By 1950, they accounted for less than two per cent.[46]

The Jews of Prague had been almost entirely annihilated. Of the 56,000 living in Prague at the start of the war, only 424 had survived by remaining in hiding, protected by Czech and German friends.[47] The Old-New Synagogue was still there, as was the ancient cemetery, but there were too few of the living to sustain a congregation. A thousand years of Jewish philosophy, literature, folklore, commerce and conversation fell into silence.

IF THE MULTI-ETHNIC flavour of the old republic was largely gone, its democratic spirit was badly wounded too. The destruction of Masaryk's idealistic republic had induced a kind of moral disorientation. Some turned to the church, but for many, communist ideology offered a more compelling explanation for what had gone wrong and a seemingly rational alternative to weak-kneed liberal democracy. For them, the problem had not been Hitler, nor the war, nor the Depression that preceded it, but the whole broken system that had produced these monsters. Becoming a communist allowed Czechs to draw a line under the catastrophe of the past decade, to dedicate themselves to a nation-building project and to face the future with optimism.

Heda Margolius, now reunited with her husband, Rudolf, was torn between her loyalty to Masaryk's 'bourgeois' democracy and the persuasive arguments made by friends who came to their apartment to make the case for a communist future. After hearing the arguments from both sides, Rudolf presented Heda with two application forms for the Czechoslovak Communist Party.

US DIPLOMAT GEORGE KENNAN, now based in Moscow, wrote to a colleague that the Soviets saw 'only vassals and enemies; and the neighbours of Russia, if they do not wish to be the one, must reconcile themselves to being the other'.[48] President Benes nonetheless remained confident that by embracing the Soviet Union, he had won some leeway to re-establish his republic as a bridge between East and West. Winston Churchill, however, realised that being in the Soviet camp put Czechoslovakia on the far side of an impenetrable barrier. In his famous 'Iron Curtain' speech of 1946, Churchill listed Prague as one of the 'famous cities' now subject to 'a very high and, in many cases, increasing measure of control from Moscow'.[49]

Two months after Churchill's speech, the Czechoslovak communists won a plurality of seats in the parliamentary elections, but fell short of a majority. Gottwald became prime minister and communists took over the critical ministries of information, finance and the interior, which gave them control of the police. Worried democrats were reassured by the presence of Jan Masaryk in the cabinet, who stayed on as foreign minister, but the interior minister, Vaclav Nosek, created several new agencies, including the State Security Police – the StB, which soon began targeting opponents of the Communist Party.

Any lingering hopes Benes and Jan Masaryk might have held that they could entertain close relations with both Washington and Moscow were dispelled in 1947, when Stalin quashed their plans to participate in the Marshall Plan, an American proposal to revive Europe's ailing economies with a massive aid program. The scale of the aid was unprecedented, and Europe's governments scrambled to take up the offer.

The Czechoslovak government had enthusiastically accepted an invitation to attend a conference in Paris to discuss the program. But as they prepared to go, Masaryk and Gottwald were summoned to an urgent late-night meeting in the Kremlin, where Stalin told them the American offer was an anti-Soviet plot and they should keep out of it. 'If you go to Paris,' he warned, 'you will show that you want to cooperate in an action aimed at isolating the Soviet Union.'[50]

Masaryk said he couldn't see the logic in his objections, but Stalin calmly directed their attention to a nearby map of Europe and said it would be a shame if Czechoslovakia ever had to face Germany alone again. After that chilling warning, the discussion moved on to finding a face-saving way of backing out of the Paris talks. Masaryk told several friends on his return, 'I went to Moscow as the foreign minister of an independent sovereign state; I returned as the lackey of the Soviet government.'[51]

THE REFUSAL TO ACCEPT Marshall Plan aid led to a slump in the popularity of the Communist Party. An opinion poll run by the Interior Ministry predicted the party would lose as many as a quarter of its seats at the upcoming parliamentary elections, scheduled for May 1948. While President Benes officially remained above the politicking, privately he happily predicted the communists would lose and that they would have to take a back seat in the new government. Benes was, as usual, optimistic that democracy could be sustained, but the democrats in his government were troubled by reports that the communists were seizing power by stealth, stacking the police force with party members. Tensions increased on 10 September 1947, when three non-communist ministers, including Jan Masaryk, received package bombs in the mail. The explosives failed to detonate and no one was hurt. The terrorists were identified as Communist Party members, led by Gottwald's son-in-law, but the trial was held off until the following year, when the charge was thrown out.

In February 1948, the non-communist ministers clashed in cabinet with Interior Minister Nosek over reports that eight divisional police commanders had been replaced with party loyalists. The cabinet meeting almost ended in a fistfight.

The democratic ministers decided to bring on a showdown. They threatened to resign en masse, expecting the crisis would bring down the government and force an election that would expose the communists' weak public standing. It was at this moment that a tragic misunderstanding arose between the president and the democrats who needed his leadership.

EDVARD BENES'S HEALTH was failing. The president had suffered a series of strokes that left him struggling to speak and write clearly. When the delegation of democratic ministers came to the castle to discuss their plan, they couldn't help but notice the president's confusion. Benes told them to 'stand firm' but did not give any clear assurances as to what would happen should the ministers leave the government.

On Friday 20 February, twelve ministers submitted their resignations in the expectation that the president would call parliamentary elections to break the deadlock. But they were one minister short: the constitution required the resignation of half of the twenty-six cabinet members to trigger an election, and Jan Masaryk had begged off, citing a bad cold. The Social Democrats declined to resign. The anti-communists couldn't count and Gottwald was ready for them. 'I knew I'd get them in the end,' he said, 'but I never thought they'd hand me their asses to kick on a platter.'[52] Gottwald rushed to the castle and told Benes he must accept the resignations and appoint replacement ministers.

The democratic ministers had left Benes in an impossible position; the failure to take half the cabinet forced the president to deal with the prime minister he had and gave him no legal latitude. The president said he would consider Gottwald's proposal.

Throughout that weekend, the dissenting ministers dithered, while the foreign minister remained in bed. Masaryk might have feared provoking a civil war or a Soviet invasion. Perhaps he was simply exhausted, like Benes, and unable to rouse himself to the emergency.

Gottwald mobilised his forces. Guns were distributed to workers' militia groups, who marched through the streets of Prague and stood guard at public buildings. Newspapers sympathetic to the communists ran headlines blasting the twelve ministers as traitors in the pay of foreign imperialists. State radio urged workers to rise up to defend Gottwald's government. Defence Minister Ludvik Svoboda addressed the communists' Central Action Committee and assured it that the army would 'always remain loyal to the people'.[53]

Benes tried to play for time, but the following day, more than two million citizens took part in a national general strike in support of Gottwald. A counter-protest by pro-democracy students failed to make an impression on the president, who had already decided to bow to the pressure.

ON THE AFTERNOON OF 25 February 1948, Klement Gottwald, accompanied by the party's general secretary, Rudolf Slansky, arrived by car in Wenceslas Square to address a cheering crowd of party supporters. Wearing a woollen Russian hat,* Gottwald grinned as he gave the crowd the stunning news, but he was drunk and slurred his words: 'I have just come from the castle, where I have seen the president of the republic, and I can tell you that he has accepted all of my proposals without making any changes.' This was, he said, 'the defeat of reaction and the victory of the working people.'[54]

Heda Margolius was watching from the window of the publishing house where she worked as an art editor. Her boss, standing beside her, softly said, 'This is a day to remember. Today, our democracy is dying.'[55]

TWO DAYS LATER, President Benes swore in the new ministers. Jan Masaryk was asked to stay on as foreign minister, but otherwise

---

* The hat was thoughtfully placed on his head by his friend and comrade Vladimir Clementis, who would be hanged as a traitor in 1952 at the end of the Stalinist show trials. Clementis was subsequently erased from the photo of Gottwald's victory speech.

Gottwald's government was entirely dominated by communists or fellow travellers.

Author Graham Greene happened to be in Prague visiting his publisher just as the coup was taking place. Arriving well after midnight, he discovered all the restaurants in Prague were closed, but the porter told him the hotel staff were having a party in the basement and there would be food there.

Downstairs, Greene found the party in full swing. He saw the Venezuelan ambassador dancing with the cook. Other diplomats were drinking with the pastry chefs and chambermaids. 'If this was really a revolution,' he thought, 'it seemed to me not so bad.'

The next day, Greene noted the parades and the shouting in the street. The joyful impression from the late-night party dimmed, and he noticed 'the bitter humour of defeat was circulating'. Greene visited his publisher twice. On the second occasion he saw an armed sentry at the door. Soon afterwards, the publisher was arrested and disappeared into prison for a decade.[56]

THE COMMUNIST VICTORY changed the face of the city almost instantly; windows were adorned with red flags. Victory processions pounded through the streets. Stalin's picture was hung in every classroom and a banner was draped over Wenceslas Square proclaiming: 'With the Soviet Union Forever!' The authorities swiftly closed the borders. Former ministers found themselves shadowed by secret policemen.

Benes did not stand down. But after having sworn in the new ministry, he left for his home in the countryside in protest. He never returned to Prague Castle. One by one, the new regime replaced members of Benes's staff with communist loyalists who kept a close eye on him. His health deteriorated further. On 12 March, a friend noticed Benes had suffered another stroke. His eyes were watery and fearful, and he moved 'like a puppet damaged by a child'.[57]

The ministers had been too dependent on Benes but, ultimately, responsibility for the failure to defend the Czechoslovak democracy rested with him. He had observed the constitutional proprieties too narrowly: this was not a contest between parties acting in good faith, but a fight against an external threat to the democracy that had been entrusted to his care. In acting too correctly, he had handed power to a clique of fifth columnists acting on behalf of a foreign power, and Benes had given legal sanction to a communist putsch. Democracy was finished and would not resurface in Prague for another forty-one years.

JAN MASARYK HAD REMAINED in his apartment in the Czernin Palace during the crisis, nursing his cold. His American lover, Marcia Davenport, had followed him to Prague, but now Masaryk asked her to leave for her own safety. She thought he looked grey and exhausted.

On the evening of 9 March, Masaryk took care of routine ministerial business in his apartment. His butler brought him a dinner of roast chicken, potatoes and salad. Masaryk reminded him to wake him at eight-thirty the next morning.

AT DAWN, HIS LIFELESS body was found in the palace courtyard. Masaryk had been dead for some hours. His bathroom window, directly above, was open and his apartment was in disarray.

The official verdict was suicide. The communist authorities claimed that Masaryk had become despondent over criticisms of him in the Western press. His English friend Bruce Lockhart supported the suicide theory, saying that Jan 'had come to the end of his physical and mental strength'.[58] But it wasn't clear why a depressed Masaryk did not use the loaded revolver he kept in his room, nor the bottle of sleeping tablets in his bathroom cabinet, and chose instead to climb up and push his paunchy frame through a narrow bathroom window.

The doctor who certified Masaryk's death as a suicide was himself found dead a few weeks later; his death was also ruled a suicide.

In 2004, a police investigation concluded Masaryk was murdered. The distance of his body from the building indicated he did not drop but was thrown from the window. The report argued that the perpetrators were most likely Soviet agents. Masaryk's death rid Stalin of the most popular democrat remaining in the government. It also put Gottwald and his ministers on notice to stay in line or suffer a similar fate.

THE DEATH OF JAN MASARYK distressed Benes terribly. He made a rare trip into Prague to attend the funeral, but he made no speech and sat grimly through the proceedings.

A new constitution was passed through the National Assembly on 9 May, but Benes refused to approve it. It was a hybrid document that kept the shopfront of the old democracy but allowed for each democratic institution to be supervised at every level by the Communist Party. Every civil rights guarantee was smothered by a blanket provision that nullified any exercise of those rights that were deemed to be a threat to the 'People's Democratic Order'.

Under the new constitution, a single list of candidates from the National Front, dominated by the Communist Party, was put before the people and duly elected to the National Assembly. Benes, who was now very ill, privately complained to Gottwald but said nothing publicly. He resigned the presidency for the second time on 7 June 1948. The official announcement cited health reasons for his departure. Gottwald replaced him as president, fulfilling his lifelong ambition of becoming master of Prague Castle.

Benes was granted a salary and allowed to remain in his country estate. For the first time in his life, the ailing ex-president had nothing to do. After suffering several more strokes, Benes fell into a coma and died on 3 September 1948. He was sixty-four years old.

TOMAS MASARYK HAD considered falseness to be the most dangerous of human vices. 'Don't lie!' he had once commanded. 'That would be the first law of a modern code of ethics.'[59] As president, he had taken Jan Hus's slogan *Pravda Vitezi* – Truth Prevails – and made it the national motto. But under this new regime, with all its weird inversions, truth would become a hostage to power once more. Reality in Prague would become slippery, mutable. Masaryk and his son Jan would simply disappear from official memory, as though they had never existed.

Today there is a bust of Jan Masaryk's noble bald head in the lobby of the Czernin Palace, but a better monument to him sits over the entrance to the family villa in Vinohrady – a bronze plaque stencilled with his sardonic reworking of Hus's motto: 'The truth prevails, but it's hard work.'

CHAPTER NINE

BE WITH US. WE ARE WITH YOU.

1949–1968

Mistakes

THE SECOND ANNIVERSARY of the Communist Party's 'Victorious February' was celebrated with a gala ball at Prague Castle. Heda Margolius, accompanied by her husband walked through one glittering state room after another, where the ancient royal treasures of Bohemia were on display. The guests, a mix of senior government figures and intellectuals, helped themselves to glasses of champagne and platters of food from the buffet table.

Five years had passed since Heda had come home to Prague in her concentration camp rags. Now her husband, Rudolf Margolius, was deputy trade minister and the couple had become members of the *nomenklatura*, the highest and most privileged echelon of party members. But on this night, despite the fine food and wine and the opulent surroundings, Heda felt the old fear creeping back into her heart.

Since taking the post, her husband had buried himself in his work, while Heda mournfully observed the arrests, the food shortages, the public displays of compulsory joyfulness. Within a year of communist rule, 25,000 people were jailed for political reasons.[1]

The abolition of private ownership had transformed every shop in Prague into a state-owned enterprise. Items in high demand were often kept under the counter, to be sold to favoured customers or bartered for other goods. When word got out that a store was about to receive new stock, workers took hours off to stand in line outside the door. Periodic rumours of a currency devaluation sent people scurrying to buy whatever goods they could find before their savings became worthless. Under these conditions, the economy seized up and refused to work.

Party propaganda nonetheless assured citizens that their nation was a model in all things for the entire world. Cinema newsreels showed footage of happy workers and grateful citizens offering floral bouquets to party leaders at public forums. The steep drop in living standards was blamed on a conspiracy of spies, saboteurs and black marketeers. Many of Prague's writers and intellectuals had become cheerleaders for the regime; the rest resigned themselves to the new system, a furtive life of 'fear, blood draining out of the face, trembling hands, talking in whispers, silence, apathy, sealing windows shut, suspicion of one's neighbours, signing up for the hated Party membership'.[2]

At the gala, Heda was in one of the smaller salons when President Gottwald entered the room, drunk, propped up on the arm of the speaker of the Assembly. Gottwald's health had sharply deteriorated since taking office from alcoholism, heart disease and the symptoms of syphilis.

The president lurched towards her and demanded to know why she wasn't drinking. A waiter speedily handed them both a glass of wine, which they drank. Gottwald waved his empty glass around, squinted at her and again demanded to know why she wasn't drinking. The speaker laughed nervously and manoeuvred the president out of the room. Heda's legs were trembling under her gown.[3]

GOTTWALD'S LIKELY SUCCESSOR was his second in command, Rudolf Slansky, the ruthless party general secretary. After taking power, Slansky had crushed the remaining voices of dissent within the country, ordering the executions of more than 100 political prisoners. Slansky was a dedicated Bolshevik, but he was also Jewish, and Stalin, in his dotage, had slid into a sump of anti-Semitic paranoia. The Soviet leader wanted a purge of the Czechoslovak Party and Slansky was the perfect candidate to play the role of string-puller of a vast and fictional conspiracy. Tearing down a figure as senior as Slansky would remind the Czechoslovak party that no one was beyond Stalin's reach. Soviet ideologues accordingly drafted a document chillingly titled 'On Several Mistakes of the Communist Party of Czechoslovakia', which laid the blame for many of these at Slansky's feet.

Moscow's evident dislike of Slansky placed an agonising burden on Gottwald; the two men were old friends and comrades-in-arms, who had supported each other before, during and after the war. Deeply worried, Gottwald and Slansky responded to these Soviet hints by sending an abject telegram to Moscow in September 1949, asking for advisors to assist the StB in locating the saboteurs within the party. In October, two colonels from Soviet state security arrived in Prague and took over the investigation. Within months, six government ministers were arrested, imprisoned and subsequently tortured.

IN JULY 1951, STALIN sent a message to Prague Castle insisting that Slansky be dismissed for having appointed 'unreliable persons and enemies' to government positions.[4] The timing of the demand, however, was supremely awkward: the party was part-way through public celebrations of Slansky's fiftieth birthday: two leather-bound editions of his written works had been published, and Gottwald had presented him with the nation's highest honour, the Order of Socialism.

On 6 September 1951, Slansky was removed as party general secretary and demoted to deputy prime minister. Knowing he was in grave danger; he performed an act of self-criticism in front of his ministerial comrades. In late November, Slansky and his wife were coming home from a party when they noticed all the lights in the house were out. Inside the darkened house, he was grabbed, handcuffed and driven away with a hood on his head.

Slansky's interrogators used well-honed Soviet methods to break him. He lost all sense of time as each day passed in endless rounds of questions and beatings from a rotating shift of officers. Still, Slansky denied being part of a Trotskyite–Zionist plot, and insisted there had been some terrible mistake. After one interrogation session, he locked himself in a room, ripped out the telephone cord, looped it around his neck and attempted to hang himself from the window. Maintenance workers broke open the door just in time to save him.

FORCED CONFESSIONS LED to more arrests. On the night of 10 January 1952, Heda Margolius's husband, Rudolf, failed to come home. At 1 am, five men came to the apartment and told her Rudolf had been arrested. Heda sat in her armchair, smoking cigarettes, glaring at the StB officers as they searched each room, confiscating items they considered suspicious.

The next day she called every high official she knew to beg for help or information. Some expressed sympathy but could do nothing. Then they, too, were arrested. People who had once fawned over her now avoided her in the street. A month later she was fired from her job. For the second time in her life, Heda was too dangerous to be seen with. A non-person.[5]

*

The Meat Queue

LATE AT NIGHT, as they lay in bed, Praguers became accustomed to the sound of cars pulling up in the street outside, the footsteps on the stairs, the scuffles and anguished cries from the neighbours down the hall that they had done nothing wrong. Then, in the morning, they would read in the party newspaper *Rude Pravo* that life was getting better and better, that humanity was reaching its full potential under party rule. Even romantic love was becoming richer and more edifying. 'People will still fall in love,' declared the culture minister Zdenek Nejedly, 'but we expect that, under socialism, as the working class, they will love each other more and better than before.'[6]

The credit for this new joyfulness was to be laid at the feet of comrade Stalin. On the occasion of the Great Helmsman's seventieth birthday, the party in Prague commissioned a gigantic monument that was to stand above the river on Letna Hill. Reaching thirty metres high, it was to be the biggest statue of the Soviet leader in the world. Stalin's shoe alone would be two metres long.

The design competition was won by a modernist sculptor named Otakar Svec, who sketched out a heroic vision of the Soviet leader, book in hand, staring benignly across the river. Behind him, there would be a procession of Soviet and Czech heroes: a soldier, a worker with a flag, a farmer, a female partisan. The model for Svec's winning design was published in the party newspapers. Praguers instantly dubbed it *fronta na maso* – the meat queue.

Svec was terrified. He had entered the competition only because failure to do so would have brought him under suspicion. He had gone so far as to plagiarise another sculptor's work, hoping he would be disqualified, but he won anyway.

Svec now found himself at the mercy of equally anxious government ministers and bureaucrats, fretting about this or that aspect of his design, worried it might unintentionally offend their Soviet masters. There were compositional issues: could he make Stalin bigger and the followers smaller? Why was he approaching the city from the west instead of the east? Why had he stopped at the riverbank and not continued? When ministers came to meet Svec in his studio, they would bring a penknife to lop off slivers of clay from bits of the model they didn't like. Months and then years passed in these bouts of hair-splitting, but the delay itself was dangerous and could be interpreted as a lack of ideological enthusiasm.

Meanwhile, huge slabs of granite were mined and delivered to the site, ready to be sculpted into Stalin's likeness. A pedestal was constructed on Letna Hill from reinforced concrete, but Svec worried it might not take the weight of the granite, and that the monument would collapse into the hill.

The sculptor began drinking heavily and socialising with other women. His wife, Vlasta, became equally miserable and took her own life. Svec discovered her in the bathtub.

On 2 March 1955, two months before the public unveiling, Svec took a taxi to the site and asked the driver what he thought of the statue. Not knowing he was in the presence of the artist, the driver pointed to the thrusting arm of the partisan woman, and said it looked like she was groping the crotch of the soldier behind her.

'I'm telling you,' he told Svec, 'when they unveil it, the guy who designed it is one-hundred-percent sure to get shot.'[7]

Svec went back to his studio and killed himself. His body wasn't discovered for another fifty days. News of his death was covered up and his name was not engraved on the completed monument. He too had become a non-person.

The massive Stalin Monument on Letna Hill.

The Terror

THE WHOLE CITY WAS now pulled into the undertow of the Stalinist terror. In these years, nearly a quarter of a million Czechs and Slovaks would be convicted of political crimes and 178 would be executed in the largest set of show trials in the Soviet bloc, scripted and orchestrated by the Soviet advisors.[8]

After two months of torture and constant interrogation, Rudolf Slansky's will broke, and he agreed to say and do everything asked of him. The beatings ended and the food improved. The interrogators spent weeks helping Slansky memorise and rehearse his confession.

Of the fourteen men indicted in the Slansky trial, eleven were Jewish, including Rudolf Margolius. The prosecutors labelled the accused as 'repulsive traitors', 'dogs', and 'wolves'.[9] Each defendant made elaborate admissions of guilt, claiming they had joined the Communist Party merely to subvert it from within. All confessed they had been part of a complex Fascist/Titoist/Zionist bourgeois nationalist plot to destroy the people's democracies.

ON 27 NOVEMBER 1952, eleven of the defendants, including Slansky and Margolius, were sentenced to death. On the scaffold at Pankrac Prison, Slansky thanked his executioner and muttered, 'I'm getting what I deserved.'[10] He was thinking, possibly, of others he had once condemned on trumped-up charges.

The method of hanging was the same used on Karl Hermann Frank: death was achieved through slow strangulation on a short drop, with a cord instead of a noose. Such a sadistic process suggests a degree of gleeful hatred for the 'traitors' on the scaffold.

The show trials were broadcast to a mass audience on state radio. If listeners held private doubts as to the victims' guilt, or of the sanity of the howling prosecutors, they mostly kept those reservations to themselves. Enormous pressure was brought to bear on people to act as though they truly believed everything was just as the authorities said it was. The people were being trained to manage a constant inner tension – the need to pay lip-service to the prevailing ideology while concealing inner disagreement. In this way, a person might know the condemned men to be innocent, but can sincerely hate them as traitors all the same.

OF THE 178 PEOPLE executed because of the Stalinist show trials in Prague, only one was a woman.

Milada Horakova was a pro-Masaryk democrat, a socialist and a sincere Christian. After she graduated from Charles University with a law degree, she became an activist in the women's movement and the Czechoslovak Red Cross. Her mentor in these years was the influential senator Frantiska Plaminkova, a Czech feminist who had formed the Committee for Women's Suffrage before the war. While attending several women's forums, Milada met and befriended another feminist pioneer, Eleanor Roosevelt, the wife of the US president.

During the Nazi occupation, Milada was arrested and tortured by the Gestapo at Terezin. At war's end she re-entered public life as a left-of-centre anti-communist and won a seat in the National Assembly. When the communists took power in 1948, she resigned her seat. A year later she was arrested and imprisoned again. Her husband escaped to West Germany and she never saw him again.

In the course of her trial, the prosecution presented 'evidence' of gun caches and swastika flags, implying that she, a Gestapo victim, was a closet Nazi. Milada expected to be sentenced to some years in prison, but the government orchestrated a public campaign of letters, meetings and petitions calling for her to be given the death penalty.

Her co-defenders confessed their guilt and agreed they deserved the death penalty, but Milada refused to play the role assigned to her in the courtroom. She said she would accept the punishment the court assigned to her, but would remain faithful to the ideals of Masaryk and Benes. 'And I want to say this,' she told the courtroom, 'no-one in this country should be made to die for their beliefs. And no-one should go to prison for them.'[11]

On 8 June 1950, the court sentenced Milada Horakova to death. Winston Churchill, Eleanor Roosevelt and Albert Einstein sent messages asking for clemency, but they were ignored.

AS SHE AWAITED HER execution, Milada wrote a series of letters to her family that were never delivered. Her daughter, Jana, who was sixteen at the time, read hers forty years later, after the fall of the communist regime:

My only little girl Jana,

God blessed my life as a woman with you ... Apart from your father's magic, amazing love, you were the greatest gift I received from fate ... Don't be frightened and sad because I am not coming back any more. Learn, my child, to look at life early as a serious matter. Life is hard, it does not pamper anybody, and for every time it strokes you it gives you ten blows. Become accustomed to that soon, but don't let it defeat you. Decide to fight. Have courage and clear goals – and you will win over life.

Much is still unclear to your young mind, and I don't have time left to explain to you things you would still like to ask me. One day, when you grow up, you will wonder and wonder, why your mother who loved you and whose greatest gift you were, managed her life so strangely. Perhaps then you will find the right solution to this problem, perhaps, a better one than I could give you today myself.

The letter concludes with a benediction:

I kiss your hair, eyes and mouth, I stroke you and hold you in my arms (I really held you so little). I shall always be with you.[12]

MILADA AND THE OTHER condemned prisoners were led into the courtyard of Pankrac Prison. Party members had been awarded special tickets to witness the hangings, and they treated the spectacle like an exciting sporting contest, littering the courtyard with cigarette butts and chocolate wrappers.[13]

As she stepped up to the scaffold, Milada was heard to say, 'I am falling, falling. I lost this battle. I am falling honourably, I love this land, I love this people, work for its prosperity! I am departing without hatred for you. I wish you, I wish you ...' And then she died.[14]

Milada Horakova on trial, 1950.

The Engineers of Human Souls

THE DEATH OF STALIN on 5 March 1953 was announced in a sombre black-bordered edition of the party newspaper *Rude Pravo*. The editorial writers reached for every kind of overwrought superlative, as though Stalin was somehow still looking over their shoulders.

President Gottwald paid tribute to the dead man as one of the two greatest geniuses in human history (Lenin was the other), then boarded a plane to attend the funeral in Moscow. But Gottwald was not a well man either. Five days after the funeral, he suffered a burst artery and died, and so Prague put on its mourning clothes for the second time in a week, with black veils draped across windows and flags at half-mast. Gottwald's coffin was ferried through the cold streets of Prague to scenes of performative weeping. His untimely death was hailed as the supreme act of loyalty to Stalin.

GOTTWALD'S REPLACEMENT as party leader (variously titled general secretary or first secretary) was Antonin Novotny, who won the job with Moscow's backing. Square-jawed, thin-lipped, with a fine head of steel-grey hair, Novotny was sometimes flattered with the nickname Krasny Tony – Beautiful Tony. One colleague, however, described him as 'a frigid political hoodlum with the approximate charm of a petulant cobra'.[15]

Trained as a locksmith and metal worker, Novotny signed up as a founding member of the nascent Czechoslovak Communist Party at the age of sixteen. When Nazi Germany invaded Prague in 1939, he went underground until the Gestapo found him and sent him to Mauthausen concentration camp.

After the war, Novotny returned to Czechoslovakia, climbed the ranks of the Communist Party and, in 1951, he entered the presidium of the central committee, the party's supreme governing body, just as the Stalinist terror was getting underway. Novotny took a leading role in preparing the case for the judicial murder of his former comrades Slansky and Clementis.

After the traitors' executions, their household possessions were passed on to senior party members. Novotny's wife, Bozena, helped herself to the Clementis family's bed linen and teaset, which she had often admired while visiting their home in happier times. Novotny, for his part, felt no qualms sleeping between the sheets of a man whom he'd connived to have executed. Having survived a Nazi invasion, internment in a concentration camp and the Stalinist terror, he may well have concluded that perpetual horror and violence were simply the way of the world.

Under Novotny's rule, Czechoslovakia became a model Soviet satellite. Moscow rewarded his loyalty by naming a mountain in Kyrgyzstan for him. But he was at a loss to know how to respond when Stalin's successor, Nikita Khrushchev, delivered a sensational 'secret' speech in Moscow denouncing Stalin's crimes and failures.

Khrushchev's speech left Novotny, the obedient Stalinist, right out on a limb. Despite his reflexive obedience to Moscow, Novotny could hardly renounce the purges and executions of the Stalinist terror because he couldn't disown his own role in them.

IF DE-STALINISATION WAS simply too hard to fully address in an open, meaningful way, it could at least be implemented at a cosmetic level, by getting rid of the party's grand folly: the super-massive Stalin monument that continued to menace the city from its perch on Letna Hill. It seemed prudent now to tear the thing down.

Typically, Novotny went about it in a manner that might allow the party to pretend the monument never existed in the first place. So, in October 1962, Prague residents were ordered to remain indoors, while the demolition crew set about razing Otakar Svec's accursed statue to the ground. The head of the crew was ordered to demolish it, 'but with dignity'.[16]

Demolishing the fifteen-metre-high 17,000-tonne monument in a single big explosion risked sending massive chunks of granite flying into the Old Town, so it would have to be demolished in stages. More than 800 kilograms of dynamite were required. The result could hardly pass unnoticed: booming explosions shook windows across the city, filling the streets with smoke and grit. It was rumoured that the first detonation had decapitated one of the observers, a party chieftain, and sent his head splashing into the Vltava River.[17]

*

IN 1957, FIRST SECRETARY Novotny assumed the mantle of president of the republic and moved into Prague Castle. In 1960, he introduced a new constitution, his proudest achievement, which hailed the Czechoslovak state as the first nation in the Soviet bloc to fully achieve socialism. But it was all downhill for him thereafter.

The Stalinist terror had scarred the country economically as well as psychologically. The purging of independent thought and enterprise had created a managerial vacuum that was filled by unqualified apparatchiks, who had nothing but their abject loyalty to recommend them for their positions. The overall effect was like putting the levers of the economy in the hands of anxiously obedient circus animals, ever watchful for cues from their masters. Bohemia, once a manufacturing powerhouse, slipped well behind its prosperous neighbours in the West. People living in the industrially poisoned borderlands could see on West German television how different life was in the capitalist world.

In 1963, the leadership was presented with statistics showing that Czechoslovakia's national income had gone into reverse.[18] Party economists responded by gingerly putting forward a set of proposals recommending decentralisation of decision-making and the introduction of price signals to make state-owned enterprises more responsive to consumer demand, rather than meeting arbitrary production targets. Novotny publicly supported the reforms, while working all the while to undermine them. He was struggling with the same problem all leaders in the Soviet bloc faced: the need to improve productivity and raise living standards without unleashing energies the party might not be able to control. Novotny forlornly placed his hopes in Marxist theory, which predicted that advances in technology would resuscitate economic activity and revive the communist project.

Novotny was thrown further off balance, when Khrushchev was removed from power in 1964 by a Politburo clique led by Leonid Brezhnev.

The new Soviet leader was a cautious and formidable political animal, who, like Stalin, was deft at pinning responsibility for policy failures on his rivals, while avoiding blame for his own. The bushy-browed, jowly Brezhnev was typical of his generation of Soviet leaders, who had survived Stalin's Great Terror and the Second World War, and now longed for security and stability. He put a stop to Khrushchev's mild liberal reforms and tightened control over free expression. The new conservative mood in Moscow put Czechoslovakia out of synch once again with its Soviet masters, because just as Moscow was clamping down, the boundaries of speech and creativity in Prague were starting to loosen up.

THE NEW INTERNATIONAL spirit of play and experimentation in the 1960s infected Prague like no other communist capital. Authors played a game of cat and mouse with the authorities, writing sly absurdist parodies that were often too subtle for the dim-witted censors to pick up until the works had already found an audience on the page, the stage or the screen.

Ivan Klima's first play, titled *The Castle* (with a nod to Kafka), was a clever allegory of the party's insidious capacity to make its favoured artists complicit in its crimes. *The Castle* was picked up by Prague's Vinohrady Theatre company and performed to full houses for weeks before party members twigged that the play was 'hostile to socialism' and shut it down.

Playwright Vaclav Havel was then in his late twenties. By the mid-1960s he had established an international reputation with *The Garden Party* (1963) and *The Memorandum* (1965). Havel was fascinated by officialdom's abuse of language, and its compulsive need to detach words from their meaning. *The Memorandum*, a black comedy, was set within the offices of an unspecified bureaucracy where the manager receives a directive from the authorities ordering him to implement a new officially mandated language called Ptydepe. This newspeak, he learns, has been created to clean up the mess and uncertainty of natural speech. Commonly used words will, logically, be composed of just two or three letters, whereas an uncommon word like 'wombat', will contain a gigantic string of 319 letters. Unfortunately for the director, the memorandum itself is written in this terrifyingly impenetrable new language. His secretary, he discovers, is able to translate Ptydepe, but she lacks the necessary official authorisation to do so.

THE HEADWINDS OF THE 1960s were also blowing through Prague's Barrandov Studios, which produced a rash of new films of startling power and originality. The films commonly used unscripted dialogue and non-professional actors to create a sense of fluidity and realism, unlike the stiff, socialist realist films of the 1950s. Excited critics in the West dubbed them the Czech New Wave.

Milos Forman, who would go on to make *Amadeus* and *One Flew Over the Cuckoo's Nest* in America, made his first classic comedy, *Black Peter* (1964), on the tensions and absurdities of teenage life in a small Bohemian town. Jan Svankmajer created surreally beautiful short films using stop-frame animation. Jiri Menzel's *Closely Watched Trains*, adapted from the book by Bohumil Hrabal, poked fun at the national myth of universal heroic anti-Nazi resistance.

The most remarkable film from this era was Vera Chytilova's *Daisies* (1966), starring two young doll-like women in bikinis, who resolve that since everything in this world is 'spoiled' they might as well be spoiled too. Accordingly, they launch themselves on a bacchanalian rampage through Prague. They gorge themselves at a vast banquet table set for party officials, start a food fight with giant slabs of cake, and bathe in a bathtub full of milk.

Vera Chytilova created an entirely new cinematic way of looking at Prague, as a colour-saturated city of Art Nouveau brasseries and pop-art apartments; it was a million miles away from the monochromatic expressionist landscapes of *Der Golem*. Like the surrealists of the 1930s, Chytilova had the great gift of knowing how to train her camera at everyday things: a field of flowers, a box of green apples, a velvet curtain – and look at them hard enough to make them seem queer and fantastical. Inevitably, *Daisies* was attacked in the Czechoslovak parliament, then pulled from the cinemas, purportedly for 'wastage of food'.

Ivana Karbanova, from Vera Chytilova's Daisies.

THE CREEPING INFLUX of rock and roll was another headache for the regime. The new music – known in Prague as Big Beat – filtered into clubs and dance halls. Charles University students made furtive contact with cultural radicals from the West. In March 1965, they invited American beat poet Allen Ginsberg to Prague.

Ginsberg, the long-haired prophet of sexual freedom, created a sensation as he read his poetry in small venues around the city. Each night he drank at the Viola wine bar on Narodni Street, surrounded by a pack of worshipful Czech beatniks.

Prague's students were so delighted with Ginsberg, they crowned him their Kral Majales, the King of their Mayday celebrations. The day itself was riotous: the gay bearded hippie king was carried through the streets of Prague in an open-topped vintage car, wearing a golden crown and love beads. Ginsberg, thoroughly enjoying himself, sang Buddhist mantras, played finger cymbals, and delivered a speech honouring Franz Kafka in front of the building where *The Trial* had been written. Students laughingly chanted mock slogans: 'All slogans were pre-approved! We agree with them all!'; 'Better a stupid system than the need to think!'[19]

LATER THAT NIGHT, the King of Mayday held a discussion with a roomful of students. Ginsberg, no fan of Western capitalism, didn't much care for communist repression either. Marxism, he explained, could only mean 'cruel spiritual terror'.[20]

The regime, by now, had become fed up with the hairy American interloper, and he was arrested on a spurious charge of public drunkenness. Ginsberg dropped out of sight for two days, then was discovered at the Viola, where three StB officers plied him with cheap Georgian cognac and stole his notebook containing the names of his sexual partners in Prague. The StB brought in the humiliated young men for questioning.

Two days later, Ginsberg was assaulted while walking down Jindrisska Street after midnight. His attacker was an StB officer codenamed Lubor, who charged after him, calling him a 'homo'.[21] Ginsberg was expelled from the country and put on a plane to London, where the incensed poet wrote one of his most famous works, 'The King of May'.

The trip ended badly, but on the whole, it had been a wild ride for Ginsberg and his student devotees, who were inspired by his vision of radical freedom. The virus of rebellion had entered the bloodstream of Prague's youth.

We Want Light

ON 27 JUNE 1967, the Fourth Congress of the Czechoslovak Union of Writers convened in Prague and almost immediately there was an uproar. Previous congresses had served as a forum for writers to declare their fealty to communism; now onlookers watched with astonishment as party members Ludvik Vaculik, Milan Kundera and Pavel Kohout attacked the regime and its leaders as a menace to free thought and creativity. 'Are they really masters of everything?' Vaculik asked. 'What, then, do they leave in the hands of others than their own? Nothing? Then we needn't be here.' The hall erupted into applause, as party loyalists walked out in protest.[22]

The backlash from the regime was swift: control of the literary magazine was taken out of the hands of the reformists. Klima and Vaculik were expelled from the party, but still, quite remarkably, no one had been arrested.

ON THE NIGHT OF 31 October 1967 the lights went out in a dormitory at Prague Technical University. Power outages had become a semi-regular event in the dormitory, but on this occasion, disgruntled students met in the quadrangle and decided to protest. The mass of students marched out towards Prague Castle, chanting,

'We want light! We want light!' The authorities, scrambling to respond, sent a mass of police cars to meet the students at the bottom of Nerudova Street. Uniformed officers chased the protestors up the hill. Then a squad of cars stormed the Strahov dormitory, assaulting the students with batons and tear gas.

No mention of the demonstration appeared in the following day's edition of *Rude Pravo*, but word of the violent police attack spread through the city. Students demanded an inquiry into police brutality. The protest, and the police's thuggish behaviour, created an expectation in the city that something had to change.

LEONID BREZHNEV VISITED Prague in late 1967 to conduct meetings with senior party figures. The Soviet leader was shocked at the depth of hostility to Novotny within the party. Before he left, he offered the embattled president only lukewarm support. He told him, 'It's your affair,' and left the Czechoslovak party to sort out its own petty squabbles.

Without Moscow's firm backing, Novotny was finished. But Brezhnev had misjudged the situation: he mistook the sniping in Prague as a reaction against Novotny's obnoxious personality when, in fact, the rift lay much deeper. The turmoil in Prague was an ideological struggle for the soul of the Communist Party, a conflict that was about to shake the world.

1968

ON 5 JANUARY 1968, the Presidium of the Central Committee issued a bland communique, announcing that Comrade Novotny had 'asked' to be relieved of his post as party first secretary, to allow him to concentrate on his important symbolic work as president of the republic. The new first secretary was Alexander Dubcek, a reformist and a Slovak. Dubcek was tall and trim, with neat, slicked-back hair and a long beak-like nose. His warm, open smile identified him as an altogether different creature from his dour predecessors.

Dubcek inherited his communist idealism from his father, who had taken his young family to the Soviet Union in the 1920s to 'help build socialism'. They travelled all the way out to Kyrgyzstan, near the Chinese border, where Dubcek spent his boyhood. The family returned to Slovakia in the crisis year of 1938, and the teenaged Alexander joined a local Communist Party cell in Bratislava.

In the later war years, Alexander and his brother, Julius, joined the Slovak partisans; Julius was killed in combat, and Alexander wounded twice in the leg. The fight against fascism in these years bound him even closer emotionally to the party and to its promise of justice and freedom for working people.

After the war, Dubcek got married, took a factory job in Bratislava and was steadily promoted from factory official to regional party secretary. As a loyal apparatchik, he supported the Stalinist purges and condemned 'bourgeois nationalism', a catch-all phrase used to condemn those who wanted greater autonomy for Slovakia. Recognising the gaps in his education, Dubcek enrolled at Moscow Political College, where he began to hear troubling stories from former prisoners of Stalin's gulags. Dubcek, who would never be deterred from his conviction in the rightness of communism's historic mission, was nonetheless shaken by these accounts. He graduated from Moscow with honours, and at home his star rose even higher. In 1960, he was elected to the Central Committee, where he formed links with reformists and fellow Slovaks alienated by the boorish Novotny, who seemed to regard Slovakia as a kind of colony within the Czech nation.

In 1963, Dubcek was named party chief in Bratislava, and Slovakia moved towards greater liberalisation. Novotny interpreted this as an attack on his authority, and the two men became enemies. Brezhnev's non-committal stance on the leadership gave Dubcek and his allies an opening and Novotny was pushed out.

PRAGUE'S WRITERS and intellectuals greeted Dubcek's appointment to the leadership with a shrug, assuming that one party hack had been replaced by another, but within weeks Dubcek gave the go-ahead to the economic proposals that had stalled under Novotny and the pace of reform began to pick up.

In late January 1968, the Writers' Union elected Dr Eduard Goldstucker, a former political prisoner, as its new chairman. Goldstucker soon began appearing on state television saying remarkable things – speaking candidly about the party's mistakes and holding up before and after photos of a senior party meeting with the various 'non-persons' airbrushed out. Circulation of the Writers' Union magazine, *Literarni Listy*, leapt to unprecedented figures, as readers enjoyed the delicious thrill of reading previously forbidden material. Exhilarated by this new atmosphere of openness, writers and intellectuals debated what the priorities for reform ought to be. Goldstucker, in a TV discussion, told a panel of students: 'The world is watching whether we shall be able to do what history has not yet known – to unite socialism with freedom.'[23]

Street demonstrations rolled across Prague, demanding freedom of speech and an inquiry into the Stalinist purges of the 1950s. This gave Dubcek the political latitude to push Novotny out of Prague Castle and appoint a new president, Ludvik Svoboda, a popular general who had been designated a Hero of the Soviet Union for his wartime leadership.

And then, with Dubcek's tacit consent, the party simply stopped bothering to enforce censorship. Baffled citizens wondered how Dubcek had managed to outfox the hardliners on the presidium. It was a simple case of competence prevailing over ineptitude. Zdenek Mlynar, one of Dubcek's closest colleagues, had set up a bureaucratic process that allowed the better educated reformers to master their complex briefs and distil party reports into concrete policy recommendations, thereby running rings around the clueless conservatives on the presidium, who were more accustomed to acting on instructions from above.

DUBCEK WAS YOUNG, open and affable, unlike any other leader in the communist bloc. His personal charisma became a major political asset. After just three months in power, the first secretary was riding a wave of popularity and hope.

As Dubcek and his allies groped towards a more humane form of communism, they took care to reassure Moscow that the party was still very much in control of events, that the changes were purely internal, and they need not worry about his country's loyalty to the Soviet bloc. For Dubcek, there was no question of dropping the party's historic commitment to socialism. So long as they remained a one-party state, firmly within the Warsaw Pact, Dubcek couldn't see why Soviet leader Brezhnev would mind their small domestic excursion into openness and freedom.

Brezhnev, however, *did* mind. Particularly when party leaders in East Berlin, Warsaw and Ukraine complained to him that the Czech 'virus' was seeping through their borders, creating unrest among their young people. The East German leader Walter Ulbricht went so far as to clamp down on all business and personal travel to Czechoslovakia, which he feared was becoming a window to the West.

Dubcek nonetheless remained confident he could keep the Soviet bear at bay. Some nervous party members recalled what had happened the last time a Soviet bloc country had tried to liberalise; Hungary's experiment with multi-party democracy in the 1950s had ended in a bloody Soviet invasion. But Dubcek told himself the mistake the Hungarians had made was to threaten to leave the Warsaw Pact. So long as he didn't stray from the alliance, Dubcek calculated that Moscow would have to learn to live with the Czechoslovak experiment. Perhaps, down the track, the Soviets might even choose to follow their example.

ON 23 MARCH, DUBCEK and senior party colleagues travelled to Dresden, ostensibly for a meeting with the Soviet bloc leaders on issues relating to economic cooperation. But Dubcek had been deceived. As he sat down at the table, he was confronted by a united front of communist leaders from Poland, Hungary, East Germany, Bulgaria and the USSR, who took turns to express their deep concern. Brezhnev put it starkly: 'We see a danger, which has brought the entire public life of Czechoslovakia to counter-revolution.' Poland's leader Wladyslaw Gomulka warned Dubcek that, although they had no intention of interfering, 'there are, of course, situations when so-called domestic affairs naturally become external affairs, thus affairs of the entire socialist camp'.

Dubcek's colleagues were taken aback. Oldrich Cernik strongly defended the reforms, explaining how the new atmosphere of openness had reignited genuine popular enthusiasm for the party, but the men across the table remained stone-faced. The chastened Czechoslovak leaders promised to take the criticisms on board and carefully re-analyse the situation, but on returning to Prague, Dubcek chose to downplay the veiled threats put to him in Dresden. 'The comrades are on our side,' he reassured party members, 'and want things to work out.'[24]

ON 1 APRIL 1968, the Central Committee in Prague shocked Brezhnev by passing an Action Program, a radical document by Soviet standards, calling for greater democratisation, the rehabilitation of the victims of Stalinism, and for greater autonomy for Slovakia. The program set the Czechoslovak Communist Party on a historic voyage into the unknown, to find a third way between the rocks of rapacious capitalism and repressive Stalinism, an approach that Dubcek called 'socialism with a human face'.

The Action Program proposed a ten-year transition period, but immediately the cry went up: why wait? Oldrich Cernik was appointed prime minister on 8 April, and the same month a new inquiry was launched into the circumstances of Jan Masaryk's death. Author Ladislav Mnacko, who had initially regarded Dubcek with scepticism, was completely disarmed by his reformist courage. 'I didn't think he could rise this high, a man like this, as good as this.'[25]

THE SEASON OF RADICAL change caught the eye and imagination of the Western media, which dubbed it the 'Prague Spring'. Journalists and photographers were sent from all over the world to capture the excitement in the streets. Zdenek Mlynar, the chief author of the Action Program, described the Prague Spring as a moment of 'sudden joy at the end of a long period of despair, at the end of oppression, and the feeling of a new beginning'.[26]

Prague's May Day parade of 1968 was a genuinely exuberant event. Alongside the groups of workers, soldiers and schoolkids massed in Wenceslas Square were long-haired hippies marching under an oversized candy-coloured umbrella that said 'Dubcek Hold out for Us'. A country girl dressed in traditional costume was spotted wearing an 'I'm on LSD' badge, while another group of young people marched under an umbrella with the slogan 'STUDENT POWER'.[27]

WHILE PRAGUE DANCED, the Kremlin shuddered. The Soviets could never shake the suspicion that the Americans and the CIA were somehow secretly guiding events in Czechoslovakia. In early May, Dubcek was summoned to Moscow, where Brezhnev issued another dead-eyed warning to pull back, to change course. 'The situation, I repeat, is very serious,' he cautioned. 'This is no longer an internal matter.' Brezhnev could hardly have made himself clearer, warning he was ready to take 'far-reaching steps' to deal with the matter.[28] Dubcek noticed one of his colleagues, Vasil Bilak, nodding along with the Soviet leader.

On his return to Prague, Dubcek tried a shift in tone. He reiterated his support for the Action Program, but insisted that change could come only through the Communist Party. Dubcek's power now rested on his public popularity, which would collapse if he was to do Moscow's bidding and abandon reform. He tried to rein in growing media criticism of the Communist Party, but to no avail. 'Why are they doing this to me?' he asked his friend Mlynar plaintively. 'They would have been afraid to do this under Novotny. Don't they realise how much harm they're causing me?'[29]

Despite Brezhnev's warning, Dubcek believed he had no alternative other than to press ahead, and in June the Central Committee officially removed all media censorship. The next day, Ludvik Vaculik published a manifesto, 'Two Thousand Words', calling for the cause of democracy to be carried further, outside the Communist Party.

Towards the end of Vaculik's essay, a premonition of disaster fluttered through the pages. 'There has been great alarm recently,' he wrote, 'over the possibility that foreign forces will intervene in our development. Whatever superior forces may face us, all we can do is stick to our own positions, behave decently, and initiate nothing ourselves.'[30]

SUCH DARK THOUGHTS could never be entirely banished from the mind, even as the excitement of the Prague Spring shifted into the warm haze of summer. Photos of this time show young women in checked miniskirts applying thick mascara before nightclub mirrors; teenagers kissing in dance halls; workers standing outside newspaper offices, reading the day's stories; bearded beatniks reclining in jazz clubs; old women with shopping bags signing petitions in the street. News footage shows a grinning boyish Dubcek being applauded in the street. The pace of change was dizzying. 'Never before or since,' Ivan Klima later wrote, 'have I lived with such haste or intensity.'[31]

Overhanging everything, was the question of whether Czechoslovakia could become a genuine multi-party democracy. There was a logic to Vaculik's argument that Dubcek's reforms, unless they were reversed, must eventually lead to something like Western-style parliamentary democracy, where the Communist Party would have to risk losing power in a free election.

As if in readiness for a multi-party future, civic organisations began to spring up outside the party. In May, a group calling itself the Club of Committed Non-Party Members (KAN) formed to promote human rights and political pluralism. The conductor and composer Dr Emil Ludvik set up a similar organisation, the Society for Human Rights, dedicated to reviving the democratic legacy of

T. G. Masaryk. Another group called K-231 emerged to campaign on behalf of former political prisoners who had been tortured, forgotten in prisons or sent into deadly work in Bohemia's uranium mines. K-231's most remarkable activist was Dagmar Simkova, who had been sent to a labour camp in the 1950s for anti-communist activities. In prison, the seemingly fearless Simkova had organised hunger strikes for better conditions, and set up a covert university with imprisoned academics. Released at last in 1966, Simkova threw herself into her work with K-231, which took its name from the law used by the regime to imprison political opponents. As the political climate warmed through 1968, K-231 petitioned the authorities to be given legal status. Dubcek was sympathetic and the group was accorded a temporary permission to exist and hold meetings.

ON 29 JULY, DUBCEK and his colleagues travelled to the Slovakian border town of Cierna nad Tisou to meet once again with the Soviet leadership. The Czech leader arrived by train to cheering crowds chanting, 'We want Dubcek! We want Dubcek!' Dubcek greeted his people with smiles and jokes. When one person shouted, 'Don't let us down! Don't let the Russians get the better of you!' Dubcek replied uncertainly, 'Nothing to be afraid of.'[32]

Brezhnev's and Dubcek's teams sat down for bilateral talks in a modest railway workers' hall. The Czechoslovak delegation was divided between Dubcek's supporters and a minority of hardliners including Bilak and Alois Indra, who were angling to be part of any new dispensation that would follow a Soviet intervention. Brezhnev cooly listed his demands: an end to anti-Soviet statements in the Czechoslovak media, and the abolition of non-party political groups like KAN and K-231. Dubcek, sensing real trouble now, agreed to do something about the press. Brezhnev took that to mean he would reintroduce censorship, but for Dubcek, it meant having a word with the authors and editors concerned and asking them to tone it down.

LUDVIK VACULIK, RETURNING to Prague from Cierna nad Tisou, remarked, 'It is hanging by a thread.'[33] Dubcek still believed he could prevail in the face of Brezhnev's hostility by remaining steadfastly loyal to the Soviet bloc. But the true note of caution for the Prague Spring was not struck in 1956 in Budapest, but six years after that in Berlin, when the Soviets had been compelled to construct a double-layered prison wall across the city with towers and armed guards, to staunch the steady outflow of people from their sector into the West.

At the time, many saw the construction of the Berlin Wall as an impressive act of Soviet resolve, when in fact it was a thing born of weakness, an admission of political failure. The Soviet world was exposed as a creature with a faulty immune system, which could only be sustained by hermetically sealing itself off against the free flow of information and people. By opening Czechoslovakia to the world, Dubcek had, unwittingly, pierced another hole in the Soviet bubble, and Moscow would again be forced to act to protect itself.

THREE DAYS LATER AT a Warsaw Pact summit, the Slovak hardliner Vasil Bilak furtively handed a letter to the Ukrainian party boss, Petro Shelest, in the men's room. The note, signed by eight members of the Czechoslovak presidium, stated that Dubcek was waging 'political and psychological terror' against communists in Prague. The signatories warned that the gains of socialism in Czechoslovakia were under threat, and requested Soviet military intervention, 'if circumstances should so warrant ... to block the path of counter-revolution'.[34]

DUBCEK, CAUGHT BETWEEN the aspirations of his people and the demands of his Soviet benefactors, was running out of time. On 15 August, he received a phone call from Brezhnev who dressed him down for failing to quash anti-Soviet press commentary. Dubcek insisted that he had spoken to the people concerned and they had agreed to put a stop to all 'polemical' articles.

'But Sasha,' Brezhnev groaned, 'we agreed that all mass media, the press, radio, television, will be brought under the control of the Central Committee of the Communist Party! . . . What I'm getting at here is that you're deceiving us! I'm not able to regard it as anything other than deceit.'

Dubcek was overcome and lost for words.

'Alexander Stepanovich,' Brezhnev said coolly, 'I'm sorry that you are getting so upset. In important matters emotions cannot save the day.'[35]

AT BREZHNEV'S REQUEST, Dubcek met with the Hungarian leader, Janos Kadar, one last time on the banks of the Danube River. Kadar, the most astute of the Warsaw Pact leaders, was sympathetic, but warned Dubcek of 'unforeseeable consequences' if he failed to do Brezhnev's bidding. As they parted, Kadar asked Dubcek, 'Do you *really* not know the kind of people you're dealing with?'[36]

Europarty

IN PRAGUE, THE CARNIVAL atmosphere whirled on through the summer heat. In mid-August, a television crew rolled into town to make an episode of a popular West German music program called *Europarty* with a group of international singing stars. Shirley

Bassey mimed 'Goldfinger' at a construction site and performed 'Big Spender' on Narodni Street, skipping past startled shoppers. The popular Czech singer Marta Kubisova performed with her group the Golden Kids, as did the French pop artist Françoise Hardy.

On the afternoon of 20 August, the *Europarty* crew set up their cameras on the Mala Strana end of the Charles Bridge to record a song from British group The Moody Blues. There was no dressing room, so the police turfed a family out of their nearby apartment so the embarrassed band members could get changed into their ruffled blouses.

French television host Albert Raisner interviewed 'Les Moody Blues' in English, smoothly translating their answers into French and German, then left them to perform 'Nights in White Satin' to a crowd of hundreds of happy young Praguers. The medieval towers seemed to complement the song's vaguely chivalric lyrics. It was a moment when Prague, for better or worse, was being welcomed into the wider world of contemporary pop culture. But the Prague Spring had just hours left to run.

Justin Hayward of The Moody Blues,
performing on the Charles Bridge, August 1968.

LATER THAT NIGHT, Jaroslav Kovaricek was walking home to his apartment in Mala Strana. Jaroslav was then a 24-year-old musicology graduate from Charles University. More recently he'd become involved with the Society for Human Rights, in the hope that his country could one day become like Austria, a neutral democratic state outside the Soviet bloc.

Jaroslav had been drinking with friends in a pub. It was past midnight when he crossed the Legion Bridge over the Vltava. Overhead, he heard planes buzzing in the moonless sky but could see nothing. He went home to his bed and fell asleep.

Several hours later, the phone jolted him awake. 'We are occupied,' a friend's voice told him. 'The Russians are here.' Jaroslav got dressed and ran downstairs, where he saw tanks clanking down the narrow street.

*

AT 1.30 AM, TWO SOVIET aircraft had landed at Prague airport. More than thirty soldiers had disembarked and seized control of the main building and control tower. With the airport secured, a succession of Soviet AN-12 transport planes touched down on the runway, one after another, in intervals of less than a minute, disgorging more Soviet paratroopers, officers and tanks. Within hours, an entire airborne division had assembled on the tarmac, ready to make its way into central Prague.

In the Central Committee building, the presidium was in late night session when Oldrich Cernik burst into the room with the news that more than 200,000 troops from the Soviet Union and four Warsaw Pact countries had just surged across the border into Czechoslovakia.

The stunned presidium tried to absorb the news. Vasil Bilak, the plotter who had known this was coming, stood up and paced nervously around the room, waiting to be called a traitor.

'Alright lynch me!' he shouted. 'Why don't you kill me?'[37]

Dubcek was devastated. 'This is my own personal tragedy,' he told the room, tearfully. 'I have always loved Russia. I have devoted my entire life to cooperating with the Soviet Union, and this is what they've done to me.'[38]

Mlynar quickly drafted a resolution condemning the invasion as a breach of international law, and it was put to a vote. Two of the plotters on the presidium lost their nerve and defected back to Dubcek's side, and the vote was passed seven to four. The message was defiant but Dubcek wanted no bloodshed, and so the defence minister gave orders for the Czechoslovak army to remain confined to barracks and not to open fire on the invaders under any circumstances.

Determined to hang on as first secretary, Dubcek retreated to his office with his allies, where he stared at the phones on his desk, still hoping someone might call and tell him this was all some kind of monstrous misunderstanding. Watching from his window, he saw a crowd of young demonstrators gathering in front of the building, chanting his name, waving national flags.

At 4 am, Dubcek looked out and saw a black Volga sedan leading a convoy of tanks and armoured cars across the Hlavka Bridge towards the building. The crowd failed to move away in time and the soldiers opened fire to clear a path, killing a young man. As the armoured vehicles pulled up at the entrance, Soviet paratroopers carrying automatic weapons leapt out and formed a tight cordon around the Central Committee building.

ACROSS THE STILL-DARK CITY, telephones rang out from house to house. Taxi drivers flicked their lights on to high beam and honked their horns to rouse people from their beds. In Hradcany, US journalist Alan Levy saw a dozen tanks coming down the ramp from the Strahov Monastery into the open space of Pohorelec Street. He saw a Soviet soldier pop his head out of a turret, looking around and squinting at an old tourist map. They were lost. The frustrated officer produced a pistol and demanded directions to the castle from the onlookers, but nobody was willing to help, even though it was just around the corner.

AS MORE PEOPLE WOKE to the crisis, they instinctively tuned into Czechoslovak Radio, which continued to broadcast the statement from Dubcek condemning the invasion. The realisation that the broadcaster had not yet been occupied encouraged thousands of listeners to rush through the early-morning darkness to defend the radio headquarters in Vinohradska Street, some still wearing pyjamas.

The swelling crowd of protestors set up a defensive barricade to protect the studio building. Buses, cars and trucks were turned over and set alight. Then a tram was halted and, with the aid of its passengers, derailed and pushed into the barricade.

As the protestors prepared for the inevitable arrival of Soviet tanks, broadcasters within the radio building sent out an urgent appeal to the city: 'Be with us. We are with you.'[39]

DAYLIGHT BROKE AND AT 8.30 am, six tanks came trundling into Vinohradska Street, rolling right over the barricaded trams and crushing them beneath their tracks. A protestor threw a Molotov cocktail and a tank burst into flames. Then an ammunition truck ignited and exploded in the street, demolishing the facade of a building and tearing a hole in the road. The panicked Soviet troops retaliated by firing wildly, killing seventeen protestors. Another sixty-five were wounded by bullets and grenade fragments.

A squad of troops stormed past dead and dying civilians and charged into the radio building. A newsreader was mid-sentence when the studio door was flung open and a soldier barked a single command in Russian: 'Out!' The Soviet troops quickly occupied the first two floors, but not one of them bothered to check the third floor, where a working studio continued to broadcast updates and messages of resistance for another two hours.

Czechoslovak Television had also been on the air, broadcasting continuous updates until 8.30 am, when Soviet troops burst into the building, ordered everyone out, then sprayed the cameras and equipment with bullets. Undaunted, the television crews reconvened and set up an improvised broadcast studio at a nearby cinema, and then at a transmitter tower outside the city. It took hours for the invaders to locate the rogue broadcasters and to send a team of paratroopers to shut them down. As the Soviet forces advanced on the tower, the crew turned their cameras on them, exposing the operation to millions of viewers.

DESPITE THE APPLICATION of overwhelming military force, the coup was coming off the rails. Brezhnev had initiated the invasion with firm expectations that Bilak, Alois Indra and the other hardliners on the presidium would mobilise their supporters, depose

Dubcek with a vote of no confidence, seize control of the media and then quickly issue the Soviets with an official invitation to cross the border to provide 'fraternal assistance', giving the invasion a fig leaf of legality. But ten hours into the invasion, none of these things had been accomplished. The hardliners had failed to dislodge Dubcek and his allies from their official positions, and so the Soviets took steps to isolate the first secretary before he could rally the party into open opposition.

At 9 am, a group of eight soldiers armed with assault rifles burst into Dubcek's office, followed by a KGB colonel with two plain-clothes StB officers in tweed jackets and open-necked shirts. Dubcek instinctively picked up the phone to make a call, but a paratrooper snatched it from him and tore the cable from the wall. Dubcek and his allies were marched into a windowless room to be held at gunpoint until the Kremlin could figure out its next move.

BY MID-MORNING, TENS of thousands of furious and distressed Praguers rushed into Wenceslas Square to confront the invaders. National flags fluttered defiantly from the windows as protestors swarmed around the tanks like angry hornets. People climbed onto the skirts of the tanks and harangued the confused troops, telling them to disobey their commanders and go home. Several trees lining the square were set alight; people tore off the burning branches and tried to flog the tanks with them. Some brazenly chalked swastikas on the back of the armoured vehicles. Old women banged on pots and pans from their balconies. Protestors old enough to recall the presence of Hitler's tanks in the square nearly thirty years earlier felt a harrowing sense of déjà vu.

The Soviet soldiers were dumbfounded, angry and frightened. Some sat on their tanks, legs outstretched, arms folded, like petulant children. Most were conscripts from Central Asia or Ukraine, unsure of where they were. They'd been told their mission was to give fraternal assistance against Western counter-revolutionaries, and were assured they would be welcomed in Prague as liberators. Instead, they were surrounded by howling, jeering locals pounding on their tanks. They began to panic. A round of bullets was shot into the air and the tanks swivelled their guns towards the protestors massed in front of the National Museum at the top of the square.

JAROSLAV KOVARICEK WAS standing near the statue of St Wenceslas as the gunfire strafed the crowd. The protestor next to him caught a bullet and fell to the ground, but it was too dangerous to stop and help.

Amid the stampede of terrified citizens, Jaroslav bolted to the top of the square into Vinohradska Street, hoping to find shelter with his friends at the radio building, but was halted by the barricades of flaming buses. In confusion, he turned into a side street and was stopped short by a column of Soviet tanks.

A Russian tank commander caught sight of Jaroslav and gestured with his hand to come forward.

Jaroslav was amazed. *This man is my enemy,* he thought. *I should want to kill him. I must not talk to him.* But there was something oddly compelling about the gesture, and so, against his better judgement, Jaroslav walked towards the Russian officer. To his astonishment, the officer came to him and embraced him. There were tears in his eyes.

'It was Brezhnev,' he said. 'It was Brezhnev who ordered us to do this. I am a soldier. I see what we have done here. And I am so sorry.'

Jaroslav, sleepless and overwhelmed by the morning's events, wept too.

Speaking Russian, Jaroslav asked him what he was doing here.

The officer explained that he'd only just completed a degree at a university in Leningrad when the army had called him into national service.

'For the last three months we've been in training,' he said miserably, 'and I haven't seen my family. My wife's had a baby boy and I don't know when I'll get to meet him. They'll keep us in isolation when we get back so we won't talk about what we've seen here. They always do that.'

Jaroslav, who was scheduled to begin national service himself, couldn't help but sympathise. 'I realised,' he said later, 'he was in a much worse situation than me, because at least I was free. So I really felt sorry for him. He and I were both ordinary people. We were really crying; it was all so tragic.'[40]

BY MID-AFTERNOON, the Soviet plan was in tatters. International television coverage brought unforgettable images to a scandalised world. Footage of tank attacks on unarmed civilians exposed the cover story of 'fraternal assistance' from the USSR as a sham. The sight of swastikas chalked onto the occupiers' tanks made the parallels to 1939 all too obvious.

To Brezhnev's disgust, the local hardliners had been revealed as hopeless bunglers. With the existing party leadership still in place, Brezhnev reluctantly concluded he would have to strike a deal.

A KGB colonel was sent to fetch Dubcek and his allies, still under house arrest in the Central Committee building. They were brought out at gunpoint and taken in an armoured vehicle to Ruzyne airport.

Inside the terminal, Dubcek was told to sit and wait, as several more hours passed. He had the dawning impression his captors didn't know what to do with him, an indication of uncertainty at the top. Then at 9 pm, the captive men were led across the airfield and into the belly of a Soviet Tupolev transport plane.

They were flown first to an airstrip in Poland, then to another in Ukraine, where they were met by KGB agents who drove them to some nearby mountain chalets. After a few hours' sleep, Dubcek was, absurdly, blindfolded with dark glasses, then driven to a Ukrainian regional party building. The dark glasses were removed and he was handed a phone. On the other end of the line was Nikolai Podgorny, from the Soviet Politburo.

'We will have to talk,' he said.

Dubcek was coming back to Moscow, this time as a prisoner.[41]

THE UNITED STATES AND other NATO powers were united in their condemnation of the invasion, but showed no inclination to risk nuclear conflict by intervening militarily. The communist world, however, was badly split. Ho Chi Minh in North Vietnam declared his support. Cuba, which had repelled a US military invasion of their island seven years earlier, was torn and said nothing. The most intensely totalitarian states, China and Romania denounced Moscow's action, as did the Italian Communist Party. Albania chose to walk out of the Warsaw Pact in protest and to align itself with Maoist China instead.

In Britain, news of the invasion was met with outrage in some quarters, indifference in others. On the night following the invasion, the Russian State Symphony Orchestra appeared at London's Albert Hall. As the musicians took their seats to perform a Dvorak concerto (of all things), the musicians were heckled from the stalls with cries of 'Shame on you!'

Other members of the audience, unhappy with the disruption, shouted back at the hecklers, 'We want to hear the music!'[42]

✳

The Hedgehog and the Elephant

WITH DUBCEK AND THE reformers out of the country, the protestors in Prague continued their self-organised campaign of civil disobedience, which disoriented and demoralised the invaders. There was something magnificent about the people of Prague that week and they knew it. The belief that they had somehow thwarted the mighty Soviet army with their bare hands bound them all together. They taunted the Russians with slogans posted all over the city:

AN ELEPHANT CANNOT SWALLOW A HEDGEHOG.
WITH BROTHERS LIKE YOU, WE BEG MOTHER RUSSIA
TO PRACTICE CONTRACEPTION.[43]

Protestors rotated street signs to point the wrong way, baffling the foreign troops. Groups of Praguers passed from tank to tank, looking for soldiers willing to talk, peppering them with unwelcome questions: 'Why are you here? What would you do if your home was invaded by foreign soldiers?' People queued in the street to sign petitions demanding the return of Dubcek.

Dissident radio stations popped up from improvised locations on different frequencies. In response, soldiers were ordered to confiscate any transistor radios they saw being used in the streets. Praguers then amused themselves by walking around with bricks of coal pressed to their ears and were delighted when the soldiers confiscated those, too.

MANY PEOPLE, HOWEVER, lost heart. Unable to see a future for themselves, they packed their suitcases and drove to the Austrian or West German border to make new lives in Western Europe or elsewhere. The border guards waved them through. Eduard Goldstucker took up an academic position in Britain; Ota Sik, the party economist, made his way to Switzerland. Josef Skvorecky and his wife, Zdena, went to Canada, where they set up a publishing house for Czech authors.

Dagmar Simkova, the co-founder of the political prisoner support organisation K-231, also chose to leave rather than risk a return to prison. This remarkable woman emigrated to Perth, Western Australia, where she completed two university degrees and found work as an artist, nurse and trained as a movie stunt woman.

Those who happened to be in the West at the time of the invasion faced an agonising choice – to build a new life as an exile away from family and friends or return to an uncertain future. Ivan Klima, who was travelling through Britain and the United States, was offered work in America but couldn't bear the thought of being alienated from the language and landscape of his literature, and came back to Prague with his family, expecting he would never be allowed to leave again.

AS THE PROTESTS IN Prague intensified, the Soviet leadership became increasingly desperate to arrive at a solution to the crisis it had initiated. Above all, they needed a compliant government in Prague. On 23 August, Soviet ambassador Stepan Chervonenko came to the castle to ask President Svoboda to lead a Workers' and Peasants' Revolutionary Government, but Svoboda refused.

'Ninety-five percent of the population are behind Dubcek and Cernik,' he warned. 'If they are not released a great deal of blood will be shed.'[44] With that, the Soviet ambassador stormed out.

The president was then asked to appoint a new government led by Indra and Bilak, but he declared, 'If I were to do anything of the sort, the nation would drive me out of this castle like a mangy dog.'[45] Instead, Svoboda proposed to lead a delegation to Russia to find an 'honourable and dignified solution' to the crisis.[46] The next morning, he flew to Moscow, accompanied by two of the key plotters, Bilak and Indra, as well as one of the leading reformers, a bespectacled Slovak named Gustav Husak.

The Moscow Protocol

DUBCEK AND HIS COLLEAGUES had been dragged to Moscow like common criminals, still wearing the same dirty clothes they'd been wearing for three days. But when Svoboda arrived a day later, he was received at the airport with full honours due to a visiting head of state.

Brezhnev spoke to Svoboda alone, asking him what he had to propose, but the president waffled. He said he would agree to Dubcek being dropped from the leadership, but had no suggestions for a replacement. The old general was past his prime.

At 11 pm Dubcek was brought into the Kremlin to meet with Brezhnev and other Soviet Politburo members, but nothing was resolved. Dubcek, exhausted and unwell, was taken to a guesthouse nearby where he slept for most of the following day. When Zdenek Mlynar arrived in Moscow, he insisted on seeing him at once. Mlynar found Dubcek lying on a bed, partially sedated and stripped to the waist in the August heat. There was a small bandage on his forehead, covering a wound incurred from having slipped in the bathroom.

Dubcek told Mlynar he was in an impossible position, caught between the demands of the Kremlin and the expectations of his people, cut off from news from home and undermined by some of his own people, like the treacherous Bilak, who was passing on information to the Soviets. Dubcek was able to join the negotiations only intermittently. Mlynar thought he was in a state of nervous collapse.

In Dubcek's absence, the Czechoslovak leadership fell into infighting. President Svoboda lost patience with the reformists, theatrically trying to shift the blame for the invasion on them. 'There you go, talk, talk, talking again!' he shouted. 'You've already talked and talked till your country's occupied. So act accordingly and do something!'[47]

Brezhnev made his position to the Czechoslovaks brutally clear: in such a crisis, he recognised no national borders, only the borders of socialism. 'Your country lies on territory where the Soviet soldier trod in the Second World War,' he told them. 'We bought that territory at the cost of enormous sacrifices and we shall never leave it.'[48] He warned that if they didn't accept Moscow's proposals, the inevitable result would be mass bloodshed.

AS THEY WRANGLED, Brezhnev and his colleagues studied the Czechoslovak delegation closely, trying to identify a viable future partner among them. They had already written off Bilak and Indra as incompetent clowns, but the cool professionalism of the Slovak leader Gustav Husak impressed them. Husak, whom Dubcek had once regarded as an ally, was now describing himself to both parties as someone 'with a sense of reality'. Acting as a helpful intermediary between the Soviets and his own group of reformists, Husak pressured Dubcek and his men to sign off on the Soviet demands.

In the negotiations, Brezhnev was able to exploit Dubcek's great weakness: his lifelong loyalty to his communist ideals. Deeply riven by his duty to defend his country and his commitment to communist solidarity, Dubcek simply fell apart. He agonised for three days, and then he consented to sign Brezhnev's ultimatum, known as the Moscow Protocol, which renounced his own Action Program, and gave formal consent to the occupation of their country. In return, Dubcek would be permitted to remain in the job as first secretary. With that, he and his colleagues were allowed to go home. Only one Czech presidium member, Dr Frantisek Kriegel, refused to sign.

'Send me to Siberia,' he said, 'or shoot me dead.'[49]

DUBCEK FLEW BACK to Prague in the early hours of 27 August, wondering what on earth he would tell his people. The Soviets had agreed that the final text of the Moscow Protocol was too provocative to be made public, so Dubcek struggled with how he would avoid revealing the full truth of it without actually lying.

At 5.50 pm he delivered a radio address to the nation. In a strained and halting voice, Dubcek said the first thing that was needed was the 'normalisation' of the situation as soon as possible. Yes, he said, the invading armies would be gradually withdrawn, but there would be a corresponding need for restraint, to avoid prolonging the 'abnormal situation'. As a result, the party would have to introduce 'some temporary exceptional measures' restricting freedom of expression. Above all, he urged his people, don't make trouble: 'We beg you, dear fellow-citizens, to help us prevent any anti-socialist, provocations by some elements which are interested in worsening the situation, which is in any case very tense indeed. In this period we need order, we need deliberate discipline on the part of all our citizens.'[50]

Dubcek's voice cracked and fell silent for long, agonising moments as he fought to compose himself. A staff member brought him a glass of water. The gentle tap of the glass on the table brought Dubcek back to his senses, and after another moment, he drew breath and resumed his speech, with tears running down his face. Just a week ago, he thought he was the bringer of dignity and freedom. Instead, he'd become yet another Czechoslovak leader who had surrendered his country's future.

IN THE LONG TERM, Moscow paid a high price for crushing the Prague Spring. The invasion destroyed the Red Army's prestige in Prague, it crippled the USSR's influence in the communist parties of Western Europe and discredited its remaining apologists elsewhere. 'Socialism with a human face' in a one-party state was exposed as a chimera. No one could now plausibly pretend that Stalinism had been a tragic aberration. For Ivan Klima, who had in his youth subscribed to the ideals of the party, the communist movement could only be seen as 'a criminal conspiracy against democracy'.[51] To this day, the Warsaw Pact remains the sole military alliance in history to ever attack one of its own members.

The invasion, the second of its kind in three decades, inflicted another generation of Praguers with a deep spiritual wound. The unarmed teenagers who pounded their fists helplessly on the tanks had witnessed the same terrible spectacle their parents had in 1939: the victory of raw power and violence over democratic values.

✳

A WEEK AFTER THE invasion, Jaroslav Kovaricek went to pick up the new edition of the Society for Human Rights' newsletter from the printer. But the elderly man at the machines told him he shouldn't bother.

'If I was young like you, I would get out,' he said. 'There's no future here.'

The same day, Jaroslav heard the radio replaying Dubcek's choking speech, calling for normalisation.

It's lost, he concluded. *I might as well leave.*

JAROSLAV SAID GOODBYE to his parents, flew out of Prague, and eventually migrated to Australia. He quickly mastered English and in time became a radio presenter for the ABC, Australia's national public broadcaster. I discovered his late-night music program, *Acoustica Nova,* while studying at university.

I remembered Jaroslav while planning to write this book and discovered he was living on the New South Wales coast, four hours north of Sydney. In June 2018, I drove there with my wife, Khym, to spend an afternoon with him. After lunch we sat down to record his story at his kitchen table.

IN AUSTRALIA, JAROSLAV had come to embrace Buddhist thought and to admire Aboriginal culture. He had developed an aversion to left-wing 'political correctness', which seemed to him another ideological imposition on free speech. From the far side of the world, he kept an eye on his lost homeland as the dreary years of 'normalisation' rolled on. Both Jaroslav's parents died while he was away; he was unable to attend their funerals.

Then came 1989, the year of miracles.

Jaroslav was watching the Velvet Revolution unfold on television when he received a call from the office of Australia's most popular TV news broadcaster, Jana Wendt. Jana's family were Czech, and Jaroslav knew her father well. Now she was proposing to fly with Jaroslav to Prague to make a prime-time TV documentary, telling the story of his emotional journey home to his lost city.

And so, after an absence of two decades, Jaroslav returned to Prague in January 1990. 'It was very strange,' he said. 'I used to have refugee dreams, where I was back but I couldn't get out. So suddenly I'm crossing the river on the Charles Bridge with Jana and her camera crew, and I think I'll wake up at any moment. I had very strong emotions.'

ONCE THE DOCUMENTARY was completed, Jaroslav had some free time to enjoy dinner with old friends. Afterwards, he wandered into Wenceslas Square to enjoy a Prague sausage and some proper Bohemian pilsener.

'It was close to midnight,' he told me. 'I went to a kiosk and ordered a beer, and I saw a group of young people, with a young man sitting on a box playing guitar, and they were all singing.'

Jaroslav noticed the guitarist was Russian. 'And I thought – that's how it *should* be: young Czech people, young Russian boy. Singing together. Enjoying it. It's just the politicians that keep pulling us apart.'

Feeling mellowed by the music and the goodwill, Jaroslav approached the Russian guitarist and bought him a beer. He asked him where he had come from.

'Leningrad,' the guitarist replied. 'And where have you come from?'

'I have just come from Australia,' Jaroslav answered. 'I had to escape in 1968, but I'm sure you don't know anything about that.'

'You mean the invasion?'

'How do you know about that?' Jaroslav asked.

'I was born that year in Leningrad,' the singer said. 'My father was sent here. He was the commander of a tank. We didn't see him for years afterwards. And when he came back, he was telling me all about what happened here, and he felt so ashamed.'

JAROSLAV LOOKS AT OUR astonished faces across his kitchen table. 'Now I can't prove it,' he says, 'but I think there was a very good chance that this boy was the son of that tank commander.'

CHAPTER TEN

THE SECOND CULTURE

1968–1988

The Prague Autumn

SEVERAL DAYS AFTER Dubcek's radio address, Paul Wilson made his way back to Prague. It was close to midnight when his train arrived at the main railway station. In the park outside, he saw a row of Soviet tanks, waiting to board military trains. He walked around the corner into Wenceslas Square, but it was empty and quiet. No one had told him a curfew was in place.

Paul found a working public phone and called friend after friend but no one was home. Eventually someone picked up and said, 'We're all here at my place, come on over.' He slipped through the back streets to an apartment on the Old Town Square where his circle of friends had gathered. They'd been handing out protest sheets, missed the curfew and were holed up there for the night.

There was no despair among this group. Not yet. They still expected something would be salvaged from the wreckage of the Prague Spring. After having come so far forward, how could they go back?

*

PAUL, A CANADIAN literature graduate, had been living in Czechoslovakia for just over a year. He had known almost nothing about the country until he attended a Czech New Wave film festival in London. Paul was enchanted and mystified by the sophisticated artlessness of these films, the sly humour, the way ordinary situations could be made sinister and chilling.

Soon afterwards, he had met a couple of Czech engineers in a London pub and they started talking about communism. Paul had tried to argue there was no reason, theoretically, why communism shouldn't work, but the Czechs laughed and insisted there was no way *practically* that it could. 'Why don't you come over and see for yourself?' they suggested.

Paul arrived in the Czechoslovak Socialist Republic in the summer of 1967, just as the demand for reform was starting to pick up. When his bus rolled into Prague, the capital looked rundown and grimy. The slow restoration of the old baroque buildings was failing to keep pace with the decay. Still, he could see something of Prague's fabled beauty shining through the scaffolding.

Paul taught English in Brno and then in Prague. Within a year, he learnt to speak passable Czech. He established friendships within Prague's flourishing counterculture, and felt the surge of hope and excitement of the Prague Spring. Giddy optimism overpowered the sense of threat. Paul thought the Russians couldn't possibly do anything as drastic as invading the country, and felt confident enough to leave town in August 1968 for a summer vacation in Yugoslavia with friends from Canada. Days later, as they watched the televised footage of tanks in Wenceslas Square, his friends advised him not to bother going back. But Paul didn't want to run out on his new gang of friends in Prague, and he was curious to find out what would happen next.

*

ALEXANDER DUBCEK'S tearful speech, pleading for the normalisation of the situation, had been followed by a winding-down
of the campaign of civil disobedience. There was a belief that the
people had made their point, that their protests had stung the
Soviet giant and forced it to come to terms with their demands for
greater freedom and dignity. The protest movement took Dubcek at
his word that the reintroduction of censorship was an unfortunate
but temporary measure to avoid bloodshed, a pause to give the
reformists time to regain their bearings and move forward again
later. The Soviets, however, shrewdly used the hiatus to demobilise
the protest movement and then demoralise it by making Dubcek
and the reformers renege on their promises.

Free speech was not curtailed with a sudden blow, but by a slow,
ever-tightening constriction, until it could no longer draw breath.
Paul Wilson observed the shifting official language with each
passing month: first he noticed the word 'invasion' was banned,
replaced with 'intervention'. Then that too was replaced with 'the
timely arrival of the fraternal armies'.[1]

All talk in the media of Dubcek's January Action Program abruptly
ceased. Independent human rights organisations such KAN and K-231
were forced to disband. The directors of the state radio and television
services were removed from their posts and replaced with more
compliant figures. The various bureaus of state censorship were not
reinstated, which at first seemed like a concession, but a more subtle
and insidious constraint was put in place: writers, journalists and
editors were now expected to monitor each other's work and practise
pre-emptive self-censorship. This had a chilling effect on once lively
newsrooms, and sowed fear and distrust between former friends and

colleagues. Many writers were prohibited from publishing altogether. Banners and posters with the depressing slogan *With the Soviet Union Forever!* reappeared in public squares and at train stations, this time with, *And never otherwise!* added for extra emphasis.

LEONID BREZHNEV USED the crisis in Czechoslovakia to assert a new principle of Soviet power that became known as the Brezhnev Doctrine, whereby the USSR reserved the right to intervene militarily in 'the near abroad' – countries within the Soviet sphere of influence – to maintain Communist Party control. Once a satellite nation had seen the light of Soviet communism, it would not be allowed to un-see it.

Brezhnev pressed for a treaty to give Soviet tanks and troops 'temporary' permission to be stationed on Czechoslovak soil. The National Assembly, which had rallied to Dubcek so strongly in the days following the invasion, approved the treaty of occupation by a vote of 280 votes to four. There was nothing 'temporary' about the agreement: Soviet forces would remain in the country for another twenty-two years.

AND YET, EVEN AS their democratic freedoms shrivelled before their eyes, there was still plenty of fight in Prague and elsewhere in the country. Students burnt copies of *Pravda* in front of the Soviet embassy; 8000 protestors showed up to heckle the Soviet deputy foreign minister at the National Theatre. In November 1968, anti-Soviet protests sprang up around the nation on the anniversary of the Russian revolution. State police retaliated with tear gas and truncheons. Dubcek, now a cowed, tragic figure, issued a statement scolding the protestors, accusing them of damaging the process of normalisation, and the 'innermost interests' of the country.[2] The next day, the new deputy prime minister, Gustav Husak, announced a ban on all demonstrations.

By the end of 1968, the message had sunk in: the people had been abandoned by their leaders.

THESE DISPIRITING DEVELOPMENTS had done little to faze the author Milan Kundera, who, even now, believed the Czechs could forge a new path between Soviet communism and Western capitalism. In his essay 'The Czech Destiny', published in the December 1968 edition of *Listy*, Kundera argued that this was not the time to go weak at the knees. Yes, he admitted, the backlash against socialism with a human face was harsher than expected, but this was no catastrophe. 'I would even venture to say,' he wrote, 'that the significance of the Czechoslovak autumn may even surpass the significance of the Czechoslovak spring.'[3]

Kundera made the case for the historic mission of his country as a small nation wedged between great powers, which had often been forced to draw on its creativity to avoid being utterly subsumed by its neighbours. It was hardly surprising, therefore, that the Czechs had managed to discover a goldmine of democratic possibilities hidden under the bedrock of Soviet communism. Just as Jan Hus had once revolutionised Catholic Europe, Kundera said, today's Czechs would continue to turn socialism on its head and give it new meaning. 'A nation thus endowed,' he concluded optimistically, 'has every right to approach the uncertainties of the coming year with complete confidence.'[4] But Kundera's essay credited too much originality to the concept of Dubcek's socialism with a human face. Socialist policies such as universal health care, state ownership of key utilities, and welfare payments to the unemployed had already been implemented in modern European nations like Sweden and Britain without the need for a one-party state.

It was a point picked up by Vaclav Havel, who wrote a stinging rebuttal in another literary monthly *Tvar*, which put a question mark on Kundera's title: 'The Czech Destiny?' The Prague Spring, Havel said, was not an inspired act of political creativity, but the work of a society simply trying to remove an abnormality from its system. Freedom of speech was 'something self-evident in most of the civilised world'; to claim there was anything special about the attempt to introduce it to Czechoslovakia was 'a pompous illusion'.[5] Havel suspected that reform communists like Kundera were fooling themselves with all this grandiose talk of national destiny. To him it looked like they were constructing an alibi so they could shrug off their own culpability as former apologists for the party's crimes, and blame it all on 'History' instead.[6]

Prague's literary community was shocked by Havel's trenchant attack on Kundera, who had been a friend and mentor to him. The breach between these men, the two most influential Czech writers of their time, would never quite be healed, but Havel's analysis was to prove the more clear-headed. Eventually, Kundera would resign his hopes for the 'Prague Autumn' and choose a life of exile in France, while Havel followed a different star.

Outside and Below

VACLAV HAVEL WAS BORN in 1936 into a family of wealthy property developers and politicians. His grandfather had constructed the glamorous Art Nouveau Lucerna Palace shopping complex on Wenceslas Square, while his father and uncle built the Barrandov Film Studios in the city's southwest.

At home, little Vaclav received all the care and comfort of a princeling, but his privileged status and chubby figure made him an object of derision in the schoolyard, where he was ridiculed as a 'fat little piglet'. No matter how low or high Havel rose or sank, he would never lose this sense of exclusion, of being an outsider in the world. This view, he once said, was the key to his plays: 'It is a view from below, a view from the outside, a view that has grown out of the experience of absurdity.'[7]

After 1948, the Havel family's wealth and property were confiscated by the state. Vaclav's bourgeois background disqualified him from higher education, and he left school at fifteen. He wrote his first plays while fulfilling his compulsory two years of military service to escape the drudgery and boredom. On his release from the army, Havel took a job as a stagehand at Prague's ABC Theatre, where he felt happy and at home. Prague's theatres would form a natural refuge for him for the rest of his life.

In the mid-1950s he found a circle of like-minded friends at the Café Slavia, the elegant Art Deco coffeehouse opposite the National Theatre. There he met and fell in love with Olga Splichalova, who became his wife. Despite their different backgrounds, the marriage was close, held together by shared hardship and their complementary characters. While Vaclav was compulsively polite, Olga was unnervingly plain-spoken. Vaclav had been born into luxury, whereas Olga was marked by her proletarian origins: four fingers from her left hand had been severed in an industrial accident. Although Havel would conduct several serious extra-marital affairs, he thought of Olga and himself as 'faithful, lifelong fellow travellers'. His infidelities and years in prison would strain the partnership but not break it.

HAVEL BEGAN TO WRITE sketches and black comedies for the experimental Theatre on the Balustrade. His first significant full-length plays, *The Garden Party* and *The Memorandum*, mocked the contorted language of bureaucracy. The result was a symbiosis of Kafkaesque weirdness and Hasekian buffoonery that left audiences rocking with laughter.

Havel's plays were translated and performed in Germany, Austria, Poland, France and Britain. During the Prague Spring, he was permitted to travel to the United States for the opening night of *The Memorandum* at New York's Public Theater. But his enjoyment of success would always be tempered by his absurdist worldview. Havel could never quite shake the suspicion that it was an illusion, that at some point an authority figure would walk into the room and tell him to go home or order him back to his prison cell.

Havel, surprisingly, was not particularly politically active during the Prague Spring. Never a party member, he wasn't interested in redeeming the communist project, and he held out little hope for socialism with a human face. He did, however, acknowledge Dubcek's decency and humanity. In July 1968, a month before the invasion, Havel was invited to an official writers' reception. To overcome his shyness, he downed a glass of cognac, which emboldened him to bowl up to Dubcek and advise him at length on how he should deal with the Soviets and handle the opposition within his party. The next morning, he was embarrassed by his behaviour and impressed by Dubcek's forbearance and his willingness to listen to advice from a half-drunk playwright.

Havel and Olga were out of town, staying with a friend in Liberec, when the Soviet tanks crossed the border. In Liberec's town square he saw tanks smashing down an arcade, burying people in the rubble, and his diffidence evaporated at once. He joined the local resistance, broadcasting messages on television and radio from the local station, calling for the world to help the people of Czechoslovakia.

As the pall of normalisation settled in, Havel became exasperated by the reform communists still trapped in their ideological cages. He thought Dubcek had acted like a fool in Moscow, folding so completely to Brezhnev. Havel believed a whole range of political options had been open to Dubcek, but he'd failed to grasp them, largely because he had gone to Moscow not as the leader of a sovereign nation but as a 'guilty servant' of communism.

Havel's impatience may go some way to explain the sharp tone of his reply to Milan Kundera's upbeat essay in the pages of *Listy*, but his anger might also be partly explained by the charged atmosphere in Prague in January 1969, caused by the death of a student in Wenceslas Square.

Torch Number One

THE DAWNING REALISATION that the revolutionary moment had passed, that the Prague Spring was finished, was unbearable to those young people who had hoped to live their lives in greater freedom and dignity than their parents' generation. The slow winding down of expectations was particularly intolerable to an idealistic, twenty-year-old economics student at Charles University named Jan Palach.

In his student ID photo, Palach's boyish face looks out at the world with a dark-eyed, soulful expression. Dubcek's reforms had sparked his youthful idealism, and so when the Soviets invaded, he joined the protest marches and painted anti-occupation slogans in the street. But as the months passed and the mood of resignation set in, he cast about desperately for ideas to galvanise the public's attention and revitalise the resistance. In his despair, he conceived of a radical gesture, an act that could neither be ignored nor forgotten.

On the morning of 16 January 1969, Palach sat down at his desk and wrote out copies of his final letter. He sent one to a close friend, another to the student leadership, a third to the Czechoslovak Writers' Union, and the original he put into his briefcase. In his letters, he identified himself as the head of a group of dissidents willing to take radical action to 'stir the sleeping conscience of the nation'. He wrote that his group had drawn lots and that he, Jan Palach, had earnt the right to become 'Torch No. 1'. But there was no group. It was just him.

After posting the letters, he took two white plastic buckets to a petrol station on Opletalova Street and filled them with gasoline. At 2.30 pm he carried the brimming buckets and his briefcase to the foot of the National Museum in Wenceslas Square, still strewn with rubble from the Soviet tank attack. Standing next to the museum's fountain, he tipped the fuel on his head, drenching himself and his clothes, and then with his trembling hands he lit a match.

THE FLAMING MAN LEAPT over the railing and ran towards the statue of St Wenceslas, narrowly avoiding a passing tram. Then he tripped and fell to the ground. Horrified onlookers ran to him and smothered the flames with their coats as best they could.

Jan Palach was still alive. Lying on the stones, trembling, smouldering, he begged the onlookers to open the briefcase he'd left near the stairs and to read the letter within. An ambulance rushed him to Vinohrady Hospital. Still conscious, he gasped to the medical staff that he wasn't a suicide case, that he had set himself on fire as a protest. 'Please tell everyone why I did it,' he repeated. 'Please tell everyone.'[8]

THE DOCTORS AT THE burns ward kept the police outside the door, while Palach's mother and brother stood at his bedside. Speaking as best he could, he repeated that he was part of a group, that he had not acted alone.

After lingering for three days, he died in hospital on 19 January. His death led the TV news that night. 'Jan Palach died quietly,' the newsreader announced with tears in her eyes. 'His body could not stand the strain of his burns.'[9]

PALACH'S FUNERAL PROCESSION on 25 January 1969 had the scale and solemnity of a state funeral. Hundreds of thousands of people stood in freezing rain in deep silence as the coffin was ferried through the streets. No one had seen such a display of public mourning since the death of Jan Masaryk. A long train of mourners filed past his coffin, faces contorted with grief. Older women sobbed helplessly; men wiped away tears with their fists, their faces filled with uncomprehending loss. Paul Wilson, who was in the crowd, felt a terrible sense of finality, 'a feeling that it was the end ... the end of hope'.[10]

THE WORLD MEDIA ASSUMED that Palach had modelled his suicide on the Buddhist monks of South Vietnam, who had self-immolated in protest against the Saigon government, but Czechs naturally saw a closer link to the burning of Jan Hus.

Palach's prediction that others were ready to burn became a self-fulfilling prophecy as other young men chose to self-immolate in protest: Jan Zajic on 25 February, Evzen Plocek on 4 April, and Michal Leucik on 11 April. Media coverage of their deaths was suppressed by the regime.

In Wenceslas Square, the site of Palach's burning was transformed into an improvised shrine, with candles and photo portraits of the young man. The site became a recurrent sore point for the authorities, as people gathered there each year on 16 January to commemorate his sacrifice. The act of remembrance, the struggle against forgetting, had become as important as Jan's deed of protest.

The human torch of Wenceslas Square succeeded in collapsing the long, drawn-out dissolution of their freedoms into a piercingly singular point in time and space. Each year the people of Prague remember Jan Palach not on the anniversary of his death, but on the date of his self-immolation. It's the flame more than the death that burns in the imagination.

The Pain Gate

NOVEMBER 2011: MY WIFE Khym has prepared a special family dinner, a Vietnamese dish that is to be cooked at the table. She places the ingredients in a large ceramic bowl, which sits atop a saucer with a little puddle of methylated spirits. Khym lights a match and carefully extends it towards the saucer. Our twelve-year-old son, Joe, is sitting next to me. Our daughter Emma is eight; she's spooked by the flame and is standing well away from the table.

Khym lights the fuel. A thin blue flame encircles the bowl and ingredients begin to sizzle. The food is cooked and eaten, and everyone's still hungry. Khym offers to cook some more, but the flame in the dish has almost expired, so she decants a tiny amount of spirits into the plastic cap, and gently tips it into the saucer.

A FIREBALL ERUPTS across the table, and my shirt and arms are on fire. I look down and see the flames rippling across it. I tear off the burning shirt and run to the bathroom.

Standing under the shower, I call out in a panic, 'Is everyone alright? Are the kids alright?'

In the distance, I hear Khym cry out that everyone is okay and that's she trying to put out the flames.

And with that, something quietens in my head. I feel the pain of the burns, but it doesn't seem to bother me as much. The confusion is replaced by a profound sense of clarity and curiosity. I open my eyes to study my wounds. The burns extend all the way up my right arm and across the fingers of both hands. The skin is blackened and ruined.

IN HOSPITAL, IT IS explained to me that hot and cold fuel are chemically different; adding cold fuel to the hot burning spirits in the saucer had caused it to spatter and ignite mid-air. That was how I'd caught fire.

A week later I go in for skin graft surgery. Afterwards, the new skin on my hands and arm doesn't hurt, but the flayed area on my thigh, the donor site for the grafts, is searingly painful. The nurses give me a mix of opioids that dim the pain but don't quite extinguish it.

Khym comes to see me one afternoon, and in the course of the hour my painkillers start to fail and I have to stop talking to concentrate on managing the throbbing in my leg. This is different from the pain I'd felt after the fire, which I'd been able to observe from a distance. This pain is closer now and it hurts much more. It troubles me more. Khym takes my hand and closes her eyes, slowly synchronising my breathing with hers. It seems as though she's drawing the pain out of me, like a poison. I fall into a deep sleep and when I wake up two hours later she's gone and I feel fine.

*

MEDICAL UNDERSTANDING of pain has advanced dramatically in recent decades. It was once thought that pain was a straightforward sensory experience, like hearing or vision. Pain, it was thought, operated like an emergency signal passing through a telephone line from the stimulus point to the brain; the bigger the stimulus, the louder the bell in the brain rings.

The first inkling that the experience of pain might be bound up in perception came from a study by an American doctor, Henry Beecher, who treated injured soldiers during the Second World War and was surprised when so many badly wounded men reported having next to no pain at all. Beecher considered the context of their pain: the men were in bad shape, but knew they had survived combat, that they were receiving the best of care, and they would return home to their loved ones as honoured veterans. For most of them, Beecher realised, the *meaning* of the pain was positive. And that meaning somehow diminished its intensity.[11]

Then in 1965, two Canadian researchers came forward with a revolutionary new theory of pain – the Gate Control Theory – which is broadly accepted today. Pain, they contended, is registered through a gate in the spinal cord, a gate that can either be opened, or closed, exposing the person to more or less pain.[12] Depression, inactivity and anxiety tend to open the pain gate wider, as does consciously focusing on the pain, like I did that afternoon in hospital. Factors that close the pain gate include a positive outlook and being reassured the pain is not harmful.

Jan Palach's anxious pleas from his hospital bed for his letter to be read can therefore be understood, not only as a dogged act of political will, but also, perhaps, as an instinctive act of pain mitigation. To think that his act of self-immolation had not been properly understood would only have compounded his agony.

Jan Palach.

The New Normal

BY EARLY 1969, Alexander Dubcek had outlived his usefulness to Brezhnev, who now looked for an excuse to eject him from his post as Czechoslovak party leader. The opportunity duly presented itself on 28 March, when Czechoslovakia played against the USSR for the world ice-hockey championship in Stockholm. In a tight match, the Czechoslovaks eked out a 4–3 victory. The team refused to shake hands with their Soviet opponents. Close to half a million Czechs rushed into the streets of Prague to exult in the triumph. In Wenceslas Square, someone picked up a cobblestone and smashed the windows of the office of the Soviet airline Aeroflot, which was all the excuse the Russians needed to intervene.*

The Soviet defence minister, Andrei Grechko, rushed to Prague to dress down his Czechoslovak counterpart, claiming

---

* Dubcek, in his memoir (p.237), claimed that the first people to throw cobblestones through the Aeroflot windows were strategically placed StB *provocateurs*, acting on orders from Moscow.

the demonstrations were not spontaneous but well planned and organised by counter-revolutionary elements. Grechko issued a dark threat: 'We warn you we shall not tolerate a repetition of such acts. We shall make short shrift even of 100,000 counter-revolutionaries.'[13]

The loyal Dubcek was demoted into oblivion. On 17 April, he was forced out of the party leadership and relegated to the position of chairman of the rebranded Federal Assembly. Later in the year he was named Ambassador to Turkey, then dismissed from that post just a few months later. Finally, a clerical position was found for him in the Western Slovak State Forests Department. His former ally, Dr Gustav Husak, was named party First Secretary.

HUSAK WAS A SOLID replacement as far as the Soviets were concerned: an ambitious Slovak, associated in the public mind with the reformists, who was nonetheless prepared to do Brezhnev's bidding in all things. Under his leadership, Czechoslovakia returned to the fold as one of Moscow's most obedient allies.

Physically, Husak was easy to overlook; with his receding hairline of neat snowy hair, thick glasses and pleasant pudgy face, he resembled an academic from a regional university. But his bland exterior concealed a complex and driven personality. Husak, whose childhood had been marked by poverty and deprivation, had joined the communists in the 1930s, and was jailed periodically during the war. Like Dubcek, he joined the Slovak partisan uprising against Nazi Germany and the puppet Tiso government.

After the war Husak became the effective leader of the Slovak communists, where he showed considerable acumen in crushing the local democratic parties. He was quick witted, hard-working and seen by his rivals as 'dangerously capable'.[14] Husak could rouse an audience with a good speech, particularly when calling for greater autonomy for Slovakia within the new socialist republic. All this marked him out for special treatment from Prague once the purges and show trials got underway. On 6 February 1951, he was arrested and denounced as 'a bourgeois nationalist'.[15]

Husak was tortured under interrogation but steadfastly refused to confess to the accusations put to him by his interrogators. He expected to be dragged to the gallows, like Slansky, but was sentenced to life imprisonment instead. Once inside, several inmates who had been put there by Husak took their revenge upon him, putting a bag over his head and beating him.[16] Husak nonetheless held tight to his ambitions and in his faith that the communist movement would get back on track one day and rehabilitate him.

In 1960, nine years into his sentence, Husak was released by President Novotny as part of his lukewarm de-Stalinisation program. Husak was a free man, but his marriage was in ruins: while he'd been away, his wife, Magda, had become a successful theatre director and had fallen in love with one of her leading men.

Husak's time in jail had hardened, not humanised, him. The reformist Zdenek Mlynar observed he had emerged from his long years of isolation as 'a powerful political personality ... eager to show the knaves and fools the proper way to conduct politics'.[17] In 1963, Husak was rehabilitated by the party with the strong support of his fellow Slovak Alexander Dubcek, who saw him as an educated communist and a natural ally.

WHEN HUSAK REPLACED DUBCEK as party leader in 1969, he might have entertained hopes he would be allowed some latitude, but the Soviets made clear from the outset that he served at their pleasure. 'The phone calls from Brezhnev started coming right away,' recalled his colleague Lubomir Strougal. In his first eight years as first secretary, Husak visited Brezhnev twenty-six times, more than three times as often as any other Soviet bloc leader, and he regularly consulted with the Soviet ambassador.[18] For all his cleverness, Husak had become another Emil Hacha, a servile cut-out for an empire that intended to run Czechoslovakia as a vassal state.

A joke circulated in Prague about a man who is eaten whole by Leonid Brezhnev. As he passes into Brezhnev's stomach, he encounters Gustav Husak.

'Comrade President!' the man calls out. 'Has Brezhnev eaten you too?'

'No,' answers Husak, 'I came in from the other end.'

AT BREZHNEV'S URGING, Husak initiated a purge of the party membership, beginning at the uppermost levels, then reaching down into every workplace. One and a half million party members were screened to decide whose membership should be renewed or cancelled. Eventually more than 300,000 were expelled.[19] Those who had expressed support for Dubcek's reforms were invited to sign a declaration renouncing their views, which would then be placed on file. The point of the 'confession' was not to incriminate but to humiliate: to make people complicit in their own subjugation. Writers, academics, doctors and journalists who refused to recant were put to work as cleaners, stokers, bricklayers and rubbish collectors. Prague soon had the most over-educated menial workforce in the world. Armed guards with automatic weapons policed the border; escape into Austria or West Germany became a near impossibility.

NORMALISATION WAS NOT a return to Stalinist violence; Husak's regime practised a subtler, wearier form of totalitarianism. There was no need for the direct application of mass terror. Instead, the party entrenched its rule by doling out small luxuries to its supporters – a car, a better apartment, a promotion. Rebellion would be met with a sliding scale of counter-incentives: demotion, defamation, relegation to a job in a factory or a uranium mine. The party no longer seriously expected to win over hearts and minds to the heroic task of building socialism in Czechoslovakia. It was enough to merely nod one's head when apparatchiks said how well everything was going. Dissidents were no longer denounced as heretics but as 'troublemakers' and 'hooligans'. The state did not require the entire person, wrote one purged party member, 'just the part that projects above the surface of public life'.[20]

The purging of independent thought and initiative, however, left the regime with the same problem it had faced in the 1950s: a severe shortage of competent professionals to keep the country running. The newly vacated posts were often filled by politically reliable people of no discernible skill or talent. Czechoslovakia became a kingdom of the mediocre and incompetent, while its most talented and imaginative people cleaned boilers and washed windows.

Access to higher education became a useful means to keep people on a short leash. Each year, lists of prospective students were compiled by regional committees, who marked the names of kids from politically reliable families with an A. These were to be accepted at once. Those marked with an N were not to be accepted under any circumstances, no matter how well they performed in their exams. Fear of spoiling their children's education led many to keep their heads down and to encourage their sons and daughters to do the same. Parents were thus exposed to their children as liars and hypocrites. Pavel Kohout observed ruefully that 'children are taught that lying is an ethic – say one thing at home, another at school. Of course it's understandable, but it is also our tragedy. *I did it for the children* is the Czech problem.'[21]

Golden Nightingales

THE EXPLOSION OF POP and rock music in the 1960s was an ongoing headache for the regime. Songs performed to a mass audience that called implicitly or explicitly for truth and personal freedom presented problems both for the state and for the people who sang them. The different fortunes of the nation's most popular male and female recording stars, Karel Gott and Marta Kubisova, illustrate the hard choices faced by Prague's creative artists under normalisation.

Karel Gott was the uncontested king of Czech Europop: a five-time winner of the Golden Nightingale award for the most popular male singer. Gott sang in German as well as Czech, and thus became a star in West Germany and Austria as well. His album and concert sales earnt him a stream of foreign royalty payments, much of which was siphoned off by the regime.

Gott had emerged in the early 1960s as a kind of Czech Cliff Richard. As the decade wound on, he grew out his hair, put on some flares and learnt to gyrate, but his songs were apolitical and his appearance was clean-cut. The regime was unnerved by Gott's popularity, and in 1971 it decided to take him down a peg. *Rude Pravo* scolded him as a bad example to the nation's youth. While recording a one-man prime-time special for state television, Gott was told by the director to cut his hair. Two full days of tense negotiations followed, between Gott's manager and the Ministry of Culture. Eventually a compromise was reached: two centimetres would have to be shorn off above the ears. He would be allowed to grow it back for his tour of West Germany but until then, it was decreed, 'the ears must show!'

The regime gave him another slap when it banned one of his songs, a ballad of a lover who flips a coin to tell if his girlfriend loves him or not. The song was deemed objectionable for its 'insulting' attitude towards the value of the Czech currency. Gott, on tour in West Germany, decided to call the regime's bluff and threatened to remain in the West indefinitely. With that, Husak backed down, and wrote a personal letter, pleading with him to return:

> *Dear Karel: We are not angry with you ... Please come back to see us and you will get your contract to sing in the West. But you must sing for us, too, and, if you agree, we will fulfil your every wish. We want to help you, but isn't it logical that you should help us, too?*[22]

Gott and the regime reached an accommodation that allowed him to keep most of his earnings and live like a rock star in Prague with the regime's blessing.

MARTA KUBISOVA'S CAREER took a different path. Young, vampish and achingly beautiful, Kubisova was the closest thing the Czechs had to Dusty Springfield. Her husky contralto voice filled any space effortlessly, and she invested her songs with genuine feeling. Adored by her fans, Kubisova was voted the winner of the female Golden Nightingale award three times in the 1960s.

When the Soviets invaded, Marta publicly supported the embattled Dubcek, dashing up to him on the steps of the Central Committee building to give him a bunch of roses and a medallion of an angel to wear on his wrist. Kubisova's most famous song 'A Prayer for Marta' was played throughout the invasion crisis on Czechoslovak Radio. Its words were taken from a prayer written by the seventeenth-century Czech exile, John Amos Comenius:

Let peace remain long within this land.
Malice, envy, fear and strife,
Let them pass, let them finally pass.

The song tapped into a deep longing for peace, freedom and independence. In February 1969, she sang it defiantly at the televised Golden Nightingale Awards ceremony. Marta had become a symbol of national resistance and inspiration.

That same year she married the charismatic Czech New Wave film director Jan Nemec, who had shot footage of the anti-Soviet protests in Wenceslas Square. When the Czechs beat the Russians at the ice-hockey championships, Nemec became so excited, he told Marta he wanted to write her name on bullets above their apartment's bay window.[23]

Marta Kubisova, from the film clip of 'Hey Jude', 1969.

IN 1970, MARTA WON the Golden Nightingale once more by popular vote, but this time there would be no ceremony; she was told she would have to pick up her award privately at the offices of *Young World* magazine.

Soon afterwards, on the eve of a concert tour, her manager was summoned to the office of the state booking agency, Pragokoncert, where the agency's director laid out a photo-montage from *Hot Kittens*, a Danish porn magazine. Marta's face had been superimposed onto one of the bodies in the pictures. When Marta saw the pages she laughed, thinking the forgery was too crude to be believed.

Copies of *Hot Kittens* were nonetheless sent to various media outlets, and Marta was dropped from the booking agency. Determined not to be undone by such a squalid fabrication, she sued the director of Pragokoncert for defamation. She won her case, but all her bookings dried up anyway, and she was led to understand that if she was to persist in singing, some other 'evidence' against her would soon appear in the newly compliant press. Marta became pregnant, but in the aftermath of the stressful court case she suffered a traumatic miscarriage at eight months, losing so much blood that doctors had to revive her from a state of clinical death.

HER CAREER ABRUPTLY TERMINATED, Marta and her husband retreated to the countryside. Jan Nemec found work as a tractor driver and she took on a job gluing bags together in a factory. Nemec found the isolation and irrelevance unbearable and migrated to West Germany; Marta chose to stay behind and the couple divorced.

Occasionally she would slip back into Prague and walk the streets. On bad days, she hoped a balcony or a cornice from a decaying building would fall on her and kill her. With her last royalty payment she bought a washing machine.[24]

✳

The Ear

THREE APPARATCHIKS CAME to Prague one month for a party conference. After the first day, they sat up late in their hotel room, drinking and telling stories. The alcohol loosened their tongues a little, and they began to complain about the secret police. One of them hushed the other two and whispered, 'What if they're listening to us right now?' The other two laughed, so the man decided to play a joke.

He went downstairs to the hotel reception and asked the woman at the desk to deliver three cups of tea to the room in fifteen minutes. When he re-joined his friends, he sat down and leant towards a vase of plastic flowers, and said, 'Hello comrade major! Could you have three cups of tea sent up to our room?'

His friends laughed, but when the tea arrived, they blanched, made their excuses and went to bed.

The next morning, the man went out for a walk, but when he returned to the hotel, his friends were gone. He asked the receptionist what had happened to them.

'They've been arrested,' she said. 'They would have arrested you too, but the comrade major really liked your joke about the tea.'

THE DREAD THAT ONE'S conversation might be overheard was the subject of many jokes from this time. Some were long shaggy dog tales, others achieved a kind of pithy perfection: an American visits a Czech relative in Prague. 'How are things going?' he asks. 'Oh, you know,' replies the Czech. 'Can't complain.'

The secret police devoted enormous resources to keeping tabs on troublemakers. The dissident writer Ludvik Vaculik and his wife, Madla, discovered tiny microphones hidden in every room in their apartment. Their phone was bugged, and another apartment in their block was taken over by StB agents to monitor their conversations. Thus, for twenty years, they avoided discussing anything of significance out loud, and wrote it down instead on flushable sheets of toilet paper.[25]

IN 1970, A TENSE psychological drama called *The Ear* ('Ucho') was released from Barrandov Studios. The movie was centred around a couple, Ludvik and Anna, who return home, drunk, after a glittering cocktail party for senior officials. The handsome Ludvik, a deputy minister, discovers his house keys have gone missing, so he climbs the garden wall to get in, but they find the front door unlocked. Just as worryingly, the phone is dead and the power is out, even though the lights are on in the other houses in the street.

Then they spot trench-coated secret police officers prowling outside. The couple snipe and bicker. Ludvik has learnt at the reception that his boss, who is Jewish, has been mysteriously detained. They anxiously go over the earlier conversations from that evening, agonising over whether Ludvik had said or done something wrong.

They discover more evidence the house has been searched. In a panic, Ludvik rifles through his documents and flushes a torn-up photo of him with his former boss down the toilet. Their fighting is abruptly halted when Anna finds a listening device in the kitchen. More bugs are found in every room of the house. Anna's fury at her husband turns to fear as the couple realise their conversations have been monitored electronically all night by what she calls 'the ear'.

Ludvik locks himself in the bathroom, intending to kill himself, but he discovers his revolver has already been confiscated by the secret police. 'When they want to do it, they do it themselves,' he mutters.

At 5 am, the phone rings. It's the president offering congratulations: Ludvik is to replace his former boss. Through the ear, the police have heard proof of his cowardice and are satisfied he'll give the regime no trouble.

THE EAR WAS DIRECTED by Karel Kachyna from a screenplay he co-wrote with Jan Prochazka, one of Prague's most outspoken writers and intellectuals. Prochazka had once been an ardent communist but had since fallen out with the party. His outspokenness had brought him to the attention of no less a figure than the Soviet Foreign Minister Andrei Gromyko.[26] Convinced that Prochazka was part of an 'elite anti-state group', the KGB had sent an agent posing as a West German tourist to befriend Prochazka, and then abduct him into East Germany. The plot was aborted when the agent realised Prochazka spoke no Russian, and he spoke no Czech.[27]

After the Soviet invasion, Prochazka continued to pen attacks on the regime, but then the chill of normalisation set in. His health declined. Prochazka was wondering if the authorities would ever let him work again when he saw a TV guide mentioning that a documentary was to be broadcast on state TV about him, titled *Report from on the Seine*. Prochazka was pleased and relieved. He saw it as an olive branch from the party, a gesture of respect towards an honourable critic of the regime.

WHEN THE PROGRAM BEGAN, Prochazka and his family were confused by what they saw. On the screen, there was a view of rolling countryside seen through the front window of a car. The driver was not visible, but his hands were on the wheel, and he could be heard talking to a companion, also out of sight. The driver laughed and said terrible, insulting things about Alexander Dubcek and various members of Prague's literary community. Prochazka was confused, until he realised, with horror, that the driver's voice was his own. Somehow, the secret police had recorded a late-night conversation where he and a friend had indulged in the classic vice of writers everywhere – drinking too much and badmouthing their fellow authors. The StB had simply dubbed the audio over some driving footage to make Prochazka look like a snide elitist, dumping on his friends while cruising around France.

The phone rang in his apartment. The caller denounced him as 'a monstrous, shameless two-faced bastard'.[28]

REPORT FROM ON THE SEINE instantly destroyed Prochazka's reputation. He was snubbed by the people he'd criticised on the tape. The broader public seemed to enjoy seeing a hypocritical writer knocked off his perch.

Prochazka tried to redeem his reputation, typing letter after letter to explain how the StB had edited the conversation out of context to make it sound so much worse than it was, but his former friends continued to shun him, despite his rapidly declining health. He was then diagnosed with bowel cancer, but his wife chose not to tell him, seeing he had not long to live. Jan Prochazka died in February 1971, at the age of forty-two.

The film he wrote, *The Ear*, was buried in the archives.

IT'S HARD TO OVERSTATE the sheer weirdness of normalisation. Amidst the dullness, there was a *Through the Looking Glass* quality to daily life, in which people were expected to accept six impossible things before breakfast. The terrible dinginess, the shortages, the suppression of honest opinion were at odds with Husak's claim that life was getting better and sweeter. Communism seemed both unsustainable and unkillable.

In 2018, on a long, four-hour flight from Perth to Sydney, I fell into conversation with the woman next to me, Anna, who had grown up in communist Poland. I asked her if she'd ever travelled to Czechoslovakia during those years, and she recalled spending a summer at a Friendship Camp in Spicak, near the German border, with a group of other kids from the Soviet bloc. One day, she said, the camp administrator informed them that an important party dignitary would be visiting to make a speech, and they would have to make the camp look nice for the official photographs.

'But there was a problem,' Anna explained. 'The lawn in front of the hostel had dried out. So all of us were given buckets of green paint to make it look good for the cameras.'

'You *painted* the lawn green?' I asked.

'We painted the lawn green.'

'With brushes or rollers?'

'With brushes,' she said.

'So what happened when the party dignitaries came?'

'They came. They made their speeches, of course. The happy photos were taken, and after they left, the lawn completely died.'

I had to ask if the news pictures of the event were published in colour, or black and white.

'Oh, black and white,' she said, smiling.[29]

Bony

IN MAY 1975, GUSTAV HUSAK replaced the ageing Svoboda as president, while retaining his post as party leader. From his high perch at Prague Castle, Husak looked down at a city frozen in time. The Old Town, New Town and Mala Strana had become precincts of flaking facades and rotting interiors, propping each other up in their old age. The wandering, tendril-like streets and the cluttered skyline of domes, towers and spires seemed so strangely at odds with the communist ideal of an orderly centrally planned society.

Prague's housing crisis was solved by the construction of estates of prefabricated tower blocks on the city's periphery. These apartment buildings, known as *panelaky*, were heroic in scale and close to tram and metro stations, but the towers were ugly, and the tower parks barren and depressing. Public areas lacked the laneways, street shops, huddled cafés and public gardens, where friends and neighbours might run into each other and socialise.

The powerful social solidarity that had bound Praguers together after the invasion atomised under the pressure of normalisation, as people concluded that political activity was either too dangerous or simply pointless. The StB compiled secret reports acknowledging a 'deep passivity' pervading the people of Prague.[30] Unable to escape state supervision, they practised a kind of inner migration and retreated into their private lives, finding satisfaction within their families or in the pursuit of good beer, pork, dumplings and cabbage. Praguers in these years lived for the weekend, finishing work early on Fridays to head for their country cottages, where they could drop their guard and enjoy their work: mowing the lawns, planting and harvesting vegetables from the garden, mending and extending their houses.

All adults were required to work during the week, but few were motivated to perform beyond the minimum requirements of the planned economy. Alcoholism was endemic and working conditions were often dangerous and unhealthy. Power generation relied on burning brown coal, which often smothered Prague in sulphurous smog. Nearby forests began to die off at an alarming rate, and many waterways became sewers of pollution.

Low-grade food could be produced in sizable quantities on the collective farms, but poor distribution meant that much of it would rot before it reached the shelves. People lined up outside shops to buy Cuban oranges, Hungarian shampoo or Moravian sausages, often joining a line without knowing what was on sale. Milk was sold in plastic sacs that often burst inside shopping bags. Women's sanitary napkins had to be washed and reused. Toilet paper was almost never available, so people improvised by using pages of *Rude Pravo.*

Manufactured goods such as cars and refrigerators were poorly constructed and spare parts almost non-existent. Electricians, plumbers and car mechanics conducted freelance work illegally after hours, which earnt them more money than their regular jobs with state-owned enterprises. When television began broadcasting in colour it hardly mattered, as almost no one owned a colour TV set to watch it on.

BUT WITHIN THIS SEA of austerity, there were a few tiny islands of plenty. Western goods of all kinds could be bought at a chain of special state-run stores called Tuzex shops, but only with special vouchers purchased with Western hard currency, nicknamed *bony* (taken from the word for coupons). Czech citizens were permitted to receive limited gifts of foreign currency from relatives living in the West. These dollars and Deutschmarks could in turn be exchanged for *bony*, giving ordinary people entry into Tuzex's cornucopia of

French cognac, Brazilian coffee, Marlboro cigarettes, Sony TV sets and Casio watches.

Inevitably, the Tuzex stores became a focal point for organised crime. Gangs of hustlers, known as *vekslaks*, would hang around banks and hotel lobbies, offering to illegally exchange foreign currency for crowns at a far better rate than that offered by the authorities. Flush with Western currency, the hustlers could exchange their cash for Tuzex vouchers, which they could then sell to citizens for Czech crowns at inflated rates.

Ideological communists deplored the brand fetishism that turned Levi's jeans into *haute couture* and made Coca-Cola a delicacy to be enjoyed at Christmas time. But the regime badly needed the hard currency that came into the Tuzex stores, so they looked the other way when the grey market blended into the black.[31]

The Secret Streamlet

PRAGUE'S BOHEMIANS SPENT the early 1970s finding solace in private parties, cheap beer and adultery. 'For me,' Havel later confessed, 'the first half of the decade is a single, shapeless fog … each of us, in his own way, was stewing in his own juices.'[32] Unable to stage plays or publish books or participate meaningfully in their own society, they killed time in bars, bedrooms and country houses, sleeping with each other's spouses. Tired of the intrigue and insularity of Prague, Havel and Olga spent more and more time at Hradecek, their cottage in the mountains. He was still writing, but with no hope that his plays would be performed in his own country.

In 1974, Havel took a labouring job at the Trutnov brewery, ten kilometres from Hradecek. He found the hard work calming and satisfying, and after a few months he was ready to step back into public life. It was time, he realised, to stop reacting to whatever the state wanted to dish out to him; instead, he would give *them* something to react to, which took the form of a long open letter to the nation's leader.

Havel's 'Letter to Dr Husak' addressed itself to the malaise of Czechoslovak society under normalisation, but it stands for all time as a classic essay on the practical and moral consequences of totalitarianism. Havel contrasted the apparently placid surface of everyday life in Czechoslovakia with the pervasive sense of fear lurking beneath. This was not, he wrote, a quaking-in-terror kind of fear, but a constant awareness of danger that might be hovering nearby or in the distance, a fear that drove people to express support for the party's decisions, enforced in the last resort by the secret police, which he likened to a hideous spider, 'whose invisible web runs right through the whole of society'.[33] But Havel noted the party would itself become paralysed by its own venom and fail to function properly. In a remarkably prescient passage, Havel foresaw the circumstances of the regime's downfall:

A secret streamlet trickles on beneath the heavy lid of inertia and pseudo-events, slowly and inconspicuously undercutting it. It may be a long process, but one day it must happen: the lid will no longer hold and will start to crack. This is the moment when once more something visibly begins to happen, something truly new and unique, something unscheduled in the official calendar of 'happenings', something that makes us no longer indifferent to what occurs and when – something truly historic, in the sense that history again demands to be heard.[34]

*

White Light, White Heat

Thanks to the Government and the Party, we're
day after day increasingly happy.

Czechoslovak Youth Union slogan.[35]

PAUL WILSON WAS UNWILLING to give up on Prague, while there was still so much going on in the city. In late 1969, Paul was introduced in the street to Ivan Jirous, an art critic with long curly chestnut hair and a forceful gaze. Jirous invited Paul to come over to his apartment for potato dumplings and beer.

At the apartment, Paul met two members of a new psychedelic band called the Plastic People of the Universe. The group, founded by four teenagers from Prague's Brevnov district, were heavily influenced by New York band the Velvet Underground, and had somehow procured a copy of the Velvets' classic first album with an Andy Warhol banana on the cover.

Somehow the numbness of normalisation had failed to penetrate this room. While Jirous cooked, the guests helped themselves to jugs of pilsner as their host held forth on Czech history and culture, in between flipping records by the Velvet Underground, The Doors and Captain Beefheart on his crude stereo.[36] Jirous, Paul discovered, was argumentative and pugnacious. 'He had arrived at a set of ideas that guided his life and he protected them with all the zeal of an ideologue.' There was always a sense, Paul felt, that the argument might end up in blows, although it never did.[37]

Paul Wilson and Ivan Jirous became part of a merry free-floating association of artists, musicians and hangers-on, who called themselves the Crusader School of Pure Humour without Jokes. In a parody of communist bureaucracy, Jirous styled himself as the group's Minister of the Interior and vetted the membership carefully. He assumed the nickname Magor, which translates as 'fool' or 'fantasist' (from the Czech word *fantazmagoria*).

Jirous was excited by the primitive, confrontational power of the Plastic People of the Universe, and had become the band's artistic director, just as Warhol had for the Velvet Underground. He invited Paul to see them perform in a village pub just north of Prague. Paul entered the dance hall and saw an audience of long-haired rock and roll fans, jostling, smoking and drinking. The Plastic People hit the stage at sundown, wearing long dirty satin gowns and sinister makeup. Fires burnt on either side of the stage. When the band broke into their opening song, a juddering cover of the Velvet Underground's 'White Light/White Heat', the crowd began to dance frantically. A fire-breather leapt onto the dance floor and shot a blast of flame from his mouth, while the singer did his best to mimic Lou Reed.

The music was crude, bacchanalian, thrilling. Jirous asked Paul what he thought. Paul said they were wonderful but needed to practise more. 'Have you any idea man,' Jirous groaned, 'just how difficult it is to get gigs right now?'

THE REGIME'S CULTURAL apparatchiks were straining to keep rock and roll within the bounds of cheerful, acceptable pop, but the Plastics had chewed through the leash. Karel Gott, with his helmet of sculpted hair was welcome; shaggy teenagers making a distorted racket in live shows that were literally inflammatory were not.

The Plastics' early repertoire was made up almost entirely of cover versions of songs by the Velvet Underground and The Fugs, sung in

English, even though the band didn't really understand the lyrics. They turned to Paul for help and he joined the group as singer and rhythm guitarist.

To perform in public, bands were required by law to audition for a licence. At the end of the Plastics' audition, a disgusted official said, 'Cut their hair and send them down the mines.'[38] The Plastics were denied professional status, which was quite acceptable to Ivan Jirous, who thought the very concept of state-sanctioned rock music was ludicrous anyway.

Unable to find a venue, Jirous circumvented the rules by organising public lectures on pop art, where he would talk about Andy Warhol and then the Plastics would perform songs from the Velvet Underground to illustrate his point. Jirous was paid an honorarium for these lectures, which he used to buy instruments for the band. But it wasn't long before the StB figured out this ruse; Jirous was interrogated and accused of earning money illegally.

While Jirous tried to ignore the authorities, sometimes he was unable to help himself. In the summer of 1973, he was jailed for insulting a retired StB officer by eating a page from *Rude Pravo* in front of him, telling him the Bolsheviks were destined to be devoured the same way. For that he was sentenced to ten months in prison.

PAUL WILSON LEFT The Plastics on friendly terms in late 1972 as the band's repertoire began to fill up with original songs, sung in Czech. Their sound matured when saxophonist Vratislav Brabenec joined and introduced jazz tonalities to their music. They dropped the props – the robes, makeup and fire – and moved towards a stripped-back, more authentic presence on stage. They joined forces with a legendary wild-man poet named Egon Bondy, whom Jirous had met at a psychiatric clinic. Bondy contributed lyrics to the band's original songs and offered the Plastics the use of his one-room apartment on Nerudova Street as a rehearsal space.

Bondy was a vocal opponent of the regime, but his criticism came from the revolutionary left, and he was just as hostile to consumer capitalism. He was a good fifteen years older than Jirous, and his connection to the Plastics made his work freshly relevant to a new generation of Bohemian misfits. The Plastics' first album of songs set to Bondy's lyrics was banned in Czechoslovakia, but was released in France under the title *Egon Bondy's Happy Hearts Club Banned*.

OTHER BANDS ATTACHED to the Plastics began springing up across the country. Another band of surrealist-anarchists called DG 307 also gained a strong following, pounding out industrial music with drums, horns and sheets of metal. Jirous named this flourishing scene the Second Culture, placing it not so much against the state as entirely outside its boundaries. The crowds of musicians, poets and concert-goers were sometimes called *androsi* – 'undergrounders'. The police began to monitor the scene closely, hovering outside concerts and taking down everyone's ID on the way out.

In March 1974, officials were shocked by the size of the crowd at an underground rock festival held outside Ceske Budejovice, and assumed it was part of a coordinated anti-state protest. The festival was broken up by police with attack dogs. Hundreds of concert-goers were rounded up and herded into an underpass towards the train station, where they were beaten with truncheons. Students and young workers were arrested and brought back to Prague, where their long hair was shaved off.

ON THE FACE OF IT, there was no real need for the regime to crack down so hard. The Plastics' style was certainly distasteful to the authorities, but there were no protest songs in their repertoire, no direct incitements to youthful rebellion. The regime simply couldn't tolerate the presence of a cultural phenomenon that could flourish so completely outside its margins.

The StB was tormented by suspicions that some kind of shadowy Western conspiracy was at work behind the underground scene. Dana Nemcova, a Prague psychologist who helped organise the Ceske Budejovice event, was pulled in and asked how it was possible to organise such a huge gathering. When she told them, 'Word of mouth,' the interrogators scoffed and told her it would take hundreds of people to pull off something like that.

'No,' she insisted, 'it just happens spontaneously. All you do is put the word out and it happens. It's all because we want to do it. You don't need a conspiracy to do this.'[39]

The party's campaign against the band shifted into high gear. *Rude Pravo* denounced the Plastics as 'long-haired, neurotic drug addicts'.[40] State media portrayed the underground music scene as a seedy hotbed of criminality. In an unintentionally comic episode of the state TV police drama *Major Zeman*, the clean-cut hero of the series was pitted against a cell of terrorist hippies with handguns who perform screeching rock music to crowds of hypnotised young people. The connection to the Plastics was unmistakable, and ridiculous.

The Trial of the Second Culture

STATE PERSECUTION WAS nerve-wracking but it heightened the sense of romance in the underground and led its members to identify with the rich history of Czech dissent. One day in 1974, between prison stints, Ivan Jirous travelled out to the village of

Lisnice with forty-five other *androsi*. They were on their way to see the debut performance of a new band, which would be playing with the Plastics and DG 307. The excited music fans got out at the train station then trudged for a mile through dusky half-frozen fields towards Lisnice. Their mood, Jirous wrote, was one of sheer joy. 'As we walked through the bleak countryside, many of us experienced an intense feeling, which some expressed in words. It reminded us of the pilgrimages of the first Hussites into the mountains.'[41]

Ivan Jirous with the Plastic People.

SOME TIME IN EARLY MARCH 1976, at the suggestion of a mutual friend Vaclav Havel agreed to meet Ivan Jirous in Prague. Despite their mutual suspicion, the two hit it off. Havel was of an older generation than the Plastics, but he quickly grasped that the underground music scene was a fine example of that 'secret streamlet' trickling beneath the surface of official communist culture. The Plastics' chaotic Dionysian music came from a very different sensibility from Havel's precise and thoughtful writing, but they shared a common approach: to create culture as though censorship didn't exist.

Jirous played Havel some music from the Plastics and other underground bands, and Havel instantly felt there was something special and authentic about it. He recognised 'a disturbing magic in the music, and a kind of inner warning'.[42] After talking for hours, the two men decided to go out to a pub, where the friendly barman locked the doors and opened the cellar vaults. They drank and talked all night. Havel agreed to come to the Plastics' next performance, scheduled in two weeks' time, but the concert never took place. On 17 March, the secret police swooped, arresting nineteen people, including Jirous, musicians from the Plastics and DG 307, and concert organisers.* Police raided apartments across Prague, confiscating letters, artwork, instruments, tapes, and home-made amplifiers that had been put together from components.

The arrests were widely reported and condemned in the Western media. *Rude Pravo* defended the police action with its usual dreary clichés: 'Our society will not tolerate any forms of hooliganism or public disorder, and quite naturally, will resist any moral filth and efforts to infect our youth.'[43]

Havel left his cottage at once and came back to Prague to see what he could do to help. He approached other prominent Czech writers and intellectuals, and was pleased to find that many of them were as ready as he was to shrug off the torpor that had set in since the Soviet invasion. Ever the pragmatist, Havel suggested they begin modestly with a simple petition to release the prisoners, which would give the regime space to retreat, rather than force them to dig in.

In the end, only four of the defendants were sent to prison. Ivan Jirous received the longest sentence of eighteen months for 'organised

---

* Paul Wilson, who knew the barman, later discovered he was an StB informant code-named Agent Fox, and suspected it was he who passed on the concert information to the authorities.

disturbance of the peace'; saxophonist Vratislav Brabenec received eight months.

THE FIGURE MOST CONSPICUOUSLY absent from the list of those arrested was the Plastics' lyricist Egon Bondy. Several times, Bondy had warned Jirous and others not to tell him too much, that he was not the kind of person who could keep a secret. That was all the warning they got. Bondy had been collaborating with the StB for more than a decade. From 1961 to 1968, the poet handed over 181 reports under the code name Klima. After a five-year hiatus, he was given a new code name, Mao, and between 1973 and 1977 he delivered another 110 reports.

It's unlikely Bondy was able to pass on any meaningful information – there was no Western-directed conspiracy to overthrow the state through rock and roll after all – but the revelation of his long-term collaboration led some old friends to keep their distance. Jirous, who had suffered more than any other figure in the underground music scene, forgave Bondy and continued to praise him as 'the patriarch of the Czech Underground'.[44]

A Fine Way to Begin a Struggle for Human Rights

HAVEL AND HIS FELLOW petitioners were dismayed by the prison sentences handed out to Jirous and the others, but also somewhat heartened by the solidarity and conviviality that had rallied a loose-knit group of writers, former party members, conservative Catholics and misfits to the musicians' defence. In December, the group reconvened to see how they might continue to press the case for human rights.

In the weeks that followed, the group drafted a joint declaration for the new year. The text praised the government for signing the human rights provisions in the 1975 Helsinki Accords but then noted, 'regrettably', that such rights only existed in Czechoslovakia on paper.

The invocation of the Helsinki Accords put the regime on the back foot. The Soviet Union and its satellites had not demurred when asked to commit to the human rights clauses at Helsinki, never imagining they would be called to account for their own abuses. The glaring gap between the noble sentiments expressed in the Accords and the regime's behaviour gave Havel and his associates the room to run a campaign that was moral rather than ostensibly political in its aims. Havel's group was therefore at pains to point out that they were not a political organisation, which would have been illegal at the time, but merely a loose, informal group of concerned citizens.

They decided to appoint three spokespersons to forestall the group from being silenced if one of its leaders was arrested. These were Havel, Jiri Hajek, a former minister under Dubcek, and Professor Jan Patocka, an elderly philosopher much admired by Havel. By January 1977, the group had discreetly gathered 242 signatures and were ready to launch themselves under the name of Charter 77.

ON 5 JANUARY, HAVEL crossed the river and walked up the hill to the apartment of a fellow Charter 77 activist, Zdenek Urbanek. Havel's car was out of action – someone had cut the hydraulic cables on the clutch – so he had to make his way through the icy streets on foot. At Urbanek's apartment, the two men began stuffing copies of the Charter into envelopes, which they planned to send to media organisations and institutions all over the world.

After a while, Havel's roguish drinking companion Pavel Landovsky showed up.* Landovsky, a popular film actor with a

---

* Landovsky played the gregarious pig farmer in Philip Kaufman's film *The Unbearable Lightness of Being.*

broken nose and a Zapata moustache, had brought along Ludvik Vaculik, another Charter signatory. When the envelopes were ready, Havel, Vaculik and Landovsky piled into the actor's Saab, intending to discreetly slot them into various postal boxes across the city. The cloak-and-dagger nature of the excursion put the three men in a merry mood, but as they drove through Prague they realised they were being followed by a squad of unmarked police cars. There are several accounts of what happened next.

The most colourful version came from Landovsky, who claimed that when he realised they were being followed, he hit the accelerator then took a sharp turn into a side street, causing two of the police cars to skate across the icy street and smash into each other. In the confusion, Landovsky was able to pull up at a mailbox. Havel flew out of the passenger seat with a bag of letters and stuffed them into the slot. He jumped back into the car and they shot off down Lenin Street, but the road was blocked by police vehicles. Two more pulled up behind them, forcing Landovsky to come to a screeching halt.

Dozens of officers ran to the car but the actor had locked the doors internally. The police pounded on the bonnet, ordering them to get out, but Landovsky turned to Havel and said cheerfully, 'See, now they'll pound away at the car, get a bit tired, and when they start pounding us it won't hurt so much.' Havel, sitting next to him, said drily that this was a fine way to begin a struggle for human rights.

Havel reasoned that since they had done nothing wrong, they should have nothing to fear. But when he unlocked his door, the police yanked him out horizontally. 'They sucked him out like a rolled-up carpet,' Landovsky said. 'All I saw was the shoes.'[45] Vaculik was hoisted out of the car in a similar fashion, but Landovsky stayed put in the driver's seat, with his big hands fixed to the steering wheel. Then an officer entered the Saab, put a gun to his head and ordered him to follow the police cars to the station. Both he and Havel were released from custody late that night, then brought in every day the following week for further questioning.

Landovsky was a natural raconteur, and the story surely grew in the telling, but the legend helped the signatories of Charter 77 to build a mythology around the group's origins, binding them together in friendship and good humour.

Devout Lackeys of Imperialism

THE LAUNCH OF CHARTER 77 made news all over the world, but in Prague its impact was muffled by censorship and by the small number of signatories. Some intellectuals had refused to sign it on principle, irked by the 'elitist' appeal to abstract human rights and the absence of a concrete call to political action. But the Charter's call for the state to observe the Helsinki human rights obligations, was in itself a political act that badly unnerved the party leadership and provoked it to lash out at the Charter signatories in *Rude Pravo* as 'washouts and self-appointees', 'devout lackeys of imperialism' and 'bitter anti-socialists'.[46] Readers must have wondered what the fuss was about, for no part of the Charter was actually quoted.

For weeks, the StB conducted house searches and interrogations of the signatories and their associates. Many lost their jobs; their telephones were removed and their driver's licences confiscated. In offices and factories, workers were asked to sign an anti-Charter document as they went to collect their wages.

THE OFFICIAL CAMPAIGN against Charter 77 culminated in a depressing event at the National Theatre on 26 January. Prominent

Czech performers and celebrities awkwardly took their seats in an orchestrated show of public support for the regime that came to be known as the Anti-Charter rally. On stage, actress and party activist Jirina Svorcova denounced the Charter signatories as 'opportunists and traitors'.[47] Jan Werich, who had hoped the event would be low-key, cringed when the TV cameras singled him out. At the end, the participants were expected to line up and sign the anti-Charter document, re-dedicating themselves to 'new works committed to socialism and peace'. *Rude Pravo* published their signatures the next day. Karel Gott later claimed he had no idea what was in the text of the document. 'I thought I was signing an attendance list,' he said.[48]

The furious backlash against the Charter gave it far more publicity than was warranted by the relatively small number of signatories, and convinced many people it must have merit. After the National Theatre event, author Ivan Klima fell into conversation with three workers delivering coal to his apartment block; one of them leant over and quietly asked if he had a copy of 'that Charter'. Klima, who had not signed it for fear his daughter would be refused entry to an art school, was nonetheless happy to fetch a copy and watched the men as they pored over the document, reading each line closely, caught up in the pleasure of reading forbidden literature.[49]

ON 14 JANUARY, Vaclav Havel was formally arrested and charged with 'subversion of the state'. With Havel in jail, Jan Patocka stepped up as spokesperson for Charter 77, but the elderly philosopher's health was failing. In March, Patocka was in bed with bronchitis but managed to rouse himself for a meeting with the Dutch foreign minister. The meeting enraged the authorities who brought him in for three consecutive days of interrogation. On the night of 3 March

1977, Patocka woke up with terrible chest pains and was admitted to hospital where he died ten days later.

Jan Patocka's death was inevitably seen as another Czech martyrdom. More than 1000 people attended his funeral. During the ceremony, StB agents hovered around the mourners, taking note of who was attending. Police helicopters flew overhead and motorcycles revved their engines to drown out the voices of the eulogies. The disruption was organised with the help of the priest, an StB collaborator.

MARTA KUBISOVA SANG a song at the funeral written especially for the occasion. Her voice had lost none of its strength and soulfulness. After Patocka's death, she became one of the three spokespersons for Charter 77 and a regular visitor at the Havels' country house.

Marta had since married another filmmaker, Jan Moravec. When she became pregnant with her daughter she resigned as Charter spokesperson, but the state continued its surveillance of her everyday activities. Marta was aware that one of her neighbours was monitoring her comings and goings, but the StB had also secretly recruited her husband to curb her 'anti-social activities'.[50] The marriage ended when Kubisova learnt of his extra-marital affairs. She only found out Moravec had been spying on her when the secret police records were made public after the Velvet Revolution.

PAUL WILSON SUSPECTED the police had stepped up their surveillance of him as well. Occasionally, the phone in his apartment rang but he heard no one on the line when he answered, just some odd sounds. He spotted people in his local pub he'd never seen before, just sitting, not talking to anybody. When a new couple moved in upstairs, one of them asked Paul to look after a package for them. Paul's wife wondered if it contained a listening device.

Paul had been secretly recording interviews with Charter 77 figures for the Canadian media. One morning, the secret police arrived at his door at 6 am. Paul was already up, dressed and ready to head out for an interview, but he asked them for a minute to get dressed, while his wife frantically tried to conceal any compromising materials lying around the living room. When he opened the door, they took him away.

As the police car zoomed along the embankment of the Vltava, Paul knew his time in Prague was coming to an end. He gazed at the spiky skyline, the Charles Bridge, the castle, in the early-dawn darkness, thinking he might never see them again.

In the interrogation room, the officers said they knew all about him, and invited him to speak more about his friends. 'I'm happy to tell you anything you want to know about what I think and what I do,' he replied. 'But if you want to know what my friends think and what they do, you ask them. Don't ask me.' Another officer entered the room, pounded his fist on the table and threatened him with jail, but Paul knew that, as the last resort, his Canadian passport would give him safe passage out of the country. The questions, threats and abuse continued until 2 pm, when they released him.

Two days later he was told he must leave the country.

After ten tumultuous years in this strange kingdom, it was time to go.

✳

The Power of the Powerless

CHARTER 77 DID SUCCEED in shining an international spotlight on human rights abuses in Czechoslovakia. Embarrassed, the regime changed tack. The Interior Ministry instituted a new policy, the *Asanace* – 'Decontamination' – campaign. Dissidents were threatened in their homes by the secret police, who urged them to leave the country before some terrible 'accident' could befall them and their families. Targets of the campaign were beaten up in their apartments, burnt with cigarette butts, and on one occasion, choked into unconsciousness. Many Chartists, including Pavel Landovsky and Pavel Kohout were terrorised into cutting their losses and leaving the country.

The Plastic People of the Universe were also battered by the unremitting hostility of the state. They were running out of venues. Three weeks after performing at a house in the countryside, the house was burnt down. The authorities pressured their saxophonist Vratislav Brabenec into emigrating to Canada, where he became a gardener. Ivan Jirous spent most of the decade in prison, where he wrote his most celebrated collection of poems, *Magor's Swan Song*, as well as a collection of poems and fairy tales for his daughter.

Jirous was changed by his years in jail. Paul Wilson noticed that prison toughened him. 'He was always very uncompromising, but prison turned him into a really tough guy. An angry guy.'[51]

THE BEATINGS, ARRESTS and forced emigrations led some of the core members of Charter 77, including Havel, to set up a new opposition group calling itself the Committee for the Unjustly Persecuted (VONS). VONS would take on a more activist role than Charter 77, monitoring and reporting on cases of 'victims of arbitrary actions by the police or judiciary'.[52]

Havel had been in an erratic mood since his release from detention. He blamed himself for Jan Patocka's death, and was deeply ashamed for having played into the regime's hands by writing a too-clever-by-half plea for release that *Rude Pravo* recast as a cowardly sell-out of Charter 77. To prove them wrong, he resumed his political activities with an almost manic intensity.

After VONS announced its existence to the world in April 1978, the StB built an observation post on the grounds of the Havels' cottage at Hradecek. A policeman followed him whenever he walked his dog around the property. Havel took the heightened surveillance with as much good humour as he could muster. He was busy drafting his most famous and influential essay, 'The Power of the Powerless', an exposition of how the state controls its citizens by pressing them into a performance of obedience. At the centre of the essay is an imaginary greengrocer, who consents to place a sign in his shop window with the slogan *Workers of the world unite!* The slogan itself is meaningless to the greengrocer, who is unlikely to feel strongly one way or the other about global worker solidarity. The real meaning, Havel argues, is embedded in the sign, not the slogan: 'It contains a subliminal but very definite message. Verbally, it might be expressed this way: *I, Greengrocer XY, live here and I know what I must do. I behave in the manner expected of me. I can be depended upon and am beyond reproach. I am obedient and therefore I have the right to be left in peace.*'

It would be a different matter, Havel wrote, if the sign had said more bluntly and truthfully: *I am afraid and therefore unquestioningly obedient.* But the regime is happy to spare the greengrocer's feelings in this matter. It makes it easier for him to hide his subservience behind an upbeat sentiment, while at the same time concealing the 'low foundations' of its own power.[53]

Havel concluded that the multitude of small gestures like the greengrocer's sign made everyone complicit in the system, to the extent that they *become* the system. The regime requires mass participation in its lies to continue to exist. But when it demands people disbelieve their own eyes, something inside them automatically rebels. It's this human need to live in truth, even under the most absurd and dangerous circumstances, that gives power to the powerless.

This longing for authenticity compelled people to create a more meaningful space outside the regime, in the shadow world that Jirous had called the Second Culture, and the Catholic dissident Vaclav Benda dubbed a Parallel Polis. Secret workshops sprang up around Prague and in the countryside, producing prohibited books, essays and albums in *samizdat* format.* The books were often produced to a high professional standard but time with them was preciously short. Readers would stay up all night or call in sick for a day just to finish a book before having to pass it on to another friend. American author Philip Roth made several visits to Prague in the 1970s, and was deeply moved by people's pursuit of literature in such dangerous circumstances. Back in the United States, Roth commented that in Prague, 'nothing goes and everything matters – here everything goes and nothing matters'.[54]

Plans for Prison

ON THE NIGHT OF 28 May 1979, Vaclav Havel was arrested again, along with other VONS members. This time the state was

---

*   *Samizdat* is a contraction of a Russian phrase, meaning 'self-published'.

determined to put them away. He and his five co-defendants stood trial together and all were found guilty of subversion. Havel was given four and a half years.

During his long sentence, he was passed on from prison to prison. At Hermanice, he spot-welded metal grates; at Bory he worked in the laundry and then was put to work stripping insulation from wires and cables.

Before going in, Havel had set himself a strict regime of self-improvement: he resolved to remain healthy, write several plays, learn to speak German and improve his English, and to study the bible closely. He achieved none of these things, but he did succeed in his most serious ambition, to reconstitute himself psychologically after years of stress, worry and shame over his perceived failures and shortcomings. This 'deeply existential and personal experience' involved a long and painful process of honest introspection. In his letters to Olga, he chided himself for his excessive politeness, his foolish overestimation of his own cleverness, his tendency to trust the wrong people, and his constant need to explain himself.[55]

PRESIDENT HUSAK WAS no less of a captive than Havel, albeit one living in a vastly larger and more comfortable cell. Husak was still haunted by his traumatic past. Shortly after becoming president, he invited his closest political ally, Lubomir Strougal, to join him on a strange excursion to Kolodeje Castle, where Husak had once been imprisoned. As they walked through the grounds, Strougal thought, 'this is bad':

> *He led me into the cellar. We were both silent and I knew what*
> *was going on. We went through that long dungeon … it was*
> *dirty and unkempt. He led me to a corner and said: 'There was*

a wooden cell here and I spent nine months in it in solitary confinement.' And he started crying. Then he said: 'I wanted you to see it. I'll never come here again.'[56]

HUSAK'S FIRST WIFE, Magda, had died years earlier. In 1973 he married Viera Milerova, a Slovak journalist and translator. Viera was a lifelong communist, but had retained a degree of creativity and humanity, and she urged Husak to rehabilitate the former friends he had expelled from the party.

Husak found some solace in his wife's warmth and conversation, but their time together was brief. In October 1977, Viera travelled to the spa town of Bardejov where she injured her shoulder in a fall. A helicopter came to fly her to Bratislava for medical treatment, but the night was foggy and the helicopter crashed in a cornfield near the runway. Everyone on board was killed.

Strougal brought Husak the awful news. 'Gustav took it calmly,' he recalled. 'Sobbed some, said nothing.' Strougal asked if there was anything he could do for him. Husak said he wanted to see the body and asked him to arrange it. Husak was a widower again; he would not re-marry.

Nineteen Years

THE 1980s BROUGHT a sense of immobility to everyday life in Prague. A visiting *New York Times* reporter noted 'the grey shroud over what was once one of Europe's most creative, articulate and communicative cities'. The gloom in the streets depressed him. 'Each individual or small group seemed to be unaware of others, bent only on fulfilling quickly the task that brought them out of their houses in the first place.'[57]

The lethargy in Prague was symptomatic of the Party's sclerotic leadership. Husak, now in his seventies, was almost blind. Each year he would read his New Year's Day speech behind reading glasses with increasingly thick lenses that made his eyes appear cartoonishly large. In Moscow, the situation was even worse: three geriatric leaders – Leonid Brezhnev, Yuri Andropov, Konstantin Chernenko – passed away in quick succession.

On 11 March 1985, the Soviet leadership held its breath and elected Mikhail Gorbachev, a bright, 52-year-old reformer, as general secretary. Unlike his hardline predecessors, Gorbachev was affable, reasonable and, by Soviet standards, quite liberal. He called for a policy of *glasnost* – greater openness, and more ambitiously, for *perestroika* – restructuring of the Soviet economy to make it more efficient and responsive to consumer needs.

IN APRIL 1987, GORBACHEV visited Prague, raising hopes that he would put Husak on the spot by publicly calling for his government to follow Moscow's lead, but the Soviet leader chose to be diplomatic. He declared that reform was 'essential', but that it was up to Czechoslovakia to choose whether to pursue it. Gorbachev's spokesperson was more direct: when asked by journalists to explain the difference between the Gorbachev reforms and those of Alexander Dubcek, he quipped, provocatively, 'Nineteen years.'[58]

Gorbachev's reformist message left Husak and the party in an excruciating bind: having frozen their society at the bidding of one Soviet leader, how were they to unfreeze it at the bidding of another? Their confusion made their public utterances nonsensical. In October, Husak declared that Czechoslovakia 'must not fall behind', but then quickly cautioned, 'We must not hasten solutions too quickly and we should minimize the risks that could occur.'[59]

In December, Husak, enfeebled by multiple strokes, was forced to resign as first secretary, but was permitted to retain his ceremonial post as president. When Prime Minister Rakowski of Poland came to visit him at Prague Castle, he noted that Husak seemed very tired, and barely able to exchange a few banal pleasantries.

Rakowski met the 'new generation' of party leaders in Prague, led by the rigidly conservative 67-year-old Milos Jakes. The Polish government, under pressure from Gorbachev and the dissident trade union Solidarity, was ready to go some way down the road of political and economic reform, but Jakes told Rakowski he felt no such pressure from his people. 'As long as Czechs have their hot dogs and beer,' he said, 'there'll be no revolution.'[60]

GUSTAV HUSAK HAD become an isolated figure. In the summer, he retreated for six weeks to the presidential country house at Lany. The housekeepers at the estate later told his successor, Vaclav Havel, that Husak passed the days in a strange manner: sitting alone in a room, not reading, simply staring at the wall, while uniformed police officers paced up and down the hall outside. Occasionally the staff would bring him food.

'And when the employees told me this,' Havel said, 'I suddenly understood that he was simulating the situation in his prison cell. He made for himself a kind of temporary, more comfortable prison at Lany.'[61]

CHAPTER ELEVEN

TO LIGHT THE MAGIC LANTERN

1988–1990

The Seven Wonders of Czechoslovakia:
Everybody has a job.
Although everybody has a job, nobody works.
Although nobody works, the Plan is fulfilled up to 105 percent.
Although the Plan is fulfilled up to 105 percent, there's nothing
*   in the shops.*
Although there's nothing in the shops, we've got enough of
everything.
Although we've got enough of everything, everybody steals.
Although everybody steals, nothing ever goes missing
anywhere.
And the Eighth Wonder of the World is that it has been
*   working for forty-one years.*

*   Velvet Revolution slogan.* [1]

Hope Rises Again

IN HIS FIFTH YEAR IN PRISON, Vaclav Havel came down with pneumonia and was admitted, belatedly, to the prison hospital. Worried that their most famous prisoner might die under incarceration, the authorities suspended Havel's sentence and released him when he was well enough to stand upright. Once recovered, he returned to writing plays but was kept under constant StB surveillance.

One spring evening in 1987, Havel stepped outside his apartment to take his dog for a walk along the Vltava embankment. As he approached the bright lights of the National Theatre, he saw a crush of police cars and a crowd of excited bystanders. Curious, he edged his way forward and saw the Soviet leader, Mikhail Gorbachev, emerge from the theatre to cheers from the crowd. Gorbachev walked past the well-wishers, smiling and waving, and then Havel realised with some embarrassment that the Soviet leader was smiling and waving directly at him. All Havel could do was grin shyly and wave back.[2]

Havel was annoyed by the cheers for Gorbachev. He despaired that the Czechs would forever look to an outside figure to liberate them rather than do it themselves. But a decade had passed since the signing of Charter 77 and nothing had changed; Gorbachev was a far more powerful symbol of hope to Praguers than the small group of Charter signatories, still living almost invisibly on the margins of society.

NONETHELESS, AS THE 1980s came to a close, the fog of fear and apathy in Prague slowly cleared, allowing a new cohort of younger activists to see a way forward. Disappointed with the Chartists' lack of visibility and frustrated with their carefully calibrated 'anti-political' approach, these students and young dissidents were the first to test the limits of state control. They had no memory of the demoralising defeat of 1968, and had less to lose from the system of threats and inducements that had daunted their parents.

In April 1988, a group of disgruntled Chartists and young Christian pacifists formed a new organisation, the Independent Peace Association (IPA), which called for the right to refuse military service, to build trust between the state and its citizens, and for the repair of the ravaged environment. The IPA operated in parallel with the older activists, but more visibly. They published their own *samizdat* journal, met with peace activists from Western Europe, staged hunger strikes and organised tree plantings in clear-felled forests.

The old absurdist instincts resurfaced. In July 1988, a group calling itself the Society for a Merrier Present paraded up and down the Charles Bridge, wearing helmets made from watermelons while holding up completely blank banners. The police arrived and hurriedly confiscated the banners, while onlookers laughed.[3] In August, performance artist Tomas Ruller publicly set himself on fire before falling face down in a pool of mud, unharmed. His performance earnt him a beating from the police. 'For some reason,' he said cheerfully, 'they see it as a political statement.'[4]

THE TWENTIETH ANNIVERSARY of the Soviet invasion was fast approaching, but Charter 77 decided to bow out of any public demonstration, not wanting to risk police violence. The departure of Havel and others for the countryside meant the authorities were caught napping on the weekend when the IPA decided to hold their own peaceful protest. On the morning of 21 August, young IPA members milled around the city centre, identifying each other by wearing prominent tricolour ribbons. At 1 pm, they gathered at the top of Wenceslas Square to lay flowers. After that, there was some uncertainty as to what would happen next. One of the IPA's founders, Hana Marvanova, gave a speech in support of peace and *perestroika*. Incredulous shoppers and passers-by stopped to listen. Nothing like this had happened for years in Prague. The crowd swelled and within an hour, a spontaneous public seminar broke out. A nine-point document was drafted calling for the departure of Soviet troops, free elections and support for human rights. The police hovered nervously at the periphery, unsure of how to respond.

By 6 pm. the crowd had become a throng of 10,000; the vast majority in their twenties. A chant went up for freedom and democracy as they marched to the Old Town Square. More passers-by joined in; others simply applauded as it passed. Then the crowd broke up peacefully and went home.

The success of the rally shook the Charter 77 leaders out of their pessimism and forced them to admit the twenty-somethings had roused the city from its apathy. They were particularly delighted by the spontaneous, improvised nature of it all. 'We won't be satisfied with things as they are,' declared the IPA's co-founder Tomas Dvorak. 'After twenty years, hope rises again in us.'[5]

IN OCTOBER, THE GOVERNMENT declared that the seventieth anniversary of Czechoslovak independence in 1918 was to be a national holiday. The announcement caught people by surprise: until now, the regime had tried to scrub Masaryk's republic from the national memory. But the decree was merely a ploy to encourage Praguers to take a long weekend in the countryside rather than be tempted to join any anti-government protests in the city. State television and *Rude Pravo* warned that unofficial demonstrations would not be tolerated.

This was no empty threat. On 28 October, 10,000 people flowed into Wenceslas Square, chanting, 'Masaryk!' and 'Freedom!' As they began their demonstration, white-helmeted riot police with attack dogs emerged from the subway entrances and side streets. They laid into the crowd with their truncheons, knocking people to the ground. Protestors on the periphery of the violence hooted with derision at the police. A young man who placed flowers at the foot of the St Wenceslas statue was dragged off while protestors chanted, 'Fascists!' Someone was seen singing the national anthem even as he was being clubbed down. Michal Docekal, a drama student, saw an isolated policeman being chased by some furious protestors. He picked up a heavy paving stone and weighed it in his hand, and for several agonising moments, he wondered if he was really the kind of person who could hurl a stone at a fellow human being. The stone did not leave his hand, but he was shaken by the experience.[6]

The demonstrators scattered and regrouped in the Old Town Square, between the Astronomical Clock and the Jan Hus monument. As soon as they resumed their protest, a line of armoured personnel carriers with machine-gun turrets entered from a side street, followed by water-cannon trucks. Clouds of tear gas and blasts of freezing cold water hit the crowd. Then the APCs lurched forward, sending the demonstrators flying in all directions, clearing the square. Afterwards, riot police scoured the streets, looking for more protestors to beat up. Some 200 people were arrested. IPA founders Hana Marvanova and Tomas Dvorak were charged, absurdly, with 'preparing to commit incitement'. The following day, *Rude Pravo* accused the two of being in the pay of foreign governments.[7]

The Neverending Symposium

THE NEW DEFIANT MOOD encouraged Charter 77 and other independent groups to announce an international symposium, provocatively titled 'Czechoslovakia 88', to be held at Prague's Hotel Paris in November. The nervous authorities neither gave nor refused permission for the symposium to go ahead. Foreign dignitaries, scholars, journalists and human rights activists accepted the invitation to come to Prague, but several days before the scheduled opening, police were given orders to arrest the Czech participants. Havel managed to dodge the police long enough to slip into the Hotel Paris's breakfast room on the symposium's opening morning. But as soon as he sat down at the table of foreign delegates and journalists, he was pulled out of his chair by a trio of police officers. Havel said, 'Well, in this moment I am arrested.' He had just enough time to declare the symposium open before he was dragged out of the room.

The startled foreigners were then approached by a muscular woman in a tight leather jacket, holding a bunch of flowers. She handed each of the delegates an unmarked envelope containing a photocopied message. The threat was more comic than sinister: 'Achtung,' it began. 'I am warning you that the action called symposium CZECHOSLOVAKIA 88 is illegal and its performance would be contrary to the interests of Czechoslovak working people and consequently illegal. In this connection your efforts to take part in this action would be considered as a manifestation of hostility to Czechoslovakia and in virtue of this we should have to draw relevant consequences against your person.'[8]

HAVEL WAS DETAINED for four days and, as convenor, never did get to officially close the symposium. The secret police searched his home and confiscated his PC. He fired off a letter of complaint to the prime minister, Ladislav Adamec, noting in passing that the police had thought the keyboard was the computer, that the computer was an 'amplifier' and the monitor was a TV.[9]

*

AS THE NEW YEAR came around, the regime steeled itself for another unwelcome anniversary. The 16th of January 1989 would mark twenty years from the day of Jan Palach's self-immolation. The week leading up to the anniversary was taken up with demonstrations in Wenceslas Square. Each day protestors were beaten and knocked off their feet by water cannons.

The young protestors gained courage with each day. At times they had run from the police, but at other critical moments they had found it in them to stand their ground, and their fear was now tempered by excitement and a sense of solidarity and possibility. As they were dragged away, they chanted, 'Tomorrow, here again!' and there would be more people in the square the next day.[10] By the end of the week, Mustek metro station was filled with the lingering stench of tear gas. Journalist Michael Zantovsky, who was soon to become Havel's press secretary, saw that many of them had crossed a psychological threshold: 'When you are faced, for the first time, with a solid line of space-helmeted grim-faced young men with their metre-long batons and Star Wars shields, with the bare-toothed snarling attack dogs straining at their leads, or with the business end of a water cannon, you wish with all your might to be somewhere else. When it happens for the fifth time, and you are still around, and still the same person, give or take a couple of bruises, it starts to feel like something you can take.'[11]

On the morning of the anniversary, police cordoned off the streets, but some 5000 protestors made it into the square anyway and were dispersed once again with tear gas. Havel tried to get in but was arrested and charged with 'incitement' and 'obstructing public order', and then sentenced to eight months' prison.

International outrage ensured it was a short stay behind bars. President Mitterrand of France wrote a personal letter of protest to Gustav Husak. A student petition demanding Havel's release was handed to the authorities and to their amazement it was accepted and the playwright was out the next day. Pankrac Prison's parole board cited Havel's good behaviour and his 'tidiness in making his bunk'.

THAT NIGHT, there was a party in the Havels' apartment. Among the guests was Alexander Dubcek, who appeared at their door like a ghost of the Prague Spring. Dubcek and Havel talked for three hours. Afterwards, Havel said he thought Dubcek's visit was significant; the former politician had sniffed a change in the wind.

Six weeks later, on 29 June, Charter 77 produced a new petition, modestly titled 'A Few Sentences'. The document called for the release of political prisoners; an end to censorship; freedom of assembly and religion; a review of the ecological impact of heavy industry; and an opening of a debate on the Stalinist era and the events of 1968. Forty thousand people put their names to the petition within three months – eighty times as many signatories as Charter 77.

A Hole in the Iron Curtain

THE HEADY SENSE of possibility in Prague chilled that month by the massacre of Chinese students and workers in Beijing's Tiananmen Square. Chinese leaders had given the Prague dissidents an insight into how a frightened communist regime might use lethal violence to protect itself against its own citizens. Czechoslovak party leader Milos Jakes welcomed the news of the Beijing massacre almost gleefully, and there were fears he too might order a military crackdown, but the presidium was paralysed between Jakes's old guard and the pro-Gorbachev reformists.

While the hardliners grimly hung on to power in Czechoslovakia and East Germany, their fraternal parties in Hungary and Poland had already travelled a long way down the road of reform. In June 1989, the Polish regime buckled to popular pressure and opened the majority of its parliamentary seats to free elections. The result was a communist wipe-out: the opposition Solidarity group won every openly contested seat in the lower house and all but one in the Senate, and a non-communist, Tadeusz Mazowiecki, was appointed prime minister. Gorbachev made no effort to interfere. The Brezhnev Doctrine was dead.

At the same time, the Hungarian government declared that its citizens would be allowed to travel freely to Austria. Crucially, they extended the same right to citizens of other communist countries. The announcement inspired thousands of East Germans to cross the border into Czechoslovakia by train or in their two-stroke Trabant cars, hoping to make the long round-trip through Hungary and Austria into prosperous, democratic West Germany, where they could claim automatic citizenship.

The Czechoslovak authorities responded to the sudden influx by closing their border with Hungary, hoping the dejected East Germans would simply go home. Instead, they drove straight towards Prague, to the West German embassy in Mala Strana, to ask for political asylum. The streets around the embassy became clogged with parked Trabants, as refugees climbed the fence and camped in the embassy's gardens.

The overcrowded refugee camp was a painful embarrassment for the East German regime and a major headache for their Czechoslovak comrades. After weeks of negotiations, an agreement was reached to transport the East German refugees by a special closed train to West Germany. The decision was announced from the embassy balcony to ecstatic cries of joy from the East Germans.

West German student Katrin Bock was among the crowd in Prague looking on as the excited refugees boarded buses to take them to the station. 'I was surrounded by happy Czechs who wished the East Germans all the best, who clapped at each bus and thought that it was high time for something to change in Czechoslovakia when even the East Germans are demonstrating and leaving the country in their thousands.'[12]

After the buses left, the abandoned Trabants were dismantled for spare parts.

Best Wishes for the Year to Come

ON 5 OCTOBER, KEEN-EYED readers of *Rude Pravo* might have caught a small birthday greeting in the personal notices to a 'Ferdinand Vanek', thanking him for all his hard work and wishing him all the best in the year to come. The birthday boy was in fact Vaclav Havel; 'Vanek' was the name he used as an alter-ego in his

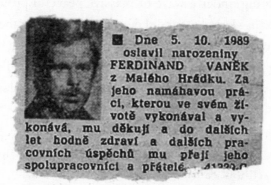

Dne 5. 10. 1989 oslavil narozeniny FERDINAND VANĚK z Malého Hrádku. Za jeho namáhavou práci, kterou ve svém životě vykonával a vykonává, mu děkují a do dalších let hodně zdraví a dalších pracovních úspěchů mu přejí jeho spolupracovníci a přátelé.

plays. The notice, along with a smudgy photo of Havel, was a prank, sent in by his friends to trick the authorities into publishing a cheery salutation to their enemy in the Communist Party daily. Dissidents who had not opened *Rude Pravo* for decades rushed out to buy a copy for a laugh. Others bought copies just to see what this notorious dissident looked like. The prank was revealed on Radio Free Europe and published all over the world.

A FEW DAYS LATER, police were sent to arrest Havel in his flat to prevent him taking part in any Independence Day protest rallies. Havel was laid up in bed, feeling unwell. When Olga demanded the police produce a warrant, he wandered out from the bedroom in his pyjamas. 'Oh, let them in, Olga,' he said. 'You could get them fired.' The police agreed to place him under hospital detention. That evening, a small coterie of well-wishers gathered on the street outside his hospital room to chant, 'Long live Havel!' [13]

Strange Beings

MEANWHILE, ACROSS THE BORDER, East German authorities were staggering under a wave of massive peaceful protest marches in East Berlin, Dresden and Leipzig. On 9 November, the East Berlin party boss Gunter Schabowski held a dramatic evening press conference to announce that East Germans would no longer be prevented from crossing into West Berlin. An Italian journalist asked when the law would come into effect. 'Uh, as I understand it,' Schabowski replied uncertainly, flipping through the pages of his document, 'it goes into effect immediately.' Then, with more certainty: 'Without delay.'[14]

The border guards at the Berlin Wall had been given no orders to this effect, but when excited East Berliners rushed to the checkpoints, the guards waved them through. They were greeted on the other side by West Berliners with champagne. Within hours, thousands of East and West Berliners began hacking into the hated wall with pickaxes and hammers. Hoisting one another on top of the twelve-foot-high concrete slabs, they danced, sang and wept with joy.

IN PRAGUE, CHARTER 77 activists ached as they watched news footage of these once unthinkable scenes. The dissidents were tormented by the suspense. Communism had collapsed, or was collapsing, in Poland, Hungary and East Germany, but they wondered if their own people would summon the courage and resolve to demand the same.

MARTA KUBISOVA WAS NOW a 47-year-old single mother with a clerical job at a construction company. Between the demands of her job and bringing up her daughter, she no longer had time for opposition activity, but to her annoyance, the StB still kept her under close surveillance. One day, she thought she'd try a trick she'd seen in *The French Connection*. She walked into a subway station, boarded a carriage and hung around close to the door, pretending to be absorbed in conversation with a friend. As the doors slid shut, she leapt back onto the platform. Marta gave herself a little round of applause as she watched the furious secret policemen inside the carriage zooming away from her.

On 14 November, Marta finished work for the day and walked from her office to a nearby recording studio. Inside, she removed her coat and scarf and began her vocal warm-up exercises in front of the microphone. The sound engineer became wide-eyed with fear as he recognised the distinctive voice coming from the speakers. 'Bloody hell,' he said, 'it's Kubisova.' He made his apologies and left. The cleaner muttered her excuses and then she was gone too.

Marta had been invited to the studio by film director Fero Fenic, who wanted Marta to sing for the closing credits of his new film about misfits and outsiders titled *Strange Beings*. Marta was still banned from public performance, but Fenic didn't care. The director felt shivers down his spine as he heard Marta's voice, dark and warm, floating above a sustained, shimmering chord from the orchestral strings. It sounded hopeful, expectant.[15]

Friday, 17 November

A STUDENT RALLY WAS planned for 17 November, but few expected much to come from it. The rally was intended to commemorate a Nazi atrocity: the murder of nine Czech students by the Gestapo in 1939. The key figure then had been a medical student named Jan Opletal, who had been shot by German civilian police and later died of his wounds in hospital. The Nazis had subsequently closed the universities and condemned a thousand more students to the concentration camps. Prague's students, to their surprise, were given permission by the communist authorities to hold an anti-fascist remembrance ceremony outside the university's medical faculty in Albertov, near the fortress of Vysehrad.

THE ORGANISERS HAD HOPED for a crowd of 4000, but by four in the afternoon, more than 15,000 people had shown up.

Observers noticed at once there was something different about this gathering. There was none of the orderliness usually seen at official events: instead the students milled about, carrying candles and flags, talking to each other excitedly. When the ceremony began, no one sang along with the official student song. A banner was held up calling for an end to one-party rule. Other handwritten banners called on students to seize the moment: *Who – if not us? When – if not now?*[16]

The restless crowd formed a candlelit procession from Albertov to Vysehrad's cemetery of national heroes. They heard an emotional speech from one of the elderly survivors of the 1939 student massacre. Another speaker urged the students to accept the lessons of the Nazi occupation: 'Our forerunners well knew that oppression was worse than death, that freedom must be fought for and that it is not possible to live without it.'[17] Afterwards, a cry went up to march on to the city centre. The authorised commemoration was now an unauthorised protest march.

The mass of students proceeded along the Vltava embankment, chanting and singing. Trams halted to allow the protestors to pass, while motorists honked their horns in approval. When the rally turned right into Narodni Street, actors and staff from the National Theatre came out on to the balcony to applaud them.

THEN HALFWAY UP Narodni Street, hundreds of riot police with helmets and perspex shields jogged out to form a defensive wall, blocking the students' path. Behind the rows of police stood members of the Red Berets, a highly trained anti-terrorist air-force regiment. The protestors further down the line kept filing into Narodni Street, unable to see the blockage up ahead. Then another line of riot police came rushing out to cordon them off from behind.

With nowhere to go, the anxious students sat down on the cold asphalt and began to sing 'We Shall Overcome'. An elderly veteran of the original Jan Opletal protest of 1939 remained upright, leaning on his walking stick, singing the national anthem, 'Where Is My Home?'

As the tension mounted, the protestors produced their keys from their pockets and jingled them musically in front of the bristling riot police, creating a reverberant cacophony that rang out through the street. More police arrived, blocking the lanes and side streets. The students realised they were boxed in on all sides. Police with loudhailers ordered them to go home, but it was impossible to go anywhere.

Then the perspex wall moved forward. The protestors rose to their feet, raised their arms and chanted, 'Our hands are empty!' Panic rippled through the crowd and the police moved in, swinging their batons, cracking heads. Students ran to the back, only to meet another line of riot police advancing from the rear. The protestors were caught in a human vice, punching, beating and kicking them to the ground. Smaller students were lifted off their feet in the crush of bodies. Armoured personnel carriers charged onto the sidewalks like motorised battering rams, sending people scattering into the side streets, where Red Berets waited to deliver a beating. A Western cameraman was hurled through a shop window, while a *Chicago Tribune* reporter had her head split open. The soldiers dragged protestors into doorways, tore off their clothes and beat them naked.[18] One protestor saw a girl about to be hit and flung himself forward; he was beaten all over his head and body with truncheon blows, while soldiers shouted, 'Give it to the motherfucker!', 'On his face!'[19] For the protestors, there was nowhere to escape, other than through a narrow passage on Narodni Trida, lined on either side by a gauntlet of police, who bashed protestors as they ran through.

Student Michael Kukral saw some frightened high-school kids dashing into a doorway and followed them in. He stepped through a red curtain and found himself in a small studio apartment crammed with dozens of whimpering teenagers. A middle-aged woman hissed at them to be quiet and then turned off the lights. In the darkened room, they heard shouts and groans, barking dogs, feet pounding on the pavement.[20]

As Narodni Street began to empty, bands of Red Berets fanned out into the nearby metro stations, attacking groups of commuters on the concourse who had stopped to help the bloodied protestors.

Katrin Bock had holed up with her friends in a nearby pub to wait out the storm of violence raging outside. At around 11 pm, she ventured out to find Narodni Street mostly empty. There was no traffic, but the street was littered with abandoned bags, hats, shoes and bloodied clothes. 'It was a strange atmosphere, completely silent,' she recalled. 'You could see blood on the walls of buildings ... and students walking around in a daze, traumatised.'[21]

AS THE SHOCKED AND wounded protestors staggered back to their homes and dormitories, word spread that the security forces had beaten a student to death. Some of the protestors recalled seeing an inert body on the pavement being picked up and carried off in an ambulance.

The nineteen-year-old victim was identified as Martin Smid by Drahomira Drazska, a porter at one of the student hostels, who claimed to be his girlfriend. News of Smid's death was passed on to Petr Uhl from Charter 77, who then gave the story to Radio Free Europe, the BBC and Reuters. Petr Uhl was subsequently arrested for 'defaming the republic by spreading slanderous information'.[22]

Milos Jakes's government angrily denied that anyone had been killed in the police action. They produced two Martin Smids for state TV, both alive and well. But having lied so often, the government simply wasn't believed.

The story jolted Praguers out of their apathy. 'Until that day,' recalled dissident Jan Urban, 'there had been a deal between the Communist regime and the people: "You shut up and we will take care of you". But the moment people had the impression that their kids were being killed, the deal was off.'[23]

FOR ONCE, HOWEVER the regime was telling the truth. The dead student, Martin Smid, did not exist. The seemingly lifeless figure seen on the pavement was Ludvik Zifcak, a young StB officer sent to infiltrate the student movement. Zifcak, who was very much alive, later claimed he'd been acting that night as a foot soldier in a complex plot hatched by the StB with the connivance of the KGB. Senior StB officers, he said, had instructed him to encourage the students to march into the city centre, where they would be confronted by the security forces. When violence broke out, he said he was instructed to play dead in the street. Drahomira Drazska, his co-conspirator, had played her part by feeding the false story of Smid's death to the dissident movement.

The idea that the StB would conspire against the communist leadership seemed bizarre, but Zifcak claimed the StB had wanted to discredit Milos Jakes and then depose him in favour of pro-Gorbachev moderates, who could cut a deal with opposition leaders and keep the party in power.[24]

The implications of Zifcak's allegations were breathtaking: if true, it would mean the 'people power' revolution in Prague had, in fact, been secretly instigated by the secret police. But the conspiracy theory collapses on closer inspection. In 1992, a parliamentary inquiry report found Zifcak's testimony to be 'technically impossible and unfeasible'.[25] It could find no connection between the StB and Drahomira Drazska, who later admitted she'd made up the story of Smid's death to get back at the security forces for the vicious attack that night.[26] Although Zifcak claimed he'd been playing dead, it seems more likely he'd been beaten unconscious in Narodni Street by the security forces, who had failed to recognise him as one of their own. Western journalists and historians reported Zifcak's bold conspiracy claims as fact, basing their stories on an interim report of the parliamentary inquiry, but the inquiry's final report demolished its earlier findings and Zifcak's allegations along with it.

Nonetheless, the widespread perception that the regime had murdered a student had set revolutionary forces in motion. Distressed students returned to Narodni Street to assemble a makeshift shrine to honour Martin Smid, lighting small candles on the spot where they believed he had fallen. They strung up a banner to commemorate the parallel student martyrdoms spaced exactly half a century apart: *Jan Opletal: 17.11.1939, Martin Smid: 17.11.1989.*

It was Prague's greatest ever literary joke: the catalyst for the fall of the regime was the death of a fictional character.

Sunday, 19 November

ON SUNDAY, GROUPS OF exhausted, frightened students came together at the university to figure out what to do next. As they debated, their outrage gave them fresh reserves of energy; they voted to go on strike and called for a nation-wide workers' strike against the regime. Prague's actors and stage workers declared their support. Prague's theatres became debating chambers and centres of political activity.

That evening, Vaclav Havel made his way to the Actors' Studio theatre to convene a meeting of dissident writers, student leaders, conservative Catholics, ex-communicated communists, actors and scientists. Ideologically diverse but socially narrow, they recognised they had to become more broadly representative of Czech society, and so they invited Petr Miller, an electrician from the CKD engineering works and Milan Hruska from the North Bohemian coal mines into their inner circle.

The group, which called itself Obcanske Forum – 'Civic Forum' – demanded the resignation of the Communist Party leadership, the release of all political prisoners and for an inquiry into Friday night's police attack. They repeated the students' call for a general workers' strike for 27 November, which would, Havel said, be a referendum on communist rule in Czechoslovakia.

Havel was ready to harness the revolutionary potential of the moment and carry it forward in a style that accorded with his convictions and his personality. This was to be a non-violent revolt, directed from the theatres of Prague, where Havel could comfortably manage the unfolding drama. As the excited Civic Forum leaders made their way home that night, the first snow of the season covered Prague with a powdery white veil.

Monday, 20 November

MAREK TOMAN, WHO WAS then a philosophy student at Charles University, had not been present at the Friday night student march; he had assumed the officially approved rally was going to be a waste of time, and had left town to see one of his favourite bands perform in the countryside.

Marek had lived all his young life under the pall of normalisation. He was born in 1967, a year before the Soviet invasion. When the tanks rolled into Prague, his father left for West Germany. He told Marek's mother he would make arrangements so they could follow him, but after a few months he called and asked them not to come; he had made a new life in Germany without them.

Marek's father's flight to the West was deemed a criminal act and a black mark was recorded against the family name. Marek's mother had to plead with the authorities to get him admitted to high school and to university, and had to assure the authorities of their loyalty. Deeply alienated by the system, Marek avoided military service by faking mental illness and was admitted to a psychiatric institution for six weeks. 'It was actually fine,' he recalled. 'I learnt interesting stories from the others in the group-therapy sessions. I didn't mind.'

Although the Berlin Wall had fallen, Marek thought the party *nomenklatura* would find some way to cling to power in Czechoslovakia. After his weekend in the country, he came back to Prague on the Monday morning not knowing what to expect. Walking around the corner from the railway station, he saw a student in a black pullover standing under the statue of St Wenceslas, reading out a statement condemning the police violence. Marek saw he was trembling with nerves. The student continued reading his statement, but then he stumbled over a line, and said, in English, 'Shit!' The use of 'shit', instead of a Czech curse word (of which there are a great many), was, he thought, a bit crazy, a bit absurd, and hopeful. 'It was a sign of a fresh wind from abroad which was starting to blow through the city. When I heard him say "shit," I thought, *maybe something really is going to happen*.'[27]

THAT EVENING, at the end of the work day, Praguers spontaneously made their way into the city centre. Soon Wenceslas Square was a shifting sea of 200,000 excited Praguers holding flags and candles.

The great majority were in their twenties or teens. An exhilarating sense of strength and solidarity surged through the crowd; there was, said one student, 'a feeling of stupendous wholeness and rightness'.[28]

A chant went up: 'Down with Jakes! Down with Husak!'

Then, in imitation of the students on Friday night, the demonstrators pulled their keys from their pockets and jingled them. The jangling noise echoed off the buildings, creating an eerie sound that carried through the streets of the city. The message to the regime was clear: time to go.

IN HINDSIGHT, the end of communist rule seems inevitable, but at the time no one knew whether they were racing towards a Berlin triumph or a Beijing massacre. Milos Jakes, supported by hardliners on the presidium, prepared for a crackdown, putting the hated people's militia on alert. These militias, known as the Armed Fist of the Working Class, were state-sanctioned regiments of armed factory workers, who wore their workers' garb so as to give the impression of 'spontaneous' worker support for the Communist Party. Jakes also put special units of the army trained to deal with public insurrection on standby, awaiting his signal to enter Prague and shut down the protests. But lacking clear support from Moscow, the presidium couldn't bring itself to give the order to risk mass bloodshed in Wenceslas Square.

In the meantime, the border garrisons were brought into the capital to maintain order, but no one had arranged accommodation for them. The troops spent the night shivering inside their buses parked outside the Interior Ministry. Students took pity on them and brought over hot soup, which was gratefully received.

Tuesday, 21 November

WENCESLAS SQUARE had become a mass open-air auditorium, and Havel, the master dramatist, saw the need for a high central stage from which Civic Forum leaders could address the crowds. Through an old school contact, he was given access to a small balcony on the Melantrich building, positioned midway up the square, which could be entered via a newspaper office. Havel's rock-musician friends set up a powerful sound system that could reach the whole of Wenceslas Square, making every word intelligible.

As Tuesday afternoon drew to a close, the square filled up to the brim again. People climbed into the trees and on top of phone booths and newspaper kiosks, waving flags. Havel stepped onto the Melantrich balcony and welcomed the cheering crowd with a rumbling, 'Dear friends!' He introduced the Civic Forum leadership, one by one. And then a woman stepped forward on the balcony, breathing heavily and emotionally in the fading afternoon light. It was Marta Kubisova.

THE CROWD HADN'T seen Marta for two decades. Her otherworldly, youthful beauty had faded, but her presence now had a different power: the crowd saw her greying hair, her everyday clothes and glasses, and

Marta Kubisova, Wenceslas Square, 21 November 1989.

recognised her as one of them. Marta lifted up her arms and tried not to cry. A thunderous chant went up: 'Long live Marta! Long live Marta!' and she thought: *no singer ever had a comeback like this.*

The chanting faded into silence and she began to sing 'A Prayer for Marta'. Her voice rang out, unaccompanied, clear and strong.

> *Let peace remain within this land.*
> *Malice, envy, fear and strife,*
> *Let them pass, let them finally pass.*

Members of the crowd raised their hands to form a V sign, for victory and for peace. 'That was the moment,' Marta recalled, 'when people started to cry.'[29] International news crews wondered who this unknown woman was and why she had unlocked such a welter of emotions from the normally restrained Praguers. No one was more surprised than Marta's ten-year-old daughter, who had no idea her mother had once been a famous singer.[30]

Thursday, 23 November

'A PRAYER FOR MARTA' had given Praguers a badly needed emotional catharsis. There was a gentleness mixed into the sense of exaltation. Even those who had chosen to sit out the uprising and watch it on television felt themselves being coaxed out of their habitual reserve and public solitariness. 'Each day people felt stronger and stood up straighter,' recalled one citizen.[31] Eye contact between people was resumed and smiles were exchanged. Citizens performed small acts of generosity on public transport and in the cafés.

Divisive party propaganda was drowned in the rising tide of goodwill. When *Rude Pravo* denounced the student protestors as saboteurs and lay-abouts, the student leaders sent platoons of volunteers to keep the national monuments tidy and to clean up the public parks and gardens. Students donated blood and volunteered at hospitals and clinics. They sent emissaries to the giant CKD plant in Smichov to make the case for change to the workers, who passed a resolution condemning the police violence and calling for free elections.[32] The students' courage and courtesy impressed their elders and shamed more than a few. How had a generation of young people raised in such a morally contaminated environment become so idealistic? 'It is a terrible dishonour,' one worker said, 'when it is the children who have to strive for the reform of our society.'[33]

Worker support for the regime was slipping away. Miroslav Stepan, the party boss in Prague, also came to the CKD plant to address the workforce. He attempted to ridicule the protest movement: 'Fifteen-year-old kids cannot decide who the president will be,' he snorted. A worker shot back, 'We are not kids!' An angry chant went up: 'We are not kids! We are not kids!'

Stepan, shocked, tried to talk over the raucous jeers and whistles. 'I will finish! I don't think you understand,' he said. 'I wasn't talking about you!'

A new chant began: 'Resign! Resign!'

Stepan gaped wordlessly at the crowd, then turned away and went back inside.[34]

A BUNKER MENTALITY set in among the party leadership. Havel, aware of the troops stationed around Prague, worried Jakes might order a military massacre. He was deeply troubled when the army's chief of staff declared on state television that the armed forces were standing by, ready to defend the party and socialism. Havel decided to plant a seed of doubt in the party's mind that if they gave the order to shoot, their soldiers might not obey. That night in Wenceslas Square, he called for the army to side with the people and, if necessary, to defend them. Choosing his words carefully, he obliquely reminded the party of the international consequences of a massacre. 'Not only our future is at stake,' he said, 'but all of Europe's.'[35]

Friday, 24 November

CIVIC FORUM'S SCOPE and reach expanded rapidly, with branches appearing in towns and cities across the country. In Bratislava, Slovaks formed their own opposition group, Public Against Violence, which coordinated their activities with their colleagues in Prague.

In the space of a week, Civic Forum had grown from a dissident coalition into an alternative government. The group commandeered the Magic Lantern Theatre on Narodni Street and converted it into an improvised shadow parliament. Meetings and debates took place in the auditorium, while activists occupied a jumble of overheated foyers, dressing rooms, offices and storage spaces. The clammy air was filled with laughter and argument, and the distinctive fug of 'cigarette smoke, sweat, damp coats, and revolution'.[36]

On Friday afternoon, Havel was on stage at the Magic Lantern chairing a meeting when Alexander Dubcek walked in. Dubcek looked very much like his old self in his neat grey coat and hat – the uniform of the communist functionary. He moved more slowly and deliberately, but there was still the same shy smile, the sad eyes and open face.

At sunset, Havel brought Dubcek to the Melantrich building. Another capacity crowd had congregated outside in Wenceslas Square. Dubcek stood back from the windows, waiting to be introduced, while Havel tried to give him tips on how to handle the crowd: 'They'll scream *Dubcek! Dubcek!* and you'll have to calm them down'. 'Thanks for your help,' Dubcek replied tersely, 'but I know how to deal with that.'[37]

Nothing, however, could prepare Dubcek for the stadium-sized roar that greeted him as he stepped onto the balcony. The crowd could hardly believe what they were seeing. It was really Dubcek, back after all these years.

'DUB-CEK! DUB-CEK! DUB-CEK!'

Dubcek faffed around awkwardly, donned his thick-rimmed glasses, then pulled them off and grinned boyishly. Leaning right over the balcony, he opened his arms and brought them in, as if to hug every single person in the square, and the crowd went wild. Havel, with his aversion to showy public gestures, would never have done such a thing.

The crowd took up a new chant: *'DUBCEK TO THE CASTLE!'*

'That depends on you,' he replied.[38]

Dubcek, a far more popular and better known leader than Havel, might have become the figurehead of the revolution at that moment, but his presence was received more enthusiastically than the speech he gave. Dubcek hadn't moved on from 1968. He still wanted to redeem socialism with a human face, and his language was still laden with clapped-out Marxist jargon. Dubcek had come back to Prague believing the times had caught up with him at last, but instead they'd passed him by.

Still, it had been a magical moment. When the spotlights were turned off, Dubcek and Havel were seen backlit against the window, gently twirling around each other in a little pirouette of joy.

Marek Toman, who had spent the week campaigning for the general strike, was still worried that people might end up settling for a more innocuous form of communism. He'd seen too much apathy over the years to be impressed by the new found courage of his fellow citizens. *How was it*, he wondered, *that all these people, who were so docile for so long, had become so bold?*[39]

DUBCEK AND HAVEL returned to the Magic Lantern that evening for the regular 7.30 pm media conference. Someone asked a question about socialism. Havel said that the word had become meaningless in Czechoslovakia. Dubcek was debating the point when a bearded aide crept on stage, crouched down beside Havel and whispered in his ear. Havel stood up and announced that the entire presidium had just resigned.

The whole theatre leapt to its feet, weeping and cheering.

Someone uncorked a champagne bottle, splashing the fizz all over the stage. Havel, revelling in the happy mayhem, hugged Dubcek and then raised a toast to 'a free Czechoslovakia'. Outside, car drivers heard the news on their radios and honked their horns. In the square, people cried, sang and danced, dizzy with joy and relief. Four soldiers in uniform ran arm in arm together, laughing and waving flags. Incredibly, only a week had passed since the student march. After decades in which accomplishing the smallest thing had been so hard and harrowing, everything was now coming to them so quickly.

*Dubcek and Havel receive the news of the presidium's resignation
at the Magic Lantern Theatre 24 November 1989.*

Now We Have This Fantastic Speed

ON THE WEEKEND, the public rallies moved to the spacious Letna Plain, near the plinth where the megalithic statue of Stalin once stood. More than 600,000 people showed up on both days – as many as half the city's entire population. There were concurrent rallies in Bratislava, in Brno, Ostrava and in other towns and cities across the nation.

On Sunday morning, thousands of Catholics and interested onlookers walked up to St Vitus Cathedral to attend a celebratory mass for the canonisation of St Agnes of Bohemia, the medieval princess who came down from the castle to live among the poor seven centuries ago. An old prophecy, which predicted Bohemia would not prosper until Agnes was canonised, was remembered. Later she would be named the Patron Saint of the Overthrow of Communism.

ELSEWHERE THAT MORNING, a Civic Forum delegation met with Prime Minister Ladislav Adamec, an apparatchik presenting himself as a reasonable, 'liberal' communist in the Gorbachev mould. Adamec had earlier dismissed Havel as a nobody and had refused to meet him. But once Adamec realised that help was not coming from Moscow, he agreed to sit down with the scruffy playwright, dressed informally in an open-necked shirt.

'We haven't met yet, have we?' Adamec said, extending his hand across the table.

'I'm Havel,' said the playwright, stating the obvious.

The meeting was brief. Adamec quickly agreed to release all political prisoners in Czechoslovakia's jails, including Ivan Jirous. Havel, in turn, invited Adamec to speak at that afternoon's rally on Letna Plain. Havel's intention was to build up Adamec's popularity and enhance his authority within the presidium as a negotiating partner. But at Letna, Adamec's speech flopped. His announcement that the government was ready to accept all of Civic Forum's demands was well received, but when he proposed the next day's general strike should be a symbolic act and last only three minutes, there were boos and whistles. Adamec walked off the stage to a cacophony of heckling and jeering. The dissident Catholic priest Vaclav Maly felt obliged to step in on his behalf. 'As democratically thinking people we must allow others to speak freely,' he told the crowd, 'even if we don't agree with them.'[40]

THAT EVENING AT the Magic Lantern, a Civic Forum subcommittee presented a multi-point 'What We Want' document to its members. It proposed a return to Masaryk's democratic republic, with rule of law, an independent judiciary, free elections, a market economy, social justice, a clean environment, a cultural and academic life free of the shackles of ideology, and a 'return to Europe'.

The document was read out to the auditorium by Vaclav Klaus, a silver-haired economist from the Academy of Sciences, who had studied at Cornell University in the United States. Klaus was a free marketeer and an admirer of British prime minister Margaret Thatcher. Havel was to become the figurehead of the new post-communist society, but Klaus would be the principal architect of its economy. 'History has begun to develop very quickly in this country,' Havel said. 'In a country that has had 20 years of timelessness, now we have this fantastic speed.'[41]

Strike

ON TUESDAY MORNING, Praguers went to work as usual, but at noon, church bells rang out across the city and all labour abruptly ceased. Workers in factories downed tools and switched off machines; shops, cafés, bookstores, pharmacies and offices closed their doors. Urban mass transit came to a halt. On television, a broadcaster announced he was joining the strike and would go off air, and for the next two hours state TV simply showed scenes of demonstrations from all over the country. Strikers marched from Narodni Street into Wenceslas Square, carrying flags, singing the national anthem. Prague's taxis formed a two-mile long blockade of the city's ring road.

The two-hour strike was a complete success. It had gathered the massive but slightly incoherent energies of the revolution and brought them to a sharp point. Havel had declared the strike would be a referendum on the regime and now the results were in. Not one institution – the army, the people's militia, the media, the unions – had come to the regime's defence.

THAT SAME DAY, after an absence of twelve years, an excited Paul Wilson made his return to Prague. Paul had been in Berlin, working on a radio documentary series, *The Gorbachev Revolution*, when news of the Wenceslas Square demonstrations broke out. He drove at once to the Czech border, but he was still officially persona non grata and couldn't get in. Then a friend told him that exiles arriving at Prague airport were being waved through, so he booked a flight. Outside the airport, Paul found the Canadian ambassador waiting with a limousine, ready to take him directly to Civic Forum headquarters.

When Paul entered the Magic Lantern, he saw Havel on stage with the other Forum leaders, delivering their nightly media conference. Paul ran into people he hadn't seen for more than a decade. The friends from his wild rock-and-roll youth had become middle-aged activists running a revolution: 'It was quite exciting,' he said, 'to say the least.'[42]

Normal All the Time

IN THE WEEK THAT followed, the central clauses of one-party rule were pulled from the constitution like rotten teeth. The National Assembly voted to abolish Article 4, which affirmed the 'leading role' of the Communist Party, along with the clause that enshrined Marxism–Leninism as the official state ideology. The parliamentary debate on Article 4 was televised live, exposing the members as confused placeholders. Some were filmed snoozing in their chairs.

On 3 December, the party made its last stand when Adamec put forward the long-awaited proposal for a new government. Civic Forum's leaders could only shake their heads in amazement: a few non-communists were to be appointed to minor posts, but fifteen of the twenty ministries were to be retained by party members, including the crucial army and interior portfolios. Adamec's lack of influence within the party was vividly exposed and it terminated his usefulness as a negotiating partner. Havel called for Adamec's resignation and for a demonstration in Wenceslas Square the next day.

AFTER WEEKS OF PROTESTS and frenetic sleepless activity, Civic Forum's energy was starting to flag. The student leaders were also exhausted and debating whether to continue their strike; some complained of feeling sidelined by the self-appointed 'grown-ups' of Civic Forum, who had commandeered the revolution they had started. But there was too much momentum now among the general public for the revolution to stall, and the next evening Wenceslas Square was filled to capacity once again. It was still the best show in town. Civic Forum's Vaclav Maly demanded free elections by June 1990; Adamec was put on notice that he had six days to come up with a much better proposal or the government would face another general strike.

The rally ended on a high note, when Karel Gott appeared on the Melantrich balcony to sing the national anthem alongside singer-songwriter Karel Kryl, who had returned from his twenty-year exile in West Germany. 'That's when we knew for sure it was a real revolution,' said Katrin Bock. 'Everybody thought: *if Karel Gott is singing here, now, then we win.*'[43]

ADAMEC RESIGNED THE NEXT day in favour of his deputy, Marian Calfa, a communist technocrat who knew how to use elements of the existing system to manage the transition to democracy. 'They knew who, and I knew how,' is how he summed up his relationship with Civic Forum.[44] Calfa, in consultation with Havel, formed a temporary 'government of national understanding', allocating half the portfolios, including the army and interior ministries, to non-communists. Jiri Dienstbier, a dissident journalist, was named as foreign minister. Jan Carnogursky, a Slovak lawyer only just released from prison, was to be deputy prime minister with responsibility for the security services. Petr Miller, the CKD electrician, was now minister for labour and social affairs. The neo-liberal economist Vaclav Klaus was to be finance minister.

President Gustav Husak swore in the new government on 10 December at Prague Castle and then resigned. After the ceremony, Husak asked Carnogursky how long he'd been in prison. 'Eight months,' he replied. Husak laughed and said it was nothing compared to the nine years he'd served back in the fifties.[45] In Husak's mind, somehow, they were both victims of communism.

After forty-one years, the Communist Party dictatorship was finished.

A slogan appeared on walls and in shop windows: *They tried to normalise us, but we were normal all the time.*[46]

Havel na Hrad

HUSAK'S RESIGNATION BROUGHT the question of who should replace him into sharp focus. As the nation's head of state, the new president would be entrusted with the critical six-month transition to democracy, with free elections scheduled for June 1990. The strong consensus among Civic Forum members was that only Havel had the leadership skills, the prestige and the moral authority to carry the nation over the threshold. On the day of Husak's resignation, Civic Forum announced its nomination of Havel for the presidency to a cheering crowd in Wenceslas Square. Posters of the smiling playwright accompanied by the slogan, *HAVEL NA HRAD* – Havel to the Castle – appeared all over the city.

NOT EVERYONE WAS CERTAIN Havel would run for the presidency or run away from it. Two years earlier, when he'd spotted Mikhail Gorbachev outside the National Theatre, Havel had felt some pity for the Soviet leader, who he assumed was yoked to the demands of high office: 'The whole day he sees the unappealing faces of his bodyguards,' he wrote, 'his schedule is busy with endless briefings, meetings and appearances, he must speak to a vast number of people, remember them all and not confuse them one with another, he must keep saying things that are witty but correct, things that the world, which is ever hungry for sensation, cannot snatch and use against him.'[47]

This passage, written only a year before the Velvet Revolution, was very likely the product of Havel wrestling with his own secret suspicion that he too might become a captive of high office before long. In October 1989, he had told a friend, 'I'm a writer, not a politician. I would like to be a kingmaker, but not a king.'[48] But by December, Havel had overcome his misgivings and had decided not to shirk the challenge of power. In public, he was already acting like a president-in-waiting, making speeches, shaking hands with the general public, holding court with an entourage of assistants and bodyguards. He claimed to be a reluctant conscript. 'I obviously don't want to be President,' he told a Civic Forum meeting. 'But if the situation sharpens in such a way that it would be in the interests of the country to have me as president for a short while, then I'm able to be president, since I have always subordinated my personal interest to the interests of the country. Otherwise I would not have gone to prison.'[49]

Havel's publicly expressed reservations were partly a political posture – far better to be pressed into high office than be seen to be hungering for it. But he did want the job, he accepted the necessity of it and was now ready to push aside those who stood in his way.

IN THE NORMAL RUN of things, it would be the National Assembly that would appoint a new president, but the communists, playing for time, now called for a public vote instead, hoping to stall the revolutionary momentum. On 15 December, Havel, the leader of a movement dedicated to transparency and democracy, held a secret meeting with Prime Minister Calfa to thwart the move for a popular vote. They met in the one government office Calfa could find that wasn't bugged. Calfa told Havel that communism was dead and buried, that he couldn't care less about the party, and that

Havel should become president and usher in a proper democracy and a market economy as soon as possible. He offered to swing the moribund parliament behind Havel's candidacy. Havel reported this conversation to a closed meeting of the Civic Forum leadership. 'The paradox of my situation,' he said, 'is that we are opponents of closed-door politics and this has to be kept a total secret … from our people and the public.'[50]

HAVEL'S DETERMINATION to win the presidency became apparent in another secret meeting held the following day with Miroslav Pavel, the director of Czechoslovak Television. Havel wanted airtime as a presidential candidate to improve his national profile, but the television executive bluntly told him he was just a minor political figure, and only deserved a late-night slot. This high-handedness ignited an explosion of long-suppressed rage in Havel, who threatened to have Pavel sacked when he came to power. Pavel relented gracelessly then left the room in a fury. Havel got his prime-time slot, and spoke to the nation that evening.[51]

In his speech, Havel maintained the posture of the reluctant candidate. He declared he would 'accept' the job as president under two conditions: that he would only serve as transitional figure until a new president could be chosen by a freely elected National Assembly; and secondly that Alexander Dubcek, a Slovak, would serve by his side. 'I will neither allow any dark powers to erect a barrier between him and me nor between our two nations.'[52]

IF HAVEL HAD OVERCOME his misgivings over the presidency, his wife, Olga, had not. When Paul Wilson came to the Havel's apartment for a breakfast interview, he found the future first lady of Czechoslovakia on her hands and knees furiously scrubbing the bathroom floor. 'Why does Vaclav have to be president?' she moaned. 'Why can't it be someone else?'

Paul sat down with Havel to begin the interview but then the phone rang. Dubcek was on the line. Havel apologised and left the room to take the call, rolling his eyes.

DUBCEK, THE VANQUISHED hero of 1968, wanted to be president at least as much as Havel did. He was still more popular and better known than the playwright, but had worn out his welcome among Civic Forum members, who were tired of his quest for vindication and uninterested in resuming an endless seminar on the viability of socialism with a human face.

Havel held five emotional meetings with Dubcek to persuade him to relinquish his claim to the presidency. Dubcek was by turns angry and tearful. In the end they struck a deal: in return for Dubcek's support, Havel would serve only as a transitional president and at the end of his six months he would step aside for the older man. In the interim, Dubcek would be awarded with the second most prestigious position in the nation – chairman of the National Assembly. It was a hollow understanding: the gift of the presidency was not Havel's to bestow, and he would never deliver on it anyway.

President Havel

ON 29 DECEMBER 1989, the members of the National Assembly convened at Prague Castle's medieval Vladislav Hall. The hall, crowned with its star-vaulted ceiling, had been built large enough to host indoor jousting tournaments between armoured knights on horseback.

Vaclav Havel watched the formal proceedings on television from an adjacent room, as the National Assembly members unanimously elected him president. He was then brought into the hall by Dubcek in his role as chairman of the National Assembly. For once, Havel was immaculately groomed, with a trim haircut and in a tailored suit. His face was a sombre mask. Havel walked slowly to the rostrum, sat down and signed his oath of office. Outside, the heaving crowd in Hradcany Square erupted into ecstatic cheers.

AFTER THE CEREMONY, Havel, Olga and their friends were admitted to the presidential palace. As they walked through the citadel of their vanquished enemies, Havel, who would never again be so exalted, felt strangely paralysed, 'deflated, spent, lacking in imagination'. Suddenly, he said, he had no idea what he was supposed to be doing.[53]

The revolutionaries introduced themselves to the staff and settled into their gloomy new offices. Some thought the castle still stank of the old regime. As they explored the rooms, they found hidden wires and microphones, and the closet with the hotline to Moscow. One assistant opened another door to discover a room full of people with headsets, still monitoring the palace's phone calls, all in the name of 'state security'.[54]

ON NEW YEAR'S DAY, a nervous President Havel sat down before the cameras to deliver the traditional presidential address on national television. He managed a shy smile, before donning his glasses and delivering an extraordinary speech, which confronted, starkly and honestly, the hard challenges that lay ahead. Havel spoke of the moribund economy, the ravaged environment and the absence of social justice. But the most serious problem, he said, was the lingering moral contamination in their society, the ingrained habit of saying one thing and thinking another. Fortunately, he said more brightly, the rising generation had given them 'something to lean on':

> *Where did the young people who never knew another system get their desire for truth, their love of free thought, their political ideas, their civic courage and civic prudence? How did it happen that their parents – the very generation that had been considered lost – joined them? How is it that so many people immediately knew what to do and none needed any advice or instruction?*

'We are a small country,' he said optimistically, 'yet at one time we were the spiritual crossroads of Europe. Is there a reason why we could not again become one?'

The president concluded his speech with a flourish – a phrase that echoed the words of John Amos Comenius, T. G. Masaryk and Marta Kubisova:

'People, your government has returned to you!'[55]

CHAPTER TWELVE

TOGETHER ALONE

1991–

APRIL 1991: SIXTEEN MONTHS after the Velvet Revolution, Khym and I are in Melbourne, having breakfast in the ground-floor restaurant of a luxurious hotel, when two powerfully built men in suits and ties enter the room, followed by a slightly stooped older man with combed-back silver hair and a familiar beak-like nose.

Khym asks me what I'm staring at.

'That guy there,' I say, pointing with my fork, 'that's Alexander Dubcek.'

'What? No …' she says, disbelieving.

Across the room, the chairman of the Czechoslovak National Assembly was slowly lowering himself into a chair at a corner table while his associates fetch his buffet breakfast. His appearance strikes me as absurdly meaningful. I'd been wandering through distorted versions of Prague in my dreams of late; now it's as though Dubcek has casually stepped from them into the waking world. Idiotically, I borrow a pen and paper from a waiter and gingerly approach Dubcek for an autograph. He signs the paper and hands it back with a faint smile, then I leave him to eat his breakfast in peace. He seems disconcertingly gloomy; I had expected him to carry himself with the glad confidence of a man vindicated by history. His natural buoyancy may well have been dampened by the long flight to Australia.

Dubcek, I later discovered, had come to Melbourne to receive a human rights award, but at the time the encounter seemed as improbable as running into Henry Kissinger in an Icelandic fjord. When I saw him that morning, he had just a year and a half left to live. On 1 September 1992, his chauffeur-driven BMW skidded off the road between Prague and Brno, and plunged into a ravine. Dubcek, who was not wearing a seatbelt, was thrown from the car, and died months later of his injuries. He was seventy years old.

The Perfect Formula for Human Happiness

IN HIS MEMOIR, Vaclav Havel likened his journey from prison to Prague Castle to the Czech fairy tale of Little Honza. Although everyone tells him it's hopeless, little Honza keeps beating his head against a wall until it collapses and he becomes king. But Havel was well aware that it was in the gift of no political leader to write the next sentence – that everyone should live happily ever after. He knew the wave of joy that had carried him into Prague Castle would place unrealistic expectations on him as president. 'We are coming in as heroes,' he warned his staff, 'but in the end, when they realise what a mess we're in and how little we can do about it, they will railroad us, tarred and feathered, out of town.'[1]

Havel, as he feared, became a captive of high office and of his status as a global celebrity. His staff of enthusiastic amateurs were too inexperienced to manage his schedule properly or to help shoulder his burdens, allowing his valuable time to be taken up with too many meetings and interviews. He rebelled against the need to bring the public around to change by repeating the same stock phrases again and again. He worked long hours, was often ill and sat through state banquets in foreign capitals dying for a cigarette.

The impressive political skills Havel had displayed as leader of Civic Forum seemed to desert him as president. He was unwilling to accept the necessity of contesting political parties in a parliamentary democracy. On his first state visit to Germany, he reportedly joked to Chancellor Helmut Kohl, 'Why don't we work together to dissolve all political parties? Why don't we set up just one big party: the Party of Europe?'[2] Civic Forum split anyway, with Vaclav Klaus forming a centre-right Civic Democratic Party which won the 1992 elections.

Without a party to stand behind him, Havel lacked the parliamentary strength to prevent the breakup of Czechoslovakia, the most serious failure of his presidency. The union had splintered once before under assault from Adolf Hitler; this time the split was achieved by a simple parliamentary vote, despite polls indicating majority support for the union in both nations. Havel, still the most admired figure in the country, backed by a solid majority of his fellow citizens, was unable to stop it. The passion of the nationalist minorities prevailed over the half-hearted unionist majority, and Czechoslovakia split into separate Czech and Slovak nations on 1 January 1993.

TODAY, MORE THAN TWO decades after the split, there are few regrets in either nation. The relationship had always been defined as much by external pressures as by their affinities. The Czechs and Slovaks were like a couple who eloped in 1918 to escape their overbearing families, the Austrians and the Hungarians. When the Cold War ended, they were free to part on reasonably good terms.

For Havel, the acquiescence to a Velvet Divorce with Slovakia was a classic triumph of Czech small-mindedness, a retreat into 'bitter provincialism'. At the end of the twentieth century, after a thousand years of co-existence, the Jews and Germans were gone, and now the Czechs had parted ways with the Slovaks. 'And who will be left?' Havel asked. 'Pure-blooded little Czechs in their own little garden.'[3]

Like T. G. Masaryk before him, President Havel was willing to draw on his immense popularity to say unpopular things to his people. He knowingly stirred controversy by suggesting it was time the nation apologised for the post-war expulsion of the Sudeten Germans, an act he described in a letter to the president of Germany as 'deeply immoral'.[4] The need for an apology was contested by Ivan Klima, who was fourteen when he was released from Terezin concentration camp. 'It is true that the behaviour of some Czechs after the war was unacceptable,' Klima said, but too many of the Sudeten Germans had chosen the Nazis in 1938 and there had been so much killing and cruelty all round.[5]

Havel worked hard nonetheless to set relations between Germany and Czechoslovakia on a better footing. Putting issues of war-related compensation to one side, both nations signed a friendship treaty at Prague Castle in 1992. The ceremony was both joyful and sombre. 'We have stood over too many graves in this century,' the German chancellor, Helmut Kohl, said. 'We have shed too many tears. The time has come for us to learn from history.'[6]

WHEN THE SPLIT WITH the Slovaks became inevitable, Havel resigned from the soon-to-be-extinct Czechoslovak presidency. Paul Wilson advised him to retire from politics and become an outspoken writer again, but Havel felt he was still needed to provide a moral centre for a disoriented people, struggling to find a way out of the post-communist morass.

Havel chose to return to the political stage but, as Wilson noted at the time, the playwright had become the protagonist in a different kind of drama. 'The Velvet Revolution in 1989 was like a morality play. The good guys and bad guys were clear. Havel was the knight on the white charger. He could do no wrong. But the situation he's in now is like one of his own plays – that's the irony of it – a play in which the hero is a deeply troubled person in a morally ambiguous situation who doesn't really know what to do, who is put upon by people from all sides, who's constantly being importuned for help, and advice, and who does not really know the right way out.'[7]

IN FEBRUARY 1993, the governing coalition nominated Havel to become the first president of the newly minted Czech Republic, but under its constitution, Havel's power was more tightly constrained, and he reigned rather than ruled as president. Unlike Tomas Masaryk, who exercised immense informal power at Prague Castle, Havel held office as a more conventional, largely ceremonial head of state.

Havel and his prime minister, Vaclav Klaus, could barely conceal their dislike for each other. Havel was polite; Klaus was blunt; Havel believed in acting in concert with Europe and the world to address climate change; Klaus denounced both the European Union and thought climate change was a leftist hoax. Klaus was a doctrinaire free marketer; Havel thought all ideologies were reductive, and that to bow before them was to betray one's own better judgement.

Havel was obliged to preside over Klaus's shock-therapy privat-isation scheme for state-owned enterprises through a controversial voucher scheme. Property confiscated by the state in 1948 was sold or returned to the original owners, with billions of dollars changing hands. The process was accompanied by numerous well-reported instances of corruption and fraud. Havel spoke of an 'ugly mood' in the country: 'Many are convinced that honest business people fare badly, while fraudulent nouveaux riche get the green light.'[8]

The Czech Communist Party retained a degree of support in the industrial regions hardest hit by the open economy, and among elderly voters nostalgic for an era when jobs were secure and not particularly onerous. Havel saw this as the dilemma of the prisoner who does not know how to cope with freedom: 'In prison everything is laid out for you; you don't have to decide on anything. They tell you when to get up, what to wear, everything is decided for you by others. If you live in this for years and are then suddenly released, freedom becomes a burden.'[9]

PRAGUE, MEANWHILE, was buoyed by an influx of income from the masses of foreign visitors attracted by the city's picturesque qualities and its cheap beer. Prague's dilapidated historic buildings were repainted and repaired.

Prague's body was healed, but she lost a little of her soul in the process. In the two decades between 2000 and 2019, annual visitor numbers jumped from 2.6 million to just under 8 million.[10] Over-tourism has driven local residents from the city centre, eroding its livability and sociability. Here and there you notice a few unmarked, hidden pubs in Mala Strana, maintained so that Praguers can enjoy each other's company, safe from the throngs of foreign pub-crawlers. Vratislav Brabenec, the Plastic People of the Universe's saxophonist, throws up his hands at the latest foreign invasion. 'Once it was Russian soldiers,' he complains, 'now it is tourists. I can't decide which is worse.'[11]

✳

Lustration

THE StB WAS OFFICIALLY dissolved on 1 February 1990, and citizens were given access to their personal files. The lists of names of those who had collaborated with the secret police made for sad reading: there were brothers who had informed on sisters, wives against their husbands. Informers were found in the ranks of former Charter 77 activists. Jan Urban, who discovered some of his best friends had been StB informers, received the news more in sorrow than in anger. 'I found out how state security broke them down,' he said. 'I don't want to judge. I don't know how I would have behaved in their shoes.'[12]

On 4 October 1991, the National Assembly passed 'lustration' laws* designed to 'purify' the civil service by naming and shaming government employees with links to the secret police. Havel signed the Act, but immediately sought to amend it, without success. He was torn between the need to keep the cynical opportunists of the old regime from getting their hooks into the new republic and the desire to avoid a poisonous, divisive witch-hunt. He admitted, 'We have not yet found a dignified and civilized way to reckon with our past.'[13]

THE QUESTION OF HOW to proceed against those who had enthusiastically participated in torture and judicial murder was less morally fraught, but just as difficult. In 2007, a Czech court found 86-year-old Ludmila Brozova-Polednova guilty of being an accomplice to murder. Brozova-Polednova had acted as a 'workers' prosecutor' at the trial of Milada Horakova in 1950, and had been one

---

* Taken from *lustrace* – a word that bundles together the concept of 'bringing to light' with 'purification'.

of the loudest voices demanding the death penalty in the courtroom. At Horakova's execution, Brozova-Polednova was heard to shout, 'Don't break her neck on the noose. Suffocate the bitch.'[14] She was sentenced to serve six years at a special geriatric prison facility, but was pardoned after a year and died five years later.

Other criminal accomplices of the old regime escaped justice entirely. In February 2019, Marek Toman brought me along to the screening of a documentary, *The Case of Uherske Hradiste*, and to meet the filmmaker, Kristina Vlachova. Marek has known Kristina since the late 1980s when he was an undergraduate and she was the receptionist at a student dormitory.

Kristina had spent a decade making the documentary – an investigation into a notorious secret police prison where political prisoners were routinely tortured throughout the 1950s. Her camera followed the survivors as they wandered through the derelict building, revisiting its former torture chambers. Some of them had never found out why they had been brought there in the first place. Kristina's film also followed the Czech justice system's half-hearted attempt to bring one of the worst of the StB torturers, Alois Grebenicek, to trial in the 1990s. Grebenicek's lawyer presented the court with a series of medical certificates stating he was too ill to attend, but Kristina's film showed him energetically haranguing a camera crew outside his house. The trial dragged on for years and Grebenicek died without ever having stepped into the courtroom. The judge, who had a communist background, came under fire from critics, who questioned the ability of the Czech judicial system to deal with the crimes of the Stalinist era.

KRISTINA'S DARK UNFLINCHING film left me breathless, and I asked if I could meet with her and Marek later that week at the

Café Slavia. We took up a corner table in the near-empty restaurant section and she told me her story.

Kristina was born in 1943 under a different name – Jana Slanska. 'Slanska' is the feminine form of 'Slansky', a name her family shared with Rudolf Slansky, the Communist Party general secretary. There was no family connection, but after the 1948 communist takeover the name alone could strike fear into a roomful of strangers. Kristina remembers waiting to see the dentist as a child; when the nurse called, 'Jana Slanska?', she saw the other patients stiffen in fear.

When Rudolf Slansky was arrested and executed as a traitor, her name drew even more unwelcome attention. After she left school, she published some poetry under a *nom de plume* and decided to keep using it. Kristina studied screen writing under Milan Kundera at Prague's film school FAMU and fell in love with Josef Koudelka, the photographer who shot some of the most dramatic images of the Soviet invasion while standing on top of a tank. Koudelka's photos were smuggled out of Prague and published in London's *Sunday Times*, making him internationally famous. He left Prague to take up a job in France, but Kristina decided to remain.

In 1969, she befriended Vaclav and Olga Havel, who came to see a play she'd written that was shut down by the state after just two performances. In 1977, when the Communist Party asked her to put her name to its anti-Charter document she refused. This was career suicide, but she knew that signing it would defame an honest man and betray a friend. After that, all her film work dried up and she was dismissed from her job at a children's publishing house. Former colleagues shunned her. 'I would run into them on the stairs in the subway,' she says, 'and they would give me a look, as if to say, "You stupid person."'

Kristina took on the job at the university as a dormitory receptionist where she organised unofficial film seminars for students and passed the days wondering if she'd ever make a film again. The Velvet Revolution liberated her. Now in her late forties, she was anxious to make up for lost time. She created more than a dozen features investigating the crimes of Nazism and communism.

While making the Grebenicek documentary, she was called at home by several people who refused to name themselves, telling her to drop the matter and not make trouble for other people. After she mentioned in a radio interview that she was taping the calls, they abruptly stopped. 'It's still present here today,' she told me. 'The spectre of communism.'[15]

PRESIDENT HAVEL'S POPULARITY, inevitably, began to wane as the national mood soured. In January 1996, Olga, his wife of thirty-two years, died of cancer. Olga had been a much-loved figure among the Czech people and when Havel married young actress Dagmar Veskrnova less than a year later, it went over poorly. Dagmar was perceived as demanding and imperious, and her husband, the moralistic president, was jeered in the tabloid media as an old man besotted by a pushy younger woman.

As someone who'd spent his life railing against utopian thinking, Havel was irritated by complaints that he'd promised to bring universal justice and happiness to his people. In a speech accepting an honorary doctorate, he said:

> *Many Czechs are angry with me because love and truth haven't*
> *yet prevailed over lies and hatred, and they hold me responsible.*
> *Those who complain that the promise remains unfulfilled have*

*turned this ideal into an illusion … No one will provide the
perfect formula for human happiness. And no one can. But there
are lights to show us the way.*[16]

HAVEL'S PRESIDENCY, for all its failures and missed opportunities, must be regarded as a success. The nation became safer, freer and more prosperous during his years in office. As head of state, he embedded and normalised democratic habits. As the nation's figurehead, he used his immense prestige to elevate his country's standing in the world, and to encourage his citizens to rise above small-minded self-interest. At the unveiling of a monument to T. G. Masaryk, Havel quoted his predecessor's words: 'We had been buried when we ceased to live the larger life.'

MASARYK'S PHRASE HAD BEEN weirdly prescient. The statues of the founder-president that had sprung up after his death in 1937 had to be buried for safekeeping two years later when the Nazis invaded. After the Allied victory in 1945, the statues were pulled up and re-installed, but had to be buried again after the communist takeover. The zombie Masaryks rose briefly from their graves once more during the Prague Spring to enjoy a few brief months in the sun until the Soviet invasion sent them back underground.

Prague is still wrestling with its communist monuments. The presence of a heroic statue of Soviet field marshal Ivan Konev, erected in 1980, was deeply resented in Prague. The marshal, who led the Red Army into the city at the end of the war, had also been complicit in the 1968 Soviet invasion. Protestors splashed pink paint on the statue. After repeated attacks, the local mayor, Ondrej Kolar, complained he was tired 'of polishing the marshal's boots', and had the statue surrounded by a tarpaulin so his council would no longer incur the cost of removing the paint and graffiti.[17] Russian diplomats objected and implied the mayor was a closet Nazi. When the statue was taken down, Kolar went into hiding after receiving numerous death threats, allegedly originating in Russia.[18]

The Soviet tank memorial in Kinsky Square (previously Soviet Tank-Crew Square) was another unwelcome monument. Like the Marian Column, it had come to signify subjugation by a foreign imperial power. In 1991, Czech artist David Cerny and a group of friends solved the problem by painting the Soviet tank entirely pink. Cerny was briefly arrested for 'hooliganism', and the tank was repainted green. But then fifteen newly elected Civic Forum parliamentarians came out to paint the monster pink again. The tank's status as a national monument was revoked, and the council moved it to Lesany, thirty kilometres south of the city. In 2011, a replica of the pink tank, with a gigantic erect middle finger sticking out of the turret, was placed on a barge and sailed down the Vltava to celebrate the twentieth anniversary of the withdrawal of Soviet troops.

VACLAV HAVEL LEFT THE presidency in 2003. In retirement, he wrote his final play, *Leaving*, which told the story of a former statesman who is stripped of the accoutrements of power and must come to terms with being defined by his years in office. *Leaving* was well received by audiences and critics and Havel, despite his poor health, was able to direct the film adaptation. After decades of chain smoking, he became increasingly ill with respiratory issues. There was a chain of hospitalisations and near-death experiences before he died in 2011.

The people of faraway Tbilisi, Georgia, have erected a statue to Vaclav Havel, but, at the time of writing, none exist in Prague. Prague's airport has been named for the playwright-president, as well as a small open space next to the new building of the National Theatre, even though he hated the glass-and-concrete edifice. The Vaclav Havel Library has found a modest home on Ostrovni Street in the New Town. The library feels warm and welcoming and it honours the memory, better than any grandiose statue could, of one of the largest human beings of his time.

PRAGUE NOW HAS a permanent memorial to the sacrifice of Jan Palach and his fellow human torch Jan Zajic. At the top of Wenceslas Square, in the place where Palach lit his match, a contorted cross is embedded in the paving stones. It twists gently and rises up at the head, implying some kind of resurrection, or the need for one.

16 JANUARY 2019: I step off the tram on Vodickova Street and join the tide of people flowing into Wenceslas Square. Television cameras are present to broadcast the event, a commemoration of the fiftieth anniversary of Jan Palach's self-immolation. A video screen displays one of his final statements: *People must fight against the evil they feel equal to at that moment.*

Tonight's ceremony is as much about the present as it is about the past. The event has been put together by a group called One Million Moments for Democracy, an organisation of citizens alarmed by the assault on the integrity of their hard-won democratic institutions by unscrupulous politicians and oligarchs.

Neither the republic's president Milos Zeman nor its prime

minister Andrej Babis is here. Zeman, a crude anti-Muslim demagogue is strongly supportive of Russian foreign policy, and has joked with Vladimir Putin about 'liquidating' journalists. His vocal support for Russia and China inspired a group of guerrilla art-activists to enter the Presidential Palace disguised as chimney sweeps; the protestors climbed onto the palace roof and hoisted a gigantic pair of red underpants on the presidential flagpole. The group later released a statement: 'Today we hung a banner over the castle for a man who is not ashamed of anything.'[19]

Prime Minister Andrej Babis, a far more powerful figure, is a billionaire who controls a large segment of the Czech media. Babis entered politics promoting himself as a businessman and a political cleanskin, but archival documents indicate that in 1980 Babis was recruited by the StB as an informant. After two years' service, he was promoted to agent status and given the code name Bures. Babis insisted he'd been wrongly identified in the documents, but a court in Bratislava dismissed his claim.

Support for the nationalist and populist parties is stronger in the regions than in Prague. Here, as in so many other places, a struggle for the nation's soul is waged between the cosmopolitan metropolis and the disgruntled hinterland. Authoritarianism is resurgent across central and eastern Europe. Neighbouring Hungary and Poland have repudiated the democratic gains of 1989 and are now governed by conspiracy-minded majoritarian regimes, unhindered by their cowed news organisations or a compliant judiciary. Prime Minister Viktor Orban of Hungary, once a liberal hero of 1989, is openly contemptuous of Western liberal democracy.

Paul Wilson remains optimistic that the Czechs will stick with liberal democracy. 'I think the Czech society is quite strong in ways that it doesn't realise itself,' he said. 'The Czechs are a very convivial people. They're natural organisers. At a time when it was basically illegal to create organisations that weren't run or monitored by the Communist Party, there were all kinds of invisible groupings. They're very good at organising on that level. This was something that Havel always tried to encourage. I think he was actually successful at that.'[20]

*

WENCESLAS SQUARE IS NOW filled to capacity. The crowd is mostly in their twenties and thirties. The man next to me hoists his daughter onto his shoulders and she taps her small hands on his head in time with the music. On stage, a succession of writers and musicians take turns making speeches and singing songs. Dana Nemcova, a Charter 77 activist, is helped to the stage. Thin taper candles are passed around and soon the square is dotted with thousands of tiny points of light. At 7.30 pm, the crowd forms a procession that flows down the ancient streets into the Old Town Square and gathers around the statue of Jan Hus. The grand monuments on the square's periphery – the Old Town Hall and its Astronomical Clock, the Tyn Church, the tall baroque houses – look down on us like a circle of giants, observing the scene from the back rows.

The speeches conclude and the crowd sings 'Where is My Home?' It sounds sweet, sad and fearful in the night air:

> *Where is my home?*
> *Where is my home?*
> *Water roars across the meadows,*
> *Pinewoods rustle among the crags …*

ACKNOWLEDGEMENTS

FIRSTLY, I WOULD LIKE to thank Prague City of Literature for generously granting me a two-month stay in 2019, and to Radka Eismannová and Kateřina Bajo from the Municipal Library of Prague for their very kind assistance and for organising a wonderful author event at the Museum of Czech Literature.

I owe a huge debt of gratitude to David Vaughan, journalist, broadcaster, academic, longstanding Prague resident and the author of *Battle of the Airwaves*, who provided excellent editorial advice on the manuscript. David has a sophisticated and compendious knowledge of his adopted city, and his journalism with Radio Prague has contributed enormously to international understanding of Czech history. He was a kind and generous host throughout my two-month stay.

It was David who introduced me to Marek Toman, author, diplomat, translator, pirate actor and prince of Vinohrady. I cannot thank Marek enough for his friendship and for introducing me to so much of the history and cultural life of his city.

'Tell me,' Marek asked me on our first meeting, 'Do you know a Czech person in Australia named Jaroslav Kovaříček?' and as it happened, I *did* know Jaroslav – his name was one of the first that came to mind when I set myself the task of writing this book, and I owe him a huge debt of gratitude for his insights into Bohemian history, literature and music.

A chance conversation with Canadian historian Gwynne Dyer put me in touch with Paul Wilson, former Plastic Person of the Universe and translator of Havel, Hrabal and Škvorecký. I had expected that writing about the normalisation era would be a gloomy business, but Paul helped me to see the passionate beating heart beneath its apparently lifeless exterior, and as a result, I enjoyed writing that chapter most of all.

I am filled with gratitude and admiration for Kristina Vlachova, both as a filmmaker and as an individual who was able to hold fast to truth and friendship in a bad time. My warm thanks also to Josephyne Oliveri, who was able to recall so many subtle and telling details of post-revolutionary Prague. I am so very glad she was there to bear witness to it all and that she had the presence of mind to take photos while we were there. I am grateful to Katrin Bock for her vivid account of the 17 November student demonstration; to Anna O'Grady for her stories of growing up under communism; to the brilliant science historian Robyn Arianrhod, author of *Einstein's Heroes* and *Thomas Harriot: A Life in Science*, who gave me editorial advice on the cavalcade of scientific geniuses that have passed through Prague over the centuries; to historian Paul Ham for his companionship over several days in the city; to Catbird Press for the kind permission to quote the poetry of Jaroslav Seifert translated by Ewald Osers; to the ghost of the late Slovak author Ladislav Mňačko for allowing me to write undisturbed in his apartment for two months; to the Cafés Slavia, Liberal, Louvre and Ideal for their coffee, soup and beer; and a tip of the hat to Richard

Flanagan – engineer of human souls and friend of the carnivorous spotted quoll, for his timely advice.

I'm so thankful as always to the utterly magnificent Brigitta Doyle and Lachlan McLaine at HarperCollins, and to Nathan Burton and Mark Campbell for the beautiful cover design, which so elegantly incorporates the Czech, German and Jewish elements of the city. Mary Rennie, my editor, was wonderful – her enthusiasm, insight and precision lifted the text and helped me weed the overgrown garden of my first draft. I must also thank Kári Gíslason and Elizabeth Troyeur for their support and advice.

And finally, all my love and thanks to my wife, Khym, who brought her prodigious skills as a librarian and researcher to this book. I cunningly beguiled her into this project by casually dangling the story of the Winter Queen and King in front of her. Khym's penetrating and sympathetic grasp of human nature, and her wise assessments of the great and not-so-great figures of history were invaluable to me.

TIMELINE

c.500 BCE	The Boii enter the Vltava basin area.
c.100 BCE	A Germanic tribe, the Marcomanni, enters Bohemia, driving out the Boii.
c.500 CE	Slavic tribes enter the Bohemian lands.
c.800	Slavic settlement established on Hradcany Hill.
862	Missionaries Cyril & Methodius enter the Czech lands to translate the bible into Slavonic.
870	Prague Castle's first stone buildings are constructed.
880s	Duke Borivoj of the Premyslids makes Hradcany his seat. Borivoj and his wife Ludmila are baptised.
921	Borivoj's grandson Wenceslas crowned duke of Bohemia.
c.926	Original church of St. Vitus constructed at Prague Castle.
935	Wenceslas assassinated by Boleslav I.
950	Bohemia incorporated into Holy Roman Empire.
970s	Prague awarded a bishopric. Vysehrad established on the right bank of the Vltava river.
1096	Pauper crusaders invade Prague and raze the original Jewish quarter.
1142	New Jewish quarter established between the Old Town and the river.
1172	Judith Bridge across the Vltava completed.

1212	Holy Roman Emperor issues Golden Bull of Sicily, making Bohemia a kingdom.
1230	King Wenceslas I grants Prague's Old Town official status.
1234	Agnes of Prague founds hospital and a cloister in the Old Town.
1235	Old Town enclosed by defensive walls and moat.
1253	Otakar II crowned King of Bohemia.
1257	Otakar II formally establishes Mala Strana, invites German craftsmen and merchants to live there.
1262	Otakar II issues *Statuta Judaeorum*, granting the Jewish community self-administration.
1270	Old-New Synagogue built in Jewish quarter.
1278	Otakar II killed at the Battle of Marchfeld.
	Prague occupied by Otto V of Brandenburg.
1306	Wenceslas III, the last Premyslid king, is assassinated.
1310	Bohemian estates elect John of Luxembourg as king.
1316	Charles IV born in Prague.
1338	Foundation of the Old Town Hall.
1342	Judith Bridge destroyed by flooding.
1344	Construction of St. Vitus Cathedral begins.
1346	King John the Blind killed at the Battle of Crecy.
1347	Charles IV crowned King of Bohemia.
	Prague becomes capital of Holy Roman Empire.
1348	Charles founds the New Town and establishes Prague University.
1357	Construction of Charles Bridge begins.
1370	Construction of Tyn Church begins on Old Town Square.
1378	Charles IV dies and is succeeded by his son Wenceslas IV.
1380	Outbreak of Black Death in Prague.
1389	Easter pogrom of Jewish quarter.
1391	Bethlehem Chapel founded in Old Town.

1393   Murder of Jan Nepomuk.

1402   Charles Bridge completed.

        Jan Hus appointed preacher at Bethlehem Chapel.

1410   Astronomical Clock installed in City Hall.

1415   Execution of Jan Hus at Constance.

1419   First defenestration of Prague.

1420   Hussite Wars begin.

        Jan Zizka triumphs at battle of Vitkov Hill.

1424   Death of Jan Zizka.

1436   *Compactata* between Church and Bohemian Utraquists brings
        Hussite wars to an end.

1437   Emperor Sigismund, the last Luxembourg King of Bohemia, dies.

1458   George of Podebrady crowned King of Bohemia.

1493   Vladislav Hall constructed at Prague Castle.

1526   Bohemian estates elect Habsburg Archduke Ferdinand as king.

1530s   Pinkas Synagogue constructed in Jewish quarter.

1560   Queen Anne's Summer Palace opens.

1573   Rabbi Loew moves to Prague.

1576   Rudolf II elected as Holy Roman Emperor.

1583   Rudolf II relocates from Vienna to Prague Castle.

1584   John Dee and Edward Kelley come to Prague.

1586   Jewish Town Hall constructed.

1599   Tycho Brahe appointed imperial mathematician by Rudolf.

        Brahe invites Johannes Kepler to assist him.

1601   Brahe and Kepler begin work on the star chart, *The Rudolfine Tables*.

        Brahe dies of uremia.

1609   Kepler publishes *Astronomia Nova* on planetary motion.

        Rudolf II signs Letter of Majesty, guaranteeing religious toleration.

1611   Passauer army invades and plunders Prague.

1612	Death of Rudolf II.
	Emperor Matthias moves imperial court back to Vienna.
1618	Second Defenestration of Prague.
	Thirty Years' War commences.
1619	Winter King and Queen crowned at St Vitus Cathedral.
1620	Defeat of the Czech nobles' uprising at White Mountain.
	Frederick and Elizabeth flee from Prague.
1621	Twenty-seven Czech Protestant leaders executed in Old Town Square.
1623	Wallenstein Palace constructed in Mala Strana.
1631	Prague occupied by Protestant Saxon army.
1635	The Peace of Prague brings civil war within the Holy Roman Empire to a close.
1648	Hradcany and Mala Strana occupied and looted by Swedish armies.
	Treaty of Westphalia ends Thirty Years' War.
	Prague's population has shrunk to 20,000.
1650	Marian column erected in the Old Town Square.
1660s	Czernin Palace constructed.
1714	Giorgio Diodato establishes Prague's first coffeehouse.
1740	Maria Theresa accedes to Austrian throne, sparking the War of Austrian Succession.
1741	Occupation of Prague by French and Bavarian armies.
1743	Austrians retake Prague.
	Maria Theresa crowned queen of Bohemia in St Vitus Cathedral.
1744	Prussian army invades Prague, but is expelled one month later.
1755	St Nicholas Church built in Mala Strana.
1771	Prague's population grows to 80,000.
1775	Maria Theresa introduces education reforms.
1784	Hradcany, Mala Strana, Old Town and New Town merge into a single civic entity.

1787   Mozart's *Don Giovanni* premieres at Estates Theatre.

1806   Holy Roman Empire dissolved during Napoleonic wars.

Bohemia incorporated into the Habsburg Austrian Empire.

1818   National Museum of Prague founded at top of Wenceslas Square.

1837   Population of Prague exceeds 100,000.

1845   Rail line established between Prague and Vienna.

1848   Slavic Congress convened in Prague.

Prague student uprising quelled by Austrian troops.

1850   Jewish quarter renamed Josefov.

1855   Bozena Nemcova publishes *The Grandmother*.

1862   Sokol athletic club founded.

1874   Bedrich Smetana begins composing *Ma Vlast*.

1881   Grand opening of National Theatre of Prague.

1884   Café Slavia opens.

1887   Ernst Mach photographs shockwaves at Charles University.

1893   Josefov's slums demolished and replaced by Parisian apartments.

1899   Hilsner trial.

1900   Prague's population exceeds 200,000.

1914   First World War breaks out.

Bohemian troops conscripted to fight for Austria-Hungary.

1918   Republic of Czechoslovakia founded by Tomas Masaryk.

Marian Column torn down in Old Town Square.

1921   Foundation of Czechoslovak Communist Party.

First performance of Capek's *RUR* in Prague.

First edition of Hasek's *The Good Soldier* Sveyk published.

1922   Greater Prague created by uniting historic centre with the suburbs.

1925   Franz Kafka's *The Trial* is published posthumously.

1933   Konrad Henlein forms Sudetendeutsche movement.

1935   Benes succeeds Masaryk as president.

        André Breton and Paul Eluard visit Prague.

1937   Death of Tomas Masaryk.

1938   Munich Agreement forces Czechoslovakia to cede its Sudeten
        territories to Nazi Germany.

1939   Nicholas Winton sets up Czech Kindertransport to rescue Jewish
        children.

        Nazi Germany invades remnant of Bohemia and Moravia.

1941   Jewish transports from Prague begin.

        Terezin refitted as a concentration camp.

1942   Reinhard Heydrich assassinated in Prague.

1945   Prague Uprising.

        The Red Army liberates the city from Nazi control.

        Benes returns as president of the third republic.

1945   Expulsion of Germans from Czechoslovakia begins.

1948   Communist coup initiates four decades of one-party rule.

        Death of Jan Masaryk.

        Benes resigns as president, succeeded by Klement Gottwald.

1950   Milada Horakova show trial and execution.

1952   Stalinist terror reaches peak with Slansky show trial and
        executions.

1953   Death of President Klement Gottwald.

        Antonin Novotny becomes party leader.

1955   World's largest Stalin statue unveiled at Letna Park.

1960   President Novotny introduces new constitution, declares
        socialism to be fully achieved.

1962   Stalin statue demolished.

1965   Prague students invite Allen Ginsberg to Prague.

        Vaclav Havel writes *The Memorandum*.

1966	Vera Chytilova's *Daisies* released.
1967	Speakers at Fourth Czechoslovak Writers' Congress criticise communist regime.
1968	Alexander Dubcek becomes party leader.
	Dubcek launches reform program and permits freedom of speech.
	Prague Spring crushed by Soviet invasion.
	Dubcek capitulates in Moscow, calls for 'normalisation'.
1969	Jan Palach self-immolates in Wenceslas Square.
	Purge of party membership.
	Dubcek replaced as party leader by Gustav Husak.
1974	Vaclav Havel writes open letter to 'Dr Husak'.
	Plastic People of the Universe concert-goers attacked by police.
1975	Czechoslovakia signs Helsinki human rights accords.
1976	Trial of the Plastic People and other musicians.
1977	Vaclav Havel and others form Charter 77.
1979	Havel sentenced to four years in prison.
1980	Prague's population exceeds 1,000,000.
1987	Mikhail Gorbachev visits Prague.
	Husak replaced as party leader by Milos Jakes.
1988	Czechoslovakia 88 Symposium in Prague.
1989	Police attack student march in Narodni Street Protests force party leadership to resign.
	Vaclav Havel elected first president of post-communist Czechoslovakia.
1990	StB officially dissolved.
1991	Lustration laws introduced.
1993	Czechs and Slovaks split into separate nations.
	Havel becomes first president of Czech Republic.
2003	Havel leaves office.
2011	Death of Vaclav Havel.

ENDNOTES

Introduction

1 Fermor, p.267.

2 Sayer, p.14.

3 Seifert, p.61.

4 Demetz, *Prague in Black and Gold*, p.329.

5 Havel, New Year's Address to the Nation.

6 www.theguardian.com/world/2016/oct/25/nobody-calls-it-czechia-czech-republic-new-fails-catch-on

7 Klapste, p.4.

8 Stach, p.23.

1. 1990

1 www.nybooks.com/articles/1990/01/18/the-revolution-of-the-magic-lantern/

2 Wilson, *Prague*, p.8.

3 Klima, p.414.

4 www.nytimes.com/1990/01/21/nyregion/insider-offers-look-at-czech-revolt.html

5 Tyrell, p.cxxi.

6 Hrabal, *I Served the King of England*, p.1.

7 www.newyorker.com/magazine/2003/02/17/exit-havel

8 Zantovsky, p.343.

9 Havel, New Year's Address to the Nation, 1990.

10 Havel, Speech to Demonstrators in Wenceslas Square, 10 December.

11 Wordsworth, 'The French Revolution as it Appeared to Enthusiasts at its Commencement'.

12 *Granta 30, New Europe*, Spring 1990, pp.127–28.

2. The Stone Crown of the World

1   Strabo, VII, ch.1.

2   Procopius, *The History of the Wars*, VII.14.

3   Teich, p.29.

4   Davies, p.829.

5   Cosmas, 1.3.

6   Vincent of Prague, quoted in Wolverton, p.ii.

7   www.christianitytoday.com/history/people/missionaries/cyril-and-methodius.html

8   Wolverton, p.152.

9   Wolverton, p.152.

10 Kantor, pp.7–8.

11 Kalhous, p.16.

12 Saunders et al., p.1015–16.

13 Saunders et al., p.1023.

14 Bažant et al., p.14.

15 Gabor, (ed.), pp.128–29.

16 Nemec, pp.41–64.

17 Cosmas, p.186.

18 Valley, p.53.

19 Demetz *Prague in Black and Gold*, p.51.

20 Fourth Letter of St. Clare, web.mit.edu/aorlando/www/SaintJohnCHI/Readings/ClareLettersAgnes.pdf

21 Demetz, *Prague in Black and Gold*, p.35.

22 Demetz, *Prague in Black and Gold*, p.35.

23 www.habsburger.net/en/stories/tu-felix-austria-nube

24 Alvarez, journals.plos.org/plosone/article?id=10.1371/journal.pone.0005174

25 Demetz, *Prague in Black and Gold*, p.63.

26 Demetz, *Prague in Black and Gold*, p.60.

27 Vlček, pp.23–24.

28 Geary (ed.), p.547.

29 Geary (ed.), p.547.

30 Demetz, *Prague in Black and Gold*, p.74.

31 Froissart, p.104.

32 Vlcek, p.21.

33 Betts, p.57.

34 Bažant et al., p.35.

35 www.nytimes.com/1977/06/05/archives/prague-a-capital-of-humane-proportions-pragues-cathedrals-castles-a.html

36 Umberto Decembrio, www.charles700.com/karluv-zivot#chapter-08

37 Boehm, pp.37–160.

38 Benes Krabice of Veitmile, *The Czech Reader*, pp.37–38.

39 The Golden Bull of the Emperor Charles IV, 1356 AD, avalon.law.yale.edu/medieval/golden.asp

40 On the flooding of Prague that occurred after continual rains', *Elizabeth Jane Weston: Collected Writings*, p.159.

41 Demetz, *Prague in Black and Gold*, p.100.

42 Vlček, p.28.

43 www.charles700.com/karluv-zivot#chapter-14

3. The Night of Antichrist

1 www.michaelhaldane.com/HusbandmanandDeath

2 Bažant et al., p.45.

3 Adler, p.72.

4 McCulloch, p.556.

5 scholarship.rollins.edu/cgi/viewcontent.cgi?article=1006&context=mls

6 web.etf.cuni.cz/ETFKCD-63-version1-disertace.pdf

7 Fudge, *The Magnificent Ride*, p.48.

8 Spinka p.38

9 Spinka, p.119.

10 Spinka, p.130.

11 Swanson, p.128.

12 Spinka, pp.138–39.

13 Pavlicek & Smahel, p.57.

14 Van Niekerk, www.academia.edu/20079397/Jan_Hus_Church_Reformer_with_an_ineradicable_influence

15 Fudge, *The Magnificent Ride*, p.210.

16 Fudge, 'Neither mine nor thine', p.25.

17   Kaminsky, pp.310–11.

18   Cosmas, p.37.

19   Fudge, *The Magnificent Ride*, p.171.

20   Kaminsky, p.372.

21   Lawrence of Bresova, quoted in Heymann, *John Zizka*, p.137.

22   Heymann, *John Zizka*, p.168.

23   Demetz, *Prague in Black and Gold*, p.165.

24   Heymann, *John Zizka*, p.442.

25   Bažant et al., pp.56–57.

26   Klassen, *Letters of the Rozmberk Sisters*, p.2.

27   Klassen, 'The Public and Domestic Faces of Ulrich of Rozmberk', p.713.

28   'Why Some People See Ghosts and Other Apparitions', *Psychology Today*, 9 July 2015, www.psychologytoday.com/au/blog/out-the-ooze/201507/why-some-people-see-ghosts-and-other-apparitions

29   Erben, 'Noonday Witch' (trans. Susan Reynolds), blogs.bl.uk/european/2013/10/the-noonday-witch.html

30   Beaune & Le Goff, pp.186–87.

31   George, p.81.

4. The Great Work

1   Kachlik, *Biographical Sketch*, p.151.

2   Marshall, p.30.

3   Bukovinska, p.203

4   Jurkowlaniec, p.18

5   Marshall, p.85.

6   Belozerskaya, pp.206–7.

7   Marshall, p.150.

8   Moryson, p.30.

9   Holeton, p.386.

10   Moryson, p.30

11   Moryson, p.29, and in Hughes, pp.491–95.

12   Wechsler, p.1.

13   Tractate Sanhedrin 38b, www.come-and-hear.com/sanhedrin/sanhedrin_38.html

14 www.jmberlin.de/en/golem-from-mysticism-to-minecraft

15 Ripellino, p.103.

16 Fitzgerald, p.69.

17 Dee, J., *The Mathematicall Praeface to Elements of Geometrie of Euclid of Megara*: www.gutenberg.org/files/22062/22062-h/main.html

18 Dee, J., *A True and Faithful Relation*, p.215

19 Dee, J., *A True and Faithful Relation*, Part III.

20 Woolley, p.270.

21 Bažant et al., p.76.

22 From *Mysterium Cosmographicum*, quoted in Sagan, publicism.info/science/cosmos/4.html

23 Koestler, p.224.

24 Koestler, p.274.

25 Koestler, p.278.

26 Wyner, p.34.

27 Koestler, p.303.

28 Koestler, p.285.

29 Evans, p.198.

30 Evans, *Rudolf II*, p.198.

31 Marshall, p.209.

32 Evans, *Rudolf II*, p.196.

33 Marshall, p.221.

34 www.habsburger.net/en/chapter/ferdinand-ii-catholic-fundamentalist

35 Matusiak, p.373.

36 Koestler, p.391.

5. A Bohemia of the Soul

1 'Epithalamion', www.luminarium.org/sevenlit/donne/palatine.php

2 Demetz, *Prague in Black and Gold*, p.226.

3 Matusiak, p.115.

4 Wedgwood, p.91.

5 Shaw & Demy (eds), p.797.

6 Wedgwood, p.460.

7 Matusiak, p.100.

8   Wedgwood, p.128.

9   Škvorecký, *Daedalus*, p.111

10   Mortimer, *The Origins of the Thirty Years War*, p.228.

11   Mortimer, Wallenstein, p.1.

12   Matusiak, p.9.

13   Wedgwood, p.391

14   blogs.helsinki.fi/natlibfi-bulletin/?page_id=794

15   Online Etymology Dictionary, www.etymonline.com/word/baroque

16   Miller, p.52.

17   Miller, p.64.

18   'Maria Theresa's Political Testament (1749-50)', germanhistorydocs.ghi-dc.org/docpage.cfm?docpage_id=3666

19   Mahan, J. Alexander, Maria Theresa of Austria, Thomas Y. Crowell, 1932, p.228

20   Blanning, *Frederick the Great*, p.230.

21   Davies, p.649.

22   Jenkins, ch.13.

23   Evans, 'Maria Theresa', p.17.

24   Duffy, p.151.

25   www.habsburger.net/en/chapter/difficult-relationship-maria-theresas-prague-legacy

26   Schieder, p.110.

27   Newman, *The Army of Maria Theresa*, p.30.

28   Demetz, *Prague in Black and Gold*, p.246.

29   Hopkins, Donald R., The Greatest Killer: Smallpox in History, University of Chicago Press, 1983, p.65.

30   www.habsburger.net/en/persons/person/gerard-van-swieten

31   www.habsburger.net/en/chapter/maria-theresas-final-years-widowhood-and-death

32   Davies, p.672.

33   Blanning, *Joseph II*, p.56.

34   Mozart, p.227.

35   Solomon, p.419.

36   Rushton, pp.124–25.

37   'When Casanova Met Mozart', *Smithsonian Magazine*, 21 March 2012.

6. Sleeping on a Volcano

1   Sked, p.28.

2   Sealsfield, pp.85–86 & 69.

3   Sealsfield, p.88.

4   Iggers, pp.52 & 56.

5   Iggers, p.79.

6   oll.libertyfund.org/titles/tocqueville-the-recollections-of-alexis-de-tocqueville-1896

7   Pech, pp.3–4.

8   Palacky, 'Letter to Frankfurt', books.openedition.org/ceup/2345?lang=en

9   Sperber, p.130.

10 Pech, p.93.

11 'Manifesto of the First Slavonic Congress to the Nations of Europe', www.jstor.org/stable/4203948

12 Large, pp.95–97.

13 Cervinka, p.150.

14 Selver, p.143.

15 Masaryk, *Talks*, p.109.

16 www.vaclavhavel.cz/en/index/calendar/1664/t-g-masaryk-the-hilsner-affair-texts-from-1898-1900

17 *In Their Own Words*, podcast, Radio Prague, Part I, 'Tomas Garrigue Masaryk: We Are All in the Same Boat'.

18 Abshire, p.41.

19 Chubykalo (ed.), p.146.

20 Wheeler et al., p.235.

21 Pawel, p.4.

22 Pawel, p.317.

23 Agnew, p.164

24 Hasek, p.213.

25 Ripellino, p.230.

26 Steiner, p.28.

27 Kennan, p.117.

28 Binet, p.119

29 Steiner, p.29.

30 Roshwald, p.163.

31 Morelon, p.173.

32 Kafka, *Letters to Felice*, January 1917.

33 Gilbert, p.158.

34 Declaration of Independence of the Czechoslovak Nation by its Provisional
    Government: archive.org/details/declarationofind00czec/page/n5/mode/2up

35 Bažant et al., p.242.

36 Pawel, p.374.

37 Orzoff, p.88.

38 Masaryk, *Talks*, p.185.

39 Orzoff, p.102.

40 Orzoff, p.101.

41 Albright, pp.85–86.

7. The Black Crow

1   Bruegel, p.89.

2   Lukes, *Czechoslovakia*, p.58.

3   Bruegel, pp.160–61.

4   Lukes, *Czechoslovakia*, p.51.

5   Bruegel, p.79.

6   Skilling, p.645.

7   Lukes, *Czechoslovakia*, p.69.

8   Skilling, p.643

9   Sayer, 'André Breton', p.67.

10 Lukes & Goldstein (eds), p.260.

11 Bouverie, p.221.

12 Manchester, p.291.

13 Sayer, *Coasts of Bohemia*, p.221.

14 Fermor, p.225.

15 Szczygiel, p.54.

16 Szczygiel, p.57.

17 Kershaw, p.171.

18 Szczygiel, p.61.

19 www.nytimes.com/2015/05/17/books/review/goebbels-a-biography-by-peter-longerich.html

20 Bouverie, p.147.

21 Rothkirchen, p.60

22 Lukes, *Czechoslovakia*, p.127.

23 Adamthwaite, p.184.

24 Robbins, p.692.

25 Bouverie, p.205.

26 Albright, pp.199–20.

27 Kershaw, p.14

28 Chamberlain & Self, p.307.

29 Gedye, p.392.

30 Faber, p.209.

31 Lukes, *Czechoslovakia*, p.185.

32 Wheeler-Bennett, p.92.

33 *British Foreign Policy Documents, 1919–1939*, p.678.

34 Lukes, *Czechoslovakia*, p.210.

35 Radio Prague: www.radio.cz/en/section/archives/the-virgin-and-child-in-the-battle-against-hitler-1

36 Davies, p.990.

37 Lukes, *Czechoslovakia*, p.219.

38 Lukes, *Czechoslovakia*, p.232.

39 Lukes, *Czechoslovakia*, p.234.

40 *British Foreign Policy Documents, 1919–1939,* pp. 519–20.

41 Zeman & Klimek, p.128.

42 www.bbc.co.uk/archive/chamberlain-addresses-the-nation-on-his-negotiations-for-peace/zjrjgwx

43 Chamberlain & Self, p.349

44 Lukes, *Czechoslovakia*, p.251.

45 *New York Times*, 1 October 1938, p.2.

46 Christofferson, p.16.

47 *New York Times*, 1 October 1938, p.4.

48 *Hansard*, House of Commons Debate, 5 October 1938, vol. 339, cols 361, 365.

49 Bažant et al., p.426.

50 Churchill, *Gathering Storm*, p.272.

51 Albright, pp.167–68.

52 Heimann, p.94.

53 Bryant, p.42.

54 Kennan, p.7.

55 Heimann, p.127.

56 www.jta.org/1938/10/12/archive/praha-jewish-editor-dies-after-suicide-pact-with-wife

57 Kennan, p.86.

58 Radio Prague, www.radio.cz/en/section/archives/occupation-and-betrayal-1

59 www.auschwitz.dk/Winton.htm#selection-211.1-216.2

60 Radio Prague, www.radio.cz/en/section/curraffrs/new-photographs-illuminate-nazi-invasion-of-czechoslovakia

8. From Darkness Into Darkness

1 Kennan, p.117.

2 Kennan, p.209.

3 Kennan, p.217 & 223.

4 Zeman & Klimek, pp.149–50.

5 Zeman & Klimek, pp.155–56.

6 *Fascism Doctrine and Institutions*, www.worldfuturefund.org/wffmaster/Reading/Germany/mussolini.htm

7 Bullock, p.527.

8 Gerwarth, p.221.

9 Bažant et al., p.322.

10 Bažant et al., p.323.

11 MacDonald, p.181.

12 Hohne, p.495.

13 Mastny, p.217.

14 parlinfo.aph.gov.au/parlInfo/search/display/display.w3p;query=Id:%22media/pressrel/P4B36%22

15 Justman, Z., 'My Terezin Diary', *New Yorker*, 16 September 2019.

16 Jelavich, p.277.

17 Klima, p.20.

18 www.holocaust.cz/en/history/events/embellishment-and-the-visit-of-the-international-committee-of-the-red-cross-to-terezin/

19 *Prisoner of Paradise,* BBC Documentary, Cineplex Odeon Films, 2002.

20 Jelavich, p.281.

21 Salle Fischermann interview, Danish Jewish Museum.

22 Judt, p.118.

23 Albright, p.502.

24 Zeman & Klimek, p.247.

25 Sayer, *Coasts of Bohemia*, p.240.

26 Bryant, p.216.

27 Kovaly, p. 39.

28 Kovaly, p. 27.

29 David Vaughan, *The Battle of the Airwaves*, www.radio.cz/en/section/curraffrs/the-battle-of-the-airwaves-the-extraordinary-story-of-czechoslovak-radio-and-the-1945-prague-uprising

30 Radio Prague, www.radio.cz/en/section/czech-history/prague-uprising-how-the-last-german-held-capital-fought-for-freedom

31 Manchester & Reid, p.918.

32 D'este, p.728.

33 Motl, Stanislav, Britons at Czechoslovakian Radio, Czech Radio, theaibs.tv/wp-content/uploads/2012/09/11378-Britons-at-Czechoslovakian-Radio-script.doc

34 Toland, p.1651.

35 Radio Prague, *Prague Uprising*, www.radio.cz/en/section/archives/prague-uprising-do-not-let-prague-be-destroyed

36 Kovaly, pp.44-45.

37 Taylor, p.185.

38 Demetz, *Prague in Danger*, p.353.

39 Quoted by Trotsky in 'Towards Capitalism or Towards Socialism?' www.marxists.org/archive/trotsky/1925/11/towards.htm

40 Albright, p.531.

41 Glassheim, *Cleansing*, p.50, and Bryant, p.237.

42 Merten, pp.116–24.

43 Glassheim, *Cleansing*, p.50.

44 Moravec, *Master of Spies*, p.221.

45 Connolly, K., 'Lida Baarova', *Guardian*, 9 November 2000.

46 Judt, p.26.

47 Adler, *Theresienstadt*, p.12.

48 Lukes, *On the Edge*, p.4.

49 www.youtube.com/watch?v=lhuhEWzQLi0

50 Schain (ed.), p.99.

51 Zeman, *The Masaryks*, p.208.

52 Sterling, p.88.

53 Zeman & Klimek, p.266.

54 www.radio.cz/en/section/czechs/klement-gottwald, and Agnew, p.232.

55 Kovaly, p.74.

56 Greene, Graham, *Ways of Escape*, Random House, 2011, pp.129–32.

57 Zeman & Klimek, p.272.

58 Lockhart, p.79.

59 www.vaclavhavel.cz/en/index/calendar/1664/t-g-masaryk-the-hilsner-affair-texts-from-1898-1900

9. Be With Us. We Are With You.

1 Lukes, 'Rudolf Slánský Affair', p.164.

2 Winder, p.508.

3 Kovaly, pp.99–100.

4 Kaplan, p.121.

5 Kovaly, p.116.

6 Szczygiel, p.86.

7 Szczygiel, p.89.

8 *The Lost World of Communism*, Episode 3, BBCTV.

9 Judt, p.186.

10 Lukes, 'Rudolf Slánský Affair', p.185.

11 www.radio.cz/en/section/arts/new-opera-brings-show-trial-of-milada-horakova-to-the-stage

12 Bažant et al., pp.349–50.

13 Škvorecký, 'Bohemia of the Soul', pp.114–15.

14 Iggers, p.302.

15 www.nytimes.com/1975/01/29/archives/antonin-novotny-70-dies-czech-dictator-195368.html

16 Szczygiel, p.93.

17 www.radio.cz/en/section/curraffrs/worlds-biggest-stalin-monument-would-have-turned-50-on-may-day

18 Skoug, p.6.

19 Blažek, p.41.

20 old.ustrcr.cz/data/pdf/publikace/bic/bic0212/034-047.pdf

21 Blažek, p.45.

22 Klima, p.213.

23 Levy, *So Many Heroes*, p.99.

24 Navratil (ed.), pp.65–67.

25 Levy, *So Many Heroes*, p.90.

26 Mlynar, *Nightfrost*, p.116.

27 Levy, *So Many Heroes*, p.194.

28 Navratil, p.86.

29 Mlynar, *Nightfrost*, p.103.

30 www.closeupfilmcentre.com/vertigo_magazine/volume-3-issue-9-spring-summer-2008/two-thousand-words-a-manifesto-for-prague/

31 Klima, p.233.

32 Levy, *So Many Heroes*, p.290.

33 www.radio.cz/en/section/one-on-one/czech-patriot-josef-cermak-i-could-not-live-under-communism

34 digitalarchive.wilsoncenter.org/document/117114

35 Transcript of Leonid Brezhnev's Telephone Conversation with Alexander Dubček, 13 August 1968, nsarchive2.gwu.edu/nsa/publications/DOC_readers/psread/doc81.htm

36 Gough, p.171.

37 Mlynar, *Nightfrost*, p.146.

38 Levy, *So Many Heroes*, p.349.

39 Levy, *So Many Heroes*, p. 234.

40 Jaroslav Kovaricek, interview with the author.

41 Dubcek, p.186.

42 www.telegraph.co.uk/news/features/3637726/Dont-forget-Czechoslovakia.html

43 Levy, *So Many Heroes*, pp.371–73.

44 Navratli (ed.), p.463.

45 Mlynar, *Nightfrost*, p.196.

46 web.stanford.edu/group/tomzgroup/pmwiki/uploads/0346-1968-09-KS-a-EYJ.pdf

47 Mlynar, *Nightfrost*, p.217.

48 Mlynar, 'Invasion 1968'.

49 www.radio.cz/en/section/arts/director-ivan-fila-on-final-cut-hollywood-kitsch-and-prague-spring-hero-frantisek-kriegel

50 web.stanford.edu/group/tomzgroup/pmwiki/uploads/0346-1968-09-KS-a-EYJ.pdf

51 Klima, p.6.

10. The Second Culture

1 Author interview with Paul Wilson.

2 Levy, *So Many Heroes*, p.508.

3 www.rferl.org/a/debate_that_wont_die_havel_and_kundera_on_whether_protest_is_worthwhile/24448679.html

4 West, p.415.

5 Zantovsky, p.120, and West, p.415.

6 Havel, *Disturbing the Peace*, p.180

7 Havel, *Disturbing the Peace*, p.6.

8 www.radio.cz/en/section/witness/jaroslava-moserova-remembering-jan-palach

9 Levy, *So Many Heroes*, p.540.

10 Author interview with Paul Wilson.

11 Author interview with Professor Michael Cousins, www.abc.net.au/radio/programs/conversations/conversations-special-whatever-doesnt-kill-me/7757358

12 Melzack& Wall, pp.971–99.

13 Navratil, doc. 138, pp.565–68.

14 Mlynar, p.223.

15 'Gustav Husak, History's Forgotten Man', Radio Prague, www.radio.cz/en/section/czechs/gustav-husak-czech-historys-forgotten-man

16 Jan Carnogursky interview, *Gustav Husak Centre Stage*, documentary, Ceske Televize, 2008.

17 Mlynar, p.224.

18 Gustav Husak obituary, *The Times*, 19 November 1991.

19 Zantovsky, p.128.

20 Šimečka, p.8

21 Stoppard, Tom, 'Prague: The Story of the Chartists', *New York Review of Books*, 4 August 1977.

22 Levy, 'Karel Gott as Hamlet', p.38.

23 *The Magic Voice of a Rebel*, documentary, Ceske Televize, 2014.

24 *The Magic Voice of a Rebel*, documentary, Ceske Televize, 2014.

25 Bolton, p.239.

26 The Prague Spring 1968: A National Security Archive Documents Reader, pp.96–7.

27 Macintyre, p.32.

28 Szczygiel, p.120.

29 Author interview with Anna O'Grady.

30 Heimann, p.279.

31 Bren, 'Tuzex and the Hustler', p.34.

32 Havel, *Disturbing the Peace*, pp.120–21.

33 Havel, *Open Letters*, p.54.

34 Havel, *Open Letters*, p.75.

35 Kovanda, *New York Review of Books*, details to come.

36 Wilson, 'What's it Like Making Rock 'n' Roll.

37 Author interview with Paul Wilson.

38 Interview with Josef Janicek, *The Lost World of Communism*, BBC TV.

39 Author interview with Paul Wilson.

40 www.slow-journalism.com/from-the-archive/they-feared-us-because-in-music-you-cannot-cheat

41 Machovec, pp.9–10.

42 Havel, *Disturbing the Peace*, p.126.

43 www.wired.com/1995/01/prague/

44 Benda et al., p.228.

45 Bolton, p.150.

46 Zantovsky, p. 179.

47 Bren, 'The Greengrocer and His TV', p.121.

48 Karel Gott interview, *The Lost World of Communism*, BBC TV.

49 Klima, p.344.

50 *The Magic Voice of a Rebel*, documentary, Ceske Televize, 2014.

51 www.slow-journalism.com/from-the-archive/they-feared-us-because-in-music-you-cannot-cheat

52 *Amnesty International Briefing*, p.3.

53 Havel, 'The Power of the Powerless'.

54 Philip Roth, 'In Prague', *The New Yorker*, 3 May 2013.

55 Havel, *Letters to Olga*, pp.14, 51, 349.

56 Lubomir Strougal interview, *Gustav Husak Centre Stage*, documentary, Ceske Televize, 2008.

57 Kamm, H., 'The Graying of Prague', *New York Times Magazine*, 29 August 1982.

58 'Gorbachev Alludes to Czech Invasion', *New York Times*, 12 April 1987.

59 'Husak Steps Down as Prague Leader', *New York Times*, 18 December 1987.

60 Mieczysław Rakowski interview, *Gustav Husak Centre Stage*, documentary, Ceske Televize, 2008.

61 Havel interview, *Gustav Husak Centre Stage*, documentary, Ceske Televize, 2008.

11. To Light the Magic Lantern

1 Wheaton & Kavan, p.10.

2 Havel, 'Meeting Gorbachev'.

3 McRae, p.39.

4 Meyer, p.139.

5 *Revolver Revue*, no.11, 1988.

6 Kenney, p.245.

7 'The Persecution of Human Rights Monitors, December 1988 to December 1989', *Human Rights Watch, Dec 1989*, p.98.

8 Ash, 'The Prague Advertisement', *New York Review of Books*, 22 December 1988.

9 Zantovsky, p.317.

10 'Charging Riot Policemen Beat Protestors in Prague Square', *New York Times*, 20 January 1989.

11 Zantovsky, p.284.

12 Author interview with Katrin Bock.

13 Zantovsky, p.333.

14 DWNews, 'The Berlin Wall: A Stroke of Fate that Changed History', *Focus on Europe*, 21 November 2014.

15 *The Magic Voice of a Rebel*, documentary, Ceske Televize, 2014.

16 Wheaton & Kavan, p.42, and Krapfl, p.46.

17 Wheaton, p.42.

18 Krapfl, p.15.

19 Krapfl, p.15.

20 Bažant et al., p.487.

21 Author interview with Katrin Bock.

22 Wheaton & Kavan, p.50.

23 'Celebrating Revolution with Roots in a Rumour', *New York Times*, 17 November 2009.

24 Sebestyen, V., 'The Accidental Uprising: How "Corpse" Killed Communism', *The Independent*, 22 November 2009.

25 www.psp.cz/eknih/1990fs/tisky/t1236_06.htm

26 ct24.ceskatelevize.cz/domaci/1372634-drahomira-drazska-strujkyne-zpravy-o-mrtvem-smidovi-promluvila

27 Author interview with Marek Toman.

28 Krapfl, p.41.

29 *Lost World of Communism*, BBC TV.

30 straysatellite.com/kubisova/

31 Sebestyen, p.374.

32 Wheaton & Kavan, p.208.

33 Wheaton & Kavan, p.77.

34 *The Czech and Slovak Velvet Revolution: A Look Back*, PBS Television documentary, 1993.

35 McRae, p.137.

36 Ash, 'The Revolution of the Magic Lantern'.

37 *The Magic Lantern*, BBC TV documentary, 1994.

38 McRae, p.144.

39 Author interview with Marek Toman.

40 Klicperová-Baker, sect. 97.

41 'The New President', *New York Times*, 30 December 1989.

42 Author interview with Paul Wilson.

43 Author interview with Katrin Bock.

44 Zantovsky, p.307.

45 McRae, p.162.

46 'Retirement for Dean of Old Guard', *New York Times*, 11 December 1989.

47 Havel, 'Meeting Gorbachev'.

48 Laber, Jeri, 'Vaclav Havel: The Playwright in Prague Castle', *New York Times*, 21 December 2011.

49 Keane, pp.365–66.

50 'Record of Meeting Between Havel and Advisors', Precan, et al., p.315.

51 Keane, pp.367–68.

52 Keane, p.371.

53 *The Czech and Slovak Velvet Revolution: A Look Back*, PBS Television documentary, 1993.

54 Zantovsky, p.343.

55 Havel, New Year's Address to the Nation.

12. Together Alone

1 Zantovsky, pp.331–32.

2 Keane, p.464.

3 granta.com/to-the-castle-and-back/

4 www.wilsoncenter.org/sites/default/files/media/documents/publication/OP%2030.pdf

5 'Memories of Wartime Brutalities Revive Czech-German Animosity', *New York Times*, 9 February 1996.

6 'Kohl and Havel Sign Pact but Issue Remains', *New York Times*, 28 February 1992.

7 *Secrets of the Fifth Estate*, CBC News 1992.

8 Havel, Address to the Senate and House of the Czech Parliament, 9 December 1997.

9 www.nytimes.com/2009/11/18/world/europe/18czech.html

10 Tait, R., 'The Fall of Prague', *The Guardian*, 25 August 2019.

11   'Children of the Revolution', *The Guardian*, 6 September 2009.

12   Laber, J., 'Witch Hunt in Prague', *New York Review of Books*, 23 April 1992,

13   Laber, J., 'Witch Hunt in Prague', *New York Review of Books*, 23 April 1992,

14   Radio Prague, 'Trial Begins of Former Prosecutor', 16 October 2007.

15   Author interview with Kristina Vlachova.

16   *Citizen Havel*, documentary, 2008.

17   Paul Wilson, 'Victims, Not Victors?', *The Guardian*, 2 December 2019.

18   www.bbc.com/news/world-europe-52500865

19   www.independent.co.uk/news/world/europe/czech-art-activists-scale-prague-castle-walls-to-replace-the-presidents-flag-with-a-huge-pair-of-10510426.html

20   Author interview with Paul Wilson.

BIBLIOGRAPHY

Abshire, David, *Einstein and the Generations of Science*, Routledge, 2017

Adamthwaite, Anthony P., *The Making of the Second World War*, Routledge, 1992

Adler, J., 'What Was Lost? The Czech Jewish Community', *European Judaism: A Journal for the New Europe*, Vol. 38, No. 2, pp. 70–76, 2005

Adler, H. G. & J., *Theresienstadt 1941–1945*, Cambridge University Press

Agnew, Hugh, *The Czechs and the Lands of the Bohemian Crown*, Hoover Institution Press, 2004

Akkerman, N. (ed.), *The Correspondence of Elizabeth Stuart, Queen of Bohemia*, Vol. I, Oxford University Press, 2015

Albright, M., *Prague Winter*, HarperCollins, 2012

Alvarez, G., 'The Role of Inbreeding in the Extinction of a European Royal Dynasty', https://journals.plos.org/plosone/article?id=10.1371/journal.pone.0005174

Amery, Leo, *The Leo Amery Diaries*, Vol. II *The Empire at Bay 1929–1945*, Hutchinson, 1988

Amnesty International Briefing: Czechoslovakia, Amnesty International Publications, 1981

Antonín, Robert, *The Ideal Ruler in Medieval Bohemia*, Brill, 2017

Applebaum, Anne, *Iron Curtain: The Crushing of Eastern Europe 1944–56*, Penguin, 2012

Arendt, Hannah, *The Origins of Totalitarianism*, Penguin Classics edition, 2017

Armand, Louis (ed.), *Abolishing Prague: Essays and Interventions*, Univerzita Karlova v Praze Filozofická Fakulta, 2014

Ash, Timothy Garton, *The Magic Lantern*, Atlantic Books, 2019

——, 'The Prague Experiment', *New York Review of Books*, 22 December 1988

——, 'The Revolution of the Magic Lantern', *New York Review of Books*, January 18, 1990

Asprey, Robert, *Frederick the Great: The Magnificent Enigma*, Ticknor & Fields, 1986

Baer, Josette, *Seven Czech Women: Portraits of Courage, Humanism, and Enlightenment*, Ibidem Press, 2015

Banville, John, *Prague Pictures: Portraits of a City*, Bloomsbury 2010

Bažant, Jan, Nina Bažantová, Nina & Starn, Frances (eds.), *The Czech Reader: History, Culture, Politics*, Duke University Press, 2010

Beaune, Colette, 'Chrétienté et Europe: Le Projet de Georges de Podiebrad au Xxve Siècle', *Chrétiens et Sociétés*, Vol. 1, 1994

Belozerskaya, Marina, *The Medici Giraffe, and Other Tales of Exotic Animals and Power*, Little Brown & Co., 2009

Benda, V., Šimečka, M., Jirous, I. M., et al., 'Parallel Polis, or An Independent Society in Central and Eastern Europe: An Inquiry', *Social Research*, Vol. 55, No. 1/2, pp. 211–46, Johns Hopkins University Press, 1988

Benes, Edvard, *My War Memoirs: From Munich to New War and New Victory* (trans. Godfrey Lias), Houghton Mifflin, 1953

Betts, R. R., 'The University of Prague: 1348', *The Slavonic and East European Review*, Vol. 27, No.68 (1948), p.57.

Binet, Laurent, *HHhH*, Vintage, 2013.

Bireley, Robert, *Ferdinand II, Counter-Reformation Emperor, 1578–1637*, Cambridge University Press, 2014

Blanning, T. C. W., *Frederick the Great: King of Prussia*, Random House, 2016

——, T. C. W., *Joseph II*, Routledge, 2013

Blažek, Petr, *The Deportation of the King of May: Allen Ginsberg and the State Security*, www.ceeol.com/search/viewpdf?id=547804

Boehm, B.D., & Jiri Fajt (eds.) *Prague: The Crown of Bohemia 1347–1437*, Yale University Press, 2005

Bolton, Jonathon, *Worlds of Dissent: Charter 77, The Plastic People of the Universe, and Czech Culture Under Communism*, Harvard University Press, 2012

Bouverie, Tim, *Appeasing Hitler: Chamberlain, Churchill and the Road to War*, Vintage, 2019

Bren, Paulina, *The Greengrocer and His TV, The Culture of Communism after the 1968 Prague Spring*, Cornell University Press, 2012

——, 'Tuzex and the Hustler', *Communism Unwrapped: Consumption in Cold War Eastern Europe*, Oxford University Press USA, 2012.

British Foreign Policy Documents, 1919–1939, Third Series, Vol II, ia802803.us.archive.org/19/items/in.ernet. dli.2015.276399/2015.276399.Documents-On.pdf

Browning, Reed, *The War of the Austrian Succession*, Alan Sutton, 1994

Bruegel, J. W., *Czechoslovakia Before Munich: The German Minority Problem and British Appeasement Policy*, Cambridge at the University Press, 1973

Brusak, Karl, 'Reflections of Heresy in Czech Fourteenth- and Fifteenth-Century Rhymed Compositions', *Slavonic and East European Review*, Vol. 76, No. 2, April 1998

Bryant, Chad, *Prague in Black: Nazi Rule and Czech Nationalism*, Harvard University Press, 2009.

Bullock, Alan, *Hitler, a Study in Tyranny*, Harper & Row, 1962.

Cadogan, Alexander, *The Diaries of Sir Alexander Cadogan, O.M., 1938–1945*, Cassell, 1971

Capek, Karel, *Capek, Four Plays* (trans. Peter Majer & Cathy Porter), Bloomsbury 2014

Carter, F. W., 'The Industrial Development of Prague 1800–1850', *The Slavonic and East European Review*, Vol. 51, No. 123 (April, 1973), pp. 243–75.

Červinka, František, 'The Hilsner Affair,' *The Blood Libel Legend: A Casebook in Anti-Semitic Folklore*, Alan Dundes, (ed.), University of Wisconsin Press, 1991

Chamberlain, Neville & Self, Robert C., *The Neville Chamberlain Diary Letters*, Routledge, 2016

Channon, Henry, *Chips: The Diary of Sir Henry Channon*, Weidenfeld & Nicolson, 1967

Charles IV, *Autobiography of Emperor Charles IV and his Legend of St. Wenceslas*, ed. Balazs Nagy & Frank Schaer, Central European University Press, 2001

Christianson, J. R., *On Tycho's Island: Tycho Brahe and His Assistants*, Cambridge University Press, 2000.

Christofferson, T. & M., *France During World War II*, Fordham University Press, 2006

Chubykalo, A. E. (ed.), *Instantaneous Action at a Distance in Modern Physics*, Nova, 1999

Churchill, Winston S., *Churchill Speaks: Winston S. Churchill in Peace and War: Collected Speeches, 1897–1963*, Chelsea House, 1980.

——, *The Second World War: The Gathering Storm*, Random House, 2002

Clapham, John, *Smetana (Master Musician Series)*, Everyman, 1972

Clarke, Lindsay, *The Chymical Wedding*, Picador, 1990

Cohen, Norman, *The Pursuit of the Millennium: Revolutionary Millenarians and Mystical Anarchists of the Middle Ages*, Vintage Digital, 2011

Cook, Bernard A. (ed.), *Europe Since 1945: An Encyclopedia*, Vol. 2, Taylor & Francis, 2001

Cornwall, Mark, 'The Czechoslovak Sphinx: "Moderate" and "Reasonable" Konrad Henlein", *In the Shadow of Hitler: Personalities of the Right in Central and Eastern Europe*, I. B. Tauris, 2011

Cosmas of Prague, *The Chronicle of the Czechs* (trans. Lisa Wolverton), Catholic University of America Press, 2009

'Cyril and Methodius, Apostles to the Slavs', *Christianity Today*, www. christianitytoday.com/history/people/missionaries/cyril-and-methodius.html

D'este, Carlo, *Patton: A Genius for War*, HarperCollins, 1995

Davenport, M., *Too Strong for Fantasy*, Scribner, 1967

David, Abraham, *A Hebrew Chronicle from Prague, c. 1615* (trans. Leon J. Weinberger with Dena Ordan), University of Alabama Press, 2008

Davies, Norman, *Europe: A History*, Pimlico, 1997

Dee, J., *A True and Faithful Relation of What Passed for Many Years Between Dr. John Dee and Some Spirits*, 1659 edition digitised by the Internet Archive, http://www.archive.org/details/truefaithfulrelaOOdeej

——, *The Private Diary of Dr. John Dee, and the Catalogue of his Library of Manuscripts*, The Camden Society, 1842.

Dekel, E. & Gurley, D., 'How the Golem Came to Prague', *The Jewish Quarterly Review*, Vol. 103, No. 2, pp. 241–58

Demetz, Peter, *Prague in Black and Gold*, Penguin, 1997

——, *Prague in Danger*, Farrar, Straus & Giroux, 2008

Dubcek, Alexander, *Hope Dies Last: The Autobiography of Alexander Dubcek* (trans. Jiri Hochman), Kodansha USA, 1993

Duffy, Christopher, *Red Storm on the Reich: The Soviet March on Germany, 1945*, Routledge, 1991

——, *The Army of Maria Theresa: The Armed Forces of Imperial Austria, 1740–1780*, David & Charles, 1977

Eisen, Norman, *The Last Palace: Europe's Extraordinary Century Through Five Lives and One House in Prague*, Hachette, 2018

Erben, Karel Jaromír, *A Bouquet* (trans. Marcela Sulak), Twisted Spoon Press, 2012

Evans, R. J. W., 'Maria Theresa and Hungary', *Austria, Hungary, and the Habsburgs: Central Europe c.1683–1867*, Oxford University Press, 2006

——, *Rudolf II and His World: A Study in Intellectual History, 1576–1612*, Oxford University Press, 1973

Faber, David, *Munich, 1938: Appeasement and World War II*, Simon & Schuster, 2009

Farley, David (ed.), *Prague and the Czech Republic: True Stories*, Traveler's Tales, 2006

Ferguson, Kitty, *Tycho and Kepler*, Transworld, 2002

Fermor, Patrick Leigh. *A Time of Gifts: On Foot to Constantinople: from the Hook of Holland to the Middle Danube*, Hodder & Stoughton, 1977

Fest, Joachim, *Hitler*, HMH, 2013

Finger, *Origins of Neuroscience*, Oxford University Press, 2001

Fitzgerald, F.S., *The Crack Up*, New Directions, 2004

Froissart, J., *The Chronicles of Froissart* (trans. J. Bourchier), Macmillan, 1908

Fučíková, Eliška (ed.), *Rudolf II and Prague: The Court and the City*, Thames & Hudson, 1997

Fudge, Thomas, '"Neither mine nor thine": communist experiments in Hussite Bohemia', *Canadian Journal of History*, Vol. 33, April 1998.

——, *The Magnificent Ride: The First Reformation in Hussite Bohemia*, Routledge, 1998.

Geary, Patrick, J. (ed.), 'The Autobiography of Charles IV', in *Readings in Medieval History Volume 11: The Later Middle Ages*, 5th edn, University of Toronto Press, 2015

Gedye, G. E. R., *Fallen Bastions: The Central European Tragedy*, Victor Gollancz, 1959

George, Timothy, *Theology of the Reformers*, B&H Publishing, 2013

Gerwarth, Robert, *Hitler's Hangman: The Life of Heydrich*, Yale University Press, 2011

Gilbert, Martin, *The Holocaust: The Human Tragedy*, Rosetta Books, 2005

——, *Winston S. Churchill*, Vol. IV, Heineman, 1975

——, *Winston Churchill – the Wilderness Years: A Lone Voice Against Hitler in the Prelude to War*, Tauris Parke Paperbacks, 2011

Glassheim, Eagle, *Cleansing the Czechoslovak Borderlands: Migration, Environment, and Health in the Former Sudetenland*, University of Pittsburgh Press, 2016

——, 'National Mythologies and Ethnic Cleansing: The Expulsion of
Czechoslovak Germans in 1945', *Central European History*, Vol. 33,
No. 4, 2000

Golan, Galia, 'Antonin Novotny: The Sources and Nature of His Power',
Canadian Slavonic Papers / Revue Canadienne Des Slavistes, Vol. 14,
No. 3 (1972), pp. 421–41

Gordin, Michael D., *Einstein in Bohemia*, Princeton University Press, 2020

Gordin, Michael D., Tilley, Helen. & Prakash, Gyan. (eds), *Utopia/Dystopia:
Conditions of Historical Possibility*, Princeton University Press, 2011

Gough, Roger, *A Good Comrade: Janos Kadar, Communism and Hungary*,
I. B. Tauris, 2006

Grayling, *The Age of Genius*, Bloomsbury, 2016

Hagen, Trever, *Living in The Merry Ghetto: The Music and Politics of the
Czech Underground*, Oxford University Press, 2019

Halevi, Z'ev ben Shimon, *Kabbalah, Tradition of Hidden Knowledge*,
Thames & Hudson, 1988

Hannaway, Owen, 'Laboratory Design and the Aim of Science: Andreas
Libavius versus Tycho Brahe', *Isis*, December, 1986, pp. 584–610

Harkness, Deborah, *John Dee's Conversations with Angels: Cabala,
Alchemy, and the End of Nature*, Cambridge University Press, 1999

Harrison, Thomson, S. 'Learning at the Court of Charles IV', *Speculum*,
Vol. XXV, January 1950

Hasek, Jaroslav, *The Good Soldier Svejk*, Penguin, 2005.

Havel, Vaclav, *Disturbing the Peace* (trans. Paul Wilson), Knopf, 1990

——, *Letters to Olga* (trans. Paul Wilson), Faber & Faber, 1990

——, *Living in Truth*, Faber & Faber, 1991

——, 'Meeting Gorbachev', *Granta*, 30 June 1988

——, New Year's Address to the Nation, 1990, chnm.gmu.edu/1989/
items/browse?search=havel

——, *Open Letters, Selected Prose 1965-1990*, (trans. Paul Wilson),
Faber & Faber, 1991

——, Speech to Demonstrators in Wenceslas Square, 10 December, www.89.usd.cas.cz/en/documents.html

——, 'The Power of the Powerless' (trans. Paul Wilson), https://www.nonviolent-conflict.org/wp-content/uploads/1979/01/the-power-of-the-powerless.pdf

Hay, Denys, *Europe in the Fourteenth and Fifteenth Centuries*, Routledge, 2016

Heimann, Mary, *Czechoslovakia, the State that Failed*, Yale University Press, 2011

Heymann, Frederick G., *George of Bohemia: King of Heretics*, Princeton University Press, 1965

——, *John Zizka and the Hussite Revolution*, Princeton University Press, 1955

Hodos, George H., *Show Trials: Stalinist Purges in Eastern Europe, 1948–1954*, Greenwood, 1984

Hodrová, Daniela, *I See a City…*, Jantar Publishing, 2015

Hohne, Heinz, *The Order of the Death's Head: The Story of Hitler's SS*, Penguin, 2000

Holeton, David R., 'Fynes Moryson's Itinerary: A Sixteenth Century English Traveller's Observations on Bohemia, its Reformation, and its Liturgy', http://brrp.org/proceedings/brrp5b/holeton.pdf

Hoogenboom, O., 'Masaryk, Charlotte Garrigue (1850–1923), First Lady of Czechoslovakia', *American National Biography*, 2000

Hoschl, C., 'Bedrich Smetana: Art and Disease', *Psychiatria Danubina*, Vol. 24, 2012

Hrabal, Bohumil, *Closely Watched Trains*, Penguin 2017

——, *I Served the King of England*, Vintage, 2009

Hughes, Charles, *Shakespeare's Europe: Unpublished Chapters of Fynes Moryson's Itinerary*, Sherrat & Hughes, 1903

Huizinga, Johann, *The Waning of the Middle Ages*, Penguin, 1955

Iggers, Wilma, *Women of Prague: Ethnic Diversity and Social Change from the Eighteenth Century to the Present*, Berghahn Books, 1995

Janouch, Gustav, *Conversations with Kafka* (trans. Goronwy Rees), New Directions, 2012

Jelavich, Peter, *Berlin Cabaret*, Harvard University Press, 1993

Jenkins, Simon, *A Short History of Europe: From Pericles to Putin*, Hachette, 2019

Jirásek, Alois, *Legends of Old Bohemia* (trans. Edith Pargeter), Paul Hamlyn, 1963

Jones, Michael, *After Hitler: The Last Days of the Second World War in Europe*, Hachette, 2015

Judt, Tony, *Postwar: A History of Europe Since 1945*, Penguin, 2005

Jurkowlaniec, Grażyna et al., *The Agency of Things in Medieval and Early Modern Art: Materials, Power and Manipulation*, Routledge, 2017

Kachlik, David, 'A Biographical Sketch of Johannes Jessenius: 410th anniversary of his Prague Dissection', *Clinical Anatomy*, Vol. 25, pp.149–54

Kachlik, David et al., 'The Life and Work of Jan Jesensky (1566–1621), the Physician of a Dying Time', *Journal of Medical Biography*, 2013, pp.153—63

Kafka, Franz, *Diaries of Franz Kafka* (Max Brod, ed.), Schocken Books, 1988

——, *Letters to Felice*, Schocken Books, 2016

——, *Letters to Friends, Family and Editors* (trans. Richard Winston), Schocken Books, 1977

Kalhous, David, *Anatomy of a Duchy: The Political and Ecclesiastical Structures of Early Premyslid Bohemia*, Brill, 2012

Kalik, J. & Uchitel, A., *Slavic Gods and Heroes*, Routledge, 2019

Kaminsky, Howard, *A History of the Hussite Revolution*, University of California Press, 1967

Kantor, Marvin, *Medieval Slavic Lives of Saints and Princes: The Life of Wenceslas*, macedonia.kroraina.com/en/kmsl/

Kaplan, Karel, *Report on the Murder of the General Secretary*, I. B. Tauris, 1990

Kaufmann, Thomas DaCosta, 'Remarks on the Collections of Rudolf II: The "Kunstkammer as a Form of Representation"', *Art Journal*, Vol. 38, No. 1 (autumn, 1978)

Keane, John, *Vaclav Havel: A Political Tragedy in Six Acts*, Bloomsbury, 2012

Kennan, George Frost, *From Prague After Munich: Diplomatic Papers, 1938–1940*, Princeton University Press, 2015

Kenney, Padraic, *A Carnival of Revolution: Central Europe 1989*, Princeton University Press, 2002

Kepler, Johannes, *Kepler's Somnium: The Dream, Or Posthumous Work on Lunar Astronomy*, Dover Publications, 2003

Kershaw, Ian, *Hitler*, Penguin, 2013

Kindleberger, Charles P., 'The Economic Crisis of 1619 to 1623', *The Journal of Economic History*, Vol. 51, No. 1 (March 1991).

Kisch, Egon, *Sensation Fair: Tales of Prague*, Plunkett Lake Press, 2012

Klaniczay, Gabor, (ed.), 'Life of Saint Adalbert', *Saints of the Christianization Age of Central Europe: Tenth to Twelfth Centuries*, Central European University Press, 2013

Klápště, Jan, *The Czech Lands in Medieval Transformation*, Brill, 2011

Klassen, John, *The Letters of the Rozmberk Sisters: Noblewomen in Fifteenth Century Bohemia*, D.S. Brewer, 2001

——, 'The Public and Domestic Faces of Ulrich of Rozmberk', *The Sixteenth Century Journal*, Vol. 31, No. 3, 2000, pp. 699–718

Klicperová-Baker, M., 'Czech Rhetoric of 1989 and Václav Havel', *Advances in the History of Rhetoric*, Vol. 18, Sup. 1

Klima, Ivan, *My Crazy Century*, Grove Press, 2009

Klossowski de Rola, Stanislaus, *The Golden Game, Alchemical Engravings of the 17th Century*, Thames & Hudson, 1998

——, *The Secret Art of Alchemy*, Thames & Hudson, 1973

Koestler, Arthur, The *Sleepwalkers: A History of Man's Changing Vision of the Universe*, Penguin, 1968

Korbel, Josef, *The Communist Subversion of Czechoslovakia, 1938–1948: The Failure of Co-existence*, Princeton University Press e-book, 2019

Kovaly, Heda Margolius, *Under A Cruel Star: A Life in Prague 1941–1968*, Plunkett Lake Press, 2010

Kovanda, Karel, 'Czechoslovakia's Imprisoned Conscience', *New York Review of Books*, 20 March 1975

Krapfl, James, *Revolution with a Human Face: Politics, Culture, and Community in Czechoslovakia, 1989–1992*, Ithaca: Cornell University Press, 2013

Kriwaczek, Paul, *Yiddish Civilisation: The Rise and Fall of a Forgotten Nation*, Hachette, 2011

Kundera, Milan, *The Book of Laughter and Forgetting*, Faber & Faber, 1996

——, *The Unbearable Lightness of Being*, Faber & Faber, 1988

Láníček, Jan, 'After the Whirlwind: Jewish Absence in Postwar Czechoslovakia', *Journal of Contemporary History*, Vol. 52 No. 2, 2017

Large, Brian, *Smetana*, Duckworth, 1970

Le Goff, Jacques, *The Birth of Europe*, Blackwell, 2005

Levy, Alan, 'Karel Gott as Hamlet', *Index on Censorship, March 1978*, pp.33–39

——, *So Many Heroes*, Second Chance Press, 1980

Lockhart, Robert Bruce, *Jan Masaryk: A Personal Memoir*, Putnam, 1956

Ludwig, E., *Defender of Democracy: Masaryk of Czechoslovakia*, Robert McBride, 1936

Lukes, Igor, *Czechoslovakia Between Stalin and Hitler: The Diplomacy of Edvard Benes in the 1930s*, Oxford University Press, 1993

——, *On the Edge of the Cold War: American Diplomats and Spies in Postwar Prague*, Oxford University Press, 2012

——, 'The Rudolf Slánský Affair: New Evidence', *Slavic Review*, Vol. 58, No. 1, Cambridge University Press, 1999

Lukes, Igor & Goldstein, Erik (eds), *The Munich Crisis, 1938: Prelude to World War II*, Frank Cass, 1999

Lützow, Francis. *The Life & Times of Master John Hus*, J. M. Dent & Co., 1909

MacCulloch, Diarmaid, *A History of Christianity*, Allen Lane, 2009

MacDonald, C. A., *The Killing of Obergruppenführer Reinhard Heydrich*, Macmillan 1989

Machovec, Martin (ed.), *Views from the Inside. Czech Underground Literature and Culture (1948–1989): Manifestos – Testimonies – Documents*, Karolinum Press, 2018.

Mackenzie, Compton, *Dr. Benes*, Harrap, 1946

Mahoney, William M., *The History of the Czech Republic and Slovakia*, ABC-CLIO, 2011

Maisky, Ivan, *The Complete Maisky Diaries*, Yale University Press, 2017

Manchester, William, *The Last Lion: Winston Spencer Churchill*, Vol. 2 *Alone*, Little, Brown and Co., 2012

Manchester, William & Reid, Paul, *The Last Lion: Winston Spencer Churchill*, Vol. 3 *Defender of the Realm, 1940–1965*, Little, Brown & Co., 2012

Manchip, J. E., *Marshal of France: The Life and Times of Maurice, Comte de Saxe, 1696–1750*, Rand McNally, 1962

Manifesto of Charter 77, chnm.gmu.edu/1989/items/show/628

Manvell, Roger & Fraenkel, Heinrich, *Doctor Goebbels: His Life and Death*, Skyhorse Publishing, 2010

Marshall, Peter, *The Mercurial Emperor: The Magic Circle of Rudolf II in Renaissance Prague*, Random House, 2006

Masaryk, T. G. & Capek, Karel, *Talks with T.G. Masaryk*, Catbird Press, 1995

Mastny, Vojtech, *The Czechs Under Nazi Rule: The Failure of National Resistance, 1939–1942*, Columbia University Press, 1971

Matusiak, John, *Europe in Flames: The Crisis of the Thirty Years War*, The History Press, 2018

McCagg, William O., *A History of Habsburg Jews, 1670–1918*, Indiana University Press, 1992,

McRae, Rob, *Resistance and Revolution: Václav Havel's Czechoslovakia*, McGill-Queen's University Press, 1997

Melzack, R. & Wall, P. D., 'Pain Mechanisms: A New Theory', *Science*, 1965, Vol. 150, Iss. 3699 (November 1965)

Mengel, David C., 'A Plague on Bohemia? Mapping the Black Death', *Past & Present*, No.211, Oxford University Press, May 2011

——, 'Emperor Charles IV (1346–1378) as the Architect of Local Religion in Prague', *Austrian History Yearbook 41*, pp.15–29, University of Minnesota, 2010

——, 'Emperor Charles IV, Jews, and Urban Space', *Christianity and Culture in the Middle Ages*, University of Notre Dame, 2015

Merten, Ulrich, *Forgotten Voices: The Expulsion of the Germans from Eastern Europe After World War II*, Routledge, 2016

Meyer, Michael, *The Year that Changed the World: The Untold Story Behind the Fall of the Berlin Wall*, Simon and Schuster, 2009

Meyrink, Gustav, *The Golem* (trans. Mike Mitchell), Dedalus European Classics, 1995

Miller, Michael, 'Rabbi David Oppenheim on Trial: Turks, Titles, and Tribute in Counter-Reformation Prague', *The Jewish Quarterly Review*, Vol. 106, No. 1 (winter 2016)

Mladenovic, Petr (d. 1451), *John Hus At the Council of Constance*, Columbia University Press, 1965

Mlynar, Zdenek, 'Invasion 1968', *New York Times*, February 5, 1980

——, *Nightfrost in Prague: The End of Humane Socialism* (trans. Paul Wilson), Karz Publishers, 1980

Mňačko, Ladislav, *The Taste of Power*, Frederick A. Praeger, 1967

Montano, Linda, *Performance Artists Talking in the Eighties*, University of California Press, 2000

Mooney, Catherine M. *Clare of Assisi and the Thirteenth-Century Church: Religious Women, Rules, and Resistance*, University of Pennsylvania Press, 2016

Moravec, Frantisek, *Master of Spies: The Memoirs of General Frantisek Moravec*, Doubleday, 1975

Morelon, Claire, *Street Fronts: War, State Legitimacy and Urban Space, Prague 1914–1920*, University of Birmingham, 2015

Mortimer, Geoff, *The Origins of the Thirty Years War and the Revolt in Bohemia, 1618*, Springer, 2015

——, *Wallenstein: The Enigma of the Thirty Years War*, Macmillan 2010

Moryson, Fynes, *The Itinerary of Fynes Moryson*, Vol. I, Glasgow University Press, 1907

Motl, Stanislav, *Britons at Czechoslovakian Radio*, Czech Radio, https://theaibs.tv/wp-content/uploads/2012/09/11378-Britons-at-Czechoslovakian-Radio-script.doc

Mozart, Wolfgang Amadeus, *Mozart's Letters*, Vol. II, Penguin, 1956

Murphy, Thomas K., *Czechoslovakia Behind the Curtain: Life, Work and Culture in the Communist Era*, McFarland, 2018

Nagler, G., *Czechoslovakia 88: A Different Seminar, Prague November 1988*, Report for International Helsinki Federation for Human Rights

Naimark, N. & Gibianskii, L.(eds), *The Establishment of Communist Regimes in Eastern Europe, 1944–1949*, Taylor & Francis, 1997.

Navratil, J. (ed.), *The Prague Spring 1968: A National Security Archive Documents Reader*, Central European University Press, 1998

Nemec, Ludvik, *The Polish Review*, Vol. 7, No. 2 (Spring, 1962), pp.41–64

Newman, Aubrey, 'The Expulsion of the Jews from Prague in 1745 and British Foreign Policy', *Jewish Historical Society of England*, Vol. 22 (1968–69), pp. 30–41

Newman, Barbara, *Medieval Crossover: Reading the Secular Against the Sacred*, University of Notre Dame Press, 2011

——, 'The Passion of the Jews of Prague: The Pogrom of 1389 and the Lessons of a Medieval Parody', *Church History*, Vol. 81, No. 1, Cambridge University Press, 2012

Nezval, Vitezslav, *Prague with Fingers of Rain* (trans. Ewald Osers), Bloodaxe Books, 2009

Nicolson, Harold, *The Harold Nicolson Diaries: 1919–1964*, Weidenfeld & Nicolson, 2004

Orzoff, Andrea, *Battle for the Castle: The Myth of Czechoslavakia, Eighteenth Century to the Present*, Berghahn Books, 1995

Paces, Cynthia, *Prague Panoramas: National Memory and Sacred Space in the Twentieth Century*, University of Pittsburgh Press, 2009

Palmitessa, James R., 'The Prague Uprising of 1611: Property, Politics, and Catholic Renewal in the Early Years of Habsburg Rule', *Central European History*, Vol. 31, No. 4, pp. 299–328, Cambridge University Press, 1998

Parker, Geoffrey, *Imprudent King: A New Life of Philip II*, Yale University Press, 2014

—— (ed.), *The Thirty Years War*, Routledge, 2006

Pavlicek, O. & Smahel, F. (eds.), *A Companion to Jan Hus*, Brill, 2015

Pawel, Ernst, *The Nightmare of Reason: A Life of Franz Kafka*, Harvill Press, 1984

Pech, Z., *The Czech Revolution of 1848*, University of North Carolina 1969

Pekař, J. 'Wallenstein and the Habsburgs', *The Slavonic and East European Review*, Vol. 16, No. 47 (January 1938)

Perett, Marcela, *Preachers, Partisans, and Rebellious Religion: Vernacular Writing and the Hussite Movement*, University of Pennsylvania Press, 2018

Pichova, Hana, 'The Lineup for Meat: The Stalin Statue in Prague', *PMLA*, Vol. 123, No. 3, 2008

Pipes, Richard (ed.), *The Unknown Lenin*, New Haven, 1996

Precan, Vilem. & Derek Paton (eds) *The Democratic Revolution in Czechoslovakia: Conference Briefing Book*, 1999

Principe, Lawrence M., *The Secrets of Alchemy*, University of Chicago Press, 2012

Procopius, *The History of the Wars,* Vol VII, http://users.clas.ufl.edu/fcurta/Procopius.htm

Rapport, Mike, *1848: Year of Revolution*, Hachette, 2010

Precam, Vilem (ed.), *The Democratic Revolution in Czechoslovakia: Its Precondition, Course and Immediate Repercussions, 1987–89,* Conference Documents, https://www.wilsoncenter.org/sites/default/files/media/documents/publication/RevolutionCzechoslovakia_TOC.pdf

Ripellino, Angelo Maria, *Magic Prague*, Picador, 1994

Robbins, Keith G. 'Konrad Henlein, the Sudeten Question and British Foreign Policy', *The Historical Journal*, Vol. 12, No. 4 (1969), pp. 674–97

Rolleston, James, *A Companion to the Works of Franz Kafka*, Boydell & Brewer, 2002

Roshwald, A. & Stites, R. (eds), *European Culture in the Great War: The Arts, Entertainment and Propaganda, 1914–1918*, Cambridge University Press, 2002

Rothkirchen, Livia, *The Jews of Bohemia and Moravia: Facing the Holocaust*, University of Nebraska Press, 2006

Rushton, J., *W. A. Mozart, Don Giovanni*, Cambridge University Press, 1981

Saunders, N., Frolík, J., & Heyd, V., 'Zeitgeist archaeology: Conflict, identity and ideology at Prague Castle, 1918–2018', *Antiquity*, Vol. 93 No. 370 (August 2019), pp. 1009–25

Sayer, Derek, 'André Breton and the Magic Capital: An Agony in Six Fits', *Bohemia – A Journal of History and Civilisation in East Central Europe*, www.bohemia-online.de/index.php/bohemia/article/view/3748/5637

——, *Prague: Capital of the Twentieth Century: A Surrealist History*, Princeton University Press, 2015

——, *The Coasts of Bohemia*, Princeton University Press, 1998

Schain, Martin (ed.), *The Marshall Plan: Fifty Years After*, St Martin's Press, 2001

Schieder, Theodor, *Frederick the Great*, Routledge, 2016

Schlosser, 'World War Three by Mistake', *The New Yorker*, 23 December 2016

Sealsfield, Charles, *Austria As It Is*, S. & R. Bentley, 1824

Sebestyen, Victor, *Revolution 1989: The Fall of the Soviet Empire*, Hachette, 2009

Sedlar, Jean W., *East Central Europe in the Middle Ages, 1000–1500*, University of Washington Press, 1993

Seifert, Jaroslav, *The Poetry of Jaroslav Seifert* (trans. Ewald Osers), Catbird Press, 1998

Selver, Paul, *Masaryk: A Biography*, Michael Joseph, 1940

Shaw, J. M., & Demy, T. J. (eds) *War and Religion: An Encyclopedia of Faith and Conflict* (3 Vols), ABC-CLIO, LLC, Santa Barbara, 2017

Shirer, William, *The Collapse of the Third Republic; An Inquiry into the Fall of France in 1940*, Rosetta Books, 2014

——, *The Rise and Fall of the Third Reich*, Simon & Schuster, 1990

Šimečka, Milan, *The Restoration of Order: The Normalization of Czechoslovakia 1969–1976*, Verso, 1984

Sked, Alan, *The Decline and Fall of the Habsburg Empire, 1815–1918*, Routledge, 2015

Skilling, H. G., 'Gottwald and the Bolshevization of the Communist Party of Czechoslovakia (1929–1939)', *Slavic Review*, Vol. 20, No. 4 (December, 1961), Cambridge University Press.

Skoug, Kenneth N., *Czechoslovakia's Lost Fight for Freedom, 1967–1969: An American Embassy Perspective*, Greenwood Publishing, 1999

Škvorecký, Josef, 'Bohemia of the Soul', *Daedalus*, Vol. 119, No. 1, 1990, pp. 111–39

——, 'The State of Europe', *Granta 30: New Europe!*, Granta, 1990

Smith, R. (ed.), *Britain and the Revolutions in Eastern Europe, 1989: Documents on British Policy Overseas*, Series 3, Vol. 12, Routledge, 2019

Smith, R. (ed.), *Britain and the Revolutions in Eastern Europe, 1989: Documents on British Policy Overseas*, Series 3, Vol. 12, Routledge, 2019

Solomon, Maynard, *Mozart: A Life*, HarperCollins, 1996

Speer, Albert, *Inside the Third Reich*, Simon & Schuster, 1970.

Sperber, Jonathan, *The European Revolutions, 1848–1851*, Cambridge University Press, 1994

Spicka, Jiri, *Francesco Petrarca Travelling and Writing to Prague's Court*, www.verbum-analectaneolatina.hu/pdf/12-1-02.pdf

Spinka, Matthew, *John Hus: A Biography*, Princeton University Press, 2017

Stach, Rainer, *Kafka: The Early Years*, Princeton University Press, 2016

Steiner, Peter, *The Deserts of Bohemia; Czech Fiction and its Social Context*, Cornell University Press 2000

Sterling, Claire, *The Masaryk Case*, Harper & Rowe, 1969

Stoppard, Tom, 'Prague: The Story of the Chartists', *New York Review of Books*, 4 August 1977

Strabo, *Geography*, Loeb Classical Library (trans. H. L. Jones), Harvard University Press, 1932

Svankmajer, Jan, 'Cabinet of Wonders: On Creating and Collecting' *The Moving Image*, Vol 11, No. 2, 2011

Swanson, R., *Promissory Notes on the Treasury of Merits: Indulgences in Late Medieval Europe*, Brill, 2006

Szczygiel, Mariusz, *Gottland: Mostly True Stories from Half of Czechoslovakia*, Melville House, 2014

Taborsky, E., *Communism in Czechoslovakia, 1948–1960*, Princeton University Press, 2015.

Taylor, A. J. P., *Origins of the Second World War*, Hamish Hamilton, 1961

Teich, Mikulas (ed.), *Bohemia in History*, Cambridge University Press, 1998

Teplitsky, Joshua, 'Jewish Money, Jesuit Censors, and the Habsburg Monarchy: Politics and Polemics in Early Modern Prague', *Jewish Social Studies: History, Culture, Society*, (Spring/Summer 2013)

——, *Prince of the Press: How One Collector Built History's Most Enduring and Remarkable Jewish Library*, Yale University Press, 2019

The Chemical Wedding of Christian Rosenkreuz (trans. Joscelyn Godwin), Phanes Press, 1991.

Thomas, Alfred, *Anne's Bohemia: Czech Literature and Society, 1310 –1420*, University of Minnesota Press, 1998

——, *Reading Women in Late Medieval Europe: Anne of Bohemia and Chaucer's Female Audience*, Palgrave Macmillan, 2015

Toland, John, *The Last 100 Days*, Random House, 2014.

Tomek, V. V., *Jewish Stories of Prague*, Sharpless House, 2015

Trotsky, Leon, *Literature and Revolution*, Haymarket Books, 2005

Tyrell, John, *Janacek: Years of a Life*, Vol. 2 (1914–1928) Tsar of the Forests, Faber & Faber, 2011

Valley, Eli, *The Great Jewish Cities of Central and Eastern Europe*, Jason
    Aaronson, 1999
Vlasto, A. P., *The Entry of the Slavs Into Christendom: An Introduction to
    the Medieval History of the Slavs*, Cambridge University Press, 1970
Vlcek, Emanuel, *Physical and Personality Traits of Charles IV, Holy
    Roman Emperor and King*, Karolinum Press, 2016
Voelkel, James, R., *Johannes Kepler and the New Astronomy*, Oxford
    University Press, 2001
Volavková, Hana, (ed.), *I Never Saw Another Butterfly: Children's
    Drawings and Poems from Terezín Concentration Camp, 1942–1944*,
    McGraw Hill, 1971
Wedgwood, C. V., *The Thirty Years War*, Penguin, 1957
Weinberg, Gerhard, *Hitler's Foreign Policy 1933–1939: The Road to World
    War II*, Enigma Books, 2010.
West, Tim, 'Destiny as Alibi: Milan Kundera, Václav Havel and the
    "Czech Question" after 1968', *The Slavonic and East European Review*,
    Vol. 87, No. 3 (July 2009), pp. 401–28
Wheaton, Bernard &, Kavan, Zdeněk, *The Velvet Revolution:
    Czechoslovakia, 1988–1991*, Routledge, 1992
Wheeler, John, *Geons, Black Holes, and Quantum Foam: A Life in Physics*,
    W. W. Norton & Co., 2010
Wheeler-Bennett, J. W., *Munich: Prologue to Tragedy*, Macmillan, 1966
Whitby, Christopher, *John Dee's Actions with Spirits* (Vols I & II),
    Routledge, 2013
Williams, Kieran, *The Prague Spring and its Aftermath*, Cambridge
    University Press, 1997
Wilson, Arthur, *The History of Great Britain: Being the Life and Reign of
    King James the First, Relating to What Passed from His First Access to
    the Crown, till His Death*, Richard Lownds, 1653
Wilson, Paul, 'Growing up with Orwell', *Best Canadian Essays*, Fifth
    House, 1991

——, *Prague: A Traveller's Literary Companion*, Whereabouts Press, Indiana University, 1995

——, 'What's it Like Making Rock 'n' Roll in a Police State?', *Musician Magazine*, 1983

Wilson, Peter, *Europe's Tragedy: A History of the Thirty Years War*, Harvard University Press, 2009

Winder, Simon, *Danubia*, Pan Macmillan, 2013

Wingfield, Nancy M., *Flag Wars and Stone Saints: How the Bohemian Lands Became Czech*, Harvard University Press, 2007

Wolverton, Lisa, *Hastening Toward Prague: Power and Society in the Medieval Czech Lands*, University of Pennsylvania Press, 2001

Woolley, Benjamin, *The Queen's Conjurer: The Science and Magic of Dr. John Dee, Advisor to Queen Elizabeth I*, Flamingo, 2002

Wotton, H., *The Life and Letters of Sir Henry Wotton*, Clarendon Press, 1907

Wyner, Lawrence M., 'Urologic Demise of Astronomer Tycho Brahe: A Cosmic Case of Urinary Retention', *Urology*, February 2016, Vol. 88, pp. 33–35

Zantovsky, Michael, *Havel, A Life*, Atlantic Books, 2014

Zeman, Zbyněk, *The Masaryks*, Taurus, 1990

Zeman, Zbyněk & Klimek, A., *The Life of Edvard Beneš 1884–1948: Czechoslovakia in Peace and War*, Oxford University Press, 1997

Zweig, Stefan, *The World of Yesterday: An Autobiography*, Viking Press, 1964.

IMAGE CREDITS

INDEX

Some sub-entries in this index are ordered chronologically instead of alphabetically, to aid useability.

Square brackets indicate parts of names that do not appear in the text (e.g. Charles [VII]); they are included for clarity.